Driving Productivity

Studies in Critical Social Sciences

VOLUME 331

The titles published in this series are listed at *brill.com/scss*

Driving Productivity

Automation, Labor, and Industrial Development in the United States and Germany

By

Anthony J. Knowles

BRILL

LEIDEN | BOSTON

Cover illustration: United Auto Workers Collection: Local 174 Mural, “Untitled” “1937” (uaw_35325). *Walter P. Reuther Library, Archives of Labor and Urban Affairs, Wayne State University*. Used with kind permission.

This book was published with the generous support of the McClure Scholarship for the Study of World Affairs and the Dr. Wanda Rushing Sociological Research Award.

The Library of Congress Cataloging-in-Publication Data is available online at https://catalog.loc.gov
LC record available at https://lccn.loc.gov/2025027894

Typeface for the Latin, Greek, and Cyrillic scripts: “Brill”. See and download: brill.com/brill-typeface.

ISSN 1573-4234
ISBN 978-90-04-73670-2 (hardback)
ISBN 978-90-04-73671-9 (e-book)
DOI 10.1163/9789004736719

This book is printed on acid-free paper and produced in a sustainable manner.

Contents

Acknowledgements

Writing this book has been an enormous challenge but has been nevertheless rewarding. Its publication marks the end of a project I have been continuously working on since 2019. In this long journey, I have encountered many people on both sides of the Atlantic who have assisted in one way or another whether they knew it or not. I cannot list them all here, but I am indebted to so many for helping me make this book a reality.

I must first and foremost thank Harry F. Dahms for his mentorship and friendship. This book and my career would never have been possible without your steadfast support, advice, and assistance over what has now been over a decade. It is no exaggeration to say that meeting you opened a world of opportunities, of which the opportunity to write this book is only one among many.

I am grateful to all the people I met in Germany, especially Ursula Mense-Petermann, Kim Anh Dang, Ulrich Jürgens, Martin Krzywdzinski, and Gert Schmidt. I am also indebted to my University of Tennessee colleagues Jon Shefner, Paul K. Gellert, Ian Down, Stephanie Bohon, and Kevin Heaslip. This would not have been possible without your feedback and support.

My family has also been an invaluable source of encouragement and assistance, Anthony and Mitzi Knowles, my in-laws Martin and Ransom Schwerzler, my siblings Aidan, Alec and August Knowles as well as my adoptive brother Garren Logsdon.

I also thank Courtney Farley for all her work as my graduate research assistant. Joel Crombez also deserves mention for his indirect assistance.

Finally, when I first met my life-partner Cole, I was still working on my first scholarship application for travel to Germany. You have been by my side every step of the way, and I am enormously thankful for all these years of companionship and love.

Abbreviations

AGV	Automated Guided Vehicle
COLA	Cost-of-Living-Adjustment
DAF	*Deutsche Arbetisfront* (German Labor Front)
DQP	Diversity Quality Production
EV	Electric Vehicle
FDI	Foreign Direct Investment
GAW	Guaranteed Annual Wage
GM	General Motors
GMAD	General Motors Assembly Division
HPV	Hours per Vehicle
IC	Internal Combustion
IMVP	International Motor Vehicle Program
IRA	Inflation Reduction Act
JV	Joint Venture
LP	Lean Production
MIT	Massachusetts Institute of Technology
NAFTA	North American Free Trade Agreement
NLRB	National Labor Relations Board
NPC	New Production Concepts
NUMMI	New United Motor Manufacturing Incorporated
SAIC	Shanghai Automobile Industry Corporation
UAW	United Automobile Workers
VER	Voluntary Export Restraints
VW	Volkswagen

Introduction: The Social Dynamics of Productivity, Automation, and Technological Displacement

1 Limits and Dynamics of Socioeconomic Transformation

Capitalist societies are structured around jobs, and there is considerable time, energy, and discussion devoted to determining how many people are working, where they are working, what they are doing, what their working conditions are and so on. Despite full employment being a nearly universally recognized social good and unemployment is treated as a scourge, history shows that the labor market fluctuates in ways not fully controllable by any social system. Despite many modern societies purporting to be democracies, ostensibly ruled by the people, the underlying anxiety and discourse over employment belies how modern societies appear—at least as far as economic issues are concerned—to be ruled not by the people, but by *something else*.

Commentators and scholars have tried to conceptualize and define this 'something else,' in a variety of ways, from notions of 'market forces' or the 'invisible hand' (Smith 2014 [1776]), to capitalism as a "perennial gale of creative destruction" (see, Schumpeter 2003 [1942]: 81–86). Setting aside the merits of any singular explanation for the vicissitudes of capitalism and of employment and unemployment, one common—though often tacit—understanding remains: who is employed, who is not, and the nature of work is neither purely arbitrary, nor simply a matter of will or political manipulation. There appear to be 'forces' that operate behind the backs of human actors which are beyond direct individual or systemic control.

In the abstract, it is possible to conceive of infinite combinations of means of production and labor power arranged in a variety of structural formations that could employ any given number of people to produce the commodities and distribute the value needed to sustain society. There are obviously choices that must be made in terms of what to produce, where to produce, and how to produce, which related decisions necessarily involve the factors of production such as land, labor, production equipment and technology. Yet the history of capitalism, especially since the first industrial revolution in Great Britain during the late 18th century, shows that only a *limited variety of organizational forms and national systemic arrangements have emerged and proven sustainable*. This prompts the question, what is it about these specific organizations and arrangements that allow not just sustainability but also growth? Are there detectable patterns of what makes them 'successful?' What combinations of labor and technology prove viable, which do not, and why?

 | DOI:10.1163/9789004736719_002

History reveals that no organizational arrangement is ever permanent, but each undergoes 'systemic adaptations' to ensure its survival. What is the nature of this change and do the adaptations also follow a discernable pattern? The primary concern of this book is whether systemic change pushes *technology* or *labor* to become more central to production processes and why. Such decisions are made by human beings, but the options considered and proven to be viable appear restricted. We proceed from the premise that there are *systemic imperatives and constraints* that limit the feasible combinations of means of production and labor power. In other words, social, economic, and organizational change is driven, in part, by changes in socially general imperatives and constraints *rooted in the dynamics of productivity*, and that understanding the historical dynamics underlying these processes is essential to grasping the dilemmas of employment and unemployment in modern capitalist societies. Historian Moishe Postone (1993) described this dynamic as a form of *social domination*, and this book seeks to expound upon and illuminate the importance of this concept.

Since the rise of modern capitalism in the late 18th century, a common narrative emerged that centers modern social change on technological development and discusses the potential dangers of automation and technological displacement (see Woirol 1996; Frey 2019; Knowles 2017). It is undeniable that innovations in technology, from steam engines to computers, have both created new jobs, eliminated 'obsolete' jobs, and transformed the nature of work since the beginning of the industrial revolution. The standard explanation is that the pursuit of higher productivity by firms results in more technology in production processes via automation because machines are supposed to be faster and more productive than human workers. Job tasks that are routine or become routinized are purported to be most susceptible to automation (Autor, Levy, and Murnane 2003; Frey and Osborne 2013; Frey 2019; Susskind 2020). However, technological development and the corresponding employment and job-changing effects have not unfolded evenly or concurrently, drawing attention to the specific ways technological development, implementation, and job displacement effects have unfolded over time and in different societal contexts. There are various organizational and national systemic arrangements that may mediate, stifle, or enable technological development. We therefore should ask, how have nationally organized arrangements handled the challenges relating to technology, employment, and productivity differently and to what extent there is convergence or divergence in technological development, deployment, and the effects on the workforce?

This book approaches these questions through a comparative historical examination of the development paths and dynamics of technology and labor in the American and Germany automobile industry since its beginnings at the turn of the 20th century. If countries possess distinctive features that enable, mediate, or stifle technological developments, productivity, and job displacement, how does each *societal context* influence the trajectory and outcomes of automation and transformations of work within each auto industry? Here, the United States and Germany are here conceptualized as two *value-regimes* (Harvey 2017) that have engendered economic systems shaped by and embedded within unique social, political, cultural, and historical circumstances.

Value-regimes are constituted by distinct constellations of *business, labor,* and *government* that shape economic and technological development. We must ask in turn, how have the structure and practices of *businesses* stifled, mediated, or enabled automation and the transformations of labor? Here, corporate managements pursue varied profits strategies within different industrial relations contexts to implement production plans that combine labor and technology in arrangements aimed at securing profit, market share, and growth. Next, how have *workers*—as individuals, or collectively coordinated as members of labor unions or works councils—responded to and resisted threats of automation, coped with technological change, job losses, job retraining, and the elimination of certain types of jobs? The powers, legal rights, and organizational frameworks of workers' organizations are especially important here as well as the degree to which the relationship between labor and management is defined by contention or cooperation. Finally, how have *governments*—in their role as rule makers and conflict mediators—enabled, mediated, or stifled the technological displacement of jobs, particularly in how they shaped the legal and institutional framework for national industrial relations regimes? The government's responsibility to protect and advance national interests by maintaining jobs and industrial capability induces intervention in domestic industries, including labor-management struggles. They also sometimes act on behalf of domestic producers against foreign competition, thereby working in favor of the domestic value-regime. These models of integrating business, labor, and government are analyzed to see how each has fared against the vagaries of the global market and the vicissitudes of automation and technological displacement. The goal is to stage an encounter between history and existing theories to develop a *critical theory of productivity, automation, and technological displacement.*

1.1 *Germany's* 'soziale Marktwirtschaft' *versus America's 'Exceptional' Economy*

The choice to examine the United States and Germany follows logically from their similarities that makes comparison fruitful as well as from their differences that can facilitate insights by observing the specific developmental paths that emerge from different organizational and systemic arrangements.

According to Hall and Soskice (2003 [2001]), advanced capitalist societies can be categorized as either *liberal market* or *coordinated market economies*. The United States is considered a prototypical liberal economy that relies more on the market to solve coordination problems. Germany, by contrast, has been a coordinated market economy that addresses challenges via non-market forms of collaboration and cooperation (Hall and Soskice 2003 [2001]: 24). Ideologically, the United States is often framed as "exceptional" among nations (Lipset 1996; Jouet 2017), whereas Germans find value in the modernist social democratic model or what has been called Germany's *soziale Marktwirtschaft* (social market economy). The 'free market' focused 'American capitalism' in the 'exceptional' nation of the United States is here systematically analyzed versus the 'Rhine' capitalism of Germany and its *soziale Marktwirtschaft* (see Albert 1993).

It is well documented that both societies experienced increases in wealth and 'progress' since the industrial revolution took hold, belatedly, during the last quarter of the 19th century, and concurrently encountered the 'creative destruction' (Schumpeter 2003 [1942]) attendant with this progress, including technological displacement of labor through automation (Frey 2019). Both countries had small but growing domestic auto industries by the beginning of the 20th century. Thereafter, numerous factors impacted their developmental trajectory. German industrial policy fostered a highly skilled labor force (Kern and Schumann 1987; Lüdtke 2009), whereas the United States often deployed technology that deskilled the labor force (see, Braverman 1998 [1974]; Crumm 2010). German factories possess *works councils* stipulated by law to entail certain *codetermination rights* that foster cooperation with management on determining working standards and conditions (e.g., Jürgens 1995; Haipeter 2006).[1] Labor law in the United States structures conflict resolution on multi-step grievance procedures (Lam, Norsworthy, and Zabala 1991; Asher and Edsforth 1995), and workers typically have a much more combative relationship with management. As Greenhouse (2019: 8) observes, the United States has an "anti-worker" exceptionalism. American capitalism is known for biasing its outlook to short-term profits, while German companies invest for long-term economic sustainability (Albert 1993). Generally, the United States is a value-regime based on *combative industrial relations*, a (relatively) *low skill labor force*, and a *capitalist orientation* toward profits, while Germany has *cooperative industrial relations*, a *high skilled workforce*, and a (comparatively) *humanist orientation* that mediates capital accumulation with humanist goals. The objective, therefore, is to examine how these divergent tendencies shaped industrial development and the response to various challenges.

1 For simplicity, referring to Germany when discussing the years 1949–1990 means *West Germany*, unless stated otherwise. The East German auto industry is not discussed in depth.

One motivation for this comparison is to determine whether the United States or Germany has the resources and sustainable systemic arrangements that can resist the loss of income, economic health, and social solidarity that is possible with automation and technological displacement in the context of the competitive global economy. Are there "humane" forms of rationalization that can preserve jobs or is deindustrialization "inevitable?" Is it possible to harness the productive power of the industrial system without negative social consequences for some workers and communities? Alternatively, can a company resist change or lag competitors if necessary for the sake of jobs without causing other negative consequences such as slower growth, loss of revenue or market share, or even bankruptcy? Through historical comparison, it is possible to evaluate which society has fared 'better' according to multiple criteria and points of view, from the struggle for job security, to the survival of the firm, and even the economic standing of nation-states. Such questions are not trivial, as identifying the advantages and disadvantages of certain 'models' of organizational and systemic arrangements helps us evaluate which value-regimes are more capable of meeting the challenges of the future.

1.2 *The Importance of the Automobile Industry*

The automobile industry is examined as an exemplar of industrial development that has also experienced profound transformations in the production process and the nature of the work (e.g., Braverman 1998 [1974]; Kern and Schumann 1984; Flink 1988; Jürgens, Malsch, and Dohse 1993). The industry has been characterized by continuous labor displacement through technological and organizational changes, including through the automation of specific production processes (e.g., Hounshell 1985; Jürgens, Malsch, and Dohse 1993; Krzywdzinski 2020a). It is also an industry whose emergence spurred on a transportation revolution that transformed and accelerated modern social life (Rosa 2015), as well as prompted the creation of many related industries such as auto repair shops and gas stations. In sum, the automobile has both transformed society and has itself been transformed by revolutions in production which thereby transform the nature of work and employment within the industry.

The auto industry has been considered vital for both the American and German economy. They represent industrial strength and are major sources of employment for major auto companies as well as for suppliers, dealers, and other automobile related jobs. This therefore means they are responsible for the generation and distribution of a large amount of value within their respective value-regime. This extensive reach and influence are reasons why the auto industry has been famously called the "industry of industries," as Drucker proclaims, "The automobile industry stands for modern industry all over the globe. It is to the twentieth century what the Lancashire cotton mills were to the nineteenth century: the industry of industries" (cited from Meyer 2004: 1; Drucker 1946). The health of the American and German auto industries has been used as a 'barometer' for the general health of the US and German economy, and their interests have been framed as coterminous. As one General Motors executive put it in the 1950s,

> for years I thought what was good for our country was good for General Motors, and vice versa. The difference did not exist. Our company is too big. It goes with the welfare of the country. Our contribution to the Nation is quite considerable. (Quoted in Terrell 2016)

It can be claimed, with perhaps only minor exaggeration, that one way to assess the overall economy in both the US and Germany is to observe the conditions of its auto industry. There is also a cultural significance of the automobile within both countries, a specific 'car culture' that generates cultural attachment and meaning to 'German' or 'American' cars, which is similarly attached to the domestic German and American auto companies (Hiott 2012; Albert 2019). Today, the global auto industry is among the largest industries in the world with revenues in the trillions and employment in the millions (Covarrubias and Ramírez Perez 2020b).

The auto industries in both countries were also major sites of labor struggle, with each developing different ways of dealing with the conflict between capital and labor (see, Brumlop and Jürgens 1983; Flink 1988; Cutler 2004; Haipeter 2006). There is a strong labor union tradition in both the American and German auto industries, but both differ greatly in their structure, size, scope, collective bargaining strategies, and relationship to the state and business. This variance helps us understand how the specific labor-business relationship in each value-regime impacted their productive development. For these reasons, by exploring the history of the auto industry, one can gain useful insights into the structure and dynamics of both value-regimes and how each has handled the transformations of labor that coincides with technological change and automation.

2 Capital as Value in Motion among Value-regimes

The theoretical basis for this analysis is a synthesis of social theories drawing primarily from the work of David Harvey, Moishe Postone, and Niklas Luhmann. The theory is actively applied and evaluated against the historical cases of the American and German experience to further develop the theory in light of the findings. The result is a fusion of theory and empirical historical experience that seeks to be greater than the sum of its parts and more illustrative and analytically powerful than what came before. The following introduces the theoretical precepts and concepts developed throughout this book, starting with the foundational concept of *capital* in modern societies.

Capital is not a 'thing,' such as money or a 'capital stock,' but rather *value in motion*: it has no fixed material embodiment but is a process that appears at different moments in the form of money and commodities in a spiraling path of movement and expansion. This process was stylized by Marx in Capital Volume 1 (1976 [1867]) in the formula *M-C-M'*, with each letter expressing a moment in the process of movement of capital. Harvey (2017) describes the whole movement this way,

> It begins as money capital before taking on commodity form passing through production systems and emerging as new commodities to be sold (monetized) in the market and distributed in different forms to different factions of claimants (in the forms of wages, interest, rent, taxes, profits) before returning to the role of money capital once more. (3)

When this expansionary trajectory of capital is imagined in conjunction with the recursive circulation process, then capital can be visualized as a "spiral in constant expansion" (Harvey 2017: 4). This capital accumulation process has no substantive end because it is at its core a *means to a means*, as capital begets more capital in a continuous movement from money to commodities to more money in an infinite spiral (Postone 1993: 181).

If capital is value in motion, then what is this *value* that is in motion? Harvey (2017) defines value as: "the social labor we do for others as organized through commodity exchanges in competitive price-fixing markets" (4). This definition centers human labor at the core of value and emphasizes commodity exchanges and competitive price-fixing markets as social practices that must be universalized for capitalism to function. Marx's (1976 [1867]: 129) definition is that value is *socially necessary labor time*. In other words, value is the labor time spent on making goods for others to purchase, representing social relations between workers, objects as commodities, and the commodities made by others. As a social relation that takes place beyond the will of individuals, value, like gravity, comes to take on the character of an *immaterial but objective force* (Harvey 2017: 5). As Harvey (2017) describes, "I cannot dissect a shirt and find atoms of value in it any more than I can dissect a stone and find atoms of gravity. Both are immaterial relations that have objective material consequences" (5).

This understanding of value—separate from money as value's imperfect representation—is vital here.[2]

Harvey (2017) describes four quasi-autonomous but interrelated moments in capital's formation process: *valorization*, *realization*, *distribution*, and *return to money capital* or *reinvestment*. First, *valorization* is the production process where means of production and labor power meet to generate saleable commodities through expended labor time. During this period, capital is produced in the form of surplus value where a gap appears between the differential labor time that valorizes the worker and that which valorizes the total commodities produced (Harvey 2017: 20–21). This form of exploitation is the source of society's total surplus value. Disturbances in production, such as strikes, work stoppages, and other interruptions can disrupt the valorization process.

Realization is the moment when value is transformed from commodities for sale back into money through the market exchange of commodities (Harvey 2017: 20). Recursive circulation processes of transportation and sale are important here because valorized commodities must be sold to realize their value. Commodities are de-valued if left unsold and therefore fail in their purpose within the schema of capital. Questions such as means of transport, turnover times of different commodities and circulation processes, infrastructures of wholesale and retail networks, availability to purchase, and the effective demand of buyers all have relevance here. Crises can also appear here too such as if commodities fail to fulfill a want, need, or desire and remain unsold, or if consumers cannot generate effective demand to buy the commodities on sale. If successful however, value fulfills its purpose in capital through sale.

Once realized, the money exchanged for commodities is subject to capture by various claimants. This claiming of the money earned through sale becomes

2 Often value is collapsed into money, but this misses key nuances that appear when the distinction is maintained. Take for example a worker who has worked for two forty-hour weeks. The money does not mysteriously appear to the worker during the production process, nor does the worker receive money after every hour worked. Until they receive their paycheck at the end of the two weeks, the worker is not "monetized," but rather valorized. This time lag is one reason why a concept of value is useful. In addition, there is a social expectation that the worker should get paid for their hours work. But the value they are owed remains value until it is realized at the end of the pay period. Imagine a scenario where the worker is owed $1,000 but only receives $500 for the pay period. The worker was valorized $1,000, but only $500 of that $1,000 in value was realized. This is one example of how value and monetary realization can differ. But taken one step further, the worker recognizes this and feels cheated. They complain to state authorities and demand receiving the owed $500. This is an expression of *valorization as a social relation*. The fact that the worker recognizes how there is a discrepancy of their value and wages is an example of how value takes on a socially immaterial but objective force. Though immaterial, value mediates social relations apart from money.

the *distribution* moment of the capital process (Harvey 2017: 21). These claimants include, but are not limited to, systems such as the state through taxes, the wages of the workers, the rent of the land or buildings where production takes place, the profit of the merchant who sold the commodity, the profit of the industrial enterprise that produced the commodity, and the interest on various debts owed to the creditors. Struggles appear here as well such as in the formation of tax codes that may be progressive or regressive in structure, in setting interest rates, or in structuring a distributive welfare state. Here, the mass of surplus value generated by the social whole is continuously divided amongst the different claimants, who then use this return to push the process of capital accumulation further.

This push is possible because of the final moment of capital, the return to money capital for purposes of *reinvestment* (Harvey 2017: 21). Here, the conditions of valorization must be maintained via continuous reinvestment. For example, reinvestment in the necessary raw materials, means of production, or labor power is needed to engage in the process of valorization. Disruptions in the other three moments can cause problems for reinvestment, which can ultimately threaten the existence of the capitalist enterprise. Difficulties valorizing commodities, maintaining warehouses of unsold commodities, or even simply poor management with too little designated for reinvestment can cause problems for individual capitals. Choices made at the reinvestment stage, aimed at the future sustainability of the firm, can produce path dependent consequences in the future as markets change, or changing standards of production *pressure* the implementation of certain patterns of reinvestment for survival.

These four moments give a schematic picture of the overall movement of capital as value in motion. While this serves as a useful model in the abstract, explaining the concrete unfolding of these processes in different times and places is a complex task. The simplicity of circular movement can be deceiving, as mere circularity misses the simultaneously upward trajectory that is taking place in the movement of capital. This is driven by the pursuit of capital accumulation as well as the effect of competition between capitalist businesses for profit, market share, and higher sales. As Harvey (2017) describes, "Competition between capitalists for market share transformed the circle of simple reproduction into the spiral form of perpetual accumulation for accumulation's sake" (26). Capital tends to expand and grow, and *how* this growth and expansion occurs changes the necessary conditions for continued growth and expansion in the future. It is also important to recognize how specific geographies operate and configure their own capital accumulation processes over time.

There are a variety of specific configurations of capitalism that have existed at different places and times. As Harvey (2017) explains, "If capital is defined as 'value in motion' then something has to be said about the time-space configuration of the world in which this occurs. Motion cannot occur in a vacuum" (127). This is where the concept of *value-regimes* becomes invaluable. Harvey (2017) defines value-regimes as: "regional configurations [of capitalism] ... which *relatively stable and geographically fixed configurations* of ... *value production, realization and distribution* form ..." (157; emphasis mine). What is most important here is the identification of historically specific practices of production, realization, distribution, and reinvestment that can become path dependent trajectories within delimited geographic regions. This is not to say that these practices are static, but that variable historical configurations of capital accumulation matter for the past development, present circumstances, and potential future of any geographic area. There are numerous ways that value-regimes can differ within the moments of value in motion. Harvey (2017) puts it this way,

> We need to shift from visualization of value in motion that is ungrounded anywhere to seeing it as it creates geographies of cities and transport networks; forms agrarian landscapes for the production of foodstuffs and raw materials; encompasses flows of people, goods, information; creates territorial configurations of land values and labor skills; organize a space of labor, structures of governance and administration. We also need to take account of the significance of accumulated working class traditions and know-how in particular places and times, of skills and social relations (not only of class), all the while acknowledging how the political and social struggles of people living in particular places leave behind memories and hopes of alternative unalienated ways of living and being. (127)

Each of these subjects can be investigated on its own for a particular time and place. The advantage of the concept of value-regimes is that it orients attention around historical and spatial configurations with both dynamic and variable as well as stable and durable characteristics. Within this framework, we are attempting to grasp the constellation of economic, political, and social forces and systems in relation to each other as specific formations of capitalism situated in time and space.

In analyzing value-regimes, one can point toward differences that characterize each of the four moments of value in motion. One could ask: what commodities are produced, what is the nature of capital-labor relations, and what characterizes the means of production and labor power employed? What are the wants, needs and desires of the people in the region, how is the circulation of commodities regulated, and to what degree are commodities produced within the value-regime circulate within the value-regime or are exported? How is the realized value and surplus value distributed among the claimants, how does distribution in the form of a welfare state affect conditions of valorization or the other moments of capital, and what is the proportional connection between distribution and reinvestment? How much profit is reinvested, how is reinvestment used to maintain and expand production, and how does the state support or hinder specific investment opportunities? All these questions have distinct answers within each value-regime. The relevant question in this book is how do the United States and Germany *as value-regimes* affect the history of automation, technical displacement, and the pursuit of productivity within their respective auto industries?

By conceptualizing value-regimes, the analytical specificity of capital's value in motion in a particular time and space can be pinpointed and analyzed. Harvey (2017) frames the importance of value-regimes this way,

> To point to the importance of all this in the formation of distinctive value-regimes is not to resort to either physical or cultural determinism but to open up, but not close, a discussion on the dialectical integration of capital accumulation with the perpetual evolution of the contextual geographical conditions of nature and human nature in which this process occurs. (165–166)

The primary subject of this book lies within production, i.e., technological, organizational, and productivity changes within the two auto industries. However, such developments in the corporations and on the shopfloor cannot be fully understood without understanding how they fit within the larger flow of the spiral circulation and expansion of capital, and how their activities are embedded within specific value-regimes.

2.1 *Communication, Social Systems, and Value-systems*

The term *value-system* reflects a theoretical synthesis between the Neo-Marxian approach with Niklas Luhmann's systems theory. It is designed to draw our attention to how concrete organizations are *oriented toward acquiring value* and *operate as social systems.* For example, corporations such as Ford or Volkswagen are businesses aimed at generating and capturing value and surplus value. Unions too attempt to secure value for their members through collective bargaining. In this sense, both are *value driven systems.*[3] What is specifically meant by social system, however, requires more elaboration.

3 Governments also operate as value-systems in a sense, though value accumulation through taxation, is not its primary, stated, function. Governments nevertheless legally define many

Luhmann's concept of system rests on the distinction between "system" and "environment," i.e., between "closed" systems and everything outside the system that is designated as the system's environment.[4] According to Luhmann (2012 [1997]) social systems are *only* constituted by communication. Human beings participate in society only insofar as they participate in communication. Communication forms the basis of all social systems as the quintessential social act, and all that is not communicated, including humans, remains outside of society as part of the environment of society (Lee 2000: 322). Communications from various social systems, e.g., businesses, governments and so on, can "irritate" these humans or other social systems to perform certain behavior or make further communications, e.g., command a work task or disseminate a report on the productivity of a firm. In this way, *communications steer individuals, society, and social systems.*

Communication stacks upon communication as social systems communicate to each other and push their *evolution* in particular directions through receiving and responding to communication (2012 [1997]: 251–358). Through processes of variation, selection, and re-stabilization within the realm of its own communications and its communications with others, social systems evolve and change (Luhmann 2012 [1997]: 275–305). This process of responding and adapting to the "irritations" from communication is understood to be highly contingent and non-teleological. Evolution is conceived of as an open-ended process with no end-goal or even a guarantee of successful adaptation. The evolutionary process allows for contingency in the developmental trajectory of social systems. Throughout the historical narrative, discourses surrounding productivity, automation, and technological displacement are highlighted to draw attention to how certain communications on these topics shape the evolution of the respective value-systems and influence the overall value-regime.

Processes of *differentiation* describe the functional aspect of society. Here, Luhmann (2013 [1997]) emphasizes how the evolutionary process of society has built multiple social systems each with their own function (1–166). There is an economic society, an educational society, a political society etc., each with its own designated functions, forms of communication, and generalized symbolic media (Lee 2000: 328). However, systems with different functions

aspects of the value-regime and therefore are oriented toward keeping value in motion for the regime and for individual value-systems.

4 Much of the following is reformulated from the summarization of Luhmann's theory in my article, "Sociology as Social System: Luhmann, Enlightenment, and the Gap Between "Facts" and "Norms"" (Knowles 2021).

still observe and communicate with each other in ways that can generate structural couplings, e.g., three-way communications and linkages between unions, firms, and governments (Lee 2000: 328; Luhmann 2013 [1997]: 115–124). Functional systems also make their own *distinctions* that only those within the system can understand or hold relevance. For example, communications about what production processes are automated or manual hold relevance in the auto industry as well as the distinction between productive/unproductive, and high quality/low quality. These systems typically *self-describe* themselves through communications that identify them with the *positive* side of the distinction (productive, high quality) and against the *negative* side (unproductive, low quality), and attempt to disseminate this self-description broadly, e.g., through advertisements. Communications on these topics, both within firms and unions and from other social systems such as governments or mass media, influence the evolution of the value-systems. Because modern society is differentiated into so many functional systems, any single event is often observed by multiple social systems at once, and given just as many different meanings, interpretations, and responses (Lee 2000: 328). The key to understanding Luhmann's theory of functional differentiation is to recognize that modern society is necessarily *polycontextural*, with each social system simultaneously observing and responding to its environment, including other social systems, in a variety of ways particular to each social system.

The auto companies, unions, governments, and other organizations are conceptualized as social systems communicating with one another trying to *influence the evolutionary trajectory* of both their own development (and rendered in their own self-description) and the other social systems that constitute their environment. The term *value-system* signifies how social systems such as governments, unions, and corporations are both social systems operated through communication *and* are concerned with the accumulation or distribution of value and are structured to achieve that purpose. The detectable patterns of communication, including their purpose, function, motivation, target audience, and content, can also help us better understand the specific *social* character of the historical dynamic of capitalism. It clarifies what precisely is 'social' about Postone's (1993) concept of 'social domination,' as explained in the following section.

3 Production under Productivity Pressure

Social domination is defined here as *the pressure to conform to continuously changing yet directionally dynamic, time-based, and generalizing productivity norms*. Each word has a specialized meaning, so the definition must be carefully unpacked. A good starting point is the famous quote from Marx in the Eighteenth Brumaire that "Men make their own history, but they do not make it just as they please; they do not make it under circumstances chosen by themselves, but under circumstances directly encountered, given and transmitted from the past" (Marx 1963 [1852]: 15). If humanity does not make history freely on our own terms, then this implies there must be *historically rooted constraints* on human agency. In the broadest sense, "social constraints on human agency" could be the most generic definition of social domination. Social scientists studying any social problem could use the term social domination to describe their work—e.g., "racism as social domination," "homophobia as social domination," or "income inequality as social domination." However, Postone's (1993, 2015) meaning of social domination is more specific, outlining the constraining effects of a *historical dynamic endemic to capitalist societies*. The following explains precisely what these limits and constraints are and how they constitute a historical dynamic. It is also necessary to explain how social domination is connected to production processes, automation, and technological displacement, and how social domination explains the root of the problem of automation.

3.1 *Commodity and Labor as the Social Basis*

Production in capitalism is for the purpose of producing commodities. However, the commodity for Marx (1976 [1867]) is *not* merely a physical object that could exist in any form of society but is a *historically specific form of social relations* that defines the core of capitalist modernity (Postone 2015: 11). In other words, the universalized social relations of producing commodities, buying commodities with money (with the power of universal exchange), and their dual nature both as use values and as values that stand in relation to all other commodities is a *historically specific form of relations only generally valid in capitalist societies*.

Labor power is a commodity as well in the sense that it too is "produced," "bought," and "sold" on the market, although labor possesses special qualities which are obscured through different terms (e.g., wages instead of price). When labor power is used in capitalist production, it serves a different purpose than labor in pre-capitalist societies. Instead of working for self-sufficiency or as part of kinship or direct-power relationships, labor time expenditure serves to *valorize* the worker in a way that, if converted into wages, allows for the commodities produced by others to be bought and used by the worker (Postone 2015: 12). This new form of interrelatedness and interdependence constitutes the foundation of capitalist society as a historically specific form of social life. In this way, labor in capitalism becomes not just a *means of production* but is also a *means of distribution* that constitutes one of the main avenues for distribution within the capitalist system (Harvey 2017). This contextualizes the stakes and importance of jobs and labor within capitalist society and posits that this importance is not transhistorical but has become so due to the predominance of capitalist social relations. It clarifies why jobs are so sought after and essential for the health of both individuals and their families as well as the capitalist system.

In addition to changes in the purpose and functions of labor, capitalist society is defined by changes in the perception and relationship to time, especially within production. Under the regime of the workshops and early factories of the industrial revolution of the late 18th and early 19th century, employers desired a synchronization of labor for the sake of efficiency and productivity, which required wage workers to adopt a new "time regime" that was qualitatively different from the perception of time in feudal society (Thompson 1967; Harvey 1990: 423–424; Martineau 2015).[5] Workers needed to demarcate the employer's time during labor and their own time and treat time as money to be spent as rationally as possible for economic ends (see Weber 2002 [1905]). This did not take place without resistance however, since time is social and therefore also political, and thus control and definition of time is always a locus of struggle (Martineau 2015: 5). However, the nature of this resistance changed with succeeding generations, and the predominance of an abstract homogenous time and capitalist time discipline eventually came to be normalized (Thompson 1967: 86; Postone 1993: 202). The widespread acceptance of both labor as a social form of interrelatedness and the preeminence of abstract time are two necessary preconditions for the emergence of social domination.

3.2 *Temporal Norms and Social Necessity*

Value is generated by labor as determined by *socially necessary labor time*. Time expended during work both valorizes the worker and their labor products simultaneously. However, because valorization takes place as one moment

5 In precapitalist societies, people related to time not by constant units such as seconds, minutes, or hours, but based on the timings of natural processes such as days, lunar cycles, or seasons. As Postone (1993) explains, this relationship to time termed "concrete time" does "not depend on a continuous succession of constant temporal units but either are based on events … or on temporal units that vary" (201). This is important because in a framework of time not determined by constant units, the concept of productivity, producing more in a standard period of time, is essentially inconceivable. Indeed, the concept of productivity was largely unknown to or was not important to people in precapitalist societies (Postone 1993: 200–211; see Knowles 2017: 186–187).

within a flow of value in motion in a larger social context, the determination of what *counts* as productive labor time is determined *apart from the workers and the individual business*. Instead, it is determined by whatever is considered a 'normal' or 'socially necessary' amount of time to complete certain work tasks. In this way, socially necessary labor time is a *temporal norm* that determines what counts as a fully productive period of work in the specific socio-historic context of production. This is not merely a descriptive term of how long it generally takes to produce a particular commodity, instead it, "delineates a socially general, compelling, norm. Production must conform to this prevailing, abstract, overarching norm if it is to generate the full value of its products" (Postone 2015: 14).

It is here that social domination starts to come into view. It is *social* in the sense that socially necessary labor time constitutes norms that are not determined by any single social, economic, or political entity—and therefore can only be attributed to the sum result of the operations of the social totality. They constitute *domination* because they are overarching norms that *must be responded to* by human actors yet are *not consciously determined* by them (Postone 2015: 6). In other words, these norms represent a constraint on agency that is difficult to overcome since there is no identifiable social system or systems responsible for their existence or effects. Capitalism thereby generates a form of social domination that differs fundamentally from domination by a capitalist class or the state; it is rather "*the domination of people by time*" (Postone 2015: 14; emphasis in original) in the form of an overarching system of compelling norms, constraints, and imperatives. As Postone (2015) explains,

> the result of this form of mediation is a historically new form of social domination ... one that subjects people to impersonal, increasingly rationalized, structural imperatives and constraints that cannot adequately be grasped in terms of class domination, or, more generally, in terms of the concrete domination of social groupings or of institutional agencies of the state and/or the economy. It has no determinate locus and, although constituted by determinate forms of social practice, appears not to be social at all. (Postone 2015: 15)

The core of this social domination is the constraints and imperatives attendant with socially necessary labor time.

For example, a company with production processes slower than the social average in that industry would not be rewarded with more value for being slower but is rather burdened with higher costs due to inefficiency and lack of control over time, and it would likely fail in the long-term without intervention or change. As Harvey (2017) explains, "it is the average labor time that counts. If I spend an inordinate amount of time on the [commodities] I make I will not get the equivalent back in exchange. That would reward inefficiency. I will receive only the average labor time equivalent" (4–5). Here, the "average labor time equivalent" is the correlate to socially necessary labor time, i.e., production processes that fulfill the time requirements of socially necessary labor time receive the expected average labor time equivalent, whereas production processes that lag behind the social average are expected to sell at the social average price, even though their production processes result in comparatively de-valued commodities due to their slowness.[6] Put simply, under capitalism, *socially necessary labor time counts rather than actual labor time*, and this pressure to conform to "social necessity" can be described as a form of social domination (Harvey 2017: 55).

3.3 *Productivity and Its Discontents*

Up to this point we have described socially necessary labor time as a static norm. However, what is truly domineering about social domination is not that there is *a single unchanging* norm to be followed, but that these norms *continuously change*. Specifically, they change based on increases in *productivity and efficiency*, or more generally, the decreasing time it takes to complete work tasks. Increasing productivity generates more surplus value for capitalists by "[increasing] surplus labor time by lowering the labor time necessary for workers' reproduction" (Postone 2015: 17). In other words, increasing productivity raises the proportion of value that goes toward capital accumulation rather than toward workers' valorization (see Marx 1976 [1867]: 492–639). The pursuit of higher levels of this relative surplus value in valorization processes pushes the simultaneous objective of more productivity in production. This pressure to increase productivity constitutes another aspect of social domination. It can be described as a "despotism of the collectivity, structured by *considerations of productivity and efficiency*, effected at the cost of the individual" (Postone 1993:

6 One choice for a commodity produced from a lagging production process is, in the attempt at realization, to sell at the expected average price. This would mean the commodity is sold at a loss because it is devalued by the proportion of additional labor time that was spent in its production above the norm of socially necessary labor time. The second option is to attempt to sell at a higher price that corresponds to the costs of the lagging production process, but in this case, it is unlikely to be sold at all if commodities that meet the norms of socially necessary labor time are available. If unsold, the commodity drops from the circulation of capital and is totally devalued. In either case, some level of devaluation is expected.

333; emphasis mine). In other words, the expectations of productivity and efficiency constitute social domination.[7]

How do productivity increases change the norms of socially necessary labor time? Productivity improvements are pursued because they increase surplus value, thus enabling increased capital accumulation. However, the key is how productivity increases material wealth (use values) in a different proportion than it increases value. Productivity increases the number of use values produced per hour. But if the number of workers and worker hours remains the same, the same mass of value is spread out over a smaller number of produced commodities.[8] This results in less value per commodity, but more total commodities. What has occurred is that material wealth increased, but total value remained the same, just distributed differently across the mass of commodities.

This happens because as productivity rises, the norms of socially necessary labor time are *redefined to match the higher level of productivity*. As Postone (2015) explains, this dynamic "[results in a] sort of ... treadmill. Higher levels of productivity result in great increases in material wealth, but not in proportional long-term increases in value per unit time. This, in turn, leads to still further increases in productivity" (14). This treadmill dynamic makes the pursuit of productivity a never-ending process as the gains in surplus value are always short-term because the social norms of production, i.e. socially necessary labor time, adjusts to match the higher levels of productivity. As Postone (1993) explains, "*the social labor hour is constituted by the level of productivity*" and that "reduction of socially necessary labor time redetermines the normative social labor hour" (288–289; emphasis in original). This treadmill analogy is useful because it conveys both the image of speed-up that corresponds to the effects of productivity increases (whether in terms of labor intensity or automation), and how the redefinition of value to match productivity gains

7 One could argue this is also an expression of domination by management. This is true insofar as norms of high productivity are also in the interests of management for the sake of capital accumulation. However, the determination of what these norms *are* is not determined by management in a vacuum free from the larger social context. Rather, the *effective* norms of socially necessary labor time are determined at the socially general or industry wide level and thus is beyond the direct determination of management. Therefore, it is more fully understood when framed as *social* domination.

8 On the surface, this appears as more output per hour, and higher outputs allow for the commodities to be sold at lower prices. Certain conditions (e.g., monopolization) can prevent lower prices in practice, but nevertheless, from the Marxian point of view, these commodities have less value and deviation from this in terms of price is an expression of the imperfect reflection of price and value in special circumstances (see Clelland 2014).

conveys how the system is in a recursive loop—running in place—in the pursuit of value and surplus value accumulation.

Value for Marx is much more than just exchange value or prices. It is, as Postone explains, "a category of efficiency, rationalization, and ongoing transformation. *Value is a category of a directionally dynamic totality*" (Postone 1993: 272; emphasis in original). Value here is not just "value" in the commonsense understanding that a given idea holds importance and is therefore valuable or a commodity is worth some amount of money. Value is determined by the social relations of capitalist society. These relations are caught up with and shaped by a historical dynamic that is continuously changing the level of productivity and nature of work in society.

Increases in productivity can occur via numerous methods. Labor intensity can increase with faster movements of the human mind and body to complete more work tasks within the given time without changes in technology. New work tools can aid human labor in producing more per unit time. Alternatively, machines can be developed that replace human labor entirely from certain tasks, which results in automation of the task and the technological displacement of the existing workers. Marx's definition of what is considered technology useful for increasing productivity is broad. As Harvey (2017) explains,

> Technology does not only refer to the machines and tools and energy systems put in motion (the hardware as it were). It also includes organizational forms (divisions of labor, structures of cooperation, corporate forms, etc.) and the software of control systems, time and motion studies, just-in-time production systems, artificial intelligence and the like. (9)

Changes of all the types listed above affected the auto industry of Germany and the United States at different times and in different ways.

Being the technological leader in the industry is theorized to have specific advantages for capital accumulation. Not only is there an increase in the ratio of value to (relative) surplus value via productivity improvements, but the higher number of commodities with lower value can correspondingly be sold at lower prices but at higher potential profit. As Marx (1976 [1867]) explains, "*surplus-value* is created for [the capitalist] as soon as the *individual* value of his product falls *below* its social value and can be sold accordingly at a price *above* its individual value" (1023; emphasis in original). Selling below the socially average price but above the individual commodity's value is a possibility for extra profit only for the productivity leader(s) and only for as long as that price does not adjust to align more closely to the value of the product developed by the technological leader.[9] It is therefore in the best interest of an individual business to not just *maintain* the norms of socially necessary labor time, but to *push them forward* through new innovations and productivity improvements that potentiate more capital accumulation.

In a situation where a small number of businesses in an industry have such a productivity advantage and are using it to generate higher profits, it is then that a process of "generalization" occurs. Whatever the innovation is that caused the rise in productivity is supposed to become adopted by all the other companies in that industry, which thereby makes the productivity advantage become a new industry standard. Once this occurs profits fall back to the normal level for all—including the innovators and early adopters—until another productivity innovation emerges. At the end of the process, there is more material wealth, yet total value remains the same (Postone 1993: 288). In the historical narrative, we observe how this "generalization" process occurs in the American and German auto industry.

It is held that the vicissitudes of capitalist competition are the primary drivers of this generalization process. Harvey (2017) argues that the laws of motion of capital, including the generalization of productivity changes, are "enforced but not created, says Marx, by inter-capitalist competition" (154). While productivity changes in production generate more material wealth and the potential of higher profits, competition is a mechanism of *compelling* the adoption of productivity changes, and thus the generalization of productivity change. Postone (1993) puts it this way, "Once the new methods of production become generalized, the value yielded per unit time returns to its older level, and the producers who have not adopted the new methods become *compelled* to do so" (290; emphasis in original). For individual businesses aimed at the accumulation of surplus value, these dynamics generate a *continuous pursuit of productivity*. Opportunities for additional profit are available if a novel method of increasing productivity is implemented, so productivity increases are desirable. Yet increases in productivity become not just desirable but can take on the *force of necessity* if competitors develop substantial productivity increases. I use the term *productivity pressure* to describe this compulsion to conform to productivity norms. Simply put, 'standing still' is not an option in the context

9 This advantage is only a *possibility*, however, and issues of realization can appear. There is a contradiction at play as Harvey (2017) explains, "The more sophisticated the technology the less labor is congealed in the individual commodity produced. Even more troubling, less total value may be created if the total output of commodities does not increase enough to compensate for the decreased value of the individual items. If the productivity doubles then I have to produce and sell twice the volume of commodities to keep the total value available constant" (9).

of competition as "competition among isolated businesses, which is brought about by the mediation of anonymous markets, necessitates a permanent increase in productivity" (Kurz 1999: 16). Harvey (2017) sums up the dynamic this way,

> In a competitively organized economy the struggle between firms for technological advantage produces a pattern of leap-frogging innovations and technological and organizational forms. For this reason … capital becomes a permanently revolutionary force in world history. The technological basis of productive activity is constantly changing. (9)

This combination of desire *and* need for productivity increases can be understood as an integral aspect of social domination.

This description explains the capitalist impetus for higher levels of productivity through a treadmill dynamic that compels productivity increases to acquire short-term increases in surplus value and avoid falling behind competitors. That the norms of socially necessary labor time change with each increase in productivity through this redefinition process is the core of Postone's (1993) notion of a *capitalist historical dynamic*. There is a historical dynamic that lies outside direct human control implies constraint on human agency, and this can be understood as form of *heteronomy*. It follows that capitals that defy these norms are generally punished, those that follow them are more likely to survive than those who don't, and those that innovate and decrease socially necessary labor time even further are typically rewarded. Simply put: *this historical dynamic is social domination and a form of unfreedom.*[10]

---

10 Luhmann's description of evolution as contingent may appear to contradict Postone's theorization of a historical dynamic of capitalism. However, while Luhmann does assert that the evolutionary processes of social systems are in principle contingent and non-teleological, this does not foreclose the possibility of perceptible patterns of communication and their effects on social systems that could result in what we could justifiably call a "historical dynamic." Postone (2015: 18) argues that such a historical dynamic is not a simple teleological unfolding, but a highly complex and non-linear dynamic with multiple complicating and countervailing forces acting upon it. Furthermore, we explore both the characteristics of the historical dynamic, and the differential historical contingencies and other forces acting for or against the historical dynamic within the two auto industries. Therefore, the combination of an approach to temporality that emphasizes contingency like Luhmann's, and an approach that seeks to outline patterns of heteronomy such as Postone's are warranted in an analysis that seeks to examine both contingency and heteronomy. In short, the Luhmannian conception of evolution through communications over time can be seen as an analytical counterbalance used in tandem with Postone's historical dynamic to aid in illuminating both the contingent as well as

This framework can be applied to understand the specific unfolding of this historical dynamic and the generalization processes within different value-regimes. The impetus for productivity change has been described as a *compulsion* (Postone 1993: 290) or a *necessity* (Kurz 1999: 16), but how do value-systems in different value-regimes react to these pressures differently? How does the generalization process differ in the context of low competition versus high competition? What potential role do states and unions play to mitigate or intensify competition? What are the consequences of not adopting 'socially necessary' productivity changes? Is it possible to circumvent social domination or diminish its influence? These are questions that can only be answered through historical investigation.

3.4 *Automation and Technological Displacement*

What are the results of this process? First, we understand why the capital accumulation process is described as a spiral, as this dynamic expands production and the total number of commodities through speeding up the production process, while also proceeding in a circular motion through the stages of valorization, realization, distribution, and reinvestment (Harvey 2017). The spiraling and directional nature of the system is enabled by a complex of imperatives and constraints on production that continually redefine standards of production or what is 'socially necessary.' This productivity pressure dialectically mediates the class struggle between capital and labor through both determining productive norms and the concrete response to social domination emanating from those norms. The norms of social necessity dominate both workers and capitalists alike: keep up with the demands of the capitalist system or else be deemed socially unnecessary.

This is where automation and technological displacement become important. Though labor by itself can be intensified for productivity gains and technological change can augment human labor, another possibility is increasing productivity through direct automation of specific tasks or jobs. There is the potential for the pursuit of productivity to reach a point where new technology redefines the norms of social necessity to go beyond human capabilities, which

heteronomous aspects of the history described in the empirical chapters. See Laurindo (2017) for an analysis that combines the systems approach of Luhmann with Adorno's negative dialectics to critique how neoliberalism comes to shape social systems on the model of the market. Here, Luhmannian evolution does not foreclose the possibility of neoliberal "marketization" of other social systems. While contingency is always in principle possible, patterns that take on path dependent and even heteronomous force are also possible. The key for social scientists is to keep both possibilities in mind and analyze accordingly without giving predominance to agency or heteronomy.

pressures the replacement of human labor with technology. This is especially likely when higher productivity, new techniques, and organizational forms of production allow job tasks to become routinized, which makes the task especially vulnerable to automation (Autor et al. 2003; Frey and Osborne 2013).

A modification of Postone's (1993) treadmill analogy may aid in visualizing this process. Imagine a worker whose production task to produce commodities is to run on a treadmill. In the beginning, the worker walks at a leisurely pace that can be sustained for long periods of time. Later, for the sake of generating more surplus value, the speed of the treadmill is raised to a jog that is difficult to sustain unless one has high cardio-vascular endurance. Then, news arrives that a competing firm is producing their commodities at an even faster pace still, and the speed of the worker increases to match that of the competitor, who is nearly sprinting. Several iterations of this ratcheting up process occur until the 'socially necessary' running pace goes beyond human ability, and the only viable solution is to replace the human worker with something else—otherwise the human will be thrown off the treadmill entirely. That something else is a machine that performs beyond all human capabilities, which, through its widespread adoption in the industry, becomes the 'socially necessary' way the work is done. The worker is displaced by technology.

In general, once machine labor supersedes the skill of human workers, with higher productivity, better control over time, and at a lower cost than human labor, the compulsions and constraints of socially necessary labor time make human labor anachronistic, ultimately resulting in technological displacement. But even if technological displacement does not occur, the continuous push for higher levels of productivity and efficiency changes the nature of work in society in various ways. Braverman (1998 [1974]) argues that deskilling is a likely consequence, as managers deploy organizational changes, e.g., a more complex division of labor, and machinery to deskill workers for the benefit of management control. Machines that replace workers may still need attending by others, with human labor taking a secondary role (Nicolaus 1968: 58). Furthermore, in the 20th century and especially after WWII we see the purposeful application of the knowledge gathered from natural science applied to production processes, a phenomenon that Kurz (2014 [1986]) terms *science as a productive force*. This developed to the point where automation technology itself became a business aimed at improving the productivity of other industries and formed an industry with its own imperatives to generate surplus value and expand its markets (Harvey 2017: 119–120). Such developments are evident in the history of the global auto industry.

Another implication of this analysis is the potential for technological unemployment. From the point of view of the total system, productivity and the norms of socially necessary labor time could hypothetically reach a point where jobs disappear faster than new jobs appear, generating a form of structural unemployment (Keynes 1963 [1930]). As the processes described above move forward, compelled by the imperatives and constraints of social domination, the possibility of technological unemployment developing as a result becomes more likely, though it is not necessarily an inevitability. There are many contingent factors that affect whether technological unemployment emerges (Postone 2015: 21).

The processes described here are in the sphere of production and valorization, but the other moments of capital as value in motion such as realization, distribution, and reinvestment all affect this development as quasi-autonomous moments within the whole (Harvey 2017). In addition, the differences within and between value-regimes have distinct historical and path dependent conditions and trajectories that shape this process. There are contingent factors that modify the effects of the historical dynamic and the consequent social domination. This book explores what mediating factors played a role in the history of the two auto industries.

The historical dynamic described here should be understood as a kind of "gravity" that pulls industries toward higher and higher magnitudes of productivity and thus experience social domination as temporal imperatives and constraints. Though agency, contingency, and choice certainly play a role—especially within different value-regimes—centering social domination and productivity pressure as a key factor in the history of the auto industry recontextualizes the history in a way that can draw new insights. An analysis of how the development of the auto industry of Germany and the US was shaped by social domination and caught up in the historical dynamic of ever ratcheting productivity can demonstrate how automation and technological displacement unfolded in both value-regimes.

The intent is to answer these questions through comparative historical analysis. On the one hand, the empirical history is evaluated against the propositions of the theory to see to what extent the theory explains the phenomena, deriving new insights from the history that is only enabled through an encounter with the theory. On the other hand, the theory can be 'tested' and thereafter improved upon based upon an encounter with historical evidence. The aim is to help clarify the nature of social domination in modern capitalist societies.

4 Transformations of Production over the Longue Durée

The two value-regimes are historically analyzed from the beginning of the 20th century to the present, starting from the beginning of the auto industry.

Each of the five empirical chapters are divided into roughly twenty-to-thirty-year blocks covering major developments in auto production. Automation, technological displacement, and the transformations of labor are understood as an undercurrent of gradual structural change that only becomes clear when observed from the point of view of the *Longue Durée* (Braudel 2009 [1960]). Taking this long view and drawing important insights and lessons from each period allows the transformations of labor and automation to be carefully tracked. In other words, the examination of a longer historical period is necessary because of the nature of the phenomena under examination. Transformations of labor, especially on the scale of value-regimes, can only be properly understood within this longer time scale of the *Longue Durée* (Braudel 2009 [1960]).

To demonstrate the importance of this approach, consider the shift in attitude towards the desirability of productivity and technological innovation from a *Longue Durée* view. In 1589, William Lee triggered one of the first recorded incidents of fear of technology and its potential automation effects on employment through his invention of a stocking frame knitting machine. With this machine, England's textile workers could be relieved of the need to hand knit clothing, which would reduce the time and relative physical effort needed per article. However, when Lee applied for a patent for his invention, Queen Elizabeth I observed the machine and was reported to have said, "Thou aimest [sic] high, Master Lee. Consider thou what the invention could do to my poor subjects. It would assuredly bring them to ruin by depriving them of employment, thus making them beggars" (Acemoglu and Robinson 2012: 182–183). This fear of *technological unemployment* was so great that William Lee was eventually coerced to leave Britain (Acemoglu and Robinson 2012: 182–184).

This episode may sound strange to modern ears. From the vantage point of the 21st century, it seems odd that a powerful monarch like Elizabeth, who was supposed to embody the interest of the British nation, would purposefully disallow the use of a technology that would very likely have *increased the productivity* of Britain's textile industry—an industry that Britain would come to dominate in the world market a few centuries later (Hobsbawm 1996 [1962]). The fear that technological innovation would rupture the status quo of production and employment was sufficient to *override the argument in favor of increasing productivity*. It apparently did not occur to, or was not convincing to, Queen Elizabeth that higher productivity through machinery would increase economic growth and wealth instead of generating unemployment, as economists centuries later would argue (Woirol 1996). This demonstrates how a *different conception and prioritization of productivity* existed in the 17th century than what exists today. It also shows the historical contingency of the modern view that typically assumes the desirability of improving productivity. Only with the historical development of capitalism, as a productive system, internalized ideology, and emergence of a type of "human nature," could the desirability of productivity become a hallmark of modern thought (Thompson 1967; Martineau 2015). Queen Elizabeth's fears and views regarding William Lee's invention would appear to only find resonance with 'reactionary' or 'backward' groups such as the Luddites who between 1811 to 1816, who rioted and smashed machines that were threatening to make their skills and their labor superfluous (Mantoux 2006 [1928]: 399–408). By the dawn of the automobile age, the association of technology and productivity with angst had lost much of its popularity, especially among those in power, and had instead become associated with 'progress' and increasing economic growth and wealth (see Woirol 1996).

We should note the sea change in orientation away from fear of technological change to its embrace—especially the close association between technological change, productivity gains, and modern progress. Such a change was contingent but has nevertheless taken on powerful rhetorical force today among nearly all social systems that appears almost omnipresent. Second, the struggle of workers, though no longer expressed as a romantic desire to abolish clock time or smash machines, shaped this historical development and remains relevant to the history of the auto industry as autoworkers in both the US and Germany struggled over shaping technology utilization, working time, and productivity norms. Ultimately, what is most important here is recognizing the *historical specificity of modern attitudes toward technology and productivity*. These attitudes have an origin, are historically constructed and conditioned, and are ultimately contingent. However, the connection between productivity and technology is powerful ideologically and in practice, as we observe how productivity norms have taken on a form of *social domination* that shaped 20th and 21st century industrial history.

In addition, by analyzing industrial history through an analysis of the historical dynamics of capitalism (Postone 1993), this book attempts to overcome a "presentist" bias common in works that diagnose the present with a simplistic view of history that projects current trends into the future. By "presentist" bias, I mean the tendency to diagnose the present and predict the future in ways that are simply extensions of the circumstances of one's own time. Examining automation, which by the nature of the topic is prone to futurist predictions, unfortunately lends itself to falling into such traps. These predictions become more and more off over time as modern society continues to change, and they frequently become increasingly problematic in retrospect.

Milanović (2016) explains the perniciousness this problem in his assessment of literatures from before the 1973 oil shock and afterward. He describes the pre-oil shock literature of the late 1960s as warning of a future where large corporations and monopoly capitalism dominates, technology allows for ever larger economies of scale, and there is a convergence of capitalism and communism (Milanović 2016: 156–157). In contrast, the post-oil shock literature was characterized by preoccupation with conserving natural resources, dealing with the limits to growth, and promoting flexible medium-sized (German *Mittlestand*) manufacturing over large corporations. By the 1990s, the literature shifted again into the famous "end of history" or "Washington Consensus" rhetoric, which celebrated neoliberalism and the spread of democracy through US power. Most important here, this literature presented the rise of Japan and Germany as representatives as an alternative model of capitalism that compete with American style "short-term focused" capitalism (Milanović 2016.: 157–158; Albert 1993).

Each of these literatures become increasingly problematic in retrospect to the degree they project the specific socio-historical circumstances of their immediate present into the future. Notably, for example, none of these literatures were able to grasp the unfolding of key developments such as the rise of China or the tumultuous geopolitical problems in the Middle East. The goal here is to overcome the problems of presentist historicity by analyzing the *underlying dynamics of capitalism* that have shaped the emergence and industrial trajectory of both the auto industries. This is what Postone (2015) describes as differentiating between the historically variant social, political, and economic configurations of capitalism such as 19th century liberal capitalism or 20th century state-centric Fordist capitalism versus an analysis that "allows for an understanding of capital as the core of the social formation, separable from its various surface configurations" (24). While each period experienced its own challenges and specific circumstances, the underlying historical logic and dynamics are posited to be at play throughout. This interplay of balancing an examination of the underlying logic of capitalism and period specific circumstances is an analytical challenge, but nonetheless an essential for sophisticated comparative historical analysis. By reckoning with the concrete history and social dynamics through the *Longue Durée* of capitalist historical dynamics, we are in a better position to understand the forces and factors that shaped the present and which might impact the future without projecting fleeting contemporary concerns into the future.

4.1 *Between Autonomy and Heteronomy*

The above theoretical framing should not be misconstrued as a monocausal or "master" factor that explains all developments in the industrial history of the US and Germany. Many other factors are discussed such as product changes, trade barriers, and geopolitical shifts, and there were times where different concerns were considered more important than increasing productivity or automating labor. This is why Harvey's (2017) framework is useful because it brings awareness to how changes or disruptions in *any* of the four quasi-autonomous moments of capital may affect all the other moments. However, it is necessary to limit additional factors to avoid theoretical incoherency or ceding that history is too complicated for anything to be explained. This requires a balancing act between focusing on the key factors and processes and including other variables that mediate these processes at different times and contexts. The treadmill dynamic and the continuously changing norms of productivity can be understood as a kind of "gravity" or "force field" that generates specific constraints and imperatives and tends to push towards even higher levels of productivity. Yet, like gravity's effects on humans versus birds, though this gravity of productivity pressure is always present, its effects and the response to those effects vary.

The historical development of each automobile industry can provide insights, especially regarding how different value-regimes deal with imperatives to grow and increase productivity. There is a constant tension between the need to control time and increase productivity, on the one hand, and a struggle to maintain jobs, on the other. Each value-regime handles such tensions differently and examining these differences may also illuminate new insights into the nature of social domination. This task is daunting. However, the challenge to explain this "gravity" and how it unfolds historically is as necessary as it is formidable, as Sewell (2008) explains,

> I am convinced that we need a concrete history of the emergence and development of capitalism's abstract forms, but such a prospect poses methodological and a rhetorical conundrums [sic] whose solution requires considerable theoretical agility and rhetorical finesse. (533)

The challenge is substantial as it requires nuance between contingency and heteronomy; agency, structure, and systemic imperative; totalizing drive and path dependencies; globalizing convergence and regional divergence. The solution to such tensions lies neither in the adoption of a unitary understanding of capitalism or the anarchy of individual developments (see Herrigel 2000; Dahms 2002), but in an analysis that identifies the necessary preconditions for divergence and an honest assessment of the possibilities of agency against totalizing tendencies.

According to Sewell (2008), the temporalities of social life are eventful, i.e., contingent, uneven, irreversible, and transformational. However, he also contends that processes of capital are "in certain respects super-eventful … core processes of capitalism ... sustain a recurrent logic at their core. This means that the temporality of capitalism is composite and contradictory, simultaneously still and hyper eventful" (Sewell 2008: 1). In other words, capitalist dynamics operate on a different logic and temporality than most other social processes. These historical dynamics unfold unevenly, but they do have a directional movement and inherent contradictions that can be observed throughout the history of capitalist society (Postone 1993). They generate dynamics, imperatives, and constraints that social systems must respond to, yet are often not directly identified, scrutinized, or confronted. Here, we historically evaluate these forms of 'unfreedom' (Postone 2017: 43), while simultaneously bearing in mind the contingency of the independent historical development of value-regimes (Harvey 2017).

Sewell (2008) argues that there is a balancing act that must be performed, and a mindset needed to take on such a task. He states that researchers should simultaneously,

> be attentive to contingency; to trace out the specific sequences of actions; keep the chronology rigorously straight; to look constantly at the changing contexts of action; and to figure out what protocols people actually drew upon when they acted. In other words, practitioners of historically engaged political economy and economic sociology need to keep on doing the sort of things they do. But we also need to recognize the strange stillness—what one might call a 'stillness-in-motion'—at the core of capital at its most abstract level. Here capital is always churning, always self-valorizing, moving endlessly in Marx's sequence of 'M–C–M' (from its money form, to its commodity form, and back again to its money form with the amount enhanced by profit). Everything is exchangeable for everything else because the money form is a universal equivalent. There is constant movement, but the movement is constantly repetitive. For capital at its most abstract, the movement is like running on a treadmill. (Sewell 2008: 526)

Here, Sewell (2008) both admonishes comparative historical scholars to keep an eye on contingency and rigorous historical study but adds this additional challenge of confronting capitalism's peculiar temporality. Here, we attempt to navigate the subtleties between autonomy and heteronomy. Through awareness that history is shaped by both acts of contingency and forces of constraint, one is in a position to advance a nuanced explanation of social phenomena that does more justice to the complex reality of social life in modern societies.

4.2 *Chapter Outline*

This book comprises six chapters. Chapter 1 covers the period between 1900–1929, detailing the beginning of the industry up to the market crash of 1929 and the beginning of the Great Depression. During this period, the fledgling automobile industry was primed to transform the nature of transportation in both countries. The industries began with a similar artisanal production system, but divergent trajectories of the respective automobile industries emerged early as the US industry adopted Fordism while the German industry maintained traditional craft production methods. Chapter 2 discusses the events between 1930 and 1949, the period of the Great Depression and the Second World War, up to the point when the Federal Republic of Germany was established in 1949. This period features the rise of the United Automobile Workers union that coincides with the repression of German labor under the Nazi regime. Chapter 3 covers the period of prosperity and expansion between 1950 and 1972 with the *Wirtschaftswunder* of Germany and the high point of US global market dominance. Automation of industrial labor greatly increased in both the US and Germany, though divergent industrial relations also affected this development. Chapter 4 covers the years 1973–1995, which encompasses the time from the oil crisis up through the crisis of the German auto industry in the early 1990s, as well as details the slow decline of market share in the American industry since the 1970s. Japanese competition and their system of *lean production* challenges conventional notions of industrial organization and productivity development in both the US and Germany during this period. Chapter 5 discusses developments from 1995 to the present, detailing the further decline and rebirth of the US industry since the bankruptcies and government bailout of GM and Chrysler in 2009, as well as the globalization of the German industry into Eastern Europe. The opening up of the Chinese market and rise of car manufacturing in China also opened opportunities and challenges for both auto industries. New technologies, and the rise of electric vehicles represent emerging challenges the auto industry will continue to face in the future. Each period demonstrates unique dynamics and important lessons on the transformations of automation, labor, and productivity development. Chapter 6 concludes the analysis with an examination of those lessons and synthesizes the insights from the historical analysis to outline a critical theory of productivity, automation, and technological displacement in modern societies.

CHAPTER 1

Fork in the Road: between Craft and Mass Production in the Early 20th Century

1 The Industrial Revolution and the Prehistory of the Automobile

The automobile is synonymous with 20th century industrialism. Though its invention may be regarded as epoch making, its emergence was only possible thanks to earlier developments in industrial technology, organization, and production philosophy. We begin by surveying the important developments that prepared for the arrival of the automobile and shaped its earliest production processes. This situates the emergence of the auto industry within the historical flow of modern industrial development.

The Industrial Revolution began in Great Britain in the late 18th century. The advent of steam power, the railroad, mechanized textile production, and the organizational revolution of the factory system made Britain the earliest industrial power. For the United States and Germany, the Industrial Revolution took hold in the second half of the 19th century. The conclusion of the American Civil War in 1865 advanced the economic agenda of the industrial North over the agricultural South. The aftermath generated a period of high economic growth with the rise of heavy industries like coal mining and steelmaking and was marked by numerous technological achievements from the light bulb to transatlantic telegraphs (Martelle 2014: 53). German industrialization was similarly pushed forward after the unification of the multitude of small German states under Prussian leadership in the early 1870s. Compared to its continental European peers, the industrialization of the German Empire was fast and far-reaching. Industrialization was led first by mining, iron, and steel industries and, starting in the 1890s, by the chemical and electrical industries (Bellon 1990: 7). Thanks to a sophisticated banking system and the emergence of large enterprises and cartels, Germany soon became a rival to Great Britain as the most advanced industrial power in continental Europe (Bellon 1990: 13). In the decades leading up to WWI, the United States was by far the most advanced industrializer of the 'New World' while Germany was fast becoming the most advanced industrializer of the 'Old World.'

1.1 *Evolution of Metalworking in the 19th Century*

During this period, technical innovations in metalworking took place that facilitated the emergence of automobile production. The reliability and quality

 | DOI:10.1163/9789004736719_003

of iron and steel at the beginning of the industrial revolution was insufficient for making the variety of components needed for automobile production. The rise of coke blast furnaces and the Bessemer process in the 1860s enabled high impurity-eliminating heat levels so that foundries could consistently produce high quality iron and steel (Jürgens 2023: 44). These innovations also reduced the need for skilled workers who utilized experience and intuition to manipulate the material and furnace to produce the desired result (Misa 1995). A shift in labor structure occurred quickly at American foundries whereby skilled workers were replaced by common laborers, which triggered many strikes and industrial conflicts (Jürgens 2023: 45). By contrast, the devaluation of the skilled foundry workers in Germany was comparatively less disruptive, yet still eventually resulted in skilled workers being replaced with less skilled workers (Jürgens 2023: 44–45; see also Ritter and Tenfelde 1992: 318). Thus, the displacement and deskilling of a traditional skilled craft was a necessary precondition to produce the materials necessary for automobile construction.

Similar developments occurred for skilled workers who cast molds by hand to shape metal. By the second half of the 19th century, machines were developed that could create molds and allow for much more precise casting of workpieces. Such machines could be operated by unskilled workers rather than the handcraft skilled workers. Thanks to technical changes in how casting mold, forging dies, and pressing tools were made, it became possible to produce large quantities of the specialized parts from steel (Jürgens 2023: 46–49). Fabricating these tools became its own profession known as the 'tool and die maker,' which remain an important job in auto production.

Machining was necessary to form the molded metal into shape for final assembly. The craft method of machining utilized hand tools or multi-purpose machine tools such as the drill press, the lathe, the planer, or the milling machine (Meyer 2004: 2). Such craft methods were tedious, slow, and demanded expert level experience and skill to be done effectively (Jürgens 2023: 49; Flink 1988: 41–42). Even with dexterous skilled workers, however, imprecision and the lack of interchangeability required that parts be 'fitted' together in the assembly process through various methods of adjusting and filing (Meyer 2004: 2). Developments in the machine tool industry—especially the arrival of a variety of highly specialized single purpose machines—revolutionized the machining process. Instead of relying on the dexterity of the skilled worker's hand, the tedious work of guiding the tool was now done by the machine using much more precise measurements, thereby making the skilled workers superfluous (Jürgens 2023: 51–52). Although these developments began in the 19th century, changes in machining processes were gradual and their implementation varied from industry to industry. Thus, traditional craft machinists were still highly represented in the auto industry of both countries at the beginning of the 20th century.

However, a divergence in the deployment of machine tools appeared between the US, where they were generally embraced, and Germany, where there was comparatively slower, more skeptical, adoption (Hounshell 1985; Jürgens 2023: 49–54). The prolonged work of adjusting and filing down of work pieces continued well into the 20th century in Germany, which partially explains the lower productivity levels in early German auto plants. Nevertheless, the development of machine tools from the 19th into the 20th centuries played an important role in the growth of the early industry. Overall, these technical developments in the 19th century were necessary for the invention and production of the automobile, even as some changes resulted in radical alterations in work requirements that displaced multiple types of skilled workers.

1.2 *Divergence in Industrial Ethos: the 'American System of Manufacturing'*

The different paths of industrialization between the United States and Germany were shaped by each value-regime's affinity for interchangeable parts, which was considered a novel enough innovation at the time that it constituted an industrial ethos known as the 'American System of Manufacturing.' As the name suggests, the system was embraced in the United States but was met with skepticism in Europe. Ferguson (1968) succinctly describes the American System as a "sequential series of operations carried out on successive special-purpose machines that produce interchangeable parts" (2). If parts are interchangeable, there is no need for fitters to fit together non-interchangeable parts together. Standardized parts enable faster assembly processes, which in turn enables higher productivity and high-volume production.

The use of single purpose machines that could be operated by unskilled workers were invaluable in achieving interchangeability and consistent standardization. The American machine tool industry specialized in single types of tools suitable for high volume production and interchangeability, while the European industry made a variety of more general-purpose-oriented tools designed for smaller markets (Flink 1988: 45). This difference is partially explained by the chronic labor shortage and scarcity of skilled workers in the US. This scarcity gave American skilled workers power in the labor market to demand high wages, which subsequently encouraged employers to demand the development of machines to replace them (Flink 1988: 44; Elbaum 1989). Single purpose machines were therefore valuable to American producers because they simultaneously achieved the desired interchangeability and lessened the reliance on skilled workers. Thanks to the growing popularity of the American System, the American machine tools industry flourished and even exported machines to European businesses interested in catching up to the productivity and quality standards set by American competitors (Flink 1988:

46; Jürgens 2023: 59–60). The first automobiles in both the US and Germany were not made with interchangeable parts, but within the first decade of the 20th century, efforts at interchangeability were pushed forward in the US industry, above all by the Ford Motor Company, which set the US auto industry apart from the German (Hounshell 1985: 221–222).

1.3 *Legacies of Craft Labor*

The technical developments and the rise of the American System of Manufacturing in the 19th and early 20th centuries point toward deskilling and the replacement of high for low skilled workers in many areas. With the deployment of machines, job tasks were often simplified, and artisanal workers could be replaced with unskilled workers. Automation contributed to deskilling. However, the timing, intensity, and character of these developments differed between the two value-regimes. The greater acceptance of machinery and the popularity of interchangeable parts manufacturing in the United States forms part of the explanation. However, another important factor is their trajectories in skill development.

Due to centuries of European craftsman and guild tradition, the independence and prevalence of skilled workers remained strong in Germany into the 20th century. German metalworkers in the late 19th and early 20th centuries, including most workers in the early German auto industry, were represented by the *Deutscher Metallarbeiter-Verband* (German Metalworkers Union), one of the largest unions in Germany. The union was politically supported by the Social Democratic Party (SPD), the socialist party which was ascendent during this period (Bellon 1990: 61–63). In Germany, the labor movement was not just a political or workplace movement, but a way of life, encompassing social democratic newspapers, reading groups, pubs, arts and sports clubs etc., which fostered a distinct and all-encompassing working-class culture (Bellon 1990: 63).

This milieu was also culturally solidified by the concept of 'German quality work' (*deutsche Qualitätsarbeit*). This idea suggests that German products should be of particularly high quality thanks to the high skills of the German workforce. German workers highly valued dexterity and skill as they allowed for both increasingly high wages as well as more independence from employer supervision (Lüdtke 2009: 178). This cultural legacy, combined with the support of large unions and a major political party, meant that German skilled workers had the motivation and means to defend their interests in self-valorization.

Skilled workers and skilled worker culture were by no means absent from the United States, but they did not have the prevalence and social support as in Germany. While the apprentice training system following the apprentice-journeyman-master trajectory was imported into colonial America by the British, the social conditions of the 18th and 19th century US did not cement such training in culture or in practice (Elbaum 1989: 346). As Elbaum (1989) explains,

> Neither guilds nor apprenticeship were well suited to a dynamic settler society in which land availability continually drained the labor supply, and adult immigration accounted for a substantial portion of population growth … In general, in the early United States, entry into skilled occupations required no certification. As a result, informal training was a viable alternative to apprenticeship, and youths had little incentive to honor indenture commitments. (339)

In such a dynamic and geographically large country, there was almost always a shortage of skilled workers in any given area, especially considering the high rates of occupational and geographic mobility among skilled workers. This scarcity stimulated technological deployment over skilled work as an alternative means of solving production problems, which had important consequences for industrial development in the United States (Elbaum 1989: 349; see Crumm 2010).

In this environment, the solidarity and political efficacy of skilled workers in the US, though by no means totally lacking, was much weaker than in Germany—especially in the absence of a popular socialist party (Lipset and Marks 2000). The automobile industry in the United States at the turn of the 20th century was still a craft trade requiring skilled craftsmen drawn primarily from the foundries, machine shops, and carriage-making companies of Detroit, but these workers were usually not organized by an employer recognized union nor advocated for in mainstream party politics (Meyer 1981; Meyer 2004: 1). Therefore, the orientation and organization of skilled labor in the United States was distinct from Germany, which ultimately led to skilled labor having comparatively less influence on the production process as well as less prestige in the cultural imagination. This had long-term impacts on the development of both auto industries.

1.4 *Scientific Management, Taylorism and Struggle over the Shopfloor*

The terms Fordism and Taylorism are often mentioned together, and their usage often leaves it unclear what distinguishes each. While Fordism was first introduced in the auto industry, Taylorism, or scientific management, predates Fordism by several decades, and does have distinguishing features. Taylorism is nevertheless an important precursor to Fordism and the assembly line.

Starting in 1870, American mechanical engineer Frederick Winslow Taylor examined the movement of steel workers with a stopwatch, observing that both the workers and machinery were working far below their capacity (Jürgens

2023: 65–66). Taylor recognized that skilled workers typically best understood their respective work processes, but their exclusive knowledge and independence on the shop floor also allowed them to purposefully withhold work effort and restrict output. Taylor aimed to end these inefficiencies and increase productivity by extracting the traditional knowledge possessed by the craftsmen and transferring them to the management's planning department staffed by industrial engineers (Meyer 2004: 2). This entailed the separation of planning and control of work from the workers on the shop floor. The planning department would be responsible for formulating work standards, conducting labor and time studies, and adjusting standards based on working conditions (Jürgens 2023: 68). The rise of the planning department also emerged synergistically with the prevalence of university educated engineers in factories and the formation of a strata of professional white-collar management to control the shop floor, especially in the United States (Shenhav 2006). By extracting knowledge of work procedures and the worker's bodily movements through time studies, the planning department could prescribe detailed production methods and productivity standards for the workers.

Scientific management represented an attempt to dismantle the wholistic craftsman who executed both mental and manual skills on the job. As Meyer (2004) explains, "Taylorism attempted to separate the mental skills, or the traditional knowledge, from the work process and to put these mental skills into the hands of industrial managers and engineers, leaving the mere manual skills with the workers" (2). This alienation of traditional worker knowledge from the labor process enabled deskilling and enhanced management control of the shop floor (Marx 1932 [1844]; Braverman 1998 [1974]). In addition, with the stopwatch measuring productivity and management's attempts to codify and enforce production standards, Taylorism represented not just more deskilling and management control, but of the *domination of workers by time* and a form of *productivity pressure* to meet productivity norms (see Hounshell 1985: 250). This pressure to meet productivity norms handed down by management entails a *micro-level instantiation of social domination*. Developed by the planning department and enforced by the watchful eye of the foremen, productivity targets were also intimately felt by workers as the *domination by management*, which could lead to industrial conflict over work standards.

On the factory floor transitioning to Taylorist methods, domination by management and domination by time standards appeared coterminous. Yet, this domination took on a social character beyond direct management control once such standards become normalized both within a single factory and especially if/when these standards become matched by competitors. Thus, Taylorism is not only about management control but entails a struggle over *micro-level control over time* on the factory floor, which became more entrenched as Taylorist practices generalized across competitors within the same industry and proliferated across industries. In sum, while first auto plants were primarily controlled by skilled workers, over time both the US and German industries became increasingly influenced by scientific management.

However, the importance of Taylorism should not be exaggerated. Taylor was first and foremost interested in optimizing *existing* production processes with the machines and workers available and did not attempt to automate or radically change existing work tasks. Rather, Taylor showed how productivity increases were possible with given machines and workers if production processes were optimized according to the standards set by the industrial engineers (Jürgens 2023: 69; Hounshell 1985: 249–253). Taylorism is not identical to Fordist assembly line production, but the ethos of Taylorism was nevertheless an important precursor to the extent that its emphasis on the subdivision of tasks, control over work processes, and the measurement and codification of productivity standards supplied ideological resources and practical tools for the development of Fordism and the assembly line.

In sum, technical innovations in the metal industries were necessary before the first automobile could be made. Automation in metal foundries and machining shops and the technological displacement and deskilling of certain workers had already occurred (Jürgens 2023: 72–73). While skilled workers predominated within the auto factories of both countries at the beginning, trends toward stripping worker control, standardization, and interchangeability had already begun in the 19th century and eventually appeared in the auto industry. However, there were divergences in the relative acceptance of these trends between both countries, which is primarily rooted in the relative prevalence and power of skilled workers. The unfolding of these different trajectories influenced the relative growth of each industry in the first decades of the 20th century.

2 The Automotive Idea and the Genesis of the Auto Industry

Horseless travel was already commonplace at the turn of the 20th century thanks to decades of reliable travel via steam powered trains and electric powered street cars. Yet, the automotive idea—the desire to combine speed, reliability, and independence in one vehicle—took decades of experimentation before transport needs could be met by the automobile powered by an internal combustion engine (IC). The practicality of automobility only became plausible in the second half of the 19th century (Flink 1988: 1–3; Albert 2019: 15–17). There were experiments with steam and electric battery powered cars between the 1860s and 1890s, but the IC automobile was perfected in Germany in the 1880s and 1890s (Flink 1988: 6–11). By around 1900, the automobile successfully transitioned from an experimentation phase to production as a commodity. Entrepreneurial and inventor led small initiatives established themselves as industrial enterprises, some of which, such as Ford and Daimler, still exist today.

The first automobiles cost far above what was affordable for the average person. The average car in the United States in 1900 cost approximately $2,000 while the average yearly income was only $450, with similar or wider price and wage differentials present in Europe (Rooke 2008). Albert (2019) describes the first car owners in Europe and the United States as "members of the trans-Atlantic elite," who treated their cars like "opulent toys" (19). Marketing to such a wealthy clientele meant that, to realize their value, the early automobiles needed to conform to standards of luxury, quality, and customization acceptable to their prospective customers.

This had a profound long-term impact on the German auto industry and its production system because most producers catered almost exclusively to this wealthy clientele. This is partially due to the highly unequal wealth distribution in Europe at this time, as well as to the high cost of materials and labor that went into making the earliest cars. This left the very wealthiest as the only ones who could afford the high prices. To engage this market, the early German companies typically produced numerous vehicle types in low production volumes. For example, by 1912 there were about 60 auto factories in Germany that typically produced four to six vehicle types, with larger companies like Daimler and Benz producing upwards of 10 to 14 different types (Jürgens 2023: 238). The first American auto companies also had to appeal to wealthier patrons during the early 20th century, but this necessity was overcome after the development of mass production Fordism.

Although Europe led the way in terms of automobile experimentation, the United States quickly leapfrogged Europe in terms of automobile production and commercialization. The US became the world leader in auto production by 1904, and by 1907 the American industry produced 44,000 cars a year compared to 25,000 made in France and a mere 5,150 made in Germany (Flink 1988: 18–25). By 1913, the United States produced 485,000 automobiles out of a total worldwide production of 606,124, approximately 80% of all vehicles (Flink 1988: 25). The gap between American and European production continued to widen in the following decades. This production gap has many contributing factors, with one of the most important being that the American production systems had higher productivity and thereby could produce at higher volumes. By comparing the respective production systems, we can determine multiple factors that contributed to the US taking global automotive leadership.

3 Earliest Craft Production Systems in the United States and Germany

Following the Ford Motor Company and the *Daimler Motoren Gesellschaft*, hereafter Daimler, we can assess the development and trajectory of each production system based on the characteristics of the respective value-regime. Both companies start with essentially the same production system, but quickly begin to take different directions that had important long-term implications for the levels of motorization, capital accumulation, and labor structure in each value-regime.

3.1 *Auto Production circa 1900 and the Importance of Interchangeability*

There was a high level of convergence among the production technologies, processes, and workers utilized in the budding automobile industries of the US and Europe. As Flink (1988) describes, before the emergence of assembly line Fordism,

> automobiles were made and sold much the same way on both sides of the Atlantic; that is, they were assembled from jobbed-out components by crews of skilled mechanics and unskilled helpers at low rates of labor productivity, and they were sold at high prices and high unit profits. (40)

This common situation is partially the result of the initial companies producing a relatively new commodity that required recently invented components such as the IC engine. Careful craftsmanship was needed to build a reliable product. Many of the first auto companies either previously or concurrently made similar products such as machine tools, bicycles, carriages, and wagons (Flink 1988: 40).[1] The expertise of skilled labor and the basic production tools used for these other products were applied to the production of the first autos (Meyer 2004; Crumm 2010). In addition, many of the first cars were assembled with parts sourced from parts suppliers making the same or similar parts for these other products. Therefore, to keep capital needs low, the first auto shops

1 This is one reason why Detroit became the hub of the early American auto industry, as it had multiple machine shops and carriage manufacturers, as well as over forty-five thousand manufacturing workers by 1900 (Martelle 2014: 71).

often focused on the assembly of parts produced by outside firms, signifying very low levels of vertical integration (Flink 1988: 41). As the companies grew, more and more parts typically became manufactured and assembled within the firm (Meyer 2004).

The first factory of the Ford Motor Company, established in 1903, serves as an illustrative example of the typical assembly shop. As Biggs (1995) describes, the factory was,

> A small wood-frame building on Mack Avenue in Detroit, it consisted of one room measuring 50 by 250 with a shop inventory of two lathes, two drill presses, one milling machine, one hand saw, one grinding wheel, and one forge, the shop contained no specialized tools and employed 'ten or a dozen boys [men] and a foreman.' (39–40).

In such a small plant, cars were built one at a time by small groups of skilled machinists using their experienced hands and universal machines to cut, file, and fit together non-interchangeable parts. Even when Ford moved to his second factory, a multi-story 402 by 52-foot building on Detroit's Piquette Avenue, the production methods initially remained the same, just scaled up with more workers and universal machines. One innovation, however, was that by 1906 instead of grouping alike machines into workshops with skilled workers producing different parts, they became arranged sequentially in the order in which they were used, speeding up production (Biggs 1995: 40–43). This arrangement represented a step in the direction of assembly line production, although final assembly was conducted at stationary workstations with teams of assemblers (Hounshell 1985: 220–225).

The early American auto plants began to diverge from European plants through their embrace of interchangeability based on the American System of Manufacturing. Ford started this process at the Piquette Avenue plant in 1906 by fitting machine tools with more fixtures that assured precise measurements and machining of parts—which also allowed less-skilled workers to do the job. An associate described Henry Ford's attitude stating,

> He realized as well as any other manufacturer realized that in order to create great quantity of production, your interchangeability must be fine and unique in order to accomplish the rapid assembly of units. There can't be much hand work or fitting if you are going to accomplish great things. (Hounshell 1985: 221)

Thus, the skills of the fitters were an early target of rationalization and de-valorization at Ford through its emphasis on interchangeability.

Indeed, standardization and interchangeability were perhaps the most important divergences between the early American and European auto industries. Henry Leland, former business partner of Henry Ford and early leader of Cadillac, once entered Cadillac cars into a "Standardization Test" that took place in London in 1908. He would later remark about this test in his autobiography that,

> The Standardization Test, as the event was called, had been open to all automobile companies, but there was only one entrant—the American Cadillac Motor Company. The test was complicated. If successful, the test would prove that all parts in Cadillac cars were interchangeable, and that parts of all automobiles, if properly manufactured, could be interchangeable. This would be a development of the first magnitude. Cadillacs were the product of machine tools, and if it could be demonstrated that they were so accurately made, this fact would smash the idea held by most Europeans that machine tools and quality do not go together, and that the finest car was one that in large part was handmade. It would also indicate that machine-made cars could be produced in larger numbers ... Experts freely predicted failure because, as one put it, 'A uniform accuracy of fitting to the two-thousandth fraction of an inch would be indispensable to prevent failure' Such precision was deemed impossible. (Leland 1966:15)

Leland attributes European manufacturers' lack of interchangeability to a belief that handmade methods create the highest quality cars and that achieving the necessary precision using machine tools would be impossible. Movements away from labor intensive craft production through the interchangeability achieved by machine driven manufacture were pursued more vigorously in the American industry, marking an early turning point in its industrial trajectory.

3.2 *Daimler as Exemplar of German Craft Production*

Daimler, home to German luxury brand Mercedes-Benz, is an exemplar of early German production. Its production processes best portray a craft production system and productive model oriented toward delivering a variety of luxury automobiles to a wealthy clientele (Boyer and Freyssenet 2002). It is also a useful example of the early craft production system common in both value-regimes at the turn of the 20th century.

Located in the south-western state of Baden-Württemberg near the state capital of Stuttgart, Daimler's Untertürkheim plant was a major European automobile factory at the turn of the 20th century and remains so to this day. Built in 1903, it comprised a dozen workshops housed within eight main buildings in the factory complex (Bellon 1990: 41). Nearly 70 percent of the workforce were skilled workers of various kinds, 11 percent were semi-skilled (or 'trained') machine tenders, and 19 percent were unskilled workers who fetch and carry unfished products across the factory to the different workshops (Bellon 1990: 26; Stahlmann 1992: 151).

Common to both the US and Germany were the highly skilled craftsmen whose job typically required years of apprenticeship, although formal vocational education was more common in Germany than the US (Bellon 1990: 26; Meyer 1981; Elbaum 1989). They were generally paid by the piece as an incentive wage to encourage higher productivity. These workers consciously performed tasks and had intimate, often comprehensive, knowledge of their job and how it was performed (Bellon 1990: 26). This helped these workers maintain partial autonomy from management. In other words, it signified a partial *lack of alienation* in the way Marx (1932 [1844]) defines it, as many workers did have conscious control over their production process, even though other forms of alienation, such as the alienation of the commodity from the worker, were still present.

In Untertürkheim, the master, head of the traditional apprentice-journeyman-master system, lead each organizational department and was responsible for his workshop, including maintaining workplace discipline. Masters possessed considerable personal prerogative over their workers by directing the production processes as well as setting piece rates, work assignments, and supervision (Bellon 1990: 38). American craft workers typically were not directed by a master but had the independence to direct their own labor, including controlling the work pace. As Meyer (2004) reports, "the piece workers worked slow or fast as they chose," and that "As long as the daily production was turned out ... what the body workers did was their own business" (2). Though directed by a master, Daimler workers generally possessed the same sense of labor control.

The departments in Untertürkheim housed a variety of skilled workers including fitters, tool makers, smiths, foundry form-makers, carpenters, upholsterers, and painters (Bellon 1990: 26). They primarily used either hand tools such as hammers or wrenches or larger tools like lathes that could cut metals into any conceivable part (Bellon 1990: 27). Skilled formers and coremakers fabricated molds using traditional methods. Smelters, casters, and cast-cleaners used power-hammers, chisels, and sand-blasting equipment to dislodge impurities (Bellon 1990: 32). Smiths were among the most traditional professions, initially organized in gangs using primarily hammers to shape metal around open fires (Bellon 1990: 33). Turners used lathes, a general-purpose machine tool, to engage in a variety of cutting operations to form parts into their proper shape. These workers also received piece-rate wages but were among the best paid worker groups (Bellon 1990: 34). A toolmaking shop staffed by skilled tool and die makers was also present at Daimler (Bellon 1990: 35–37). Due to the imprecise methods used in the metal forming processes, many fitters were needed at Daimler. In fact, fitters were the largest group of skilled workers at the plant, with 503 fitters out of a production workforce of 1,677 in 1908 (Bellon 1990: 34; 56). Bellon (1990) describes how "Fitters using hammers and drills cajoled and coaxed together parts which were only approximately compatible" (34). They formed gangs of between five to ten workers who assembled two or three cars at a time (Bellon 1990: 34–35). Fitting was an incredibly slow process. A minimum of a month was needed for assembly work, including between 8 to 14 days of testing certain components and the final vehicle (Bellon 1990: 35). This process was protracted but necessary given the productive methods, and careful scrutiny assured the level of quality demanded by Daimler's wealthy customers (Stahlmann 1992: 162–163). Time was saved and productivity increased to the degree that fitting was reduced or eliminated, as was the goal of most American manufacturers.

On the opposite end of the worker hierarchy were the day laborers, often called "help workers," who either assisted skilled workers or carried workpieces between stations or departments across the factory grounds (Stahlmann 1992: 152). These workers, who also existed in the earliest US plants (Meyer 1981, 2004), were the lowest paid workers as their work required no outside training (Bellon 1990: 48). Their labor-intensive work was among the first to be the target of rationalization and automation, especially in the US (Jürgens 2023: 89).

Machine tenders, though initially the smallest group of workers between the skilled and unskilled workers, were nevertheless an increasingly important contingent of workers. They operated special machines such as grinding and milling machines or fully automatic lathes that were gradually replacing the use of universal machines at the plant (Stahlmann 1992: 150). These machines could be used by an average dexterous worker with only a few months of training. Such machines also decreased the workers' relative control over the production process. As Bellon (1990) explains,

> The workers tending the milling, grinding, and planing machines at Daimler exercised little control over what they did, save for starting up and shutting off the machine, for loading the pieces to be cut, and for guiding the machine through its preset paces. To be sure, dexterity and experience were still important, but there was no longer much room for exercising independent intelligence and creativity in the labor process in the machine departments. (28)

Though the factory was dominated by skilled workers, the number of special machines and machine operators increased over time. In 1910, 43 special machines were used compared to 174 deployed by 1914 (Bellon 1990: 28). One split between the American and German production systems were the speed and proportion by which such machines and their semi-skilled operators would come to proliferate in automobile factories.

The production processes and general structure of labor at Daimler depicts the strikingly similar production system utilized across Europe and the United States before the advent of Fordism. Though Untertürkheim was a large factory for its time with relatively high internalization of parts production, the basic production processes and labor structure illustrated here describe what was necessary to construct an automobile at the turn of the 20th century. In general, highly paid skilled labor worked with general purpose machines, with the aid of low paid and unskilled transport workers, to construct a variety of high-end automobile models for a small number of wealthy clients.

3.3 *Pursuing Productivity at Daimler*

In describing early craft production systems, modern values are often retrospectively projected onto the past. In one view, craft production had many inherent flaws, such as low productivity that necessitated high prices, that only 'nostalgists' would appreciate. Economies of scale were not possible due to the meticulous and labor-intensive work so that production costs stayed roughly the same no matter how many cars were produced. Craft producers are caricatured as frozen in time, holding onto tradition and unwilling to change (see Womack et al. 1990 [2007]: 19–24). In an opposing depiction, this productive model is viewed as coherent and sustainable as long as there is a luxury market, but the internal and external pressures to increase productivity are often underappreciated (e.g., Boyer and Freyssenet 2002: 36–48). Neither approach *historicizes* the continuous pursuit of productivity that existed in these early production systems. The pursuit of productivity is obvious in the US as the industry, led by Ford, quickly moved away from craft production and towards mass production and the assembly line. However, less discussed are productivity measures pursued at Daimler, and the role that mechanization and automation played in this process. The path taken at Daimler was not the same as Ford or Cadillac in terms of interchangeability or the assembly line but were nevertheless earnest efforts at rationalization and increasing productivity.

There were concerted movements toward mechanization at Daimler. According to the firm's leading engineers, the increasing deployment of special machines was crucial to Daimler's effort to reduce production costs

(Bellon 1990: 28). There were movements away from the lathe-turning machines and toward special machines, such as cylindrical grinding machines, that required less labor and decreased labor costs and time (Bellon 1990: 27; Stahlmann 1992: 150). Increasingly, less skilled workers were attending to several machines at the same time, which meant "one is less dependent on the skill of the workers; the machines are more fully utilized, and time is saved on labor—all points which together further the highest achievement in quality and quantity" (Bellon 1990: 37). By the early 1910s, the open fires of the smiths had been replaced by furnaces and mechanical hammers powered by steam replaced the smith's traditional hammer (Bellon 1990: 33). It was the task of the toolmaking department, in conjunction with management, to come up with "labor-saving and machine-maximizing ways of building Daimler's products" (Bellon 1990: 37). These developments were not unique at Daimler, as automakers across Germany were also interested in replacing skilled workers for semi-skilled workers (Stahlmann 1992: 148; Jürgens 2023: 239–240).

There were also organizational and product changes that achieved similar goals. After 1908, several sections of the automobile were standardized as were the requisite parts (Bellon 1990: 30; Stahlmann 1992: 148). By 1911, individual fitters had been assigned to assemble only specific sections of the car at their stationary work areas, thereby dividing and simplifying the labor (Bellon 1990: 35). There was movement away from a management style that only generally set work tasks and toward the principle that management can dictate to the worker the way in which work was to be performed and subdivide the division of labor. Though there is no evidence that Daimler directly followed the advice of F. W. Taylor, there is evidence that similar production principles were increasingly exercised at the company (Bellon 1990: 37; Stahlmann 1992: 156). These efforts appeared to bear fruit as production doubled at Daimler between 1909 and 1913, with 671 cars in 1909 increased to 1,567 in 1913 (Bellon 1990: 30, 16). Though productivity was still far lower than US auto plants, the "*challenge posed by foreign and domestic competition to cut costs*" gave Daimler the impetus to increase productivity (Bellon 1990: 25; emphasis mine). The drive to increase productivity through the introduction of special machines and increasing standardization was an important means to achieve these goals.

However, these changes do not mean Daimler was pursuing the *same path* toward mass production and the assembly line, albeit at a slower pace. Production based on skilled fitters and mechanics remained the foundational at Daimler into the 1920s. This was in part due to a priority at the firm to portray the quality and "careful hand work" that went into its luxury autos as superior compared to the "shoddy" work methods that Daimler claimed were employed in the US (Bellon 1990: 40; see Stahlmann 1992: 163). As a *value-system* that promoted and supported its capital accumulation through communication with social systems, Daimler disseminated its self-description as a superior high-quality producer. This complemented the realization demands of wealthy customers for a 'variety and diversity' of high-end luxury models, the production of which required a high level of flexibility best handled by skilled workers (Boyer and Freyssenet 2002). However, the production system at Daimler was also not ossified. Numerous production changes aimed at rationalization and higher productivity. This occurred *within* a craft system and *despite* the small demand for automobiles in Germany, luxury or otherwise. Both external (e.g., competition) and internal (e.g., increasing management control) *productivity pressures* were apparent, despite the relative insularity and uniqueness of the German value-regime.

Workers at Daimler were primarily organized through the German Metalworkers Union, (*Deutscher Metallarbeiter-Verband* or DMV), a workers' committee that represented workers interests at the factory, and numerous smaller trade unions (Bellon 1990: 81). These strong labor organizations pushed for worker codetermination (*Mitbestimmung*) in auto factories. In a codetermined production system, workers and their organizations work jointly with management to shape production processes and working conditions as stipulated by legal rights, contracts, or customs (Haipeter 2006). Codetermination practices go beyond formal recognition of the union and dispute resolution procedures into worker voice and input into practical production concerns. The struggle to establish and expand codetermination rights and practices is a central characteristic of the German value-regime. In contrast to autoworkers in the US, unionized German autoworkers did gain recognition (though not yet legally mandated recognition) from the firm and fought management on various points of conflict. Though much more contentious than industrial relations would be post-WWII, there were already indications of a closer and more cooperative relationship between workers and management here than in the US. The firm made concessions to the workforce on overtime, the length of the working day, and piece wages while remaining profitable, and the union learned that tenaciously defending worker-management agreements was crucial (Bellon 1990: 75–76; Stahlmann 1992: 152).

Craft production characterized both the US and German auto industries at the beginning of the 20th century, though both quickly diverged soon thereafter. The US industry moved toward interchangeability which was complemented by mechanization and standardization as precursors to mass production. However, the German industry was by no means static. Though lacking interchangeability and relying on skilled craft-workers, there were nevertheless moves toward rationalization and higher productivity. *The commonality is the pursuit of productivity for the sake of capital accumulation*, but this pursuit was shaped by the historical legacies of each value-regime, especially the prevalence of *organized skilled labor* in Germany and the *popularity of interchangeability* in the US. Market limitations also greatly shaped the direction, as neither Daimler nor any other German auto producer operated as if a large automobile market was possible, and therefore targeted the high-end luxury market almost exclusively (Jürgens 2023: 244–246). A historical dynamic toward productivity increase can be detected, yet divergence in productivity increasing strategies complemented path dependent trajectories that had profound impacts on the future of the industries. This divergence would expand further with the emergence of assembly line Fordism and the outbreak of WWI.

4 Fordist Mass Production and German 'Mass-Craft Production'

Fordism, the assembly line, and mass production are so ubiquitous in 20th century history that an introduction is hardly necessary. A culmination of the socio-technical developments in production that came before, e.g., Taylorism, the American System, and advances in automation, mass production Fordism emerged in 1913–14 and forever changed the way commodities were produced. Its implementation engendered both rapid rises in productivity as well as the transformation of many production processes and the elimination of many job categories. At the same time, the enormous growth that mass production generated allowed displaced workers to fill other jobs within the Fordist system. Here, the key elements of Fordism, the assembly line, and mass production are described in terms of how they transformed labor and advanced automation and productivity. Workers' responses to these changes are also discussed, as labor turnover and other tensions ultimately led to the introduction of the famous 'five-dollar day' at Ford.

At the same time that Ford was perfecting the assembly line, The German state recruited Daimler and other German auto companies into war production and impressed upon these companies the need to rationalize production for the sake of the war effort. This ultimately ramped up the scale of production, which increased total output but was achieved *without* substantial productivity gains. In a sense, Germany developed a *type* of mass production at the same time as Ford that retained most characteristics of craft production. I term this 'mass-craft production' to signify the scaling up of a craft system that achieves higher production differently from Fordist mass production. The war also set precedence for a close relationship between state, firm, and labor in Germany that proved to have an enduring legacy in the German auto industry.

4.1 *The Model T as a 'Reasonable' People's Car*

For the Model T, the unique characteristics of the product play directly into the evolution of the production system. Perhaps nowhere else has there been a stronger connection between product *and* production philosophy than with the Model T. Ford began integrating interchangeability in 1906, with the Model T fully embodying this ethos when it appeared in 1908 (Biggs 1995). It was reported that the Model T's parts were so interchangeable that they could be disassembled, mixed up, and rebuilt from the same parts, which was still a rarity among low priced cars even by 1913 (Chandler 1964: 29). The Model T was designed for technical simplicity, reliability, durability, and ease of handling and repair (Schmidt 2007: 5). Henry Ford declared it "a car for the great multitude" that would be produced cheaply enough to be affordable for the average American (Flink 1988: 36–37). At a starting price of $850, its closest competitor, the Buick, cost $1,250 and was 300 pounds heavier (Albert 2019: 43). At the same time, it was not so cheaply made that it was of poor quality or unreliable for long distance travel. After its invention, Ford dedicated his company to making the Model T as its primary product with very few variants or options (Jürgens 2023: 82), which made it an ideal candidate for experimenting with production techniques to increase output.

The Model T also embodied a distinctly American ethos of populism and independence. It represented 'reasonable' automobility, that economical and reliable transport was what Americans needed (Schmidt 2007). The idea that automobiles were reserved for the rich was soundly refuted. Absent mass production and the Model T, mass automobility in the US would have likely spread out from urban centers to rural areas and gradually down the economic ladder—as would largely be the case in Germany before WWII. Instead, the *cheap and cheapening* prices of the Model T allowed mass motorization to explode in both the countryside and urban centers and eventually saturate the entire nation (Albert 2019: 36). Ford's business model focused on low costs through productivity increases that enabled permanent cost reductions and continuous market expansion (Jürgens 2023: 83). This constituted a cycle of productivity improvements leading to lower costs leading to further productivity gains leading to still further cost reductions, increasing the level of material wealth faster than the growth of the combined machine and human labor (see Postone 1993). Starting at $850 in 1908, the price first dropped below the yearly average wage in the US in 1912 at $575 and its original price was more than cut in half by 1916 at around $360 (Flink 1988: 37–38). By the end of production in 1927, the Model T had sold over 15 million units and was selling at its lowest price of $290 (Flink 1988: 38). Ultimately, the system of mass production led to the United States becoming the first mass motorized society. Productivity development allowed the value of autos to drop to the point where mass production engendered mass automobility.

4.2 *Mass Production at Ford: Flow, Single Purpose Machines, and the Assembly Line*

Fordist mass production first took place at the Highland Park factory. Completed in 1910, the plant was one of the most modern auto manufacturing facilities of its day comprised of four large, electrified buildings several times larger than the Piquette Avenue shop (Biggs 1995: 43–44). This was a space suitable for experimentation to discover the best ways to achieve large scale production. Mass production did not arise from a set plan, but from dozens of small experiments aimed at improving productivity throughout the numerous manufacturing processes around the complex. Nearly all aspects of production were tested to see if they could be run more efficiently, including experiments with materials, product design, process layout, and the division of labor (Jürgens 2023: 119–122). Hounshell (1985) argues that the experimentation bordered on reckless; there was "a surprising rate of scrapping processes and machine tools when they did not suit the immediate fancy of his production engineers" (220). This often entailed scrapping old machines as soon as new or better machines were available, even if the old machines were relatively new (Meyer 1981: 25). Such experimentation was possible, in part, because of Ford's continued financial success, which both enabled and allowed for such potentially expensive behavior. Nevertheless, the openness to new ideas and orientation toward improving productivity was ultimately fruitful for the company as the sum results of these small experiments helped form the Fordist mass production system. Even the assembly line was just one experiment among many, although it received the most attention and credit for the productivity leap (e.g., Arnold and Faurote 1915). The following discusses the development and effects of Fordist mass production by focusing on a few key aspects: prioritizing production flow, the deployment of single-purpose machines, and the assembly line.

A key objective at Highland Park was to enable a smooth workflow in all aspects of production. The workpieces and materials should move within the factory with as little human handling as possible so that work would come to the stationary workers instead of the other way around (Jürgens 2023: 88–89). To achieve this, workers and machines were continuously rearranged to find the most efficient route. For example, machine tools were grouped closely together to generate an economy of space that mitigated against work pieces accumulating on the shop floor and smooth out production (Hounshell 1985: 229). Machines and departments were arranged sequentially so that "the work-in-progress moved from foundry to machine shop to assembly department, seemingly flowing from tiny streams to small rivers and ultimately to the final assembly line" (Meyer 2004: 3). The overall goal was to discover the shortest lines possible to produce each component and arrange production to match this ideal shortest route as closely as possible (Arnold and Faurote 1915: 38).

Flow was also achieved by replacing many unskilled transport workers with tools such as chutes, conveyor belts, cranes, and transport vehicles (Jürgens 2023: 89). The constant bustle of such workers that filled other auto plants—comprising 19% of the workforce at Daimler (Stahlmann 1992: 151)—was *comparatively inefficient*. According to contemporaneous commentators Arnold and Faurote (1915), "In every instance of work-slide placing there was a gain of from 30 to 100 per cent in the production volume, with the same methods, machines, small tools, and men; seemingly nothing done to decrease labor costs, yet large savings shown immediately" (274; see Mortier 1924). The work of gravity and electrically powered conveyor belts automated the work of these unskilled hand transport workers, as the *socially necessary temporal norm* for transport work at Ford became the faster speeds of the conveyors. Though transport workers were among the lowest paid workers, "Henry Ford was known for his efforts to reduce costs anywhere he could, even if the savings amounted to only a few cents, and he was determined to eliminate as many of the unskilled, nonproductive workers as possible" (Biggs 1995: 50). This form of automation was rudimentary but nevertheless increased productivity and reduced the need for human material handling—setting a new standard of production flow.

Scientific management also contributed to the flow of individual tasks. The rigid standardization of the Model T was synergistic with the aim of rigidly standardizing work tasks in a detailed division of labor (Meyer 2004). Standardization also made it easier for industrial engineers to monitor and assess labor. As early as 1912, Ford established a time study or "work standards" department at Highland Park responsible for conducting time-and-motion studies to determine the most effective ways to perform a job (Hounshell 1985: 250). Like Daimler, it appeared that Ford did not consciously follow Taylorism, although clearly Ford had become 'Taylorized' without Taylor (Hounshell 1985: 251). Nevertheless, this development pointed to the importance of efficient flow, the rise of deskilling, and the determination and enforcement of production norms by management.

The simplified work tasks also complemented the use of single purpose machines "that would duplicate the simplified work operations" (Meyer 2004: 3). The automation of labor through machinery separates Fordism from Taylorism since Taylor aimed to improve efficiency given a pre-established set of production equipment and workers, while Ford engineers "mechanized work processes and found workers to feed and tend their machines" (Hounshell 1985: 252). Taylorism *lacked the imperative to automate* of Fordism, even as they shared the common drive for efficiency and improving productivity.

As the American machine tool industry developed machines with improved precision accuracy and consistency, machines for the first time could be relied upon to generate large quantities of consistently accurate work (Hounshell 1985: 233). Whether the machines were originally general-purpose machines modified to be single purpose or totally new tools invented in-house at Ford, over $2.8 million had been spent on machine tool equipment by 1914. In fact, there were more machines at Highland Park than workers, with roughly 15,000 machines and 13,000 workers in 1914 (Meyer 1981: 24–25). The deployment of machinery at Ford was so pervasive that extensive use of machinery was considered by many contemporaries—including within the German auto industry—to be the primary distinguishing feature of Fordism, rather than the assembly line (Jürgens 2023: 91).

Simplified single purpose machines only required low-skilled workers to operate them. As Meyer (1981) explains:

> These new machines produced only a single part and enabled the production of large numbers of identical parts by unskilled workmen. In the end, the new specialized machines established the need for a new generation of specialized machine operators. These new workers had no skills and simply placed a piece in and removed it from the machine. (24)

Deskilling and repetitive work thus appears as a feature of Fordist mass production. This also represented an automation push as operations that were previously carried out by skilled workers on general purpose machines were now done by the machines with little assistance from the workers.

Before the assembly line, automobile assembly was static as assembly teams moved from station to station for each car (Hounshell 1985: 236; Stahlmann 1992). The ethos of the assembly line was the opposite—move the work to the workers (Hounshell 1985: 237). With a smooth flow achieved throughout the factory via conveyors, gravity slides, and other devices, as well as machines that guaranteed interchangeability, assembly line production without the need for fitters could be attained. Experiments began in 1913, and—with the help of careful time study and trial and error—impressive gains in productivity were achieved (Jürgens 2023 93).

Numerous examples speak to the effectiveness of the assembly line. After much experimentation, engine assembly time was lowered from 594 to 226 man-minutes (Hounshell 1985: 249). By 1914, the productivity of assembling flywheel magnetos doubled thanks to the assembly line. Chassis assembly time had dropped from 12.5 hours in October 1913 to only 2 hours and 40 minutes by December 1913 (Flink 1988: 46). By April 1914, workers along three chassis assembly lines could assemble 1,212 chassis in 8 hours, or 93 man-minutes each (Hounshell 1985: 255). In department after department, assembly line production proved to decrease the time per workpiece and set new productivity records. The time for each task was measured before and after, with the shorter production process becoming the accepted standard of socially necessary labor time at Ford.

The assembly line was later driven by an electric chain run at a constant speed, which sped up slower workers and slowed down faster workers to achieve consistent flow (Meyer 2004: 4). As one contemporaneous commentator put it, "the output is regulated by the speed at which the traveling chains are operated. Speed up the electric motors a notch and—presto! Ford production has increased another hundred cars per day without hiring a single workman" (Meyer 2004: 4). This gave considerable power over production speed to management, who frequently increased the speed of the line to levels nearly intolerable for the workers (Edsforth and Asher 1995). The assembly line remained an essentially exclusive American invention for many years, with European competitors such as Daimler not adopting it fully until the 1920s or 1930s (Stahlmann 1992: 167; Asher and Edsforth 1995: 9).

It is difficult to assess which of these factors, flow, machinery, or the assembly line, is the most important explanatory factor for the productivity increases at Highland Park. Writing in 1923, Henry Ford put great emphasis on the new production tools and machinery used at Ford versus the traditional hand methods, "Sufficiently skilled men to the number needed could not have been trained in a hundred years. A million men working by hand could not even approximate our daily output" (Ford 1922: 46). This is plausible considering Daimler did not breach producing over 2,000 cars per year until 1926 with a workforce that was usually larger than the number of cars it produced per year (Bellon 1990: 16). Compare this to Ford's production of 1.6 million vehicles in 1926 with a workforce of a little over 40,000 (Nevins and Hill 1963; Peterson 1987). It therefore may not be an exaggeration that it would take millions of skilled workers to produce 1.6 million vehicles a year using Daimler's craft production processes. In addition, other US automobile manufacturers were both adopting similar machines as Ford even before 1913 and recorded large increases in productivity, giving credence to the idea that automation was a crucial factor for productivity (Mortier 1924; Jürgens 2023: 125).

Interchangeability and the elimination of fitters as a job classification also saved time and labor (Hounshell 1985). Efforts at achieving flow through rationalized process design and use of simple devices for moving parts also increased productivity and heavily reduced the need for transport workers. Finally, the assembly line must also be given credit for regulating production and saving time. It can be estimated that between the beginning of Highland Park production in 1910 until 1926, there was an approximately 724% increase in productivity, decreasing the hours it takes to make a Model T from 384 to merely 53 hours on average (Jürgens 2023: 123). Therefore, Fordist mass production was not simply one change, e.g., the assembly line alone, but multiple changes discovered through trial and error and experimentation oriented towards saving time and labor in each part of the production process.

4.3 *Spreading Fordism beyond Ford in the United States*

Thanks to Ford's product strategy and the immense productivity increases occurring in Ford's factories, the Ford Motor Company quickly rose to the top of the automobile market in the US, producing millions of Model Ts during the 1910s and 20s. Ford's total US market share was 55 percent in 1921 but decreased to 30 percent by 1926, being surpassed by General Motors in 1927 (Hounshell 1985: 263–264; Klier and Rubenstein 2020: 47). What caused the decline in Ford's dominance? The attractiveness of new competing models partially explains this. The Model T was considered technologically outmoded by the mid-1920s (Flink 1988: 38). Wants, needs, and desires changed as American consumers started to demand more variety in their choice of car. Thus, challenges in value realization became relevant. However, more important for our purposes was how Fordist production methods were *generalized* by American auto companies and later spread around the world, which diminished Ford's competitive advantage in production.

Other US auto companies were interested in improving productivity apart from directly copying Fordist methods. The arrival of low-priced cars such as the Model T and Buick Model 10 prompted competitors to search for ways to increase productivity and lower manufacturing costs to compete against these models. For example, Walter P. Chrysler, as head of Buick, independently made changes to production techniques that resembled Fordism (Flink 1988: 46). One Bureau of Labor Statistics study from 1924 found that six (anonymous) American auto companies experienced productivity improvements similar in magnitude to Ford from 1912 to 1923. One company decreased the number of hours to produce a vehicle from 4,664 in 1912 to 813 by 1923. Similarly, another firm dropped production time from 1,260 hours to 228 hours in the same period (Mortier 1924 737; Jürgens 2023: 125). For comparison, Ford took 274 hours to make a car in 1912 which dropped to 70 hours per vehicle in 1923 (Jürgens 2023: 121–123). Just as with Daimler in Germany, drives to increase productivity, regardless of the product strategy or target clientele, appeared to be universal, *a productivity pressure applicable regardless of circumstance.*

Yet special attention was paid to Ford's efforts as market and productivity leader. Many contemporaries and competitors of Ford "closely watched" the production changes at Highland Park and attempted to understand and emulate their development (Hounshell 1985: 260). Unlike companies that conceal production processes as proprietary information, Henry Ford was openly proud about what his company had achieved. Numerous journalistic articles appeared in the popular and trade press covering all aspects of Ford's production methods (e.g., Arnold and Faroute 1915). As Horace Arnold stated in 1914, "The Ford company is willing to have any part of its commercial, managerial or mechanical practice given full and unrestricted publicity in print" (cited in Hounshell 1985: 260). Henry Ford even divulged his industrial ethos and how Fordism works in his autobiography from a spirit that "progress comes from a generous form of rivalry" (Ford 1922: 175). Through the 1910s and 1920s, Fordist production processes and technologies were "diffused rapidly throughout American manufacturing," with auto companies moving to adopt the assembly line mere days after the first articles appeared (Hounshell 1985: 260–261; see Meyer 2004: 4). Competitors from Europe also visited Highland Park, where Ford was "remarkably open in discussing his techniques with them," although diffusion was much slower in Europe (Womack et al. 2007 [1990]: 43). Ford soon no longer held unambiguous technological or productivity advantages because Fordist methods became the *socially necessary standard* across the American industry. Some had even overtaken Ford in terms of efficiency, e.g., Hudson cars could be assembled in 90 minutes by 1926 with one car rolling off the assembly line every 30 seconds (Flink 1988: 50).

The rapid adoption of Fordism is an example of the *generalization of productivity norms.* Ford quickly exceeded all competition with its unique product strategy aimed at motorizing the masses matched with continuous experimentation in production processes that led to enormous gains in productivity. To compete with Ford in the largely untapped US market, increasing productivity and efficiency in ways similar or equal to Ford was not just desirable but *necessary.* Achieving higher productivity entailed eliminating the jobs of fitters through interchangeability and reducing indirect transport workers through mechanical devices, as Ford did. Thus, adaptation for these auto companies, and the automation of both the class of skilled fitters and unskilled transport workers was not purely a matter of choice but pressured as *social necessity.*

As Asher and Edsforth (1995) describe, "Although a few low-volume, quality car makers did not embrace the Ford Motor Company's widely-publicized new methods, the industry's other large producers were *forced to follow Ford's lead* to stay competitive" (66; emphasis mine). Maintaining competitiveness was important because the market was overflowing with auto companies. Hundreds of these US auto companies closed from the 1910s to the 1930s, while the market concentration of a few leaders who had mastered Fordism increased rapidly (Peterson 1987: 8). Therefore, survival for these American auto companies hinged on keeping up with the established productivity standard set by Highland Park.

Because Ford openly shared details about its production processes with the public, generalization was straightforward. Note also the role of different social systems in facilitating this process. Journalistic articles were the "primary agents of this diffusion" (Hounshell 1985: 260). Detailing the temporally compressed work processes, competitors reading such articles *recognized the existence of a higher productivity standard and acted to emulate it* in their own factories. Factory tours for journalists, competitors, or interested onlookers was another means of knowledge diffusion. In this way, communication via article or factory tour convinced competitors to change their operations to achieve comparable productivity levels. Productivity pressure was both a 'market pressure,' reflected in Ford's market success that squeezed out competitors, but also a *social process* via communication among social systems that seek to *identify and emulate* new productivity norms.

4.4 *Worker Reaction and the Five-Dollar-Day*

Fordism entailed dramatic changes to work processes and labor composition. The typical workforce in American pre-Fordist auto factories comprised around 40% skilled craftsmen with machine operators and unskilled laborers constituting approximately 30% each (Meyer 2004: 3). For Ford in 1913, skilled operators had fallen to 26 percent of the workforce (3,431 out of 13,304), and unskilled workers, e.g., transport workers, assistants to skilled workers and cleaners, had fallen to 21 percent (2795 total). Machine operators had risen to 51 percent (6,749), dwarfing the other two groups (Meyer 1981: 50). By 1917, machine specialists and assemblers rose to 55% of the workforce, or 22,652 out of 40,996. Meanwhile, the unskilled workers formed 14.6 percent of the workforce (5,986) and the skilled trades and technical workers only composed 15.6 percent of the workforce (6,394) (Meyer 1981: 51). The absolute numbers of all categories rose during this period due to Ford's explosive growth. Nevertheless, a trend toward less reliance on skilled trades and unskilled day laborers was apparent.

The rapid increase of the unskilled machine tenders and assembly line workers meant the rise of the "repetitive, monotonous, and alienating work" (Meyer 2004: 3). Both jobs were unskilled because,

> the skilled dimension of the work task was designed into the machines. The worker simply inserted a piece into the machine, turned a switch, and the machine performed its operation and automatically stopped. Then the worker removed it and passed it on for the next machine operation. (Meyer 2004: 3)

Work was primarily driven by the pace of the machine rather than by the operator, the dictates of a master, or even a foreman. As one worker starkly put it, "The machine that I am on goes at such a terrific speed that I can't help stepping on it in order to keep up with it. The machine is my boss" (Meyer 2004: 3). Studies of the life of these "on the line" workers frequently cite how they suffered from the monotony of their repetitive work, felt powerless from strict management control, and had no time for breaks from the fast paced work that stressed both psychological and physical limits (Asher and Edsforth 1995: 8). In short, Fordism entailed a harsh form of alienation that was cemented in its legacy (Marx 1932 [1844]; see Thompson 1995; Edsforth and Asher 1995).

Skilled workers nevertheless still formed an important part of the mass production workforce. While some skilled jobs such as molders, coremakers, and machinists were no longer needed thanks to the rise of unskilled machine operators, Ford still hired large numbers of other skilled jobs such as tool and die makers and tool setters, while other skilled workers took supervisory roles (Meyer 1981: 52–55). Under craft production, skilled workers typically self-regulated and maintained their own craftsmen 'stint' by restricting output to what they considered reasonable (Peterson 1987: 153; Meyer 2004: 4). However, with the increase in foremen and the application of scientific management, stint had to be practiced as a covert act of disrupting management control (Peterson 1987: 153). Therefore, while skilled workers were still present in Fordist mass production factories, their traditional craft ways of working changed when they became placed under management's watchful eye.

Indeed, management maintained order by hiring more supervisory personnel, with over 2,500 foremen at Ford in 1917 (Meyer 1981: 51). These foremen, straw bosses, inspectors, and clerks had the task of directly supervising labor and exhorting workers to "hurry up and work faster" (Meyer 2004: 4). The foreman was seen by workers as a "petty tyrant with an inflated sense of importance and authority," who frequently exercised their power to fire slow or unsatisfactory workers (Meyer 1981: 55). They enforced the productive norms at the factory with zeal while the ununionized workers had little recourse to dispute beyond covert action or quitting. Overall, the jobs of most Ford workers, both skilled and unskilled, had changed dramatically from the earlier craft system. This is partially why the arrival of Fordist mass production is often viewed as epoch defining (see Womack et al. 2007 [1990]: 24–46).

In the wake of such tremendous changes under harsh working conditions, workers responded through quits, absenteeism, and 'soldiering' on the line. In 1913, during the height of the experimental phase of mass production techniques, the daily absenteeism rate averaged 10 percent per day, which meant an additional 1,300–1,400 workers were needed to maintain production (Meyer 2004: 4). In the same year, the labor turnover rate was 370 percent, so that 52,000 workers were hired that year to maintain Highland Park 's workforce of about 13,304 (Meyer 2004: 4; Meyer 1981: 50).[2] These actions had negative productivity effects as Highland Park was experiencing lower levels of output than expected in all departments despite the technological innovations and transformations of the production process (Meyer 2004: 4). This is consistent with research that indicates that worker actions such as quits, absenteeism, and strikes have negative productivity and cost effects (e.g., Norsworthy and Zabala 1985; Lam, Norsworthy, and Zabala 1991). These actions demonstrated a deep-seated discontent among Ford workers.

Such dissatisfaction left Ford vulnerable to one of Henry Ford's greatest fears: unionization. Union organizing posed little threat in the US auto industry before 1913 because Detroit was famous at the time for its staunch antiunionism. Detroit was an 'open shop' city that deployed tactics such as company spies, blacklists, and private disciplinary forces to prevent unionization (Peterson 1987: 151). If deterrents were not enough, companies simply refused to negotiate with unions over working conditions, pay, or other concerns (Peterson 1987: 151). However, in response to extreme worker discontent, campaigns were launched by the radical Industrial Workers of the World and the comparatively conservative American Federation of Labor in 1913 to organize the Ford workers (Meyer 1981: 89–93). Both attempts ultimately failed but nevertheless represented a serious threat to Henry Ford's plans. He was

2 The turnover problem was not unique to Ford, but its relative scale was. As Asher and Edsforth (1995) explain, "In 1913 and 1914, the turnover rate in the auto industry was 156 percent (annually), while a sample of eighty four other industries had an average turnover rate of 93 percent" (7). In addition, 80 percent of the turnover is accounted for by resignations from new hires who quit after only a few days of repetitive work, so the hire and fire policies of the foremen are not entirely to blame here (Jürgens 2023: 112–113).

afraid unions would push for strikes, lower productivity, and output restriction, all of which directly contradicted the purpose of the Fordist production model to achieve high volume production (Meyer 1981: 90). The unionization threat, turnover, and productivity problems prompted Ford to implement the five-dollar day to counteract these developments.

Announced in January 1914, the five-dollar day promised to double the income of ordinary Ford workers (Meyer 2004: 4). Combining a wage raise and a profit-sharing scheme, the five-dollars day program assuaged the tense labor relations at Ford (Meyer 2004: 4). The raise was not unconditional however, as Ford's paternalism was extended through the practices of the so-called 'sociological department' that determined whether a given worker was sufficiently 'American' enough to deserve five dollars a day. The expectation was that high wages would be paid to workers if their daily lives expressed 'American' values and were willing to fit themselves into Ford's vast productive apparatus (Hounshell 1985: 259).

Though the actual wage fluctuated, the five-dollar day nevertheless mostly produced the intended effect of inculcating work discipline and stabilizing industrial relations. It became famous as an expression of industrial paternalism and the potential wage benefits of high-volume industrial production (Meyer 1981). It also became paradigmatic for labor relations in the US auto industry. Under this model, the primary relationship between capital and labor was characterized by labor receiving increasing compensation and benefits in exchange for management maintaining control over production processes and their development. By the 1920s, there was an implicit bargain within the auto industry that workers would accept strict discipline and monotonous, repetitive, and routinized work in exchange for high wages, plentiful jobs, and an improving standard of living (Peterson 1987: 152). As Asher and Edsforth (1995) described,

> The main compensation for unpleasant, alienating work was financial: U.S. auto workers received, and continue to receive, hourly wages close to the top of the scale for the nation's manufacturing workers. High wages led workers to expect that as long as they held onto their jobs, they could buy a home, purchase desired consumer durables, or save to start a small business that offered a way to gain more direct control over their work life. (8)

Workers' *interest in self-valorization* thereby moderated the desire for *control over the valorization process*. Nevertheless, frequent conflict between labor and capital characterized the American auto industry, but the general pattern of managing that conflict since the five-dollar day has been to compensate workers for highly alienated and intense working conditions. This tendency forms one element of path dependence that characterizes the US value-regime.

4.5 *German 'Mass-Craft Production' in World War 1*

The eruption of war in Europe in 1914 caused all capable industrial firms to be recruited into the war effort, including Daimler and the rest of the auto industry. The experience of war production and the subsequent German Revolution of 1918–1919 had profound effects on German industrial production. The relationship between business, labor, and government was tested and strained but also clarified and reforged in ways that had long-term ramifications for Germany's industrial trajectory.

Daimler was no stranger to government partnership. Their vehicles were already being used for military maneuvers by 1900, and the firm received subsidies to develop new vehicles for the military by 1910 (Bellon 1990: 86). This relationship expanded in scale and scope after the advent of war in 1914. Daimler supplied a variety of products such as heavy transport vehicles, parts for submarine engines, and airplane motors (Bellon 1990: 86–87). Such transactions were handled through military contracts worth hundreds of millions of marks—significantly more than what Daimler typically made selling automobiles. Car production fell considerably over the war years and replaced by military production (Bellon 1990: 90).

Such lucrative contracts allowed for an expansion of Untertürkheim, with several new buildings built between 1915 and 1917, as well as the opening of a whole new factory at Sindelfingen located to the south of Stuttgart—a quadrupling of Daimler's capital (Bellon 1990: 91; Flink 1988: 76). Daimler also hired thousands of additional workers and bought thousands of new machines to expand productive capacity. The workforce at Untertürkheim rose from 3,376 workers in July 1914 to a peak of around 15,130 workers on the eve of the armistice in November 1918 (Bellon 1990: 93). With an additional 5,068 workers at Sindelfingen by 1918, Daimler had over 20,000 workers for war production (Bellon 1990: 93).

This enlarged workforce was only about half the size of the Ford workforce in 1917 (Meyer 1981: 51). While Daimler produced 19,876 airplane engines and approximately 9,000 cars and heavy vehicles for the war effort from 1914–1918, Ford produced 2,576,029 cars in the same years (Bellon 1990: 87–90; Congressional Quarterly 1927). The differences between the products obviously played a role in these production gaps but cannot explain the entire disparity.

The productivity gap between Fordist and the non-Fordist mass-craft production systems was enormous.

The German state, under the urgent necessity of war production, pressured companies to pursue standardization and rationalization strategies to improve productivity, but these efforts did not come close to matching the productivity gains experienced in the United States at this time. The military instructed companies manufacturing weapons and ammunition to examine and implement all possibilities for standardization. A "German Industry Standards Committee" (*Normenausschuss der Deutschen Industrie*) was established as a partnership between the military and various engineering and mechanical industries to prepare them to become internationally competitive mass producers. Committees and task forces were developed to address production issues, which laid important foundations for a joint state-company-union institutional system that emerged during and after the war (Jürgens 2023: 239–240). Therefore, war mobilization pushed the German state, rather than entrepreneurs as in the US, to take the lead in industrial modernization.

This development also played out at Daimler. The military required vehicles and airplane engines in only a few types, which helped standardize the production processes to speed up production (Bellon 1990: 88). The mass orders of a few set models did help reduce production costs, which enabled increased profits for the firm (Bellon 1990: 104). Military officials cajoled Daimler to increase productivity in the "interest of the defense of the nation" (Bellon 1990: 87). However, these military-led efforts were not enough to spark a productivity revolution at Daimler as it had at Ford. The basic labor structure, with skilled workers and fitters, machine tenders, and unskilled day laborers, persisted at Daimler just on a larger scale. In fact, despite efforts at standardization, fitting was still necessary for the airplane motors, meaning that interchangeability of parts—a standard that became ubiquitous years ago in the US—had yet to be achieved at Daimler (Bellon 1990: 88). Bellon (1990) describes the situation this way,

> Legions of skilled hand workers and unskilled day laborers who had no machine duties were still essential to the firm's productive enterprises after years of war. Economies of scale guaranteed by the state, not a revolution in the production processes, made possible huge profits at Daimler. (91)

The war experience benefited Daimler through the expansion of capacity with new buildings, machines, and a new factory. It also brought forward some productivity enhancing standardization efforts. However, the general system of “artisanal production by skilled mechanics” remained virtually unchanged during the war (Flink 1988: 76). This form of mass-craft production was mass in the sense that it was a scaled up version of the craft production processes swelled with the thousands of skilled workers and day laborers necessary to get the craft production system producing at higher volumes. These developments at Daimler demonstrate how both productivity and employment growth in Germany differed greatly from that of Fordist mass production.

4.6 *Revolutionary Workers Slow Down German Production*

The end of WWI, the fall of the German Empire, and the rise of the Weimar Republic were fraught with political twists and turns that do not concern us here. There are, however, few points relevant to the development and trajectory of Daimler and the German auto industry. The Stinnes-Legien pact made in November 1918 solidified and legitimated many important industrial relations characteristics that define the German value-regime. The official right of union recognition, the right to organize, and to bargain collectively was established. Works councils were recognized in the Weimar Constitution and the first rights of codetermination were codified with the aim of allowing labor and management to act as co-participants in economic and productive development (Jürgens 2023: 240–241). In addition, the first region-wide collective bargaining agreement for southwestern Germany was agreed to in 1919, regulating wages and working conditions for tens of thousands of workers. In Germany at this time, large unions and employers’ associations concocted large regional collective agreements covering multiple companies and industries, rather than on a company-by-company basis as would become typical in the US in the 1930s. This agreement affirmed the role of the works councils and set up means to resolve industrial conflict through arbitration committees as per the Stinnes-Legien pact. It also included provisions for piece-rates, vacation time, the length of the working day, and overtime pay, signifying that a high degree of regulation was achievable in Germany on a broad range of labor issues (Bellon 1990: 164). Many such questions would be left unregulated in the United States for decades, leaving programs like the five-dollar day solely up to management prerogative (see Meyer 1981; Greenhouse 2019). The contracts made during the immediate postwar period had profound long-term implications as they formed much of the foundational legal basis for the German value-regime for decades to come.

The immediate aftermath for the workers at Daimler, however, was not as favorable. The end of the war meant the end of military contracts and thus the end of high-volume mass-craft production. In mere weeks after the war, approximately 4,000 of the over 15,000 workers at Untertürkheim voluntarily left the factory (Bellon 1990: 144). Others were released due to overcapacity, chosen based on a set of criteria such as age, gender, seniority, and political belief—shedding many of the most radically left workers (Bellon 1990: 145–147). Even with this shedding of workers, the factory remained full of radical leftists, Spartacists, social democrats, and various socialists who staged multiple strikes and demonstrations between 1918–1920 (Bellon 1990: 169).

At the height of revolutionary fervor at Daimler, the workers effectively rebuffed management efforts to surveille, entice, or pressure workers to work any faster than what they themselves decided. For example, workers, with the support of the socialist dominated works council, often slowed down the pace of work at Untertürkheim (Bellon 1990: 178). A few examples are given by Bellon (1990),

> One worker, who began his employment in 1917 and left in August 1920, reported that he was often told by his fellow workers to either work more slowly or to leave Daimler. A trade unionist, for example, told the workers in his department to work more slowly. When one worker refused, the steward demanded that he be sacked immediately. A member of the *Betriebsrat* [works council] from the foundry prevented a piece-worker there from doing his customary 77 pieces of work a week, a total considered too high. (178)

Such examples demonstrate both worker discontent and the rebellion against it that emerges when workers feel empowered. These also serve as examples of the output restricting and productivity decreasing form of worker activity that Henry Ford feared (Meyer 1981: 90). Unlike the US, Daimler workers wanted *control over valorization processes* rather than *tolerate higher work intensely for increased self-valorization.*

This revolutionary period of increased worker power ended abruptly with a lock out of the 7,000 workers at the Untertürkheim factory in 1920 (Bellon 1990: 184–199). The success of the lockout allowed management to cut the workforce to about 3,000 workers (Bellon 1990: 199). This labor defeat left a less revolutionary and more docile workforce that was more receptive to the rationalization methods the company pursued in the 1920s.

Though many of the workers' revolutionary victories and concessions would not last, especially during the Third Reich, they nevertheless set precedents for industrial relations in Germany that are still important today. The rights of works councils, unions, and codetermination were formally legalized, and this industrial relations in Germany which survived in altered forms after WWII. This also set the precedent for *state led rationalization initiatives* as well as state-firm partnership which would also be characteristic of the German value-regime in subsequent decades. At the same time, the vast differences in productivity and output levels remained between the US and German value-regimes. While both industries essentially began with very similar forms of craft production, differences in labor formation, machine use and automation, and productivity subsequently emerged. The results of these choices have indicated a clear productivity leader and laggard, even as there are multifactorial reasons based within the value-regime for why the choices were made. The socially necessary labor time of production differed between the two value-regimes, and this difference is reflected in their wildly different output capabilities. This output and productivity gap grew wider during the 1920s up to the eve of the Great Depression.

5 Growth, Maturation, and Rationalization in the 1920s

The end of WWI signified the beginning of the 'roaring 20s' in the United States and tough economic circumstances in the Weimar Republic. With the high productivity and automation at Ford's facilities, the heyday of Ford and the Model T continued well into the 1920s. The decade started, however, with a severe recession. The post WWI recession in 1920–1921 hit the entire US auto industry hard, including Ford which—thanks to management prerogative to hire and fire—laid off tens of thousands of workers to weather the severe drop in demand. Nearing bankruptcy, the recession prompted Ford to engage in renewed rationalization efforts including scrapping unnecessary tools, and fixtures and replacing old machines (Flink 1988: 84–85). This led to increased labor efficiency so that it was possible to operate Ford plants with 80 percent capacity with only 60 percent of the labor (Nevins and Hill 1957: 519).

The recession also prompted the retrenchment of the paternalistic 'progressive' regime of labor relations at Ford, ending the five-dollar day profit sharing plan and the sociological department in 1920–1921 (Meyer 1981: 197). This paternalism was replaced by an increase in repressive methods of worker control, signifying the 'Prussianization' of the Ford Motor Company (Nevins and Hill 1957: 349; Flink 1988: 83–86; Jürgens 2023: 117). As a family-owned business with Henry Ford at its helm, such top-down centralized control was easily achieved. From the use of spies and informants to coerce and repress labor, this policy appeared less expensive than the so-called 'welfare state' programs (Meyer 1981: 199).

What was falling into place, therefore, was the general pattern of labor relations that would reign in the US up to the present—though without union representation. On the one hand, management had control over production processes, which entailed repetitive, monotonous, and alienating work to achieve high productivity. On the other hand, labor was financially compensated for this 'inhumane' work and were among the most well-paid workers in the country. Collective struggle would not truly begin until the rise of the United Automobile Workers in the 1930s, but nevertheless this pattern of labor relations had precursors in the nonunion era of the 1910s and 1920s due to the legacy of the five-dollar day and repressive management control.

Ford survived the recession and soon entered a period of boom in the mid-1920s. The company reached yearly production of over one million vehicles in 1920, which doubled by 1923 with peak production of over two million Model Ts (Congressional Quarterly 1927). Reaching this height was possible in part due to the rise in production at Ford's River Rouge factory complex. Beginning construction in 1916, the enormous fifteen million square foot, 93 building complex was gradually built until 1928 where it progressively produced more and more parts of the Model T until taking over production of the new Model A in 1927 (Martelle 2014: 101; Hounshell 1985: 267–268). The production capacities of the Rouge dwarfed Highland Park, which itself was large and modern for its time. For example, by 1924 the Rouge foundry casted over 10,000 Model T cylinder blocks a day, and by 1926 housed over 43,000 machine tools and employing over 8,000 tool and die makers (Flink 1988: 49). Though assembly of the Model T remained at Highland Park, the River Rouge became the primary plant for Ford in all aspects of production after 1927 and became the hub of new production technologies and automation in the coming decades.

During the peak year of 1923, Ford produced over two million vehicles out of a total US production of over four million vehicles (Congressional Quarterly 1927). Reliance on a single model could not last forever however, as Ford's production declined slightly until reaching only 1.4 million autos in 1926. This decline was partially attributed to the US market reaching a saturation point where there were very few prospective first time car buyers, which contemporary reports speculated was a contributing factor for lower Model T sales (Congressional Quarterly 1927). Regardless of the cause, the decline signaled to Ford the need to produce a new model with updated technology—both in terms of the product and its production—and a new marketing approach (see Hounshell 1985: 263–267). Ford's answer to this challenge would ultimately be the Model A.

The 'classical' Fordist production schema of producing one model as efficiently as possible was experiencing limitations. Competitors, General Motors above all, were attempting to appeal to American consumers not through the low price of a basic model, which was technologically outmoded by the mid-1920s, but via styling and yearly model changes. This signified a shift in the sphere of realization as changing wants, needs, and desires meant that the Model T was encountering difficulty realizing its value. These new realization demands had important implications for not just product design and development but for the entire production system. Ford encountered problems retooling from Model T to Model A production, necessitating a total plant shutdown in 1927 (Hounshell 1985: 263–301). After the changeover, Ford was unable to regain the lead in production and market share that was lost to General Motors, and GM would remain the world's largest automobile producer for the rest of the 20th century (Klier and Rubenstein 2020: 47).

Despite this setback, Ford remained a major leader in an increasingly concentrated industry. During the 1920s, the giant firms of Ford, General Motors, and Chrysler took their stranglehold on the US market. The total number of auto firms in the US dropped from 253 in 1908 to 108 in 1920, and to 44 in 1929, showing increasing concentration and the failure of many smaller auto ventures who could not find a market niche or compete with bigger companies' productive advantages and economies of scale (Flink 1988: 70–72). The market share of larger firms grew rapidly. In 1911, Ford and General Motors accounted for about 38 percent of the market while other significant players such as Hudson, Packard, Nash and Studebaker had about 15 percent, with the remaining 47 percent held by other firms. By 1929, Ford, General Motors, and Chrysler had attained 72 percent of the market while Hudson, Packard, Nash and Studebaker held onto only 12 percent, with the remaining 16 percent going to smaller firms (Peterson 1987: 8). This concentration became even more extreme into the 1930s and beyond.

The generalization of Fordism and an expanding market made the United States essentially the only motorized society by the end of the 1920s. The century began with only approximately 8,000 cars registered in the United States, but by 1914 the country was over one million, ten million by 1921, and end the decade with over twenty-six million cars registered by 1929, out of thirty-five million car registrations in the world (Patch 1932; Peterson 1987: 4). The number of persons per automobile was 5.1 in the US in 1929 compared to 23.8 in Great Britain, 36.6 in France, and a mere 73.4 per person in Germany (Riefler 1929). The US already had an early lead on Germany by 1903 with 1,310 cars produced in Germany (Daimler: 232) while the US was already producing 11,235 (Ford: 1,708). A decade later in 1913, the gap had expanded dramatically with 17,162 produced in Germany (Daimler: 1,567) and 461,500 made in the United States (Ford: 248,307). Even as late as 1925 Germany was producing only 38,988 vehicles (Daimler: 1,406) while the US was producing 4,312,456 (Ford: 1,587,821) (Bellon 1990: 14). The lack of a mass market obviously hindered the German industry's development, but autos were similarly unobtainable for the average American when they were produced under the craft production system. Expanding the market through aggressive price reductions was enabled by the *eleven-fold increase in worker productivity* experienced in the industry between 1904 and 1925 due to the Fordist revolution (Reynolds 1989: 70). Whether it would have been possible to achieve comparable levels of motorization in Europe if Fordist production methods had taken hold is unknown, but what is certain is that adherence to the craft production system kept automobility an exclusive domain of the wealthiest Germans.

This success allowed Ford and GM to become multinational firms. Necessitated by high tariffs on US imported vehicles, foreign branches of US auto companies appeared and spread Fordism to these foreign locations, beginning with Ford in 1911 (Noyes 1938; Flink 1988: 252–254). By 1928 Ford was assembling cars in twenty-one countries and GM in sixteen, with their total foreign output exceeding the total of both the French and German auto industries (Flink 1988: 251). In Germany, Ford established a factory in Cologne and GM bought Opel in 1929, making GM the owner of the largest manufacturer in Germany (Flink 1988: 253).[3] This demonstrates how rapid capital accumulation enabled by high productivity production systems allows for market expansion as a virtuous cycle. Even as tariffs attempted to lessen the cost advantage of Fordist American firms, which simultaneously *reduced the productivity pressure to adopt Fordism for survival*, the immense capital accumulation of US firms still meant that foreign investments were possible as an alternative, thus reapplying the productivity pressure, but in a different way. The German craft producers did not expand abroad yet now faced domestic challenges from American owned firms.

The growth of the American industry also led to the explosive growth of the workforce. Starting in 1899, the infant industry employed 2,241 workers. By 1914, there were 127,092 workers, 212,777 by 1921, and the decade ended with a peak of 447,448 workers in 1929 (Peterson 1987: 4). This rapid expansion occurred during the transition from craft to mass production in the US auto industry. Such employment growth was predicated on the incredible rise in sales due to an expanding market, which was *only possible due to the transformations of the labor process*. In other words, the high employment went hand in hand with

3 It was chosen for purchase in part because it had the most modern factory and work organization in Germany with the highest productivity (Stahlmann 1992: 148, 175).

transformations of labor that made fitters superfluous and shifted the composition of the workforce away from unskilled day laborers and skilled craftsmen and toward the alienating work on the assembly line and beside the single purpose machine.

However, this staggering growth also meant that there was little perceived threat of automation in terms of total numbers of jobs—even if many job categories were eliminated. So long as workers were willing to accept these mass production jobs, including technologically displaced or deskilled workers, then there was plenty of work to be found. This indicates how economic growth can render large scale structural transformations of labor, the automation of job classes, and technological displacement *invisible*, at least when viewed from the macro level of large aggregates. Many fitters, transport workers, and other skilled trade workers did indeed lose their jobs, but their displacement was easily reabsorbed under these conditions—even without union protections. Under the precedent set by Ford, productivity norms of socially necessary labor time were pushed forward so that *firm survival depended on adaptation to Fordist methods*, which meant the adoption of interchangeability and the assembly line that eliminated the skilled fitters and prompted the need for more machinery and rationalized transport systems that swelled the ranks of machine tenders and diminished the role of transport workers. Firms that could not approximate, match, or exceed the productive norms set by Ford, or find an *alternative* selling point for their cars such as luxury quality, would likely fail—which is precisely what happened as the industry concentrated (Flink 1988: 70–72). In this way, the push for change is not rooted in Ford itself—Ford has no direct control over the production processes of other companies—but is best understood as a form of *social domination* that applies productivity pressure at a *macro-social level* apart from the value-systems involved.

Overall, the developments of the 1920s in the US witnessed a maturing of the auto market and an industry consensus around Fordist mass production. The maturing of the market meant the industry could no longer rely on first time buyers for growth. This helped lead to the decline of the Model T and the end of Ford's dominance in the American market. In a sense, Henry Ford had become a victim of his own success. Achieving the mass motorization he desired in only a few decades meant that the period of high growth and the saturation of the market arrived that much sooner. From now on, additional considerations besides productivity and the lowest cost, such as styling to encourage realization, would come to the fore. This does not, however, entail a disregard for productivity, but a need to balance it with these other factors. The challenges of the 1920s were ultimately dwarfed by the unprecedented shocks of the Great Depression and WWII that unfolded over the next two decades.

5.1 *Group Production and Rationalization at Daimler in the 1920s*

There were also important developments in the German industry during this period. The first is the experiments in group production conducted in 1919 at Daimler that aimed at increasing productivity in an alternative path to Fordism. The second is the rationalization program engaged in by Daimler (officially Daimler-Benz after a merger) in the late 1920s. Both expressed efforts by German auto firms to rationalize production and increase productivity, with the former as an alternative to Fordism and the latter moving closer to it.

The first experiments with group production (*Gruppenfabrikation*) began in 1919 during the immediate postwar revolutionary period. The expanded mass-craft war production had seriously strained the limits of the prevailing craft production system (Stahlmann 1992: 155). The expansion of the factory complex at Untertürkheim revealed the disadvantages and slowness of transporting workpieces through the different workshops or from one building to another by hand (Bellon 1990: 161; Stahlmann 1992: 154). Before and during the war, unfinished components had "wandered" between the workshops,

> first into the milling or planing department, then over to the drills, then to the fitters to be screwed together, next to the lathe machines to bore out the reservoirs, then to the drills again to make the passageways for the circulating oil, then into another lathe shop for another set of cuts, and finally back to the drilling workshop. (Bellon 1990: 162)

This haphazard, untransparent, and anarchic product flow was very slow compared to the Fordist system, and the inefficiencies of the system were only heightened during the war as production ramped up and the complex expanded (Stahlmann 1992: 154).

The proposed solution was to group production of components together to be assembled by independent groups. The process was described this way:

> The ordering of production which we describe as group production begins with the placing together in one group of a certain number of parts belonging together (e.g. all the parts of the carburetor, water pump, linkage, transmission) to carry out the whole fabrication in a production group. Such a production group is constituted from all kinds of machines

> and encompasses fitters and other hand workers besides machine workers. It is self-contained and independent from other work departments. (Bellon 1990: 161)

This resembles contemporary module production of sub-assemblies, i.e., the manufacturing of specific components from smaller independent production units. The organization of these groups within the factory was designed to take the shortest possible route both within the group and between groups to save on time and transport labor (Jürgens 2023: 240–243).

This new system disrupted the workshop system where all workers of a single skill or machine worked in the same workshop, even if workers were simultaneously producing completely different products. The priority shifted from grouping workers together to grouping produced parts together because it could save time and increase productivity. The reorganization made some interim storage facilities superfluous and eliminated a large part of transport activities (Stahlmann 1992: 157). The rationalized flow arrangement of these groups in the factory space also made the overall system resemble the organization of the assembly line, although the actual implementation of an assembly line was still years away (Bellon 1990: 163).

There was, however, a concern that organizing groups to make the same product threatened to "adversely affect the workers and even cause them to feel alienated and bored" (Bellon 1990: 163). The workforce was being atomized and divided into a more specialized and rigid division of labor (Stahlmann 1992: 157–158). However, it was also argued that group production could allow for work satisfaction because group teams could observe the production of a whole component within the group and holistically work together on the task at hand (Jürgens 2023: 240–243). This system was a precursor to the stationary group work experiments in Germany and Sweden during the 1980s and 1990s aimed at humanizing work without the assembly line (see Berggren 1994, 1995). Regardless of the potential downsides for workers, the orientation of these changes was toward rationalization and increasing productivity without resorting to copying Fordist methods.

Fordist and Taylorist rationalization was viewed positively in the Weimar Republic, especially by employers, as a 'magic formula' (*Zauberformel*) that could rescue Germany from postwar economic problems (Hachtmann and von Saldern 2009: 195; see Jürgens 2023 243–246). However, there was a yawning gap between the high expectations of public discourse and practical implementation. Nevertheless, Daimler worked to implement rationalization measures after the 1920 lockout and workforce restructuring. In a company study conducted in 1920, it was determined that a "fundamental restructuring must be carried through with all means and without delay" (Bellon 1990: 190). The report criticized the large number of unproductive workers who achieved "extraordinarily meager productivity," in part due to the "old-fashioned … machinery and factory organization" (Bellon 1990: 190). They reported that productive performance lagged far behind similar competitors, which pressured Daimler to sell their vehicles below cost (Stahlmann 1992: 155). Thus, *falling behind the norms of socially necessary labor time* made their production processes costlier than the socially expected value, which could force commodities to sell at prices below their value. The proposed solution to this problem was the deployment of "more and better machine work and less [skilled] hand work," as the "highly developed, obedient machines" were "preferable to the whims of the hand workers" (Bellon 1990: 190). Methods to lower production costs and save labor time on parts production were implemented (Bellon 1990: 191). The stated goal was to, "With far fewer personnel, produce more; save and save, but in the right places" (Bellon 1990: 190). To achieve this, Daimler aimed to reduce the number of employees, including paying workers to leave voluntarily (Bellon 1990: 190). Management's intention to decrease the workforce, automate and deskill tasks with more machinery, and increase all around productivity is clear from these statements. In addition, the productivity advantage of limiting the number of products produced during the war led Daimler to conclude that it was advantageous to offer only a few types of cars for "cheaper, more precise, and more continuous production" (Bellon 1990: 191; see Stahlmann 1992: 155).

Daimler argued these changes were necessary because, "we stand in very sharp competition with the Entente countries, chiefly with the United States" (Bellon 1990: 192). Similar problems were experienced at Benz, with management arguing that prices of foreign cars were much lower than at Benz because of their high-volume production enabling proportionally lower costs (Stahlmann 1992: 159). With it taking Benz approximately 1,800 hours to make one chassis, they argued that it was necessary to adopt American production methods because "it is impossible for us to compete on the world market with such working hours" (Stahlmann 1992: 159).[4] Measures to reduce product types, introducing more machinery, and intensifying the division of labor were all suggested to reduce the high working hours per vehicle (Stahlmann 1992: 159).

4 Original German text: "Meine Herren mit solcher Arbeitsstundenzahl ist es uns unmöglich, auf dem Weltmarkt zu konkurrieren" (Stahlmann 1992: 159).

Both Daimler and Benz's survival was at stake in the success of rationalization measures. The early 1920s were a struggle for survival for the entire German economy in the context of hyperinflation and economic turmoil. In response to the economic malaise, the powerful Deutsche Bank, which had considerable presence on Daimler's board of trustees, made calls for the merger of Germany's auto companies. In 1924, Daimler and Benz announced a partnership that resulted in a merger in 1926 creating the new *Daimler-Benz Aktien-Gesellschaft*. This added three additional German facilities to the corporation and made Daimler-Benz the second largest auto company in Germany next to Opel (Bellon 1990: 210). The merger also provided an opportunity to join the "great wave of the rationalization movement" that took place in the German auto industry between 1925 and 1928 (Bellon 1990: 210).

The workers' movement at Daimler had lost much of its vigor since the defeat of the revolution and the restructuring of the workforce after the 1920 lockout (Bellon 1990: 207). Social-democratic workers were in favor of Fordist rationalization as they believed it would bring increased wages and mass consumption, yet they also wanted to avoid the increased labor intensity characteristic of Fordism and maintain the autonomy of German quality production (Hachtmann and von Saldern 2009: 190, 195; Jürgens 2023: 243–246). Reconciling these conflicting desires was not resolved in the 1920s as rationalization efforts were ultimately only a half-step toward Fordism.

There were, nevertheless, numerous production changes. First, the group production system was expanded to further reduce the time spent between moving parts and materials from station to station and achieve better flow. More time studies were conducted which broke down holistic working into repetitive partial work (Stahlmann 1992: 162). New special machines were purchased, including from the United States, which "simplified and accelerated many of the labor processes and allowed the firm to employ cheaper, unskilled labor" (Bellon 1900: 210). The number of machine tools doubled from around 8000 in 1926 to 16,000 in 1928 (Bellon 1990: 213). The auto body plant at Sindelfingen installed an assembly line, which, although it moved at a leisurely 4 meters per hour, allowed for the assembly of an auto body in ten hours (Bellon 1990: 211). In a board of directors meeting in 1928, an engineer reported that such reforms had been a success because they allowed Daimler-Benz to cut its costs through the effective use of new machines and employing more low-paid unskilled workers in place of skilled workers (Bellon 1990: 213). Indeed, there was a noticeable trend toward a labor composition that favored less skilled over more skilled workers (Bellon 1990: 211). With many radical leftist workers purged and the workers' movement generally weakened, it appeared that the remaining workers were pressured to comply with the rationalization measures. Nevertheless, the orientation toward quality work was maintained, meaning the core skilled workforce were still essential for flexible deployment in production (Stahlmann 1992: 163).

With these developments during the 1920s, a pattern emerges. On the one hand, most of the German auto industry remained reliant on skilled craft workers to produce and assemble parts. However, there was also a conscious movement *away* from skilled work and *toward* machines and unskilled machine tenders. This appears like what was done in the United States in the 1910s in terms of deskilling and automation. On the other hand, wholly unique concepts for reorganizing production such as group production emerged that have little resemblance to Fordist methods. Stahlmann (1992: 175) argues that this compromise was the result of 'modernists' and 'traditionalists' in both management and the works councils working to increase productivity while maintaining German quality to stay competitive. This is an early example of German auto makers forging their own rationalization path judged more suitable for their special circumstances. In the case of Daimler-Benz, not only would it be difficult to radically reorganize production and lower costs enough for higher volume production, Daimler-Benz appeared mostly uninterested in reaching substantially higher volumes, instead aiming at producing for only the 'noblest' clientele (Bellon 1990: 190). Skilled workers helped ensure that Daimler-Benz could flexibly produce the high-quality autos demanded by their exclusive group of customers both domestically and abroad.

However, Daimler-Benz was still concerned about productivity, as improving productivity was a means of ensuring long-term sustainability. Reliance on wealthy customers willing to pay high prices for their cars did not insulate Daimler from the need to improve productivity, especially as both domestic and foreign auto companies also engaged in rationalization measures (Bellon 1990: 210). They recognized that their market niche was *realization based on quality rather than price*, yet they also recognized that without improved productivity, high quality at costs well above competitors was not sustainable (Stahlmann 1992: 159). This productivity pressure resulted in transforming work processes in terms of group work, flow restructuring, and increased machine utilization. Ultimately, Daimler-Benz was pushed forward by the imperatives of productivity norms even when working under a very different business model and labor structure. The German industry continued to navigate between commitments to both 'flexible quality production' and 'economic rationality' in the following decades (Stahlmann 1992: 175; see Sorge and Streeck 2016).

6 Evaluating Outcomes of Craft and Mass Production

The years 1900 to 1929 saw the rise of the auto industry in the two value-regimes. The initial production systems began nearly identically, i.e., craft production systems based on skilled labor operating general purpose machines to fabricate non-identical components. With such methods, it took hundreds or thousands of hours to make each vehicle, a time-and-labor-intensive process that produced low volumes of high-value vehicles. With these conditions combined with the highly unequal distribution of income, it was inevitable that the earliest cars could only be afforded by the extremely wealthy. The earliest companies were therefore beholden to the wants, needs, and desires of these wealthy patrons, who demanded luxury and speed above all else (Flink 1988: 15–25; Albert 2019).

The crux of the divergence between the US and German industry was whether this early status quo was acceptable or not, which the Germans affirmed but the Americans denied. Escaping this status quo in the US required abandoning the craft production system through radical restructuring of the labor process with an orientation toward flow, standardization, and automation. This was accomplished through interchangeability, scientific management, and advances in the machine tool industry. Thanks to high growth rates, the absolute number of skilled workers grew, even as their work was transformed (Meyer 2004).

For German automakers, unless there was confidence that a mass market for autos existed in Germany, then they were content to build low volumes of Germany's famous high quality vehicles (Lüdtke 2009). Without a more equitable distribution of wealth or growth in the income of average Germans—the spirit of the five-dollar day, i.e., making your workers also your customers did not occur—then no company was willing to engage in the wide-ranging reforms necessary to increase volumes and bring down the value per unit.

The rapid growth in motorization and capital accumulation in the US was known in Germany (Stahlmann 1992: 175), so why did the German automakers not also pursue this route? The most common explanation was that there was not enough effective demand, but the same was also true in the United States under the craft production system (see Flink 1988; Tolliday 1995a). It is true that per capita income in Germany was about half that of the United States in 1914, but this does not explain why means were not pursued to become more productive and decrease the per unit value so gradually more and more lower-income Germans could afford automobility (Flink 1988: 44). The justification for the dilemma is tautological: there is no effective mass market demand at existing prices, so no method is used to decrease prices, so no effective mass market demand develops, so no method is used to decrease prices, and so on. The solution is increasing productivity to increase volume and lower value per unit, but strategies at achieving higher productivity in Germany were only pursued within certain limits and thus did not foster mass motorization during this period.

However, there is no reason why motorization, *in principle*, could not have been achieved in Germany. Low wages did not have to be an obstacle, as Ford had proven when it set in motion a spiral of price reductions, market expansions, wage raises, and productivity increases (see Jürgens 2023: 245). Such a strategy would have been more difficult, to be sure, given the economic conditions of Germany, but there is no reason to believe that the strategy could not have been pursued. German mass motorization *did eventually* occur through Fordist methods and principles, but, instead of being led by entrepreneurialism, the rationalization movement was spearheaded by the Nazi state.

Instead of accepting this tautological argument, analysis of the characteristics of the value-regime provides a more wholistic explanation. For Daimler-Benz, both the firm and workers took pride in the 'high-quality' work that necessitated the low productivity and high skilled labor techniques (Bellon 1990). The self-description of German autos as made by 'German quality work' was used as a selling point for to ensure value realization (Lüdtke 2009). In this linkage, Daimler-Benz acted as a *value-system* oriented toward accumulating capital through projecting its self-description as a German quality producer and backed up its claims through its reliance on the high skilled craft production system. To grab the attention of the rich, whose price sensitivity is typically low, there was an interest in making *cost considerations secondary to quality* as the primary means to secure value realization.

This strategy was not merely ideological, but a concrete reality for the skilled workers at Daimler-Benz who had material interests in protecting their skills and valorization. Skilled Daimler-Benz workers enjoyed high levels of work autonomy and a substantial wage premium (Stahlmann 1992). Even though American firms hired thousands of skilled workers due to the high growth of mass production, their relative numbers and autonomy within the factory were radically transformed (Meyer 2004). Even if Fordism was quickly adopted in Germany and the absolute number of skilled workers increased, it would have also required higher work intensity and less autonomy. Considering Daimler-Benz was filled with socialist and communist workers empowered by unions and works councils and with a history of resistance to management control up to and including revolution, it is reasonable to speculate that skilled workers would have been willing to fight against a radical Fordist transformation that limited worker autonomy and power (Bellon 1990: 63; Stahlmann 1992:

165). Thus, skilled German workers enjoyed generally less alienated working conditions and maintained use of their skills.

However, there were costs to this arrangement, namely that neither the workers nor most other Germans were able to afford cars and benefit from the use value automobiles offer.[5] Pursuing this strategy delayed the motorization of Germany by a generation and meant the German auto industry as *value-systems* generated and distributed far less value than the American industry. In this sense, maintaining German craft production entailed *opportunity costs* for German workers, the industry, and society.

At the same time, Fordism also *entailed high costs* in the US. Work intensity increased, craft skills were lost or deskilled, the remaining skilled workers operated under increased management control, thousands of repetitive and alienating unskilled jobs in machine operation and assembly were created, and some skilled trades such as fitters were eliminated entirely (Meyer 1981, 2004; Crumm 2010). Therefore, while the US achieved mass motorization, generated more use values, and accumulated more capital, this also came at a price that German workers did not experience in the same way. It is impossible to objectively judge which value-regime is preferable when the costs and benefits of each system are laid bare and assessed without ideological bias. It would be a mistake to interpret the above narrative as supporting the idea that Fordism is 'objectively' superior to Daimler-Benz's craft system or vice versa. However, from the *unobjective* perspective of modern ideology, Fordism *is* superior. This ideological hierarchy of production systems based on productivity is itself an expression of *social* domination.

Social domination is understood in multiple senses here. First is the recognition that modern capitalist society ideologically favors high productivity and high capital accumulation. Fordism has been historically framed as an epoch making development that transformed world manufacturing irrevocably, as evidenced in the overwhelming amount of scholarly and journalistic writing on Fordism for over a century (e.g., Arnold and Faurote 1915; Barclay 1936; Nevins and Hill 1957; Chandler 1964; Flink 1988; Womack et al. 2007 [1990]). Value-systems that generate high levels of value flow and capital accumulation are polycontexturally observed by other social systems to be systems that

5 Whether one believes the lack of automobiles or the motorization of a society is positive or negative depends on one's opinion of the automobile and how it transformed the infrastructure and means of transportation in modern societies in fundamental ways. Leaving aside this subjective dimension, what is undeniable is that the German auto industry produced less use values and accumulated less capital than the American industry because of its production system.

generate *modern progress*. In *capitalist* society, systems that are especially adept at accumulating capital are often framed as *embodying this progress*, and therefore many social systems concluded that Fordism was the superior form of manufacturing. Scholars, journalists, and unions had their critiques of Fordism, (e.g., Meyer 1981, 2004; Asher and Edsforth 1995; Greenhouse 2019) but the most powerful and largest social systems from government, industry, and media placed *value*, in Marx's (1976 [1867]) sense, above *human values* such as autonomy. That this was the case and remains so today should not be surprising in the context of a socio-economic system that is first and foremost oriented toward making profits. This social-communicative aspect reflects the *social* logic of capital.

Yet, this communicative element is only part of the story. The ideological concepts of progress and modernity are tied to *concrete realities of time and productivity*. What is termed 'progress' for capital oriented social systems is *measured concretely by temporal shortening of production processes*, e.g., how Ford built its engines in less and less time year after year, and how the productive apparatuses at Highland Park turned out increasing numbers of Model Ts. Effective *control over time and increasing operational speed* through changes in technology and labor organization *grounded* the social-communicative claims. It is through mastery over time and pushing forward the historical dynamic of increasing productivity that claims of making 'progress' or being 'productive' are accepted by social systems.[6]

By contrast, German automakers, by *comparing* themselves to the temporal productive standards set by the US, self-described themselves as falling on the *unproductive* side of the productive/unproductive divide (Stahlmann 1992: 155). The German system was not unproductive in an objective sense, but only when *compared* to the productive standard of the US. In this sense, who or what is 'productive' is *socially* determined by reference to the standard of necessary labor time set by the most productive system in existence at that time. This is one reason why interest in 'rationalization' increased during the Weimar Republic as there was recognition that Germany was behind the US, even as the rationalization programs failed to achieve mass production (Hachtmann and von Saldern 2009: 195). The German automakers made up for this by self-describing themselves as providing *high quality* vehicles, but this,

6 However, the cost of achieving high productivity was increased alienation and the degradation of work. Therefore, from a critical perspective whether Fordism represents "progress" or not depends on whether progress is defined through a modern capitalist perspective or from an alternative humanist view.

while convincing for their wealthy customers, still meant less capital accumulation overall. In this case, high quality at the expense of productivity could not accumulate value at the level of Fordist firms.

Ford continuously redefined the productive norms with multiple productive innovations, which prompted a response from the rest of the American industry. No longer limited to a narrow wealthy consumer base, the potential market was continuously expanded with each price decrease which simultaneously increased effective demand. Ford's competitors understood that potential opportunities to accumulate capital would be lost if they did not respond quickly (Hounshell 1985: 260–261). This *required* rapid transformation from craft to mass production methods. Besides the potential generating profits, improving productivity by adopting Fordism legitimated claims to 'progress,' 'modernity,' and being a 'productive' enterprise, thus giving a *social* incentive for competitors to become Fordist.

Many companies, such as GM, differentiated themselves by offering styling or new technology to compete against Ford, but even competing on these other criteria still required a *fundamental baseline of high productivity* so that any additional competitive edge would not be offset by the high prices or selling at a loss that is possible if production processes are too slow. This situation was what Daimler-Benz actively feared in the 1920s and was one reason behind its rationalization program. In this way, Ford's competitors on both sides of the Atlantic faced *productivity pressure* from the productivity standards set by Ford.

For the workers at these companies, the changes put in motion therefore were more than just originating from management but *pressured* by overarching productive norms deemed 'socially necessary' *because* of their successful implementation at Ford. Therefore, while the deskilling of the Ford workers came directly from Ford management, it is incomplete to say that the deskilling or elimination of workers at other factories were *only* a result of management fiat. Rather, a more wholistic picture is that the labor was transformed due to *social domination*, i.e., through *pressure to conform to a new set of productive norms* that received both economic power from Ford's increasing market share, *and* social power through claims of productiveness, progress, and modernness. Many companies that did not or could not afford to adopt Fordism eventually failed (Peterson 1987: 8). Such reforms were easier to achieve in Detroit rather than Germany because Detroit workers had no union power and management had the unlimited ability to hire and fire (Peterson 1987: 151). Quality producers in the US and Germany could choose the alternative path of a quality model that maintained skilled labor autonomy, but that necessarily meant giving up the opportunity for increased capital accumulation from mass markets.

Even as US firms came to dominate the global auto industry, Daimler-Benz was not static or a 'model' that could be sustained indefinitely (e.g., Boyer and Freyssenet 2002). They too experienced productivity pressure and social domination, such as the entrance of US foreign investment, the potential social-communicative consequences of being comparatively 'unproductive,' and avoiding having unjustifiably high prices. They made productivity improvements through a flexible quality production system that borrowed selectively from Fordism in some respects and forged a uniquely German rationalization path in others. Their rationalization efforts brought profits by the end of the 1920s, but there was also an opportunity cost of capital accumulation eschewed by committing to craft methods and low volumes (Stahlmann 1992: 176). Yet, Ford and American firms faced their own social costs through the degradation of work and technological displacement. This was the 'price of progress,' but for Daimler-Benz there was also a price for the 'lack of progress.' In capitalist modernity, the questions of automation and increasing productivity appears to be a dilemma of "damned if you do, dammed if you don't."

CHAPTER 2

State Guided Rationalization Through Depression and World War

1 The Great Depression and World War Transforms Industry

By 1929, the world auto industry appeared to have coalesced into a stable development pattern. The American industry had experienced a rapid expansion thanks to the mass production techniques pioneered by Ford, though only a few could maintain the size, scale, and speed necessary to compete with the Big Three of Ford, GM, and Chrysler. Due to increasing concentration and a maturing market, competition was increasingly based around styling and yearly model changes rather than on pure production prowess and productivity. Nevertheless, Fordist mass production was a key component of the prosperous American automobile industry that dominated the globe. In 1929, the US contained over twenty-six of the thirty-five million vehicle registrations worldwide (Patch 1932: 9). Meanwhile, the European preference to maintain craft production or inability to implement mass production meant that automobility in Europe grew slowly and the industry's productivity was too low to challenge American mass-producers. Though lagging, it was conceivable in 1929 that either native European carmakers would gradually rationalize production and slowly expand automobility, or American producers would increasingly dominate both continents through foreign investments such as Ford's European factories or GM owned Opel and Vauxhall. The onset of the Great Depression and later World War II disrupted any straightforward evolutionary path. The following describes the consequences of these momentous world events on the development of production, productivity, labor, and automation in the auto industry of both value-regimes.

Although the US industry remained globally dominant, the depression exacerbated the highly contentious labor relations in the US industry that could only be kept suppressed by draconian management control. The rapid drop from 4.6 million cars sold in 1929 to a nadir of 1.2 million in 1932 resulted in widespread layoffs and unemployment for auto workers (Noyes 1938: 7). By July 1930, nearly a third of Detroit's auto jobs had been eliminated, adding about 150,000 unemployed in Detroit alone (Martelle 2014: 114; Reynolds 1989: 74; Rooke 2008: 3). Without any effective social safety net, the prospects for unemployed workers were grim, and homelessness and poverty grew rapidly.

 | DOI:10.1163/9789004736719_004

The remaining workers faced increasingly harsh working conditions and surveillance as management pushed for the continuous speed-up of production to improve productivity and save costs (Edsforth and Asher 1995). Franklin Roosevelt's presidency beginning in 1932 established the federal welfare state and transformed labor-management relations by establishing new legal procedures and systems for handling industrial relations, which eventually led to the unionization of the US auto industry in the late 1930s.

The union and the legal framework that outlines its rights and duties 'completes' the American value-regime in the sense that the system set in place by the end of this period defines the domestic US auto industry centered around the Big Three up to the present. In this way, the New Deal can be described as a *state-initiated form of rationalization* that regulated the industrial relations and state-labor-business relationship into the form that characterizes the US value-regime.

For Germany, this period is also characterized by a form of *state led rationalization* of a very different kind. The ascendance of Adolf Hitler disrupted the established pattern of industrial development and initiated a massive state-coordinated wave of rationalization. The explicit aim was to approximate the productivity and methods of the American mass production system and engage in expanding automobility as aggressively as Ford had decades earlier. This resulted in a swift expansion and rationalization of Daimler-Benz and the erection of the massive Volkswagen factory in Wolfsburg in the rural outskirts of Lower Saxony. This generated a leap in German production from 52,088 units in 1932 to 342,169 on the eve of WWII in 1938 (Flink 1988: 262). This was achieved in part through the heavy suppression of the workforce and the forced reorganization of the industrial unions under Nazi control.

World War II disrupted this development and ultimately led to Germany's destruction. Much of the war armaments produced by the auto companies were built by war prisoners and concentration camp inmates. In this way, the rationalization and equipment and factory build up necessary for the German *Wirtschaftswunder* or 'economic miracle' was only possible with the oppression of German workers as well as Jewish, Eastern European, and Soviet slaves. This period is therefore a story of the extreme degradation and transformation of the German value-regime. It is a period of transition for the German production system and value-regime as the full contours of the value-regime recognizable today was developed after the war. The reaction to the traumatic events of this period provided the impetus for Germany to develop a robust system of state-labor-management cooperation. At the same time, the post-war value-regime would not have been possible without the procurement of facilities and equipment capable of mass production, as well as the experience and expertise with mass production that rapidly developed in the 1930s. This period is therefore important because the collapse of Nazi Germany did not signify a *tabula rasa* for Germany, but contained a certain amount of continuity, the most important here being the development of mass production capabilities in Germany (see Tolliday 1995a).

The global response to the Great Depression led to the emergence of forms of *modernization* in the US and Germany that had important long-term implications. The following discusses these divergent instantiations of modernization as they played out in the auto industry of both countries and ultimately shaped their value-regimes.

2 German 'Modernization' and Motorization during the Third Reich

The Great Depression began in the United States but echoed throughout the world. Germany, which had already been wracked by economic turmoil in the interwar years, fell into another decline. Auto production and employment—already a fraction of that in the US—was nearly halved from 1928 to 1932 (Jürgens 2023: 246). This ended the possibility of a gradual expansion of automobility via incrementally improved productivity resulting from a combination of Fordist and non-Fordist methods of rationalization (see Stahlmann 1992). Instead, the widespread poverty mixed with far-right nationalism provided fertile ground for the rise of the National Socialists. This had important long-term consequences for Germany's industrial development, especially in the auto industry. Hitler and the Nazis aspired to make Germany a modern motorized nation like the United States, and they explicitly understood that this *required matching the productivity levels* of the American automakers (Hachtmann and von Saldern 2009: 196–197). To achieve this, factories, machine tools, labor processes, and the workforce would have to approximate Fordist system pioneered in the US. This was ultimately achieved through a combination of state investment and worker suppression, constituting a state enforced modernization project. Two major exemplars of this endeavor were Daimler-Benz as it became a 'model' Nazi corporation and the rise of Volkswagen as the flagship project aimed at achieving mass motorization in Germany.

2.1 *Daimler-Benz and Rationalization under the Nazis*

The status quo at Daimler-Benz on the eve of the Great Depression looked relatively optimistic. After surviving near bankruptcy in the mid-1920s, the merger with Benz, loans from the Deutsche Bank, and the rationalization measures to increase productivity and reduce costs had all had a positive effect on

Daimler-Benz's business prospects, going from losses in 1926 to yearly profits from 1927–1929 (Bellon 1990: 215; Stahlmann 1992: 176).[1] The post-revolution restructuring and strengthened management left the workers and their trade unions in a defensive position (Bellon 1990: 215). The business turnaround was quickly reversed with the onset of the Great Depression.

The depression was devastating. From 1929–1930, over 4,000 workers were laid off across the Daimler-Benz industrial empire, with a low of around 9,000 workers in 1932. Business similarly declined from 1929 to 1932 with approximately 130 million reichsmarks worth of production falling to 65 million (Bellon 1990: 220). Automobile demand is always sensitive to economic fluctuations, since car purchases can typically be delayed in hard times—especially for luxury cars. Therefore, it is unsurprising that it was increasingly difficult for Daimler-Benz to realize the value of its cars.

The ascension of the Nazi party dramatically changed this situation. In early 1933, the government announced the elimination of the heavy taxes on automobiles which contributed to retarding mass automobility (Bellon 1990: 221). Policies to encourage automobility were adopted such as making it easier to get a driver's license, less strict traffic laws, and the building of the *Autobahn* highway system (Flink 1988: 262). By the fall of 1933, Daimler-Benz received its first orders from the military for armored vehicles, heavy trucks, tanks, and airplane engines (Bellon 1990: 222). Military production increasingly defined the business, with military production rising from 19 percent in 1932 to 51 percent at the outset of war in 1938. This increased to a peak of 93 percent military production by 1944 (Bellon 1990: 220). The military buildup allowed for the erection of new factories and the expansion of old ones, increasing Daimler-Benz's production capacity (Bellon 1990: 221). Thanks in part to the close ties between Daimler-Benz and the Nazi party—which was fostered before they took power—Daimler-Benz became a major resource for motorizing the German army and creating the Luftwaffe (Bellon 1990: 221).

These orders provided enormous demand for workers, which would quickly turn around the conditions of the company and bring many unemployed out of poverty and desperation. The total workforce increased by 485% from 1932 to 1938, or from about 9,000 to over 46 thousand workers (Bellon 1990: 220–229). Production likewise climbed significantly to 710% of 1932 levels by 1938 (Bellon 1990: 229). Unlike during WWI under the mass-craft system where productivity barely increased even when production facilities and number

1 The productivity improvements were particularly important as one member of the board of trustees stated in June 1931 that the company's rationalization measures *would have secured a profit* in 1930 if not for the decline in business caused by the depression (Bellon 1990: 216).

of workers had expanded, productivity during this period increased faster than employment. This is largely due to the Fordist rationalization measures adopted under the Nazi regime.

The new military contracts "put the corporation under pressure to produce more efficiently" (Bellon 1990: 224; see Stahlmann 1992: 169). The adoption of the Fordist methods became the key to rapidly increasing productivity. Assembly line production was finally implemented on a large scale at Daimler-Benz, as well as the use of various conveyors and moving belts to transport materials across the factories at Untertürkheim, Mannheim, and Sindelfingen (Bellon 1990: 224). Instead of requiring thousands of skilled fitters as had been utilized during the first world war, now Daimler-Benz's assembly lines could be assembled by untrained workers or, later during the war, slaves—indicating the advance of interchangeability achieved in German auto plants (Bellon 1990: 243). Indeed, the need for skilled fitters was rapidly shrinking during the Nazi rationalization program, which signified the exchange of low productivity skilled work for high productivity unskilled work as had been done in American factories decades before (Bellon 1990: 225). The proportion of skilled workers was still higher than in the US but fell from 62 percent in 1928 to 53 percent in 1940, with semiskilled workers rising from 22 to 36 percent, and unskilled workers falling from 16 percent to 11 percent (Stahlmann 1992: 167). Investments in new special machines manufactured by German and American firms also increased rapidly throughout the 1930s, including new milling, grinding, and polishing machines (Bellon 1990: 224; 240). These new machines increased the level of automation at Daimler factories, as Moll (1961) reports that the automation level at Daimler-Benz before and during the war had already reached between 60 and 80 percent in many production processes (58). Increased specialization and rationalization of the division of labor occurred as factories were rearranged to secure the flow of parts from one end of the plant to the other (Bellon 1990: 240–243). The essentials of Fordist mass production, including flow, special machine deployment, and assembly line production, were all being implemented at Daimler-Benz. The alternative strategies of achieving higher productivity that avoided direct imitation of Fordism appeared to be abandoned as the Fordist revolution swept across Daimler-Benz factories.

Daimler-Benz workers had previously enjoyed high levels of autonomy and control over their work. Even with the weakening of the labor unions during the 1920s, one might still expect resistance to these radical production changes, especially since so many of them deskilled and degraded the autonomy of skilled workers. However, the strict disciplinary regime of the Nazis deterred organized resistance against rationalization. In May 1933, the independent unions were dissolved by the Nazi regime and replaced by a single union the *Deutsche Arbetisfront* (DAF) or German Labor Front (Bellon 1990: 234; Ewing 2017: 7). All Daimler workers were nominally part of this country-wide union, yet the DAF was Nazi controlled and not meaningfully separate from government interests, propagandizing Fordism and integration into the Nazi state (Bellon 1990: 237; Hachtmann and von Saldern 2009: 201). In addition, the DAF confiscated all trade union funds and exacted a monthly levy on all German workers (Tolliday 1995a: 282). Therefore, under single party rule and the dissolution of the unions into one state-controlled union, most of the social systems and resources dedicated to worker power and advocacy had essentially disappeared.

At the factory level, the works councils, associations, and arbitration committees that had formed the backbone of the post-WWI labor relations regime also crumbled, leaving a new system based on fear, discipline, and order. Power in the factory was vested in the leader who "has decision-making power in all matters pertaining to the plant," and "In his decisions on social matters … is unhampered by any rights of codetermination on the part of his followers" (Bellon 1990: 223). The workers thus had no legal right to codetermine the production processes and had very little recourse to dispute any aspect of their work, whether regarding pay, work hours, production standards, or technology adoption. Though the Nazis declared the 'abolition' of class conflict, the relatively 'peaceful' industrial relations were not a result of labor-management cooperation but state-management repression of labor (Bellon 1990: 223). Management shared mutual interests with the Nazi regime, and, while there is anecdotal evidence of intermittent individual or small group actions and strikes throughout the Daimler-Benz factories from 1933–1945, a united anti-Nazi front to resist the regime never emerged (Bellon 1990: 231–238).

Daimler-Benz was designed to serve as a 'model' Nazi company, demonstrating the power of fascist organization. Yet what had emerged was strikingly like the labor regime and production processes commonplace in the American auto industry for decades. With the *de facto* elimination of the unions and works councils, the auto workers had about as much worker voice and control as American workers. The production processes at Daimler-Benz had essentially forcibly undergone rapid Fordist transformation under state directive. Many workers were deskilled, and the assembly line and machine-based production had essentially eliminated the traditional craft system, albeit with a larger contingent of skilled workers (Stahlmann 1992). Mandatory overtime and long hours became the norm, even though wages also increased (Bellon 1990: 225–227). Even the surveillance and disciplinary regime could be described as comparable to what was occurring in the United States—at least before the onset of war when slaves began working in German factories (see Peterson 1987; Stahlmann 1992: 178; Greenhouse 2019: 80–93). The Nazis had succeeded at improving productivity and rapidly motorizing the country, but at great human cost. However, note that many of these costs had long been the reality for US workers, especially in terms of deskilling, repetitive work, and strict management control (see Meyer 2004).

It is thought provoking to speculate how the German auto industry may have developed in the absence of the Great Depression and the Nazis. Would the Fordist revolution have ever taken place with strong unions and codetermination rights? Or would a distinctly German path of rationalization emerged—as it appeared to have been developing in the 1920s—that would have gradually enlarged the sphere of automobility from the upper classes downward? It is also conceivable that the American companies in Germany, Ford and Opel, could have mustered the resources necessary to firmly establish mass production and eventually designed a 'people's car' instead of Volkswagen. In this scenario, domestic German companies like Daimler-Benz may have felt pressured to eventually conform to mass production—just as had happened to many American firms—or dedicate themselves to the Taylorist productive model of selling luxury vehicles at low volumes (see Boyer and Freyssenet 2002) but sacrificing the capital accumulation that higher productivity and a mass market can bring. Such scenarios remain speculative as what actually occurred was the suppression of labor resistance to the rapid adoption of Fordist principles.

2.2 *Volkswagen and the Plans for a People's Car*

Also consequential for the long-term trajectory of the German auto industry was the establishment of Volkswagen. In the early years of the regime, mass motorization was considered equally if not more important than rearmament. As Flink (1988) argues, the German economic recovery "can be explained with reference to cars and roads rather than tanks and aircraft" (262). Yet Hitler, who had read Henry Ford's biography *My Life and Work* (1922) during the same prison sentence in which he wrote *Mein Kampf*, understood that, just as American motorization was driven by the low value but high volume Model T, Germany needed an equivalent to drive its own mass motorization campaign (Flink 1988: 261). The idea of a German 'people's car' had circulated in public consciousness as early as 1904 (Grieger and Lupa 2015: 4–5). However, no domestic automaker appeared interested in or capable of developing the design and production capacity necessary to produce a low-cost car in high volumes (Tolliday 1995a: 277). Not even Ford's factory in Cologne or GM's Opel appeared to have the intention or resources to tackle this challenge, even though some "halfhearted" attempts were made (Tolliday 1995a: 278). Ultimately, the Nazis took on the task of building the people's car as a state project. Whether they were unwilling to take the risk in an unproven mass market or simply lacked the productive capacity or technology for mass production, Tolliday (1995a) sums up the situation bluntly, "there is no evidence that the German auto industry could have developed a cheap small car without Hitler" (284).

Hitler and automobile designer Ferdinand Porsche began discussing designs of the people's car in 1934 (Ewing 2017: 6). The initial project was funded and managed by the *Reichsverband der Deutschen Automobilindustrie* or Society of German Automobile Manufacturers, with the first prototype appearing in 1935 (Flink 1988: 263–264). However, the established automakers resented having to assist a state-run competitor, so the project was instead taken over by the German Labor Front (DAF) in 1937, officially forming the Volkswagen GmbH (Ewing 2017: 7). The DAF was financed by confiscated union funds, had its own building societies, and a major bank, so it was well positioned to fund the project (Tolliday 1995a: 282). This had a long-term impact on the development of Volkswagen because using confiscated union funds to establish Volkswagen became a justification after the war that workers should have representation on the company board, giving Volkswagen a unique labor-management cooperative structure (Ewing 2017: 7–8). During this period, however, Volkswagen remained a state-directed project.

The prototype car that became the Beetle, was, according to Porsche, explicitly designed to mirror the Model T as a cheap yet reliable car for the masses (Jürgens 2023: 246–248). It represented 'reasonable' automobility with its ease of use and maintenance, rear mounted air-cooled engine, and streamlined rounded design (Schmidt 2007:6–7). It was also designed to be simple to manufacture to take advantage of single purpose machines and the assembly line. The product design of the Beetle was highly suitable for Fordist mass production, just like Model T decades earlier.

To achieve the low price necessary for mass realization, it was important to emulate the production processes that built the Model T. For this reason, the Volkswagen plant in Wolfsburg, nestled in a rural area of Lower Saxony, was explicitly modeled on the Ford River Rouge factory to copy its "most modern production procedures" (Jürgens 1994: 94). Indeed, Volkswagen's management visited the River Rouge plant and decided that their factory ought to closely imitate the Ford factory. The delegation took detailed pictures of the plant layouts and technical equipment and lured nearly 20 German-born engineers from Ford to return with them to Germany (Jürgens 2023: 248–249). The completed Wolfsburg plant became the largest auto plant in the world, with 50 percent more floor space than Ford's enormous wartime plant at Willow Run. The factory also imported large numbers of single-purpose machines from the

United States (Tolliday 1995a: 282). The plan was to use this extremely large factory and specialized equipment to build 150,000 cars in its first year and adding 150,000 per year until reaching maximum capacity of 1.5 million Volkswagens per year—enormous by European standards (Grieger and Lupa 2015: 10). This was especially ambitious in the German context, which had merely 1.67 total vehicle registrations by 1938 (Flink 1988: 251). Though the factory was nearly complete and equipped by 1939, the start of WWII in September 1939 foiled the ambitious plans to begin mass production (Tolliday 1995a: 283).

Though Volkswagen did not have a chance to mass produce cars before the start of the war, its development indicates the extreme lengths the National Socialists were willing to go to achieve mass motorization in Germany. Seemingly no cost was too high to achieve their goals, with state and stolen union funds building the enormous Wolfsburg factory rather than the private incumbent automakers. It also confirms that Ford was the explicit model Volkswagen was based on, both in terms of product design and production processes.

2.3 *State Directed Motorization in Germany*

In contrast to the American industry that emerged through private enterprise, Germany did not move toward *mass* motorization until the initiatives of the National Socialist government. The Nazi motorization program transformed the industry from a 'backwater,' that produced primarily 'quality' models for the wealthy, into Germany's largest industry by sales (Tolliday 1995a: 285). State support generated both the demand and the infrastructure necessary for mass production and the corresponding mass market (Tolliday 1995a: 285). Daimler-Benz, Ford Europe, and Opel all benefitted from the policies and rationalized their factories to make them closer to American Fordism (Bellon 1990; Stahlmann 1992; Tolliday 1995a: 283–284). The establishment of Volkswagen, the Beetle, and the gigantic Wolfsburg factory proved to be an enormous economic boon in the postwar years. Overall, Germany produced 1.82 million cars between 1930–1939 (Flink 1988: 252). This was still far below the over 4 million cars produced in the US per year during the 1920s (Peterson 1987: 4) but nevertheless demonstrated massive progress toward mass production.

The rapid industrial build-up and the adoption of Fordism also demonstrates the *gravitational pull of social domination*. Though the Nazis are directly responsible for the oppression of labor and spearheading Germany's Fordist revolution, this would not be possible without *reference to productivity standards* emanating from the United States. The rise of the Nazis and their plans for motorization and military buildup required raising productive capacity and productivity in a short time to levels unprecedented in Germany. Because of the clear technological and productive leadership of the United States, the simplest solution to the productivity problem was imitating Fordism, both at Daimler-Benz and especially in the designs for Wolfsburg and the Beetle. In this case, productivity norms were *not* generalized through 'adapt or die' pressures of economic competition but through state directives.

This illustrates an instance of productivity norms being generalized via state mandate rather than economic competition. This is partially why the term *social* domination is more appropriate than 'economic domination,' as this example demonstrates how the generalization of productive norms can spread in ways other than 'pressure' from economic competition. The adoption of these production techniques simultaneously brought German production capacity and productivity much closer to the US level, which made certain forms of automation and transformations of labor *socially necessary*. The increased alienation, surveillance, lack of autonomy, and decline of skilled jobs such as fitters went hand in hand with the implementation of German mass production just as it had for American mass production decades earlier. Therefore, given their goals and a well-known productivity leader to imitate, the convergence of the US and German production system around mass production is unsurprising—though the speed and manner this was achieved perhaps is.

In this context, it appears plausible that dismantling and reconsolidating the unions under the DAF served the dual purpose of solidifying political power and *de facto* eliminating the unions as sources of resistance against the Fordist Transformation. For the sake of productivity, codetermination was set aside. On the surface, it appears obvious that the Nazi regime is responsible for the oppression of labor. Yet, it is also clear that Fordism's productive norms *provided the model* for the transformation. Thus, the experience of the workers was not just domination by the German state but the *social domination of productivity norms* under the aegis of the Nazis.

If, hypothetically, German craft production in 1933 was the most productive production system in the world, then the Nazi regime would have likely still repressed workers, but they would not have been able to refer to a higher productivity system to imitate to inform the concrete substance of that repression. For example, the shopfloor power relations between labor and management and the opportunities to intensify labor are different in a system that is reliant on skilled workers and fitters vs a system based on unskilled repetitive labor. In this hypothetical scenario, therefore, the productive trajectory and industrial relations would have looked very different. The existence of Fordism as a productivity benchmark provided a framework for the Nazis to follow, and therefore the productive transformation is not just the product of the regime, but a *globally sourced social product*—a product of the social domination of productivity norms. The specific transformation of labor was not an original Nazi idea, but an attempt to match the productivity standard of the most productive system in the world. Thus, the transformations of production and the degradation of the workers were not rooted in the Nazi regime alone, but were also influenced by the temporal productive norms established in the United States.

3 The Great Depression and Unionization

The Great Depression disrupted the upward industrial trajectory of the United States. The cyclical pattern of auto production and employment was exacerbated by the sharp decline in production and subsequent layoffs. With a saturated domestic market and lower sales, the industry needed to adapt production. The resulting speed-up of the work pace, in addition to the simmering issues over wages, autonomy, and control, brought a successful wave of unionization. This was made possible thanks to the New Deal legal framework for unionization. In this way, state policy and union organizing transformed the American value-regime into a struggle between the auto industry and the United Automobile Workers (UAW), with the US government as the rule maker and regulator of the industrial relations system. Important here are the forms of automation and the transformations of labor that appeared during this time as well as the rise of the UAW and how it transformed US industrial relations.

3.1 *Fordism Meets Sloanism: The Yearly Model Changeover*

Since the early 1930s, General Motors was the leading producer of automobiles throughout the world during the 20th century. In the early 1920s, Alfred P. Sloan became chief executive of GM and implemented a new mode of management that became a model for corporate governance imitated all over the world (Drucker 1946; Chandler 1964, 1977, 1990; Hilger 2003). This involved decentralized independent divisions that were answerable to central management and evaluated on a strict financial basis (Sloan 1964). Setting corporate goals and allocating resources was centralized, but the deployment and management of those resources was left to the decisions of the decentralized operating divisions (Flink 1988: 232). The objective of this arrangement was to maximize capital accumulation, or in Sloan's words, "The primary object of the corporation, therefore, we declared was to make money, not just to make cars" (cited in Albert 2019: 67). To that end, it was first necessary to adopt proven Fordist methods to decrease per unit value and produce vehicles at high volumes.

However, in the context of a corporation with multiple car divisions and an increasingly saturated market, Fordist product policy focusing on a single mass market model was not viable or desirable for GM.

Instead, Sloan pioneered the marketing and styling of automobiles so that the car was no longer a mere utilitarian use value for transportation but was also a symbol of one's place in the socioeconomic hierarchy. Aiming to deliver a car for "every purse and purpose," each division catered to a specific economic class ranging from the low-price Chevrolet, that competed with the Model T, to the high-class Cadillac, that competed for the same customers as the luxury Mercedes-Benz (Meyer 2004: 5; Albert 2019: 69–71). GM also pioneered the 'yearly model change' product strategy where a brand's styling periodically changes to encourage buying a new model each year. For example, since 1923 GM implemented similar frames on each car, but with differently designed bodies. There is almost never a *practical* reason to replace one's car each year, as they are designed to be durable consumer goods. Yet, the advertising and marketing campaigns that GM launched nevertheless encouraged the replacement of one's car as soon as possible, resulting in 'planned obsolescence' (Rooke 2008: 3). This intention was explicit as GM head designer Harley Earl once admitted, "our big job is to hasten obsolescence" (Rooke 2008: 3). This is advantageous for capital accumulation as it speeds up the turnover time for the realization of a new car's value, which thereby accelerates production and the entire circuit of value in motion (see Marx 1978 [1885]; Rosa 2015: 108–120; Harvey 2017).

The routinization of the model changeover affected production processes. Though Fordist objectives of flow, machine use, and the assembly line were maintained, production needed to adapt to the challenges of building a new model in the factory every year. The first major change applied to the types of machines deployed in production. Under 'classical' Fordism, building the same product year after year required investments in single purpose machines to manufacture unchanging parts. This produced reliable and efficient results. But a *single* purpose machine is, by definition, not designed to produce more than one part and therefore cannot meet the *flexibility needs* of a factory undergoing yearly model changeovers. As one engineer posed the problem in 1921, such special machines "faced the ever-present danger that a change of design may render the machine of no value whatsoever" (Meyer 2004: 5). Therefore, a fundamental change in technological design was needed.

The solution was to develop *flexible* machine tools that could be adjusted as needed to make new parts that fit the new model. These machines could be "reconfigured periodically by a skilled machinist yet still be operated by an unskilled worker" (Albert 2019: 72). Though the relationship of the machine and unskilled worker had not fundamentally changed, the annual model changes did increase the demand for skilled workers who, although technologically displaced from direct production, were reabsorbed to build the flexible machine tools, dies, cutting tools, and fixtures operated by unskilled workers (Reynolds 1989: 71–72). A skilled worker was also responsible for machine set up, readjustment, and to reset components for changes in design (Meyer 2004: 5). These tool and die makers and other skilled maintenance workers formed about 15 percent of the GM workforce between 1925 and 1940 and represented the last remnants of quasi-craft skilled worker autonomy in the Fordist system (Reynolds 1989: 71). For the average machine operator or assembly line worker, however, the annual model changes primarily meant the inconvenience of readjusting to new work routines after each changeover (Meyer 2004: 6).

By 1929, model changeovers were "pervasive and touched every corner of every plant in the industry" (Reynolds 1989: 70). The changeover period typically lasted over a six-to-ten-week period in which new dies are produced, presses are reset, machines are installed or adjusted, and all workers besides the skilled workers making these adjustments are temporarily laid off (Reynolds 1989: 70). This process was both long and expensive. In the early 1940s, GM spent around 35 million dollars a year on the model changeover (Rooke 2008: 3). The high costs of money and time also contributed to the concentration of the industry as small producers who could not make massive investments in model changes eventually fell by the wayside (Rooke 2008: 3).

The rise of the model changeover raises questions regarding the interaction between *product innovation* and *process innovation*. On the one hand, process innovations such as the replacement of human workers with machines transform the labor process and put negative pressure on employment requirements. Product innovations, on the other hand, whether through the yearly model change or through adding new components or features, typically stimulates new labor demand or makes the production process more labor intensive, which applies a positive employment pressure (Jürgens and Meißner 2005: 42). While adding components, e.g., on board computers or catalytic converters, may increase the overall demand for labor, efforts to simplify the product in other areas, e.g., sharing components across platforms, mitigate some of the positive employment effects. Nevertheless, standardization of parts *between* companies remains rare, so the design and manufacture of components is usually more labor intensive by virtue of companies producing proprietary versions of parts (Sturgeon et al. 2009: 20). The increasing complexity of the automobile from the Model T to today is undeniable, so the sum employment effect of net product changes on employment requirements is most likely positive. In addition, process innovations that increase productivity typically contributes to the growth of the company, which can increase the overall workforce even as productivity increases, and the work structure becomes less labor intensive (Jürgens and Meißner 2005: 42).

Mass production at Ford radically transformed the labor process to become far less labor-intensive than the craft production system, yet Ford's massive growth as industry leader in an expanding market more than offset the negative employment effects to result in overall employment growth. By the late 1920s, considerations of product innovation, including the primarily aesthetic changes of the annual model change, took on considerable importance and ultimately became the norm. Therefore, questions of how to optimize efficiency while simultaneously fulfilling flexibility and product innovation requirements gained increasing importance and influenced the deployment of technology and labor.

This can also be described as the influence of changing wants, needs, and desires on production processes within the flow of value in motion. Though producing a standardized product like the Model T would be the most productive and cost-effective strategy, analysis of value flows within the value-regime reveals how successful capital accumulation requires acceding to the realization requirements of consumers (Harvey 2017). This *imposes requirements on the valorization processes* to innovate and change commodities in ways that better ensure realization. This is necessary because the value of an unsold commodity—no matter how efficiently made—counts for nothing in capital accumulation processes and breaks the flow of value in motion. Therefore, despite imposing labor intensive model changeovers which usually decrease the levels of automation and productivity, such changes become necessary for capital accumulation. This tension between the continuous drive toward higher productivity and automation, on the one hand, and efforts to better ensure value realization through model changeovers and product innovations, on the other, proves to be a constant challenge for the auto industry (see Abernathy 1978).

3.2 *Auto Production in the Depths of Depression*

The Great Depression hit the auto industry hard with falling sales and hundreds of thousands of laid off workers. Without unions or means to resist hire and fire policies, the ranks of unemployed autoworkers climbed unabated. The drop in employment was not only due to the drop in demand, but also because of technological changes. However, integrating new machines slowed down during the depths of the depression. In 1931, GM started a policy of 'rehabilitating' older machines rather than buying new equipment. In addition, to better utilize existing machinery, multiple divisions came to share common production facilities and products, which further reduced costs and labor requirements (Reynolds 1989: 72–74).

This policy had negative ramifications for skilled workers, who often worked in independent machine tool shops when it was not retooling season (Reynolds 1989: 73). The policy drastically reduced demand for their labor in both the auto and machine tool industry. This also affected the semi-skilled and unskilled workers because demands for higher productivity fell on the workers as 'speed-up.' As Meyer (2004) explains,

> Since workers were cheaper and more flexible than machines and since machinery was quite expensive, manufacturers increasingly relied on human labor rather than technical innovation to increase productivity. In the worst years of the Great Depression, work standards seriously deteriorated as the 'speed-up' and the 'stretch-out' characterized automobile work. (6)

GM's strategy was to find ways of decreasing the labor requirements through increased labor intensity rather than new equipment. This saved more labor than the decline in sales warranted as, "GM undoubtedly laid off more than the slump in retail sales justified. Almost fifty percent of the work force was laid off between 1928 and 1932, yet employee productivity continued to rise" (Reynolds 1989: 74). This represented a general shift away from relying on machines to increase productivity to intensifying labor instead.

By 1935, recovering auto sales and more union organizing prompted another policy shift. The nadir of sales in 1932 at 1.3 million reached pre-depression levels by 1937 at 4.8 million (Noyes 1938: 7). Union organizing increased after the election of Franklin Roosevelt in 1932, who set in motion dramatic changes in state-labor-business relations starting with the National Industrial Recovery Act in 1933. This law guaranteed workers the right to collectively bargain with employers through chosen representatives and set up federal systems to regulate company-union relations (Reynolds 1989: 76). This "Magna Carta for American labor" prompted a surge in unionization across the country, after having degraded from four million unionized workers in 1919 to two million in 1933 (Greenhouse 2019: 75). This also encouraged another unionization wave in the auto industry, which had failed to unionize after multiple previous attempts decades prior (see Meyer 1981: 89–94). A year later in 1934, most GM workers had either joined a union or appeared to sympathize with the union movement (Reynolds 1989: 77).

Numerous tactics were used to suppress unionization, from company spies to infiltrate and guards to intimidate, the renewal of corporate paternalism to pacify, to the establishment of 'company unions' designed to be aligned with management interests and blunt the independent union movement (Reynolds 1989: 78; see Greenhouse 2019: 80–83). This also included a $50 million production adjustment program at GM designed to "reorganize, readjust, and expand manufacturing operations" in light of the new relationship between business, government, and the emerging unions. The aim of this program was to reduce the number of hours worked per week and to deskill and technologically displace the politically conscious skilled workers who led the union movement (Reynolds 1989: 79–80).

Much of the program entailed automation through "combining production tasks and replacing several machines and several operators with a single, complex machine and an unskilled operator" (Reynolds 1989: 81). For the 1935 changeover, 250-ton body presses were installed that could stamp the entire auto body, which resulted in "a whole department with hundreds of men and hundreds of thousands of dollars in labor costs [being] eliminated by the stroke of a designer's pen" (Reynolds 1989: 81). In the late 1930s, an improved Keller machine was installed that could mechanically cast dies in one hundred hours what skilled workers formally did in 2,000 man hours. As a final example, automatic die-cutting machines were installed to deskill the tool and die makers—who were among the most politically active workers at GM (Reynolds 1989: 85). The program did not negatively affect all skilled workers, however, as more machinery meant more demand for maintenance and repair workers, whose numbers increased between 1935 and 1940. Efforts at reorganization, deskilling, and automation abounded at GM, and other companies followed similar patterns (Reynolds 1989: 84–85).

Technological advances also appeared at Ford's River Rouge plant. Ford was a pioneer in developing automatic transfer machines in the early 1930s. A transfer machine can be defined as a "multi-head automatic machine which performs a sequence of operations simultaneously on a series of product-units which are automatically indexed forward from one machine station to the next" (Hounshell 2000: 100–101). Such machine complexes not only automated the machining process, as could be done by single purpose machines, but also transfer the part in between operations, thus reducing the need for human transport labor. The first experiments started small, with a two-station transfer machine developed in 1932 and a seven-station transfer machine in 1936 (Hounshell 2000: 107). However, these were primarily self-contained experiments that did not become prominent until the 1940s and 1950s, where they became the centerpiece of “Detroit automation” (Hounshell 2000: 101–109; see Jürgens 2023: 141–142). This development was also aided by pneumatic transmitters for machines that “brought automatic control to many industrial processes previously difficult to regulate at all, even manually” (Beniger 1986: 301).

By the late 1920s, wood frames covered by metal were replaced by building cars with all steel bodies. This meant assembling the car body now required welding instead of riveting, soldering, or nailing (Jürgens 2023: 145–148). Though welding initially required a “veritable forest of single spot welders,” welding operations were automated as much as possible, as evidenced by the 600 automatic welding machines at the River Rouge by 1936 (Barclay 1936: 82–83). Automatic welding machines could weld 72-inch seams in seven seconds, which was far outside human capability (Barclay 1936: 83). The changeover to steel bodies technologically displaced riveters, which meant less human labor since one spot welder replaced eight riveters who were in turn increasingly replaced by automatic welders (Jürgens 2023: 145–148). Welding automation reduced costs and improved quality (Abernathy 1978: 183).

The River Rouge housed nearly all production processes within the factory complex. While there were advances in automation, many processes, like painting with spray guns and assembly continued to be labor intensive (see Jürgens 2023: 139–152). The entire complex was designed to achieve a continuous flow, though this was difficult to master in practice due to the size and complexity of the plant. Processes were linked by an over two-mile-long conveyor system, which one Ford worker described as a “mechanical monster with its tributaries of chains, belts, and slides” (Meyer 2004: 5). The technological developments of the 1930s did improve productivity as the entire process to build an automobile from foundry to delivery that took fifty hours in 1929 had fallen to twenty-eight hours by 1940 (Jürgens 2023: 136).

The 1930s were therefore a polarizing decade in terms of automation and productivity development. During the depths of the depression, technological development was mostly paused and increasing labor intensity became the primary means of increasing productivity. As the economy recovered and unions began organizing, automation became viable not just to improve productivity, but was *wielded politically* to deskill, technologically displace, and weaken worker power (Reynolds 1989). Although politically active skilled workers were the most targeted, neither these tactics nor the oppressive spying or intimidation halted unionization efforts. According to Meyer (2004: 6), the 1930s were a time of “economic and technical stagnation,” yet there were some technological advancements and experiments with technologies such as transfer machines that took on increasing importance after WWII (Hounshell 2000).

Even in this era of social and economic turmoil, the pursuit of productivity was pushed forward both through new technical developments and increased performance pressure on workers.

3.3 *Labor Intensity and Speed-Up*

The temporary slowdown of technologically driven productivity improvements and the glut of unemployed autoworkers—it took ten years for employment to recover to 1927 levels (Jürgens 2023: 155)—gave automakers both the incentive and opportunity to intensify labor processes. In the context of too few jobs, high unemployment, and an unrestricted ability to hire and fire, production standards could essentially be set at will with no viable recourse for the workers. The magnitude of speed-up was unparalleled before or since then as Asher and Edsforth (1995) describe, "It is clear that the significant speedup of auto work that has been implemented in the last twenty years is not even remotely comparable to the grueling intensity of labor that existed in most auto plants in the 1930s" (10). Speed-up was a major grievance in this period.

The harsh labor intensity was so well known that the working conditions were investigated by the federal government. In 1934, The National Recovery Administration summarized the situation as follows:

> Everywhere workers indicated that they were being forced to work harder and harder, to put out more and more products in the same amount of time with less workers doing the job. There was a tendency to excuse the automobile manufacturer for a lack of steady work ... but when it comes to increasing their workloads they are vigorous in denouncing management as slave drivers, and worse. (Edsforth and Asher 1995: 70)

Multiple tactics encouraged speed-up. Directly increasing line speed was a straightforward tactic because workers paced by the line "must keep up with the belt or else the work piles up and the line gets clogged" (Meyer 2004: 5). The lines were so fast that often only fit young workers could bear it. As one worker commented in the early 1930s, "We had line speeds and people couldn't keep up and if you weren't in A-1 shape and you were sick or anything it was just too bad. You didn't keep the job; that's all" (Meyer 2004: 6). Higher production quotas and line speeds were frequently implemented after each model changeover (Edsforth and Asher 1995: 73). Production quotas were sometimes adjusted at random, as one foreman reported being commanded by his supervisor to raise production from 15 to 25 jobs per hour in the middle of the shift without adding manpower (Edsforth and Asher 1995: 80). Such foremen engaged in "constant exhortation and intimidation" to enforce the frequently retimed work standards (Edsforth and Asher 1995: 73).

Speed-up degraded working conditions and harmed workers both physically and mentally. As one Fisher Body plant worker reported in 1933, after returning from work he would, "get home at ten o'clock and I would be so tired I could not eat my supper. I would drop in a chair and cry myself to sleep" (Edsforth and Asher 1995: 82). The high level of stress and alienation took mental and personal tolls as one worker reported,

> When I come in the gate in the morning I throw off my personality and assume a personality which expresses the institution of which I am a part … The only personal thing required of me is just enough consciousness to operate my body as a machine … We are working so fast I don't see how anyone can think of quality … I seldom make a mistake, yet I never have my mind on my work … my subconscious is more capable of this monotony than my personality. (Edsforth and Asher 1995: 87)

For management, the ideal production system is comprised of workers who could work without physical injury and who could mentally endure the monotony. Autoworkers were essentially treated by management as if they did not have these limits and could be pushed to work continuously faster without negative short- and long-term consequences. The workers craved certainty, i.e., if they had to perform alienating assembly line work, it should be at a steady pace and not sped up to the point of absolute exhaustion (Asher 1995: 130).

Under such harsh conditions, the union movement was seen as a source of hope for change. As Meyer (2004) put it,

> Aroused and angered by impossible production-line speeds and work standards, serious safety and health concerns, fears of unemployment, and overly abusive foremen, the United Automobile Workers Union was at the center of the social and economic revolution associated with the rise of industrial unionism. (7)

Thus, one of the primary goals of the union movement was to end the speed-up, and the early UAW victories gave the workers optimism (Meyer 2004: 7). As one Fisher Body worker stated after the successful GM sit-down strike,

> The inhuman high speed is no more. We now have a voice, and have slowed the speed of the line. And [we] are now treated as human beings,

> and not as part of the machinery. The high pressure is taken off ... it proves clearly that united we stand, divided or alone we fall. (Meyer 1981: 200)

Speed-up therefore helps explain how the UAW gained popularity by promising that unionization would end the inhumane work pace and regain some control over the conditions of valorization.

3.4 *Unionizing the American Auto Industry*

Before 1937, the US auto industry was famous for its antiunionism. Though there had been numerous attempts to unionize over the decades, no union drive had succeeded at forcing GM, Chrysler, or Ford to recognize a union as the sole bargaining agent of the workers (see Meyer 1981: 89–93; Peterson 1987). Even by 1936, on the eve of the famous sit down strikes, only 15 percent of autoworkers were organized (Flink 1988: 226). The 1935 National Labor Relations Act reaffirmed the right to unionize and collectively bargain with an employer. It set up the National Labor Relations Board (NLRB) which oversees union organizing, conducts union elections, and enforces the rules for legal and illegal actions related to unionization efforts and unfair labor practices (see Greenhouse 2019: 82; Flink 1988: 224–225). This laws provided the rights and legal tools that unions needed to unionize American industry, and these unionization drives forever changed the nature of the US value-regime.

GM, the largest of the Big Three, was the United Automobile Workers' (UAW) first target. Their plan was to perform sit-down strikes at key Fisher Body plants whose operations were crucial to the supply chain. On December 30, 1936, the strike began at two plants, and within days, conventional and sit-down strikes appeared at GM plants in Michigan, Wisconsin, and Ohio (Greenhouse 2019: 84–85). The sit-down strike is a particularly useful tactic for applying pressure on employers because they disrupt valorization processes within the flow of value in motion. Since workers occupy the space of production and prevent strikebreakers from working, value production is totally stopped and cannot be restarted without either eviction by force or negotiated settlement. In this case, the company was compelled to parley with the UAW to end the strike on February 11, 1937 (see Fine 1969).

The strike was successful for multiple reasons. First, it wrecked economic havoc on GM by coordinating the strike on several key facilities that idled 136,000 workers. This move caused production to decline dramatically from 53,000 cars and trucks a day in December 1936 to a mere 1,500 a day in early February 1937 (Greenhouse 2019: 91). Because the pro-New Deal Governor refused to use the National Guard to evict the strikers, GM executives had to settle with the strikers with Governor Murphy serving as mediator (Flink 1988: 227). Full union recognition across the company solidified in the years after the sit-down strikes (Reynolds 1989: 90; Greenhouse 2019: 91–92).

The success of the sit-down echoed across the industry with UAW membership rising from 88,000 in February 1937 to 400,000 by October (Greenhouse 2019: 92). Chrysler also faced UAW sit-down strikes and quickly conceded in March 1937 (Flink 1988: 227). The GM strike also prompted contracts from smaller auto firms such as Hudson, Packard, and Studebaker as well as some auto parts firms (Meyer 2004: 7).

This left Ford as the final major holdout against the UAW. Despite multiple confrontations between the company and union—including the beatings of Walter Reuther and other organizers by the Ford Service Department at the infamous 'battle of the overpass' in 1937—Ford did not become unionized until 1941. The full dictatorial and oppressive nature of Ford's management regime is revealed in the struggle against unionization. As Nevins and Hill (1963) describe, "The River Rouge plant has taken on many aspects of a community in which martial law has been declared, and in which a huge military organization … has been superimposed upon the regular civil authorities" (150). Parallels can be drawn between the oppressive regimes of auto management in the US and Germany under the Nazis. Nevertheless, by late 1941 the Big Three was union organized, and the membership of the UAW rose to over 649,000 (Greenhouse 2019: 92).

However, strike victory and recognition were only the beginning of labor-capital struggles. The predominant pattern of US labor-management relations did not solidify until the 1950 'Treaty of Detroit.' Until then, the UAW leadership struggled with questions of how to work with management *and* the rank-and-file to win agreements on a variety of operational levels to improve working conditions. Questions emerged such as, what were the union goals and how much priority should be placed on each goal? What tactics should be used to achieve those goals? On what level of organization should the priorities be worked out, on the shopfloor, plant, or company level?

In these early years, numerous strategies were tested to effect change. One priority was to reduce abusive management practices. In response, grievance procedures were established, and union shop stewards appeared "to patrol the shop floor and settle disputes between workers and shop supervisors" (Meyer 2004: 7). The interactions between management and shopfloor workers were often direct with auto workers forming informal work groups to directly bargain with foremen (Asher and Edsforth 1995: 4). Typical grievance negotiations included questions of wages, seniority, workplace safety, and the line speed (Boyle 1995: 104). Many grievances centered around labor valorization, whether through increasing the value of labor power or negotiating on working conditions and relative output.

Eliminating speed-up was another important goal, especially among the rank-and-file. Workers aimed at *decreasing productivity* because "auto workers refused to be sacrificial lambs for the industry's god of greater productivity, and the union backed them up" (Edsforth and Asher 1995: 95–96). Thanks to organizing and union pressure, line speed was reduced in many factories (Asher and Edsforth 1995: 10). Some workers even felt empowered to take "direct action to diminish the work pace by using physical assaults, slowdowns, sit downs, quickie strikes, and even sabotage. Some workers threatened bodily harm to foremen who enforced production standards" (Asher and Edsforth 1995: 11). The spontaneity and unmediated nature of these actions prompted management to work toward *reestablishing predictability* into the labor process, but unilateral coercion and enforcement was no longer viable. Therefore, the task of establishing 'labor peace' among the rank-and-file labor became a joint problem for the UAW leadership and management. In 1937, GM coerced the UAW to accept a contract revision that obligated the union to discipline workers who participate in wild cat strikes or other spontaneous job actions or else the contract would be voided, with similar contracts later adopted at Chrysler and Ford (Asher and Edsforth 1995: 11; Edsforth and Asher 1995: 96). Management understood that their profits depended on the flow and coordination of thousands of production processes and that they could not operate efficiently if there are frequent production interruptions (Asher and Edsforth 1995: 11). Slowing down line speed, and therefore productivity, for the sake of predictable production flow was preferable over a fast line speed plagued with unpredictable stoppages resulting in a slower and therefore costlier production process. A compromise for consistent and predictable valorization and control over labor time processes was desirable. A durable agreement was not yet reached, however, as evidence by the around 2000 sit downs, slowdowns, and other work stoppages throughout the auto industry between 1937 and 1939 (Edsforth and Asher 1995: 92; Boyle 1995: 103).

In the late 1930s and early 1940s, militant rank-and-file workers wanted *direct shopfloor control* over questions of speed-up and technology use, while the UAW bureaucracy wanted to protect the fragile union by *self-limiting its demands on production control* (see Boyle 1995; Asher and Edsforth 1995: 13). The union's legitimacy was in danger because after the strike wave of 1937, the public began to harbor increasingly anti-union sentiments. This was spurred on by a 1939 Supreme Court case that allowed sit-down strikers to be fired without legal recourse and the anticommunist campaigns that targeted many of the most active unionists (Reynolds 1989: 88). Without a strong labor-oriented party to advocate for unions, UAW leaders understood that the union could be crushed at any time if their actions provoked too much negative attention from management or the federal government (Asher and Edsforth 1995: 12; see Lipset and Marks 2000). As Edsforth and Asher (1995) describe the dilemma,

> UAW leaders could neither endorse a level of militancy that would bring the union down, or refuse to resist the speedup that so angered their membership. UAW leaders thus accepted management's goal of uninterrupted production, but also insisted that management, as well as workers, had to honor contracts that defined production standards and stipulated that they would not be altered capriciously. (97)

To accomplish such a compromise, routinized grievance resolution procedures were needed.

In 1940, GM proposed that a neutral arbitrator selected via consensus by the firm and union would make binding rulings on all grievances that could not be settled between workers and management (Asher and Edsforth 1995: 13). The grievance process comprised four stages. It started with the worker and union steward negotiating with the foreman or manager. If the grievance was not satisfactorily resolved here, the grievance moved to plant level negotiation. If this also did not work, then the process moved to the national level with corporate management negotiating with UAW national department officials. If the issue still could not be resolved, then the neutral umpire stepped in to engage in binding arbitration (Asher and Edsforth 1995: 13–14). These procedures became standard at GM in 1940 and at Chrysler and Ford in 1943 (Asher and Edsforth 1995: 14). This process typically handled questions such as seniority or pay. By formalizing the grievance settlement process, the UAW agreed not to authorize a strike based on these issues which helped avoid production interruptions (Zabala 1995).

However, questions of production standards and labor intensity were *exempt* from this process. In fact, contracts signed by the UAW and Big Three specifically stipulated that production standards disputes would *not* be decided by arbitration (Asher and Edsforth 1995: 14). The rationale was that the UAW would be severely weakened if it gave up the right to strike on production issues, *especially without* codetermination rights to cooperatively determine production standards. Management accepted this because they were unwilling to risk a neutral umpire delivering a binding rule that restricted management power over production standards (Asher and Edsforth 1995: 14). Therefore, the union retained the legal right to strike over production standards.[2] This

2 Asher and Edsforth (1995) describe the process stating, "If workers in a particular factory were not pleased with management's final response to a production standard grievance, they

system provided authorized parameters of union and management dispute and represented a clear departure from the pre-union system of strict management control and suppression as well as spontaneous union resistance in the early union years. Unplanned worker actions could not be stopped altogether, but the mutual agreement to this system obliged the UAW to discipline its rank-and file-members to follow the grievance system rather than disrupt production. This system also distinguishes the US value-regime from the German, as American workers could pressure production standards through strike threats, whereas postwar German workers influenced work standards through codetermination.

This system also affected management behavior. General Motors self-imposed managerial consistency by agreeing that,

> Once production standards were set at a GM plant—and they were certainly demanding standards—the company generally stuck to them. It did not alter assembly line speeds and production standards for bench workers and machinists during the life of a particular model. (Edsforth and Asher 1995: 97)

This policy generally lowered the incidences of wildcat strikes and production disruptions, especially compared to Ford and Chrysler which frequently changed production standards—often in violation of UAW local agreements. Indeed, between 1939 and 1956, GM had far lower incidences of slowdowns and wildcat strikes compared to Ford and Chrysler (Edsforth and Asher 1995: 97). *This represents two styles of managing production among value-systems within the same value-regime.* Is it more advantageous for capital accumulation to produce at a consistent, though slower, rate with less production interruptions, or to manufacture at a faster line speed but at the cost of more frequent interruptions? Although this question cannot be answered definitively, the market dominance of GM over Ford and Chrysler suggests that consistent production with less disturbances may be one contributing factor that explains GM's decades long industry leadership (see Asher and Edsforth 1995: 21).

This dynamic also illuminates another aspect of *social domination*. Possessing the most productive production system and thereby exerting *productivity pressure* on competitors is not just about achieving the fastest production speeds at any given time in any given process but about achieving *consistent*

---

could hold a strike vote. A majority vote for a strike did not automatically begin the strike. Next, the International Executive Board would discuss the situation, and after notifying management of the strike vote, the IEB could authorize a legal strike" (14).

control over time in all its aspects, e.g., the speed of the assembly line *and* preventing time loss from strikes. If capital is *value in motion*, then the key is both to always stay in motion *and* for that motion to be at speeds deemed 'socially necessary.' Staying in motion is achieved by preventing interruptions to valorization processes as much as possible, which makes preventing strikes preferable for capital. This is what makes strikes a powerful tool for labor as they endanger capital accumulation at the stage of valorization. There is a mutual interest for both capital and labor to prevent a strike and achieve labor peace, as management wants to avoid production interruptions, and workers want management to address their grievances. These immediate concerns have deeper roots as capital wants to keep value in motion, and labor wants to maintain self-valorization within favorable working conditions.

At the same time, however, production speed cannot be lowered beyond a certain limit, even for the sake of risking a strike, because slowed down production processes may go below the socially necessary labor time standard to produce that commodity within the value-regime. Therefore, there is a struggle, on the one hand, to determine production standards agreeable to labor to prevent disruptions, and, on the other hand, to not relax production standards to such a low level that the *socially dominant standard of valorization* cannot be achieved. In addition, there is not one *unchanging* production standard, but *ever-changing* production standards by which production is expected to conform. For this reason, GM needed to maintain demanding production standards—though not too demanding as to trigger a strike—and invest in new equipment to increase productivity for each model changeover. GM tended toward reducing the frequency of production changes to maintain relatively consistent production flow, whereas Ford and Chrysler opted for more frequent changes in work standards at the cost of more frequent production interruptions. Though this factor alone cannot explain relative firm success, especially considering the oligopolistic conditions, we can hypothesize that the different strategies may have contributed to GM's dominance (see Asher 1995; Asher and Edsforth 1995: 21).

4 The Arsenal of Democracy vs the Arsenal of Fascism

The outbreak of World War II sent a shockwave throughout global industry as production shifted to total war production. A few wartime developments are important here, particularly how war production—subsidized by national governments—generated the capital and infrastructure that played a key role in the postwar boom.

4.1 *German Industry during World War II*

Germany engaged in rapid industrialization and modernization after the Nazis took power in 1933. Much of this effort was aimed at motorization and war preparation. However, with the invasion of Poland in September 1939, motorization took on secondary importance. Daimler-Benz already dedicated 51 percent of its production to military use by 1938. This increased every year until reaching a peak of 93 percent military production by 1944 (Bellon 1990: 220). The firm produced a variety of war materials including "tanks, trucks, engines for warships, parts for the V-2, and especially enormous lots of airplane engines" (Bellon 1990: 239).

Wartime production demanded maximum capacity utilization of workers, factories, and equipment to fully engage the mass production war machine. The number of workers at Daimler-Benz rose dramatically from a low of 9,000 during the depression, to 46,000 in 1938, and 64,000 in 1943 (Bellon 1990: 220). Daimler-Benz grew from five German facilities in 1926 to thirteen facilities across occupied Europe, including in occupied France, the Czech Republic, Poland, Austria, and Belarus (Bellon 1990: 210, 231). Ford facilities across Europe and Opel were also seized by the state for war production by 1941 (Flink 1988: 269–270).

Just as foreign factories were seized for the German war machine, so had millions of foreign workers, prisoners of war, and concentration camp inmates. This accelerated after March 21, 1942 when Hitler ordered mobilization of all available labor power, which ramped up the enlisting, inducing, and kidnapping of millions of people (Bellon 1990: 241). By 1944, over seven million people, or one out of every five workers in Germany were induced foreign workers or POWs (Bellon 1990: 241). At Daimler-Benz, 36,147 or 44.6 percent of the total 81,059 production workers were foreign workers by 1944 (Bellon 1990: 230). In some factories, almost the entire workforce was comprised of foreigners hailing from the Soviet Union, France, Czechoslovakia, the Netherlands, Italy, Belgium, Poland, and Armenia (Bellon 1990: 252).

These workers toiled in poor living conditions, often housed in barracks and paid only one mark per day—if paid at all (Bellon 1990: 252). Grieger and Lupa (2015) describes the general treatment of foreign workers stating, "In Nazi Germany forced laborers had no rights, and were subjected to varying levels of racial discrimination. Insufficient food, physical violence and exploitation undermined their health and endangered their lives" (11). At work, they faced the degraded working conditions of Fordist mass production driven by the pace of the machine and the assembly line (Hachtmann and von Saldern 2009: 192). Their exploitation in such high numbers was only possible due to the high amount of unskilled labor required for repetitive assembly line work. In other words, the adoption of mass production Fordism in conditions of total war gave the *impetus and incentive* to exploit forced labor. The arsenal of fascism was built by racism and forced labor *alongside* Fordist principles structurally suitable to exploit labor with high efficiency.

The situation was similar at Volkswagen. Though no Beetles were produced before or during the war, the enormous Wolfsburg factory was retooled for production of war materials (Grieger and Lupa 2015: 11; Ewing 2019: 10). Starting in 1942, Wolfsburg began producing the Kübelwagen, a militarized version of the Beetle and the German answer to the Allied Jeep (Ewing 2017: 10). A total of 66,285 Kübelwagens were produced by war's end, far below Hitler's expected scale of mass production (Grieger and Lupa 2015: 11). Forced labor was also used at Volkswagen since 1940. Approximately 20,000 Foreign workers, prisoners of war and concentration camp inmates were brought to Wolfsburg from across occupied Europe (Grieger and Lupa 2015: 11). By 1942, Wolfsburg was comprised of 60 percent forced foreign labor, which increased to 66% by 1944 (Grieger and Lupa 2015: 11; Jürgens 2023: 250).

The relative preservation of the facilities and equipment built by the Third Reich during the war was crucial to the postwar recovery. The Allied Air Forces raided the Untertürkheim factory five times in 1943 and 1944, with the September 1944 raid destroying 41 percent of the built-up area and destroying 12.7 percent of the machinery, with another 43 percent being heavily damaged (Bellon 1990: 253–254). However, by this point much of the machinery had already been transported to fourteen locations throughout Württemberg, lessening the total impact on future productive capacity (Bellon 1990: 254). The Volkswagen factory in Wolfsburg was raided three times in July and August 1944 (Tolliday 1995a: 286). These raids only rendered 20 percent of the floor area unusable with an additional 14 percent being partially damaged. Furthermore, only 225 of the 2,776 machine tools (8.1 percent) were damaged (Tolliday 1995a: 286). The raids did little damage partially because the most important machines had been moved to the basements while others were dispersed to small factories not targeted by air raids. The pre-raid production level was reached again by December 1944 (Tolliday 1995a: 286). In explaining Volkswagen's postwar success, there is a tendency to exaggerate the wartime damage to frame the company as "a phoenix from the ashes" (Tolliday 1995a: 288). Yet, it is more accurate to portray the general damage to German industry to be relatively light. The overall quality and quantity of industrial capital in Germany may have been more superior in 1945 than it was in 1939—despite the bombings (Tolliday 1995a: 288; see Abelshauser 1975).

This history helps explain the origins of the *Wirtschaftswunder*. Both the productive development under the Nazis and the relatively light damage during the war allowed German industry to recover quickly thereafter. Though the infrastructure and production equipment were relatively preserved, the end of the war brought a total socio-political-economic collapse. A new democratic government and industrial relations system were necessary before the *Wirtschaftswunder* could begin in earnest.

4.2 *Capital Buildup and the Arsenal of Democracy*

The United States formally entered World War II after the bombing of Pearl Harbor in December 1941. While both Ford and GM secured military contracts before the Pearl Harbor attacks, the auto industry only became the 'arsenal of democracy' after war was declared (Flink 1988: 274–275; Hyde 2013). Thanks to decades of experience with mass production and the massive influx of government funds, the auto industry alone produced millions of military vehicles, over 4 million engines for vehicles, aircraft, and sea vessels, nearly 6 million guns, and over 27,000 airplanes, as well as seventy-five other military items. The total value was estimated at $29 billion or one fifth of total war production (Flink 1988: 276). This staggering output is reflective of the strength of US industry and its position as global productivity leader.

This is also impressive considering only 12 percent of the automakers' machine tools could be used to fabricate war supplies (Martelle 2014: 139). The tool-and-die industry was also converted to create the capital equipment necessary for war production, and workers of all skill levels were retrained for the new production processes (Martelle 2014: 139). Meyer (2004) describes the situation this way,

> For auto workers, the major technological issue was the conversion to and the reconversion from defense production and the introduction of new workers to the advanced production methods. Always problematic for workers, the shift in production, in this instance from the civilian production of automobiles to military production of war materials and back again, created problems in unlearning and relearning day-to-day work tasks and routines. (8)

These issues were amplified as hundreds of thousands of new workers entered auto factories. Because nearly 500,000 men left Michigan to fight, hundreds of thousands of people flocked to the Detroit area (Martelle 2014: 140). This influx caused the total number of autoworkers to exceed one million for the first time. By 1943, approximately 50 percent of Detroit auto workers were new to the auto industry (Boyle 1995: 101). The city that was blighted by unemployment a decade earlier was now running at full speed with an expanded workforce.

This influx of activity and government demand stimulated the need for massive investments in new plants and equipment. For example, General Motors invested $911 million in new factories and machines between 1940 and 1944, with $809 million being taxpayer funded. This was a sum greater than the company's total capital assets in 1939, and the investments doubled the total value of GM's assets (Flink 1988: 275; Boyle 1995: 101). Approximately 60 percent of the $1.9 billion of defense contracts for the auto industry in 1941 were dedicated to building new facilities, including the Ford Willow Run and Chrysler Warren facility to manufacture airplanes and tanks respectively (Boyle 1995: 112; Flink 1988: 276). The industry also used government funds to experiment with new technologies, including new automated equipment (Meyer 2004: 8). These experiments directly led to major technological breakthroughs in manufacturing technology such as transfer machines, which became major automation technologies after the war (Hounshell 2000: 112–113). The US value-regime reoriented value distribution to war production, which generated massive capital accumulation for the auto industry that was then reinvested into facilities and equipment that set up the industry for postwar expansion and productivity gains.

Wartime conditions modified industrial relations with mixed results for labor. On the one hand, unions were legitimated as partners in many joint government-business-labor programs (Lee 1943; Greenhouse 2019: 95). On the other hand, the government's desire for smooth production created a 'state of exception' that suspended some aspects of the industrial relations system between the industry and union that had only begun to take shape less than a decade earlier. Most unions, including the UAW, adopted a no-strike pledge for the duration of the war as a sign of loyalty and support for the war effort, which constrained the power to protest labor issues. However, because the military contracts guaranteed a profit rate for the companies and covered the costs of production, including costs from potential production disturbances, management often acceded to worker challenges on production standards (Asher and Edsforth 1995: 16). Simply threatening a work stoppage or wildcat strike would sometimes convince foremen to settle shopfloor disputes in favor of the workers (Asher and Edsforth 1995: 16; Boyle 1995). However, the no strike pledge also meant managers could relax their processing of worker grievances, and workers had no recourse against this. Workers often accused automakers of ignoring or refusing to process grievances (Boyle 1995: 119–120).

Therefore, despite the no-strike pledge, wildcat strikes and rank-and-file militancy increased, with nearly one-fourth of all auto workers committing a wildcat strike or job action in 1943, rising to one half of auto workers in 1944 (Asher and Edsforth 1995: 17; Boyle 1995: 125). Federal officials feared that the

UAW leadership may have lost the ability to control the union. However, the end of the war also ended the strike wave. Thereafter, the UAW ended the no-strike pledge, and the union leadership swiftly repositioned toward rank-and-file militancy (Boyle 1995: 125). This resulted in a series of post war strikes and negotiations that eventually led to 'labor peace' with the 1950 'Treaty of Detroit.' The war both solidified the UAW presence and legitimacy as a social system, but the unique circumstances of the war years generated the conditions for increased labor radicalism that both the companies and federal government wanted to address.

4.3 *Productivity Superiority and Geo-political Domination*

Comparing the wartime experience in the US and Germany, preparation for war and war production promoted industrial expansion in both countries. This meant adopting mass production in Germany, and rapid retooling in the United States. The situation for workers differed immensely, with oppression and forced labor in Germany, while efforts at state-business-labor cooperation were attempted in the US. Though the contradictions of the US system resulted in increased strikes and militancy, wartime production nevertheless generated conditions that led to the 'Treaty of Detroit' which set the long-term trajectory of the US value-regime. The German war experience also enabled the postwar *Wirtschaftswunder*, though in a perverse manner. Because the horrors of forced labor during the war were so morally reprehensible, the postwar state-business-labor systems were radically transformed away from the oppressive practices of the Nazis (Fisher 1951). This begat the system of codetermination that remains the hallmark of the German value-regime. At the same time, the buildup of facilities and machines for the war and their relative survival helped jumpstart the German economy in the postwar years.

Also note how differences in production capacity and productivity helped determine the outcome of the war. As a measure of industrial strength, the combined automobile production in Germany, Italy, and Japan in 1938 was only 436,918 units (Flink 1988: 273). Though German production more than tripled between 1928 and 1938 (Jürgens 2023: 246), a testament to the rapid adoption of mass production, this was still far below the productive capabilities of the Allies. German production paled in comparison to the US industry where tens of millions of cars were produced in the 1920s and 1930s (see Noyes 1938). Therefore, though war is full of contingencies, the eventual outcome of WWII is hardly surprising given the stark differences in production capacity, production technology, and productivity.

This reveals another distinct advantage of being productivity leader. Not only did higher capacity and productivity give the US relative economic dominance, setting the productivity standard Nazi Germany sought to emulate through its rationalization program, the mobilization of the US labor-industry-government complex *translated US productive capacity into geo-political power* capable of winning a world war. Tracing back stepwise, we observe how American geo-political power during WWII is rooted in productive capacity, which is rooted in highly productive combinations of technology and labor power, which is ultimately rooted in the ability to control time an execute production processes significantly faster than anywhere else in the world at that time. As Flink (1988) succinctly explains, "American superiority in mass-production techniques—techniques developed in the automobile industry—was indeed the main reason for the Allied victory" (276). German accounts also support this conclusion. After Ferdinand Porsche, the designer of the Beetle, returned from his meetings with Henry Ford at the River Rouge factory, he wondered how Germany could possibly expect to win considering the "great American superiority in mass production that he had witnessed" (Flink 1988: 268). Considering the poor relative position of the German forces, "Germany was ill prepared to fight the global automotive war that it had initiated" (Flink 1988: 269). Clear differences in productivity standards confer advantages to the productivity leader—in this case transforming productive power into geopolitical power. *Social* domination becomes *geo-political* domination.

5 Postwar Reconstruction and Reconfiguration

The war's conclusion brought the collapse of the Nazi regime and the beginning of postwar reconstruction. For the United States, it ushered in the Cold War with the US positioned as the sole capitalist superpower counterposed to the Soviet Union as the communist superpower. The following recounts the German reconstruction under Allied occupation and the immediate postwar years in the US leading up to the epochal 'Treaty of Detroit.' These events serve as a prelude to the production and competitive dynamics at play in the world auto industry during the postwar decades.

5.1 *German Reconstruction and Occupation*

Under the Potsdam Agreement, Daimler-Benz's assets abroad were confiscated and used for reparations. By 1945, the company only kept the plants it possessed before 1933. By 1947, production had resumed at all plants, and reconstruction of damaged facilities was completed by 1951 (Mercedes-Benz 2023). By 1949, the company was beginning to show a profit through exports and a growing domestic market in the new Federal Republic.

The Volkswagen factory in Lower Saxony fell in the British occupation zone. Compared to the French, Americans, and especially the Soviets, the British were the least committed to reparations or interested in eliminating German competition and instead worked toward pragmatic reconstruction of the factory (Tolliday 1995a: 288–289). The Allied Military Government placed an order for 20,000 Beetles and ordered the plant to increase output as quickly as possible (Tolliday 1995a: 298). The original aim was to produce 4,000 cars a month, but supply issues reduced this to the modest goal of 1,000 per month (Grieger and Lupa 2015: 37). The British allowed Volkswagen exports to nearby countries starting in 1948 with around 4,000 Beetle deliveries to the Netherlands, Switzerland, Belgium, Luxembourg, Sweden, and Denmark (Grieger and Lupa 2015: 39). This increased to over 7,000 in 1949, with 15 percent of Beetle production sold in foreign markets (Grieger and Lupa 2015: 39).

The British intended to relinquish stewardship of VW as soon as possible. They chose Heinrich Nordhoff, a former senior manager at Opel's Brandenburg truck factory, to lead the firm (Tolliday 1995a: 300). His experience at Opel gave him considerable knowledge and experience with American mass production methods, which played a key role in future developments at Volkswagen (Tolliday 1995a: 300). Control over Volkswagen passed from the British Military Government to the state of Lower Saxony and the Federal Republic of Germany in September 1949, making Volkswagen a fully state-owned enterprise (Grieger and Lupa 2015: 50).

Despite scarcity issues and a lack of housing (Grieger and Lupa 2015: 37), worker organizations and independent unions soon emerged from the defunct DAF. By November 1945 a works council was elected, and by May 1947 the first agreement between management and workers came into effect (Grieger and Lupa 2015: 40; 44). Empowered by the Allied Works Council Law of 1946, the works council gave workers' representatives a decision-making voice at Volkswagen. The works council was given the right to participate in issues of hiring and firing, wages, reassignment, and operational changes. The production program was also shaped by the works council, and it was allowed to examine company books when formulating decisions (Grieger and Lupa 2015: 45). These parameters for cooperation between management and labor went beyond anything experienced in the United States. Codetermination remains the primary distinguishing factor between American and German labor relations. In addition, by 1948 negotiations between the newly reorganized post-DAF German metalworkers' union called *Industriegewerkschaft Metall* (hereafter IG Metall) and Volkswagen took place (Grieger and Lupa 2015: 46). German-style industrial relations systems were quickly establishing themselves even under occupation, including the crucial relationship between IG Metall, the works council, the federal and state governments, and the company.

The weakness of Volkswagen's domestic competitors after the war is another contingency that explains Volkswagen's ascendency. Wolfsburg was one of the least damaged German plants and was not subject to reparations or seizures, unlike companies such as Auto-Union or Daimler-Benz (Tolliday 1995a: 301; see Bellon 1990: 254). GM only reluctantly resumed control of Opel by late 1948 (Sloan 1964: 331). Despite leading the industry in 1938, Opel's early postwar operations were hobbled by the lack of commitment from GM to support Opel (Tolliday 1995a: 301–302). Likewise, Ford's German presence was smaller and weaker compared to their establishments in France and Britain. The lack of investment and support from the corporate headquarters in Michigan meant Ford did not take the opportunity to spearhead the economic boom (Tolliday 1995a: 302–304). The weak competition helped VW grow within the largely untapped German market.

Thus, Volkswagen led in automobile production because of its relatively undamaged plant and equipment, its rescue from dismantlement or designation as reparations, and the lack of competition to fill the demand of the recovering German economy. Tolliday (1995a) sums up the situation stating, "VW thus had an exceptional position compared to its competitors because of its modern equipment, large capacity, and room for expansion and because it was favored by the occupying power for its own pragmatic reasons" (301). After the introduction of the Deutschmark and the establishment of the German Federal Republic in 1949, Germany could build its postwar economy on its own terms. By the time of the handover of VW to the Federal Republic and Lower Saxony in 1949, the company had grown from 6,000 to 10,000 employees and could achieve a monthly output of 4,000 vehicles (Grieger and Lupa 2015: 39). In 1948 and 1949 VW was building just under half of all automobiles produced in West Germany and began exporting primarily to European countries (Grieger and Lupa 2015: 39). Volkswagen was therefore poised to become a major industrial producer in both the domestic and international arena.

Volkswagen began the postwar era with an auspicious and unusual combination of circumstances. It was controlled by a German manager who possessed considerable experience with American production methods. The company possessed a large American-inspired factory complex that was highly vertically integrated with thousands of advanced machine tools as well as a product inspired by the Model T and designed for mass production. A 'technologically deterministic' assumption may be that Volkswagen would walk down a nearly identical path as American firms. However, other factors led Volkswagen down a characteristically German path. VW was a publicly owned company with the state of Lower Saxony and the Federal Republic as the primary owners, and it possessed a strong works council and union that pushed for codetermination early on. Therefore, Volkswagen was in an interesting position to develop a particularly *German form of mass production* that mixed American and German characteristics.

5.2 *Postwar Reconfiguration of American Industrial Relations*

Just as the war reconfigured US labor relations, those relations were again modified in immediate aftermath before some regularity was achieved with the 1950 'Treaty of Detroit.' During the war, American unions gained significant strength, increasing from 8.7 million members in 1940 to 14.3 million by 1945 (Greenhouse 2019: 94). Workers were restless because wages had stagnated during the war and the no-strike pledge built up frustrations with management and unresolved grievances. In this context, the UAW GM division, led by Walter Reuther and representing 175,000 members, spearheaded an ambitious strike in 1946 intending to fundamentally reshape labor-management relations. The demands were ambitious, asking for a 30 percent raise and a call that GM not raise car prices, which the UAW feared would trigger inflation that would mitigate the purchasing power of the raise (Greenhouse 2019: 98).

Reuther argued the proposal was sustainable for GM because their production had risen by 50 percent since 1941, productivity increased 3 percent per year, and its profit rate had risen as high as 28 percent. GM instead offered a 12 percent raise but refused to keep down its prices (Greenhouse 2019: 98). The UAW counter-proposed that demands would be lowered if GM agreed to transparency and prove to the union and the federal government via company records that GM could not afford such a raise (Greenhouse 2019: 98; Asher and Edsforth 1995: 18). While the first ask is standard union pay-based bargaining, the second is deceivingly radical. It was essentially a proposal to force GM to accept a *form of codetermination* where "decisions about pricing and production would be made by labor, capital, and government" (Asher and Edsforth 1995: 18). Such a proposal would have set a precedent of codetermination in the US by expanding the number of joint decisions made between management and labor. Because GM was then the world's largest corporation and highly influential (Hilgar 2003), if it agreed to such a policy, this type of codetermination may have become standard in American companies and perhaps globally.

GM, however, rejected the proposals, giving Reuther and the restless UAW workers the impetus to strike. The 175,000 UAW workers walked out at eighty GM plants in nineteen states, beginning an enormous 114-day conflict (Greenhouse

2019: 99). Ultimately, the UAW lost the strike and accepted a 17 percent raise that was essentially nullified by the 18 percent inflation spike in 1946 (Greenhouse 2019: 101). This was the last time a large-scale effort was made to secure codetermination rights in the US auto industry. Management maintained their prerogative in pricing and production issues, though the grievance resolution system still countered management power, and strikes could be authorized over production standards issues (Lichtenstein 1986: 250). This constituted the general pattern of US industrial relations in the following decades.

Thus, at the same time postwar Germany reconstituted its codetermination system, efforts to establish an American version of codetermination failed, despite the strong position of American unions in the immediate aftermath. Though contingent, the factors in favor of reestablishing codetermination in Germany and their failure in the US are reflective of differences in the respective value-regimes and the path dependent trajectories that began at the turn of the 20th century. The long history of relative (skilled) worker autonomy, labor-management cooperation, and strong unions in Germany made it so codetermination systems were only *temporarily repressed* under the National Socialists, while the equally long history of dominant management prerogative, combative relationship labor relations, and relatively new unions made it so similar codetermination systems were not established in the United States. The characteristic pattern of each value-regime has path dependent effects. This is not to say that contingencies were not open, but that the fate of codetermination was influenced by the history of the value-regime and the development of the value-systems within that regime.

Despite this defeat, this strike and the 409 other UAW authorized strikes in 1947 and 1948 had a lasting effect. GM's president 'Engine' Charlie Wilson wanted to invest $3.5 billion to expand GM's production capacity in anticipation of returning veterans and increased consumer demand. To prevent continued production disruption at this crucial moment, Wilson made a proposal to the UAW that was critical to the future of labor-capital relations. In exchange for a promise of two years with no strikes, GM would provide a raise, a quarterly cost-of-living adjustment (COLA), and a two percent annual improvement factor (Greenhouse 2019: 101–102). The annual improvement factor gave GM workers a two percent additional raise that reflected productivity increases. Therefore, the workers directly benefit from GM's improving productivity and expect a consistently rising standard of living. By accepting this deal, autoworkers tied pay increases to rising productivity, which limited the rate of surplus value extraction in exchange for 'labor peace.' Yet, it also gave structural incentives for workers to consent to management control over production standards and blunted incentives for codetermination of those standards.

There was also a political backlash against the strike wave. The Democratic Party, which generally supported unions, lost control of Congress in the 1946 elections. As a result, Republicans passed the 1947 Taft-Hartley act which allowed states to pass antiunion "right-to-work" laws (Greenhouse 2019: 103). The law also banned wildcat strikes and held unions responsible for the employer's economic losses in the event of such strikes (Asher and Edsforth 1995: 19). The onus of worker discipline thereby shifted from management to the union as unauthorized rank-and-file action could legally and financially hurt the union. The interests between the rank-and-file and the union bureaucracy split as the legal and contractual landscape made practices of shopfloor bargaining and spontaneous worker actions increasingly risky.

The immediate postwar years were defined by a struggle between labor, business, and government to define postwar industrial relations. The UAW attempted to seize the mood of strong union militancy to establish a form of cooperation between labor, management, and government but ultimately failed. A different compromise was reached instead that both maintained management prerogative but allowed labor to share in productivity gains and the success of the industry. The failure to establish codetermination and the acceptance of sharing productivity gains to ensure industrial peace had important consequences in shaping the US auto industry and defining the US value-regime for decades to come. The Taft-Hartley Act also shaped labor relations because it disincentivized wildcat strikes as a tool for worker protest. These developments shaped the monumental 1950 'Treaty of Detroit.'

6 Fordist Transformations between Depression and War

The US and German value-regimes changed dramatically during the 1930s and 1940s. In the United States, the depression generated high unemployment, low sales, and a posture of technological conservatism in the auto industry. A loose labor market structure and the fervor to cut costs intensified speed-up which exacerbated workers' frustration. When the New Deal legally empowered unionization, the UAW emerged to address workers' grievances over long-standing issues. The battle for union recognition between 1937–1941 transformed the industry, making the UAW the third social system in the tripartite relationship between government, business, and labor in the American value-regime. The new relationship between management and labor was hammered out on the shopfloor where workers battled management directly through spontaneous job actions to reduce productivity to levels that workers considered reasonable. The outbreak of WWII interrupted the formalization of this developing relationship, leaving many questions unresolved. With war production, the entire value-regime transformed, and the auto industry became the 'arsenal of democracy' (Hyde 2013). Government became directly involved with industry, encouraging 'labor peace' through military contracts and the no-strike pledge (Boyle 1995). Although war production was temporary, the buildup of surplus value and equipment along with labor's pent-up irritation with wartime constraints had important effects on the long-term trajectory of the industry after the war. Postwar strikes and negotiations formalized long-term industrial relations in the US, culminating in the 'Treaty of Detroit.'

Overall, four industrial transformations occurred in these years: industrial decline during the Great Depression, the New Deal and the UAW transformed labor relations, World War II created a state of exception, and the immediate postwar struggles reformulated and formalized capital-labor relations. Each experience irrevocably changed the auto industry from the development path of the 1920s. By 1950, the industry had a strong union, more business concentration, and substantially more capital equipment and facilities thanks to military contracts. All four developments shaped the impending postwar boom.

Germany experienced a similar four-phase evolutionary path that primarily stemmed from the decisions of the Nazis. The depression restricted the already miniscule industry, but the economic malaise helped the fascists rise to power, whose industrial goals included the motorization of Germany. The generally Fordist rationalization plan allowed Germany to catch up with its European peers and may have reached the industrial capacity and productivity of the US if not for Germany's war ambitions. While American labor was organizing and gaining recognition, German labor's social systems were dismantled and consolidated, which *de facto* revoked substantive worker voice. The disempowerment of labor facilitated the implementation of American-inspired Fordist mass production in Germany, as no worker organization could stop the rationalization plans or influence them via codetermination. Working conditions were further degraded as forced foreign labor entered German and occupied European factories. In this respect, the differences between US and German government treatment of labor during the war could hardly be starker. The end of the war brought Allied occupation, and the country was divided into East and West. In the aftermath, Volkswagen was relatively undamaged while Daimler-Benz scaled back to its core facilities. The result was a West Germany that benefited from the capital buildup and was primed to begin mass production, even as all this came at an incalculable cost.

From these world-changing events emerged *state-led* modernization movements aimed at accumulating capital by reformulating the flow of value in motion. The New Deal redefined labor relations and redistributed the flow of value through Keynesianism and unions as a countervailing force (Keynes 1964 [1936]; Galbraith 1993 [1952]). In other words, the New Deal empowered labor to be an effective counterweight to management prerogative, even if the finalized system still did not include codetermination. Furthermore, forming the 'arsenal of democracy' took government led modernization to a new extreme through both government investment and intervention in industrial relations. The Nazi modernization program likewise made value in motion flow better to accumulate capital (Hachtmann and von Saldern 2009). To accomplish this, craft methods were largely replaced with Fordist assembly line production to bring commodity valorization down to enable mass consumption. The government also spearheaded these efforts through investment and changing industrial relations, though here labor relations became *more* authoritarian and oppressive rather than less. The mass motorization programs were government initiatives rather than the work of private capital alone (Hachtmann 2008: 22–23).

Despite both being state-led approaches, the outcomes for workers differed greatly. Just as US workers were increasing control over their conditions of valorization, German workers were losing control. Cooperative labor-management relations before 1933 were dismantled and labor was forcefully suppressed. Just as German workers became repressed after a history of cooperation, American workers began organized resistance against their history of repression. However, the US system did not become cooperative, but *combative* now that the state empowered unionization and the legal and contractual boundaries of struggle were drawn. Fascist worker oppression—especially of forced foreign workers—violated social justice but was nevertheless a boon for capital accumulation as it built up mass production capacities that enabled the postwar boom. Therefore, beyond the incomparable horrors of forced labor, was German fascism's contribution to production just a transplantation of American Fordism both in terms of productivity development *and* the authoritarian suppression of labor? Comparing the pre-union US industry and the German industry under the Nazis reveals parallels between Fordist and fascist logic (see Peterson 1987: 151; Flink 1988: 224–228; Bellon 1990: 243; Hachtmann and von Saldern 2009: 192).

The pre-union period of authoritarian labor suppression in the US was irrevocably transformed by the end of the 1940s. Collective bargaining became the norm with management control over production exchanged for higher valorization based on productivity gains. This left technological development to management. Management used technology both as a means of productivity development *and* as a means of worker control and deskilling (Reynolds 1989). This had implications for the long-term evolution of the US value-regime as management directed technological development displaced thousands of workers in the postwar decades (Steigerwald 2010: 440).

Nevertheless, the UAW had the means to resist management prerogative through the grievance system and strikes. Technology deployment and labor intensity standards became battlegrounds between labor and management. As Asher and Edsforth (1995) describes,

> From the end of the 1930s to the 1970s, legal and illegal worker/actions had forced the auto makers to abandon the brutal Depression era labor policies that had dehumanized workers. The agency of the UAW allowed auto workers to achieve a safer, more predictable work environment. After 1937 auto manufacturers and workers were locked in a continuous tug of war over the intensity of labor in the auto plants. (30)

In this way, even if the primary relationship between labor and capital in the US reflected the struggle for the *distribution* of value and surplus value, struggles over *controlling the conditions* of valorization, e.g., reducing speed-up and improving safety, were also fought out—just through more combative relations rather than codetermination. Capital-labor struggles were not exclusively about pay and benefits, but also about maintaining humanistic norms and values in the workplace.

The struggle appeared at a *mezzo level* of monopoly union versus oligopolistic firms in the US value-regime. It was contained at this level without concern for foreign competition because of the mutually advantageous constraints of oligopolistic domestic competition, monopoly unionism, and the *advantages of being productivity leader*. In the struggle over labor intensity, the line may become slower than what management prefers but achieving the regularity and predictability workers prefer also usually means less production disruption. Potential productivity gains may be forgone, but this can be maintained without competitive disadvantages if no other company within the value-regime or foreign competition speeds up to attain a productivity advantage. If all firms in the value-regime are under the same contractual rules that restrain productivity in similar ways, then the *socially necessary standard of productivity can drop* to the agreed upon lower level *without* impeding capital accumulation. Oligopolistic corporations negotiating with a monopolistic union makes this possible so that no company gains a competitive advantage. Thus, the Depression era speed-up ended, and the arena for competition and productivity development shifted from speed-up to technological development in the 1950s and 1960s (Hounshell 2000; Meyer 2002).

In addition, because the US had the highest productivity and capacity, restricting productivity to maintain 'labor peace' could be afforded without reference to foreign competitors. The combination of union monopoly, firm oligopoly, and productivity leadership formed a situation where speed-up is contained and the gains from productivity are shared broadly within the value-systems, including sharing with labor. Struggles against speed-up and for better pay and benefits still occurred, but this combination of factors made these fights primarily a *distributional struggle* over the gains of growth, rather than a *struggle for survival*.

However, high productivity *remained imperative* even in these ideal conditions. Imagine if GM in 1940, to ensure labor peace, committed itself to a new UAW contract that reverted production to the craft system dominant in the US before the rise of Fordism. GM workers would have more autonomy and work at a less demanding work pace—no longer paced by the machine or the assembly line. Perhaps labor peace would reign with few disruptions, yet GM would encounter other problems. The standards of *socially necessary labor time* in 1940 required that use of certain machines operating at certain speeds and workers operating on the line at certain speeds was socially necessary to produce automobiles in high volumes and at the expected price that yielded a profit. Under this scenario, it would be impossible for GM to produce at high enough volumes or with low enough production costs if the pre-Fordist system was implemented. Ultimately, labor peace would be achieved temporarily until GM declared bankruptcy.

Conversely, imagine a scenario whereby highly productive machines or speed-up produce at a significantly higher speed than any other company, but this resulted in protracted work stoppages due to extremely alienating conditions. The inconsistency of production could negate the productivity advantages when the line is operational and could also be ruinous in the long-term. The balanced path, whereby management-labor strife is kept to a minimum, yet productivity continues to rise with new work standards and faster machines and workers, is the most ideal for capital accumulation. This is a balance that capital and labor must work together to achieve as the interests of capital and labor are diametrically opposed here. Capital wants to maximize productivity to secure competitive advantage and accumulate capital, while workers want to maintain self-valorization *and* sustainable working conditions. Nevertheless, note how operating beyond capital and labor in both scenarios are the *productive standards dominant in that socio-historic context*. Both capital and labor must contend with socially necessary productivity norms. In this way, both capital and labor face *social domination*.

Even with monopolistic labor organizations and oligopolistic corporations, world productivity leadership *confers advantages* so that productivity development can be *contractually limited without obvious downsides*. At the same time, the drive to improve productivity cannot be eschewed entirely if productivity leadership is to be maintained. In Germany before 1933, productivity development appeared constrained by codetermination, compromise, and ambivalence, maintaining worker autonomy and a quality orientation at the cost of mass production and consumption (Stahlmann 1992; Hachtmann and von Saldern 2009). Yet after 1933, the Nazi regime eluded the issue of worker disruption through extreme discipline and fear, allowing rapid technological and productivity catch up. In these cases, the challenge is an *omnipresent productivity pressure* operating on multiple levels, yet the concrete solutions differ between industrial relations systems, work structures, and labor-capital combinations working to meet socially necessary productive norms.

Productivity pressure took on *social-communicative importance* in Germany during the 1920s where Fordism and Taylorism was euphorically discussed as a solution to Germany's problems (Hachtmann and von Saldern 2009: 188). There was a *societal longing* for mass consumption, but mass production conflicted with German sensibilities of honoring quality work and skilled labor (Hachtmann and von Saldern 2009: 190–195). The compromise resulted in a tentative rationalization still far behind the US standard. The Nazi state 'resolved' these contradictions through force, incorporating Fordist rationalization into fascist ideology (see Neuman 1942; Hachtmann and von Saldern 2009: 196). The motorization program turned the German auto industry from what Tolliday (1995a: 285) described as a "backwater" to Germany's largest industry by sales before WWII.

This transformation was not prompted by market competition, but by *social and political* motivations. Even with American owned firms in Germany, the domestic competitive landscape and socially necessary productivity standard was far lower than in the US, e.g., the first factory based entirely on the assembly line did not appear until Opel's Brandenburg plant in 1936 (Hachtmann 2008: 23). Therefore, the leap in productivity and spread of Fordism is better understood as the *German value-regime politically enforcing rationalization* to reach the globally dominant productive standard of the US (see Smith and Meiksins 1995). The geo-political reference point, *not market competition*, motivated and oriented Germany's modernization, making Nazi rationalization impossible without the American example. This helps explain why productivity is a *social* and not exclusively economic criterion.

Thus, German development during the interwar years was marked by the slow decline of German labor fueled by the adopted Fordist logic. As Bellon (1990) describes,

> During the First World War, the assembly of Daimler's airplane motors had required hundreds, even thousands, of skilled fitters. A quarter century of industrial and technical change had radically altered the production

> processes at Daimler. The move from skilled metalworkers to concentration camp inmates for fitting together the components of Daimler-Benz motors is symbolic of the changes in the labor process in the German motor building industry during a half-century which was marked in production technology by the accomplishments of men like Taylor and Ford. The widely touted 'German precision labor' at Daimler-Benz had become an advertising gambit; untrained women—industrial slaves—could assemble the Mercedes-Benz airplane engines. (243)

While this degradation touched nearly all workers in occupied Europe, exploiting foreign workers 'resolved' the dilemma facing German skilled workers since the 1920s. The racist assignment of repetitive assembly line jobs to foreign workers and efforts to maintain the German skilled workforce constitute a *two-tier hierarchy* based on race, gender, and skill (Stahlmann 1992: 179; Hachtmann 2008, Hachtmann and von Saldern 2009: 192). In this way, many German skilled workers did not face the expected work degradation of Fordism, thus finding a perverse "solution" to German fears of alienation on the assembly line. The work hierarchy of German skilled workers supported by (usually foreign) unskilled workers reappears continuously in the history of the German auto industry.

Taken together, is it appropriate to characterize German modernization during the 30s and 40s as a forced Americanization, or is this broadly characteristic of modernization? Though nearly universally condemned, the contradictions of German modernization appeared as a *species of capitalist modernization* rather than something aberrant. Authoritarianism characterized both the US and Germany, even if Germany reached higher extremes of exploitation and American authoritarianism had its limits. Both the US and Germany first enacted Fordism through repressing, deskilling, and alienating labor, but nevertheless experienced rapid buildup of industrial capacity and productive power (see Peterson 1987; Meyer 2004; Hachtmann and von Saldern 2009). This contradictory process between instrumental exploitation of humanity and the "progress" this enables is one of the main lessons of Horkheimer and Adorno's (2001 [1947]) diagnosis of enlightenment, where modernization entails progress and regress simultaneously. In this way, Nazi modernization is not aberrant, but an example where the usually hidden dark side of modernity is exposed and incorrectly singled out as unique. Misrecognition makes it harder to see the darker side reflected in the modernization of the victors and obscures the *social domination of productivity norms that drive modernization efforts*. The postwar question was how to proceed once consensus emerged around the necessity of mass production.

CHAPTER 3

Prosperity or Automation Hysteria? Contradictions of Growth, Productivity, and Mechanization in the Postwar Decades

1 Postwar Growth and the Economic Miracle

The postwar decades are often looked back on with nostalgia, with social scientists framing the period as exceptional for its 'social democratic' inequality regime characterized by high taxes and a strong welfare state (Piketty 2020). Keynesian policies focused on increasing consumer purchasing power to drive demand generated high economic growth and prosperity for most population segments in the United States as well as Europe. Satisfying mass demand required *mass supply* provided by increasingly productive and technologically sophisticated systems for producing mass consumer commodities. In the US, the auto industry led the charge with the adoption of transfer machines, or 'Detroit automation,' to make parts at even faster speeds (Hounshell 2000). That the US sustained its leadership is unsurprising, but what is surprising is the dramatic rise of Europe—especially Germany. The *Wirtschaftswunder*, or economic miracle, is aptly named as the German economy boomed and the auto industry, spearheaded by Volkswagen, produced millions of cars per year. The following examines the 1950s to the early 1970s as a period of growth for the auto industries of both value-regimes.

The picture is not entirely rosy however, as technological change both increased production volumes and accelerated technological displacement. Concerns over automation, a 'great automation debate,' emerged in public discourse in both the US and Germany as a policy dispute between management, labor, and government. By the 1970s, there was fraying of the apparent consensus of this era as the single model policy declined at Volkswagen and the American industry experienced mounting industrial conflict.

1.1 *The American Automobile Oligopoly*

The US automobile industry dominated the world during the 1950s and 1960s, maintaining the highest production and sales by far. By 1955, the industry produced around 75 percent of world car production and the Big Three had 95 percent of the US auto market in 1955 (Womack et al. 2007 [1990]: 42–43). The industry continued to concentrate as smaller companies such as Packard

 | DOI:10.1163/9789004736719_005

and Studebaker either merged or went bankrupt, leaving the Big Three to dominate the largest auto market in the world. The lack of competition from either domestic or foreign competitors meant that the Big Three functioned as an oligopoly, reaping high profits from a booming postwar market. The peak of around 5 million cars sold in 1929 was far surpassed when production reached 8 million in 1950, 9 million in 1955, and 11 million by 1965 (Klier and Rubenstein 2020: 51). The oligopolistic conditions even enabled price increases by 36 percent during the 1950s—despite increasing productivity—since no competitor could compete with the expected price and product quality of the Big Three (Rooke 2008: 4). Being supplied by major industries such as oil, glass, and steel, and receiving the support of local, state, and federal governments through road and highway construction, the automobile became the locus of national transportation policy, constituting an 'automobile-industrial complex' centered around the Big Three (Sweezy 2009; see Flink 1988: 358–376).

Most US autoworkers also benefited from the postwar boom, not from the postwar expansion alone but through collective bargaining. After the 1948 GM contract guaranteed raises, cost-of-living-adjustments (COLA), and an annual improvement factor for auto workers in exchange for two years of no strikes, the 1950 contract built upon this agreement to become a landmark in labor-management collective bargaining. The unprecedented five-year contract increased the COLA and annual improvement factor, established a generous pension plan, and GM agreed to pay 50 percent of worker's healthcare insurance. This amounted to a 20 percent income increase over the five-year period *after* factoring in inflation. This generous contract stunned journalists who termed it the 'Treaty of Detroit.' In exchange, management was promised 'labor peace' for the duration of the contract while retaining many management prerogatives including planning production and technology deployment. The contract became very influential, not just because Ford and Chrysler quickly adopted nearly identical contracts, but because hundreds of businesses across the country, both union and nonunion alike, emulated aspects of the agreement in their own benefits packages (Greenhouse 2019: 104). This contract became the foundation that built the American middle class and solidified the general pattern of the US value-regime where companies pay workers well in exchange for management maintaining Taylorist control over production. Workers negotiated for *increased valorization* over more *control over the conditions of valorization*. As Asher and Edsforth (1995) summarize,

> Reuther … eschewed radical attempts to challenge management control over decisions about pricing and plant location. Rather, the UAW sought, and won, higher wages, greater income security (productivity increases,

> cost-of-living-adjustments, supplementary unemployment benefits, and job retraining programs) and greater social security (group life, health, and dental insurance plans), a safe work environment, and management observance of the rights workers were accorded in the contracts signed by the auto companies. (18)

This arrangement was viable during this period of sustained economic growth but became increasingly difficult to maintain as the rest of the world caught up to the United States in terms of mass production technology and production capacity.

The early 1970s saw the erosion of Big Three dominance as weaknesses within the US value-regime contributed to the long-term decline. Signs were already apparent by the 1960s, as the 95 percent domestic market held in 1955 had dropped to 84 percent by 1960 and to 83 percent by 1970 (Womack et al. 2007 [1990]: 42–43; Klier and Rubenstein 2020: 48). In 1960, 7 percent of market share came from European imports, which would have been unthinkable before WWII. In addition, the around 75 percent share of global auto production from US producers between 1950–1955 dropped to only 48 percent in 1960 and to 28 percent by 1970 (Klier and Rubenstein 2020: 51). This shows the dramatic rise of the, primarily European, production systems that followed Fordist mass production methods to produce high volumes. Because the US was by far the largest auto market in the world, foreign companies, above all Volkswagen, aimed to penetrate the US market. The success of the Beetle in the United States demonstrated that the Big Three *no longer possessed decisive advantages* in terms of product and production technologies. There was, nevertheless, still little cause for concern for the Big Three because they remained remarkably successful during postwar decades.

1.2 *The German Wirtschaftswunder*

Equipped with the production materials made under the Nazi regime, Germany launched into a sustained period of economic growth known as the *Wirtschaftswunder* or economic miracle. The magnitude of this staggering growth is reflected in the growth in the auto industry. With a little over 300,000 autos produced in 1950, the industry grew to produce over 2 million in 1960, 42 percent of which was manufactured by Volkswagen (Flink 1988: 297, 322). This surpassed the production numbers of France, Italy, and Britain, with Germany surpassing Britain as the second largest automobile producer in the world by 1956 (Flink 1988: 297). Germany quickly became a motorized country with nearly a million registrations in 1952, jumping to 4.5 million by 1960 and 8.3 million by 1964 (Tolliday 1995a: 327). In addition, German passenger car production was oriented toward foreign markets, with 46.7 percent of production being exported in 1960 compared to 2.2 percent of passenger car production in the US (Flink 1988: 297). Like the US, the industry became highly concentrated, as 87 percent of production occurred in Volkswagen, Opel, Daimler-Benz, and Ford by 1960, while 28 smaller firms closed between 1956 and 1960 (IG Metall 1962: 65; Flink 1988: 297). In these same years, the industry grew by 99,000 workers (a 32.6 percent increase) while productivity increased by 47.7 percent (IG Metall 1962: 65). Europe was a sellers' market for the first two postwar decades as the continent rebuilt from war.

The German production system in the postwar era is, however, *not* a mere adoption of the American production system. Although the production technologies and organization were similar to American Fordism, the industrial relations in greatly differed. Systems of codetermination, works councils, and trade union bargaining reemerged after the war and were enshrined in the German Basic Law. Works councils made up of both blue and white collar worker representatives became the foundation for the codetermination system in the Works Constitution Act of 1952 (Jürgens 1995: 295; see Fisher 1951). This act established works councils at multiple levels in a company and guaranteed their right to access certain business information and consultation rights on various management decisions, including the ability to veto certain management prerogatives. The production issues covered by codetermination have expanded over time and cover concerns that in the US are the sole responsibility of management. These include selection of personnel in the case of layoffs, scheduling overtime, determining the system of wages and salaries, defining work organization, training protocols, and introducing new technologies (Jürgens 1995: 295).

The codetermination rights also extend to the supervisory board. Whereas in the United States company boards are comprised solely by shareholders, in Germany, large firms are legally obligated to structure their supervisory boards with an equal number of managers and workers with one neutral member (Horst and Sabel 1991). At Volkswagen, after its partial privatization in 1960, the board contained two members each from the federal government and the state of Lower Saxony. Government representatives were often sympathetic to labor, meaning that workers were almost always favored in supervisory board decisions (Ewing 2017: 25).

Trade unions bargain with employers' associations at the industry and regional level, rather than at the company level as in the US. IG Metall negotiated wages and other trade union issues with auto industry employers' associations within each region rather than having to negotiate with each company and expecting that the agreement of one company is mirrored in the others.

Although German law draws distinctions between works councils and trade unions, IG Metall quickly organized the autoworkers and gained sufficient membership and influence in the works councils so that, though distinct organizations, their interests are essentially coterminous (McKenney 2018: 81). As Turner (2009) explains, "in a process that would only deepen, unions had largely taken over the works councils, in effect turning these legally protected bodies to their own purposes" (296). Together, these social systems formed the foundations of German industrial relations that define the German value-regime. They structure the basis for Germany's *soziale Marktwirtschaft* or social market economy based on non-market coordination (see Hall and Soskice 2003 [2001]).

Many Europeans also recognized that rebuilding a prosperous Europe meant competing with the economically and politically dominant United States. This was framed as meeting the 'American Challenge' through the transfer of American cultural and economic practices so European firms could compete on equal terms with the US (Servan-Schreiber 1968; Hilger 2003: 15). This involved the "implementation of growth-oriented productivity concepts such as rationalization, automation, and 'economies of scale,'" as well as adapting US corporate structures and professionalizing management (see Sloan 1964; Hilger 2003: 3). This signified convergence toward a US model of production, management ethos, firm culture, organizational structure, and global orientation. This was necessary because German firms needed exports to grow, and American technological systems and efficient industrial management system were framed as the "universally accepted model for globalization" (Hilger 2003: 2; Ewing 2017: 33–34). According to Hilger (2003: 7) German companies succeeded by "adopting management practices and technological expertise from the United States," until "German companies started catching up to their American competitors." Therefore, both convergence *and* divergence occurred within the German value-regime, with convergence tendencies in production technology, work organization, and corporate structure, yet divergence in terms of industrial relations, workforce composition, and quality orientation. *Productivity pressure* to catch up to the socially necessary standards of productivity set by the United States generated confluence around similar solutions to production problems and productive development, yet *how* production questions were handled differed due to Germany's industrial relations system and codetermination.

The Volkswagen Beetle was an exemplar of Europe's response to the 'American Challenge' as VW adopted the high productivity of American firms while forging their own path in terms of industrial relations, product ethos, and marketing strategy (see Hilger 2003; Hiott 2012). The breakout success of the Beetle in the US contributed to high exports and high profits for VW that were reinvested in new production technology that closely rivaled American productivity standards. Ultimately, Volkswagen pursued mass production with a single model strategy that was "more Fordist than Ford" to generate mass economies of scale suitable for rationalization and automation (Tolliday 1995a: 329). However, just like The Ford Model T in the 1920s, the single model strategy began to show weakness in the late 1960s just as Germany's staggering economic growth began to slow. Therefore, the narrative here is both one of meteoric rise and hidden fragilities in industrial policy that resulted in a crisis by the mid-1970s.

2 Transfer Machine Automation in the US and Germany

The term automation was coined by Delmar S. Harder, Ford vice president of manufacturing, in 1947. Automation first referred to transfer machine technology that "permits the progressive machining of parts through long series of transfer machines without manual handling" (Ford Motor Company Archives 1953a: 1). This original meaning quickly expanded to encompass a wide range of labor-saving activities in the 1950s and 1960s, e.g., computers (Steigerwald 2010: 431). Because of its origin in the auto industry, the transfer machine soon became known as 'Detroit automation.' The discussion tracks the development and spread of Detroit automation and its effects on workers.

2.1 *Detroit Automation in the United States*

There were isolated experiments with transfer machine technology in the 1920s and 1930s, but the primary impetus for its development was the high level of investment during WWII and the postwar explosion of consumer demand (see Hounshell 2000: 102–109). The first major application of the transfer machine was in 1946 when Buick rebuilt its engine plant. Here, eleven transfer machines with between six and twelve stations were installed that automatically drilled, milled, bored, and reamed different parts of the engine block (Hounshell 2000: 114–115). The system was interconnected between roller conveyors and several standalone machine tools to connect the machining complex into a single production flow. After this initial small-scale installation, the race to implement transfer machines began with billions of dollars invested between 1945–1955, including engine plants at Ford's River Rouge as well as at Packard and Chrysler (Hounshell 2000: 114–117).

Ford was the most aggressive promoter of automation. The company formed an 'Automation Department' in 1947 and issued numerous press releases and publicity tours to display the 'modernness' of Ford plants (Jürgens 2023: 173–174). Ford's most famous example of Detroit automation was the Cleveland Engine Plant that opened in 1951. The factory consisted of three buildings, two engine plants and a foundry, that produced seventeen types of engine models by 1955 (Meyer 2004: 8; Jürgens 2023: 174). The transfer machines deployed in Cleveland dwarfed the simple system at Buick. Touted as the "world's most modern automotive facility," the transfer machine complex comprised of 42 machines linked by automatic transfer devices that effectively made the separate machines one automatic and interconnected mechanism (Ford Motor Company Archives 1952a). If laid out in a straight line, the total process would extend out to 1,545 feet, covering 46,200 square feet in space. The complex performed 530 precise cutting and drilling movements, moving workpieces sequentially from operation to operation without human intervention from rough casting to finished engine block (Ford Motor Company Archives 1952a; see Meyer 2002: 71). It not only transferred parts between machines, but automatically turned and adjusted pieces to achieve the necessary precision (Steigerwald 2010: 431). The system was directed by "electric nerve-centers" that direct the machines as workers supervise the multi-station push-button control mechanisms (Ford Motor Company Archives 1952b: 2; Steigerwald 2010: 431). The theory behind the transfer machine was no different from the Fordist principles of flow production on the assembly line, but now the machining activity was performed automatically through interlocking mechanisms and conveyors. At the same time, the individual machines were not intrinsically different from the single purpose machines deployed in Ford's factories for decades. What is new and makes transfer machines 'automation' is the *elimination of manual effort and attention* needed to move work pieces through the process, meaning that Detroit automation was essentially an innovation in mechanical handling rather than a fundamentally new production machine (see Bright 1958: 61).

When running continuously at normal speed, transfer machines performed metal machining faster and with more precision than human workers and saved the time and manual work needed to load and unload parts. This resulted in higher parts per hour and lower direct labor costs (Meyer 2002: 70). For example, one plant reported it previously required four hundred workers forty minutes to machine an engine block, while the automated system only required forty-eight workers and fewer than twenty minutes (Meyer 2002: 71). The production capacity at the Cleveland Engine plant was enormous, with a planned output of 4,500 engines per day or 1.5 million engines per year (Ford Motor Company Archives 1952b: 3). Transfer machines ensured lower per unit value thanks to the high speed of the machines and lowered value expenditure on direct workers.

The productivity gains, while usually net positive, were often less than their potential due to the frequent downtime and maintenance issues. With such large and complicated machinery, numerous problems can emerge from the failure of electrical equipment, to wear on hydraulic devices, to tool breakage (Hounshell 2000: 121). Standalone machines also encounter such problems, but downtime issues take on higher stakes in an interlocked transfer line, where failure in one part of the machine complex can breakdown the entire line. As one Oldsmobile engineer explained, "Not everything is wonderful about these machines. The greatest problem is keeping them running. When one [station] is down, all are down" (Hounshell 2000: 121). One company reported that their machine downtime was so extreme that the equipment was inoperable as much as 50 percent of the time (Hounshell 2000: 123). The net cost calculation, therefore, was between saving labor costs and cost per unit when the machines are working versus the additional costs accrued during machine downtime and hiring the necessary maintenance and repair workers needed to service the machines. As one Packard engineer reported in 1949, direct labor costs were reduced by 34 percent due to automation, but the costs of indirect labor had risen considerably, resulting in only a 17 percent net cost reduction (Hounshell 2000: 125).

Automakers therefore needed to respond to the problem of downtime. GM, for example, organized their automation to be less complex and susceptible to breakdown through segmenting the transfer line and providing in-between machine inventory areas (Hounshell 2000: 123–124). This made it possible to shut down sections of the transfer line for repairs or maintenance without having to shut down the entire complex, thus working to "assure full operation even in the event of a shut-down of any station or section" (Hounshell 2000: 124). Ford, by contrast, maintained interconnected transfer machines at the Cleveland plant, but had a 'police force' of maintenance personnel who continually performed preventative maintenance (Hounshell 2000: 126). In either case, efforts were made to control the performance of the machines as much as possible to maximize machine uptime.

The struggles against downtime reflect the fundamental valorization goal of keeping value in motion within production processes. In terms of the *time of valorization*, an hour-long strike is *equally* disruptive to the flow of value as an hour of machine downtime. Even though they have different origins and motivations, both are problems to solve from the point of view of capital accumulation. This also has implications for the *social domination of productivity pressure*, as widely differential downtime rates can impact costs, with those who are better able to control production time and manage production stoppages, whether from workers *or* equipment, are in a better position to secure productivity and cost advantages. At this micro shopfloor level, maintaining production at expected time standards is experienced as productivity pressure. At a mezzo or macro-competitive level, differential rates of machine downtime result in competitive disadvantages for those with high downtime, exerting another form of productivity pressure.

Another issue was the relative inflexibility of transfer lines. Here, realization demands for yearly model changes were in tension with the high productive capability of transfer lines (see Meyer 2004: 8). Transfer machines were inflexible and time consuming to retool, so their ideal deployment was for long runs of standardized products. However, the 'horsepower race' began in the mid-1950s where a variety of high-powered engines were in demand, so engine plants needed to adapt their transfer machines to become more flexible (Hounshell 2000: 130). A degree of standardization and interchangeability of transfer machine stations was eventually achieved thanks to the combined efforts of Ford engineers and the machine tool industry. Yet, the relative inflexibility of transfer line technology meant that even exchanging and retooling the more flexible machines was still an expensive and time-consuming process (Hounshell 2000: 130–134). This new generation of transfer machines were "enormously productive when machining long runs of standardized parts. They could accommodate change in product. But by no means were they remotely akin to … idealized, perfectly flexible universal machining centers" (Hounshell 2000: 134). Decentralizing production and producing fewer types of parts at each plant also helped the flexibility issue, though no fast and inexpensive method of adding flexibility to the transfer machine emerged (Jürgens 2023: 186–187).

Transfer lines also appeared for many other automobile production processes in the mid-1950s through the 1960s. Pontiac attempted to match Ford's Cleveland plant with their own 70,000 square foot facility that housed transfer lines not just for the engine blocks, but for cylinder heads, pistons, connecting rods, camshafts, and crankshafts, thereby automating nearly the entirety of engine production (Edsforth 1995: 164). For Ford, "advanced" transfer machines that reduce "manual handling of materials to a minimum" were used in the company's foundries, stamping plants, and engine manufacturers (Ford Motor Company Archives 1953b: 2–3). By 1957, new equipment automated the nickel and chrome plating processes in the body plants, which became widespread by the early 1960s (Edsforth 1995: 164). Automating the manufacture of major components and machining processes was pursued throughout the industry.

How did the transfer machine transform labor for the autoworkers? The Fordist division of labor since the mid-1910s comprised a small stratum of skilled workers performing tasks such as tool and die making, a large middle layer of unskilled or semi-skilled machine operators and assemblers, and a lower layer of unskilled workers. Final assembly remained labor intensive, but Detroit automation directly affected the semi-skilled machine operators and some factions of skilled workers. Instead of single machines with several machine tools performing separate tasks that required workers to load and unload parts, inspect them, and move them from one machine to the next, the transfer machine moved the part to each subsequent step without manual transport (Steigerwald 2010: 431). Previously, operators had some control over work pace and output because they controlled loading, cycle starting, and unloading the machine. With the transfer line, the work speed is determined by the automated machinery (Meyer 2004: 8).

Therefore, the transfer machine made the job class of 'machine operator' essentially superfluous. Transfer machines typically only needed one supervisor and two maintenance workers to occasionally replace tools and conduct repairs, whereas previously around 150 worker operated individual machines were needed (Nevins and Hill 1963: 365; Meyer 2002: 66). As Steigerwald (2010) explains, the semiskilled workers who "previously handled and moved parts were rendered obsolete. So too were machinists, press operators, and other skilled workers who previously had been responsible for the most intricate parts of an automobile" (431). In some automated areas, this resulted in a 90 percent reduction of direct workers (Abernathy 1978: 193). For new facilities, the reduced need for direct workers is rendered invisible because the machine operators who otherwise would need to be hired if not for the transfer machine simply do not get hired, obviating the need for their employment rather than directly eliminating it (see Hicks and Devaraj 2015). Thus, less skilled workers declined in automated plants through "a process of 'silent firing' with the loss of new entry-level machine and assembly positions" (Meyer 2002: 87). Updated older plants, however, did experience layoffs, such as Ford's Dearborn iron foundry where 1,000 jobs were eliminated when their cylinder block operations were automated in 1953 (Edsforth 1995: 166). This was a serious problem, as Willoughby Abner (1963), assistant director of the UAW, stated in 1963,

> Even where normal attrition is consciously used to prevent layoffs—from the standpoint of society—the net result may well be simply to shift the burden from the worker who is not laid off to the one who wasn't hired by that company. Or the burden may fall on the worker who gets laid off in the next recession and never gets called back. (2–3)

The employment and displacement effects of automation are obvious for some and invisible for others as some opportunities for labor valorization are destroyed while others fail to materialize.

Though many machine operators faced technological displacement, automation proponents argued not to fear technological unemployment because many more indirect skilled workers were needed to maintain and repair the automated equipment. As Ford Vice President Ray H. Sullivan (1953) argued,

> We may need fewer sweepers, fewer unskilled workers with monkey wrenches, but we need many more engineers, electricians, mechanics, electronics experts, tool and die designers and makers, and the hundred and one other specially skilled workers required to keep the tremendously complex production lines in working order. (13)

It appeared there was partial compensation for direct labor loss with indirect labor gain, as described by a Ford representative speaking before the 1955 Subcommittee on Automation,

> During the year 1950, a monthly average of 8,253 direct labor employees worked on engine production, compared to a monthly average of 6,339 such employees in 1954. What happened to the people apparently displaced by automation? Although there were 1,854 less direct labor personnel employed in 1954 than in 1950 on engine production, these people were absorbed in our other operations. In addition, in 1954 there were 976 more skilled maintenance personnel employed on engine manufacture than in 1950. (Cited in Hounshell 2000: 127)

Thus, labor costs shifted from direct to indirect labor and the net balance of workers was generally negative.

The nature of skilled work also changed for those working with automated equipment. At the Cleveland Engine Plant in 1953, the local contract specified two new automation based job classifications for skilled workers (Meyer 2002: 75). Both jobs required the skills to adjust and repair the machines, but they also entailed less autonomy because the workers were closely attached to the machine complex (Meyer 2002: 76–87). This became a source of grievance for many skilled workers who resented the loss of independence and resisted performing deskilled tasks (Meyer 2002: 80–81). Therefore, in contrast to claims that automated plants require more skilled workers with upgraded skills, automation deskilled most of the transfer line workers, making them a patrolling observer performing tasks that take less than a week of training to master (Bright 1958: 176–185; see Jürgens 2023: 173–185).

The automobile boom in the postwar decades did increase total blue and white collar employment in the auto industry. Thanks to automation, "heavy physical labor was reduced, more skilled and technical positions were created, and plant safety did improve" (Edsforth 1995: 166). However, automation shifted labor force composition, resulting in a decline in production workers. For example, though auto output rose by 90 percent between 1947 and 1963, production jobs declined by 9 percent (Edsforth 1995: 166). The UAW reported "160,000 autoworkers displaced between 1947 and 1960 … while productivity increased 50%. Retirements, displacements, and jobs not re-filled cost the union nearly a half million members between 1955 and 1963" (Steigerwald 2010: 440). Other industries such as oil refining, petroleum, steel manufacturing, and railroads also experienced simultaneous production employment decline and productivity rise, with 1.1 million production jobs lost between 1957 to 1961 with an hourly output gain of 18 percent (Steigerwald 2010: 440). Framing the postwar decades as a period of economic prosperity shadows the substantial job displacement that occurred. The American economy was already moving away from an industrial foundation of semi or unskilled production work by the 1960s. Though many workers were absorbed into other industries, many social scientists, unions, and government officials attributed the stubbornly high unemployment rate from 1957 to the mid-1960s to structural causes like automation (Steigerwald 2010: 439; Woirol 1996: 77–143).

2.2 *Becoming More Fordist Than Ford and the Source of the Wirtschaftswunder*

Rebuilding the German auto industry required establishing a mass auto market. The necessary production equipment and facilities were present, but the key was execution. Western European countries were not oriented just toward their own development but also toward globalization, entailing closer integration with each other and the United States as the 'capitalist West' became a political-economic block (see Hilger 2003). Because of American geopolitical hegemony and the economic power and reach of their multinational corporations, European countries understood the project of postwar renewal as an 'American Challenge' (Servan-Schreiber 1968; Hilger 2003). This entailed becoming not just a motorized country, but a value-regime based on export driven growth—especially exports *to* the United States. According to Baccaro and Pontusson's (2016) growth model paradigm, Germany generally favored export driven growth over domestic consumption growth (see Klein and Pettis 2020). The rise of the Volkswagen Beetle demonstrates this evolution of the German value-regime and illustrates how technological deployment, automation, and increased productivity helped accomplish economic renewal. The thesis is that Volkswagen claimed leadership of the German auto industry by becoming, to paraphrase Tolliday (1995a: 329), "more Fordist than Ford." Considering the ambivalent reception of Fordism in Germany, this may appear surprising. Nevertheless, by embracing Fordist principles, Volkswagen became a major player in the world automotive industry.

Volkswagen became "more Fordist than Ford" through its "single-minded pursuit of a single-model policy" (Tolliday 1995a: 329). Up to the early-1970s, the Beetle was Volkswagen's primary product, just as Ford from 1908 to 1927 was focused on the Model T. Rejecting yearly model runs or even modest styling changes, Volkswagen CEO Heinrich Nordhoff focused on improving quality and incremental refinements rather than fundamentally changing Porsche's design (Tolliday 1995a: 330). A single highly standardized product allows for uniform production processes that could be performed at high speeds. Committing to one model synergized with the standardized production equipment to generate a highly productive system that rivaled US competitors.

Other companies also recognized the need for increased standardization. Daimler-Benz drew upon American manufacturing methods to base their new models on a uniform construction platform because "economies of scale contribute to global competitiveness by decreasing productivity costs" (Hilger 2003: 11). However, it took time for German companies to perfect interchangeability. As Hilger (2003) states,

> As far as standardizing components such as engines, gearboxes, axles, and chassis was concerned, most of the German companies still lagged behind their American counterparts in the 1960s. In 1963, Ford plants in Cleveland produced up to 2,500 engines per day; it took Daimler-Benz in Stuttgart 17 hours to produce only one. (11)

The postwar ethos was nevertheless oriented toward closing this productivity gap through mastering mass production.

In 1950, Volkswagen produced 90,038 vehicles with a production workforce of 13,322 (Grieger and Lupa 2015: 59; Flink 1988: 322). There was not much need for new investment at this time because the existing equipment was not yet used at full capacity, with many machines that had been idled since the end of the war. Therefore, the limited investment was aimed primarily at bringing the existing lines to full utilization in addition to mechanizing transportation and materials handling (Tolliday 1995a: 336). Production capacity rose through adding labor to the line rather than new investments (Tolliday 1995a: 331). In September 1954, Nordhoff proposed a rationalization and expansion program that would implement conveyor belt assembly and increased automation (Grieger and Lupa 2015: 66). By this point, Volkswagen had grown rapidly to become the world's fourth largest automaker, but the rationalization program promised to enable Volkswagen to approximate the output of the Big Three (Flink 1988: 324).

The 1954 rationalization program sought to mechanize production (Nordhoff 1958a: 4). The equipment that survived the war was primarily individual multi-purpose machines, but the rationalization program replaced these tools with single-purpose tools (Tolliday 1995a: 311). Deploying single-purpose machines was the same move Ford made to synergize standardized production processes with the single model in the 1910s and 1920s. Production process flow was also rationally rearranged, and welding processes were upgraded (Tolliday 1995a: 331). Though Nordhoff was familiar with transfer machines, they were not implemented in this rationalization wave because "the workflow in the machine lines of mechanical production is running smoothly—even if not automatically. There is no intention, therefore, to undertake fundamental changes in the framework of this project" (Volkswagen 1954: 3; translation mine).[1] Nevertheless, Nordhoff instructed his management team to stay in contact with firms familiar with transfer lines so VW can closely watch future developments (Jürgens 2023: 254). In this memo to management, he also emphasized the importance of technology in saving costs,

> I would like to make it clear (...) that the need to save costs and labor through modern machines and equipment and through the greatest possible mechanization and automation remains the highest law of development. We are entering a period of tough competition, especially against firms of American background in Germany and England. (Jürgens 2023: 254; translation mine)[2]

This reflects how Germany's earlier ambivalence toward technology has subsided, at least among corporate leaders like Nordhoff (see Hachtmann and von Saldern 2009).

Productivity and output rose enormously with 329,893 autos built in 1955, with a production workforce of 28,606 (Flink 1988: 322; Grieger and Lupa 2015: 69). Two years later, the production output of 40,000 cars per month was a

1 Original German text: "weil der Arbeitsfluss in den Maschinenstraßen bei der mechanischen Fertigung reibungslos—wenn auch nicht automatisch—abläuft. Es besteht deshalb vorerst nicht die Absicht, hier grundlegende Änderungen im Rahmen dieses Projektes vorzunehmen" (Volkswagen 1954: 3).

2 Original German text: "Ich möchte klarstellen, (...) daß die Notwendigkeit, durch moderne Maschinen und Einrichtungen und durch weitestgehende Mechanisierung und Automatisierung Kosten und Arbeitskräfte einzusparen, oberstes Gesetz der Entwicklung bleibt. Wir gehen einer Periode des härtesten Konkurrenzkampfes, insbesondere gegen Firmen mit amerikanischem Hintergrund in Deutschland und in England, entgegen." (Jürgens 2023: 254).

figure on par with Ford or GM factories in the US (Tolliday 1995a: 338). With new technology, increased capacity, and Fordist strategy, Volkswagen was approaching the productivity standards of US firms.

At first, German domestic demand was underestimated by Ford, Opel, and VW. Yet around 1958, VW could not fulfill approximately 32,000 export orders and 70,000 domestic orders, signifying a lack of capacity. Nordhoff feared that if production capacity was not expanded that VW would lose market share to Ford and Opel as they raced to increase capacity in anticipation of burgeoning demand (Tolliday 1995a: 330–335). From 1957–1960, a 668 million Deutschmark plan was initiated to aggressively invest in new productive technology to meet the explosive demand for the Beetle.

Detroit automation first appeared in Wolfsburg in 1958, replacing many single purpose machines (Tolliday 1995a: 331).[3] Transfer machines were applied in many production areas to increase productivity and deploy less workers. For example, buffer rod production in 1961 entailed a team of twenty-one workers deployed on single purpose machines producing 400 parts per shift or 19 per person. By 1965, a transfer machine complex required three workers who produced 800 parts per shift or 266 per worker, thereby doubling the output with a fraction of the labor power (Volkswagen 1965). Much of the new investment between 1958–1960 modernized such component and sub-assembly plants (Tolliday 1995a: 338). The press shop shifted to transfer lines in 1957, making it so pressed parts only needed materials handlers at the end of the presses, rather than placing them into and out of each press one by one (Jürgens 2023: 256–257).

Body construction became one of the most automated areas. Previously, work groups performed body construction with manual welding equipment at stationary assembly areas (Jürgens 2023: 257–258). By 1958, a specialized circular transfer line was developed in-house for body construction that performed hundreds of spot welds while monitored by a few workers (Jürgens 2023: 259). Automated box shell construction took only 18 seconds, which was double the speed of GM's Lordstown plant and three times as fast as Ford's factories (Abernathy 178: 137; Jürgens 2023: 260). Finished bodies were then transported via the so-called 'rocket conveyor' (*Raketenband*), known for its high speed (Jürgens 2023: 260). By the late 1960s, the Wolfsburg body shop was the most automated area with up to 80 percent of tasks automated (Jürgens 1994: 95). Because of this, 440 body shop workers were displaced and absorbed into other

3 Daimler-Benz also pursued automation, as Moll (1961) reports that mechanical production at Untertürkheim had reached 57 percent in 1948 and advanced to 67 percent in 1956 (55–58). Beginning in 1951, transfer lines were used at Daimler-Benz to produce engine blocks, axles, and other parts (Woltereck 1956a).

production areas, while the new system produced 3,300 units a day (Grieger and Lupa 2015: 90). Assembly processes remained primarily manual or aided by electric hand tools, but by now German manufacturers had mastered the assembly line (Jürgens 2023: 263–265).

Thus, Beetle production became highly automated thanks to multiple waves of rationalization and capital investment. The Beetle's high standardization and lack of yearly model changes made the Beetle *even more* compatible with the relatively inflexible Detroit automation than Detroit's automobiles. As Jürgens (1994) describes,

> The standard product was produced with highly standardized process equipment. The high production volume justified, economically, high investments in process equipment; thus the degree of mechanization in the machining and in the body shop areas for the Beetle production was very high at the end of the 1960s already. (95)

The strategy proved fruitful. Between 1948 and 1968, the necessary production time to manufacture the Beetle fell from 196 to 56 hours—an efficiency gain of 350 percent (Jürgens 2023: 266). Combining rationalization, expanded capacity, and automation, Volkswagen first produced over one million cars a year in 1962, with production of the Beetle passing one million by 1965 (Grieger and Lupa 2015: 89; 97). Volkswagen manufactured twice as many cars as Opel in 1964 and held a 33 percent share of the passenger car market in Germany (Grieger and Lupa 2015: 82).

For the first time, a German auto company came to an equivalent level of productivity and production capacity as US firms—a feat unthinkable in the 1920s or even the 1930s. This was accomplished through conscious efforts to reach the productivity and productive scale of the Big Three. To stand on the level of the American corporations, Volkswagen had to become "more Fordist than Ford," through its embrace of mass production and automation. Direct comparison was intentional as Nordhoff claimed that automation at Volkswagen was at the same level as American auto factories (Wolfsburger Allgemeine 1966). Nordhoff also appeared to have a cost-benefit mindset characteristic of US firms. In a 1958 speech, Nordhoff (1958b) declared that the purpose of automation at vw is to achieve "top economic performance" through the criterion of "superior cost-effectiveness" rather than achieving "technical perfection" (1; translation mine).[4] Considering Germany's tight labor market,

4 Original German text: "Nein, es geht hier nicht im die technische Perfektion, sondern um die wirtschaftliche Bestleistung, und allein die überlegene Wirtschaftlichkeit ist das Kriterium." (Nordhoff 1958: 11).

rationalization according to Nordhoff was not about saving labor, but about "obtaining a higher production output with the limited number of workers available" (Enz und Metter Bote 1958; translation mine).[5] Such statements convey a *convergence of mindset* or *consensus* around the value of automation between German and American management (see Hilger 2003).

Just as in the United States, rationalization and automation had dramatic effects on the workforce. However, Germany's unique circumstances, such as the limited labor market in the 1950s and 1960s and the cultural preference for skilled labor and qualifications, created a distinct labor structure in postwar Germany (see Lüdtke 2009). Increased automation led to the development of new job types such as the *Anlagenführer* (automated systems controller) who controlled and directed the automated equipment. Thus, increasing automation provided many jobs for skilled workers who developed and manufactured the automation equipment in-house (Kern and Schumann 1984, 1987; Jürgens 1994: 95; Jürgens 1998: 281). However, there were typically more workers with qualified skills then there were positions within the skilled trades, so many skilled workers performed production tasks that did not require their skills. Approximately 60–50 percent of the workforce had some type of skill qualification between 1955 and 1965, but only 30–40 percent of the workforce was formally designated as a skilled worker (Jürgens 2023: 271–272). Therefore, a relatively large portion of the qualified workforce performed semi-skilled or unskilled jobs.

Nevertheless, German workers continued to pursue credentials. This partially stemmed from the fact that apprenticeship training was seen as an intrinsic good and the number of trainees accepted for training was not based on need. Much of the willingness of skilled workers to work in jobs 'inferior' to their qualifications was based on the expectation that they could be chosen to fill a vacancy in a skilled trade should one arise. It was also expected that future developments in technology and automation would require increasingly more skilled workers even at the 'lowest' levels of production (Jürgens 2023: 273). As Jürgens (2023) describes, "These were all essential qualification-related and socio-cultural pillars of automation, and they shaped the mindset of the workforce to be oriented toward mastering technological change and the demands of automated production" (274).[6] Therefore, many skilled workers did not view automation with fear but hoped it would enable them to exercise their skills.

5 Original German text: "Es handelt sich nicht darum, durch die Rationalisierung und Automatisierung Arbeitskräfte einzusparen, sondern mit den vorhanden in der Zahl beschrankten Arbeitern eine höhere Produktionsleistung zu erzielen" (Enz und Metter Bote 1958).

6 Original German text:"Dies alles waren wesentliche qualifikationsmäßige und sozialkulturelle Stützen der Automatisierung, und sie prägten ein Mind-Set der Belegschaft, das

The labor structure was also shaped by the arrival of foreign guest workers (*Gastarbeiter*). The continued growth of the German auto industry required an influx of new workers—despite the displacement and obviating effects of automation. During the late 40s and early 1950s, Volkswagen was a major employer of refugees from Eastern Europe in the postwar migration (Jürgens 1994: 95). But refugees were unavailable in the late 50s and early 60s when capacity expansion was needed urgently. Therefore, in the early 1960s Italian guest workers were recruited, becoming 5.5 percent of the workforce in 1967 and growing to a peak of 16 percent in 1973 (Jürgens 1998: 281; Brumlop and Jürgens 1983: 29). This generated job polarization in the division of labor, with Italians tending to do repetitive unskilled work on the line while skilled German workers performed skilled tasks such as quality control or rework (Jürgens 2023: 268–270). While there was never an official policy to arrange a polarized core-and-fringe workforce, it was a recognizable trend (Jürgens 2021: 8; Jürgens 2023: 268–270). The presence of foreign workers generated less pressure to improve working conditions in the most unskilled tasks (Jürgens 1994: 95). After the mass layoffs of foreign workers during the mid-1970s, however, there emerged an earnest effort at humanizing work in German auto factories (see Brumlop and Jürgens 1983).

Overall, the German workforce benefitted from automation for two reasons. First, increasingly sophisticated technology served both the interests of management for increasing capacity and productivity and the interests of skilled workers who had a strong affinity for skilled 'quality' work (Lüdtke 2009). Even qualified workers who worked unskilled jobs anticipated future waves of automation that may allow them to eventually employ their skills. Secondly, automation, increased productivity, and higher capacity grew the company rapidly, thus ensuring that displaced workers are reabsorbed into another production area. It was generally understood that automation was unlikely to threaten one's employment at Volkswagen, even if transfers often occurred due to technological change. However, this does not mean workers were totally unconcerned about automation. The complex orientation and attitudes of workers toward automation in both countries is discussed further below.

auf technologischen Wandel und die Beherrschung der Anforderungen einer automatisierten Produktion ausgerichtet ist" (Jürgens 2023: 274).

3 The Great Automation Debate

Detroit automation was one technological development among many driving an international debate on the significance, impacts, and potential of automation. The debate triggered discussion of a range of topics such as scarcity and abundance, work and leisure, and the future of jobs, education, and skills. For the auto industry, automation transformed work in many areas, which caused renewed negotiations between management and labor on issues such as job demarcation and transfers. It also altered the priorities of collective bargaining as policies were proposed to regulate automation and ameliorate technological displacement. Government policies were based either on an expansionist view that automation is positive because it drives economic growth, or a structuralist view that automation was causing structural unemployment (Woirol 1996). The contours of these debates in both the US and Germany are discussed here. Comparison is fruitful because the points of agreement between labor or management in both countries are just as illuminative as the differences in priority and policy.

3.1 *UAW Ambivalence towards Automation: Expansion or Structure?*

American workers were generally ambivalent about automation due to their structural position and the personal and systemic stakes (see Steigerwald 2010). The 'great automation debate' in the 1950s and 1960s was the first time a sustained automation discourse emerged simultaneously among numerous social systems, and the UAW was positioned to influence that discourse and suggest policy. Yet, the efficacy of labor advocacy is ambiguous partially because of this ambivalence. On the one hand, many workers stood to lose from automation as they can be laid off or transferred when their skills become embodied in the machine. On the other hand, the higher productivity from automation increased material wealth while decreasing the value per unit so commodities could become cheaper, thus benefiting workers. For auto workers, the annual improvement factor meant they directly benefited financially from the improved productivity. The contradictory desire to contain or manage the downsides of automation while maximizing the positive benefits characterized American labor's ambivalent stance (Automation Committee 1954; Conway 1955). The following examines worker views on automation, including both the rank-and-file and the national leadership, and the efficacy of their collective bargaining and national political strategies.

On the shopfloor, no codetermination rights meant that the UAW had no legal or contractual right to influence the implementation of new production technology. Nonetheless, Detroit automation triggered novel collective bargaining issues. Examining the Cleveland Engine plant during the 1950s, Meyer (2002: 88) describes how collective bargaining issues such as wage rates and classifications, delimiting skilled trades, and worker displacement—especially older workers—were crucial problems for UAW Local 1250. For new automation workers, the union wanted management to recognize their expanded work content and area of responsibility and raise wages accordingly (Meyer 2002: 78–79). The Preliminary Report of the UAW-CIO Committee on Automation argued that "management must be brought around to the acceptance of the principle that automated and semi-automated jobs require new classifications and rates whether in new plants or old" because of the increased responsibility and output, even if there is less physical effort (Automation Committee 1954: 2). It was, however, troublesome to classify these new job types as they combined aspects of numerous skilled trades. Even after positions like the 'automation equipment operator' and 'automation equipment setter' solidified, conflict arose over defining their work domains and wages (Meyer 2002: 75–83). One UAW shop chairman described the problem this way:

> Our entire wage structures are being distorted and disrupted due to automation. We can't argue where a job is changed, where the skill has been reduced in that job, where the responsibility is reduced, where the human effort is reduced, for higher wages ... As far as skill is concerned, the skill is in the machine. It isn't in the individual anymore. Our entire wage structure, the basis on which we had to argue our wage demands ... has been disrupted. (Cutler 1998: 351)

Automation made renegotiating valorization a thorny issue, especially considering how scarce skilled labor secures high wages through market leverage. If previously scarce skills were now performed by machines, then such skills cannot demand a wage at all, let alone a high wage, if "employers were learning to be less dependent on skill, and less dependent upon living labor itself" (Cutler 1998: 352). How to handle new classifications with cobbled together skills was a dilemma for the union.

Automation also generated novel production-standards issues as workers adjusting to the new equipment often complained of speed-up from "antagonistic" foremen who pushed production beyond humane limits (Meyer 2002: 72). Union representatives and foremen "squabbled continually on the shop floor" as absenteeism and shop floor grievances rose (Meyer 2002: 79). There were four unauthorized work stoppages in 1953 and two unauthorized walkouts in 1954, which idled 1970 workers and resulted in 8,439 lost man hours

(Meyer 2002: 84). Tensions, wildcats, and grievances over automation became commonplace thereafter (Meyer 2002: 86).

Another hotbed of rank-and-file resistance was Ford's River Rouge plant. As the largest local in the UAW, with a peak of 89,000 members, the bargaining priorities of Local 600 had special importance for the entire union (Cutler 1998: 32). As a response to Local 600's experience with automation and reports of similar experiences across the country, the local spearheaded a movement to fight for thirty hours work for forty hours pay, hereafter the '30 for 40' movement, where weekly hours would be reduced to thirty with total pay remaining the same as a forty hour week (see Cutler 1998, 2004; Edsforth 1995).

The appeal of 30 for 40 is basic supply and demand. If a constricted labor supply gives workers more market leverage and drives up the price of labor power, then reducing the number of working hours for the same pay has the *same labor restricting effect* that can deliver a similar wage premium. This is also advantageous because labor replacing technology typically has the opposite effect of decreasing the demand for labor and increasing the leverage of employers. This was a result of automation and company efforts to decentralize production by "seeking out geographic locations where labor markets were, at least temporarily, more flooded and workers were more modest and self-sacrificing" (Cutler 1998: 7). If automation, decentralization, and outsourcing were weapons to loosen the labor market, then 30 for 40 was a means to tighten it again. The labor shortage from 1941–1945 was due to the war, but a 30 for 40 program could deliver analogous peacetime results (Cutler 1998: 6).

The ideological core of the 30 for 40 movement is *labor market syndicalism*, i.e., a movement to withdraw "supply of a commodity in a sustainable manner" collectively as "Self-valorizing movements of market sellers" (Cutler 1998: 8). Syndicalist policies were often proposed by the rank-and-file to improve the workers' opportunities for self-valorization within the capitalist labor market, both in terms of increased wages and for spreading the work, thereby blunting the impact of technological displacement. As one Local 600 pamphlet put it, "a 30-hour week, with no reduction in pay, so that workers share the fruits of automation, instead of becoming victims of it. THIS IS THE KEY TO ENLIGHTENED LABOR UNION WELCOMING TECHNOLOGICAL IMPROVEMENTS" (Cutler 1998: 292; emphasis in original). Here, 30 for 40 turns workers from victims into beneficiaries of automation if the available work is broadly distributed through purposeful restriction of labor supply. Hypothetically, if labor hours with no changes in pay were freely flexible, then *no technological displacement would occur* if the necessary work was spread among enough workers, instead of concentrated in the hands of a few while the others are displaced. Even if inter-company job transfers were available, reducing working hours also lessens the need for transfers, thereby avoiding retraining and adjustment problems. This was an important motivating logic behind the 30 for 40 movement.

By contrast, *corporatist policies* that "set aside *market leverage* in exchange for *political sovereignty*" were supported by the UAW national leadership (Cutler 1998: 11; emphasis in original). Corporatism resembles socialist policies for increased worker control over the means of production or codetermination rights in Germany. They seek to give worker voice in decision-making and the opportunity to change objectionable conditions (Cutler 1998: 10–12). Walter Reuther aspired to corporatist co-management when the UAW pushed to influence prices in the 1946 strike (see Greenhouse 2019: 98–101), but the union ultimately had to settle for less control over industry than the codetermination rights guaranteed in Germany. Nevertheless, Reuther's collective bargaining strategy tended toward pursuing *political power over market leverage*.

Because of this split in tactics and policy, there were considerable tensions between Local 600 and Reuther's administration (see Cutler 2004). Although many UAW publications in the early 1950s included discussions on "Automation and the Shorter Workweek" with promises to "place [the shorter workweek] at the top of our collective bargaining agenda," they hedged by stating that this would be the next demand *after* winning the guaranteed annual wage (Cutler 1998: 353). Walter Reuther insisted that the timing was not right to fight for shorter hours,

> I would like that thirty hour week with forty hours pay. I would like to even go them one better. As a matter of fact, I'd like a twenty hour week. But I know damn well we are not going to get it in 1955, and I don't want to make any worker believe that we are even going to try, because we can't. (Cutler 1998: 357–358)

Furthermore, in the debate whether workers should aim for more leisure or more consumerism, Reuther revealed his Keynesian tendencies by arguing that "our basic fight is to get the purchasing power to buy the things we make … We don't want more leisure. We want more goods, and when we have enough goods, then we will fight for more leisure" (Steigerwald 2010: 435; see Schor 1992). The UAW would keep the forty hour week in the immediate bargaining plans if higher productivity improved the pay for UAW workers and increased material wealth. But Local 600 was concerned that automation was generating layoffs, and redistributing jobs through lower working hours was more important than higher wages for those who remain. They argued the fight for shorter hours should not be postponed:

> We are of the opinion that that time has arrived. Industry has made tremendous strides in installing automation which resulted in thousands of workers being laid off every day. We are concerned with jobs for all—not a guaranteed wage for the few who will be lucky enough to remain at work. We believe that now is the time to begin preparing for the fight for the 30-hour week with 40 hours' pay because we believe that is the only foreseeable solution to create jobs for the jobless ... We call on the International Union officers to change their position and join with Local 600 in fighting for a better life for all Americans—NOW. (Cutler 1998: 310)

Reuther's refusal to push for 30 for 40 hurt the rank-and-file movement. Because the Reuther administration had tight control over the UAW's agenda, the 30 for 40 movement did not become a serious UAW demand, despite the advocacy from its largest local. Local 600 was right that automation and decentralization would heavily impact the River Rouge, as employment dropped from 85,000 workers in 1941 to 28,000 by 1961 with around 4,000 unemployed union members (Cutler 1998: 461). The 30 for 40 movement of the 1950s and early 1960s was one of the last major rank-and-file pushes for reduced working hours in the US auto industry. It also reflected the split between rank-and-file advocacy and union leadership, as less solidarity and identification with the union became more common among US rank-and-file workers (see Yates 1992). By contrast, solidarity with the works councils and IG Metall is ubiquitous in Germany, and lower hours movements in Germany won concessions over the years, demonstrating that corporatist and syndicalist tactics need not be mutually exclusive (Brumlop and Jürgens 1983).

The UAW leadership was, however, not apathetic toward automation and its effects on the workers but were instead ambivalent. They held optimism, shared with many employers, that automation could usher in an age of abundance and reduce the drudgery of assembly line work, but they were also cautious about its potential effects on workers and employment (Steigerwald 2010: 432–433). This sentiment was described by Jack Conway, the head of the UAW's Automation Committee, when he stated, "We do not fear the automatic machine. We welcome better tools that take the danger and drudgery out of our work. What we oppose is blind, irresponsible use of these new tools" (Conway 1955: 2). This expressed both the hope that automation would benefit workers and the potential for automation to harm workers, especially when deployed by American corporations. Reuther also argued automation could result in abundance, as he stated his official position in 1954 that,

> Automation must be met sanely and constructively … so that the miracle of mass production—and the ever greater abundance made possible by automation—can find expression in the lives of people through improved economic security and a fuller share of happiness and human dignity. (Steigerwald 2010: 434)

Here, Reuther saw potential in automation to improve living standards, but only when it was managed well.

However, by 1955, as over 150,000 auto workers were laid off and Detroit unemployment sat at 8.3 percent, despite the success of the Big Three, it was obvious to the UAW leadership that collective bargaining policies were urgently needed to shield workers from automation (Steigerwald 2010: 436). The Reuther administration's primary policy to defend from automation was the guaranteed annual wage (GAW). The logic behind the GAW was that because the "wealth producing potential of automation is matched only by its potential for disruption and chaos" workers should have enhanced employment and income security so that "the nation can meet these revolutionary possibilities within the framework of employment security" (Automation Committee 1954: 4). Originally proposed as an income and employment security program, the national automation discourse prompted the UAW to "graft" the GAW onto the union's automation program (Meyer 2002: 88). The GAW's primary goal was to stimulate management to provide steady full-time employment by guaranteeing income protection for a full year of layoff for workers with sufficient seniority (CIO 1953: 75). Companies would make payments to laid off workers, in combination with state unemployment insurance, so that they are paid the same amount as on the job, thus making their annual wage guaranteed whether in good or bad economic conditions.

Such a program also restructures corporate incentives. First, it incentivizes firms to advocate for more generous unemployment insurance, because the more generous the welfare system the less employers would have to pay through the GAW to laid off workers (CIO 1953: 78). Second, it disincentivizes implementing automation during economic downturns when major layoffs may occur, as the program places financial responsibility for dismissals on the company. Instead, the "introduction of new and more efficient equipment would be geared to periods of expanding markets so that other jobs would be available for the workers displaced by automation" (Automation Committee 1954: 4). Finally, the program discourages outsourcing, as moving production or closing factories generates layoffs whose costs are borne by the company. Without the GAW, workers could be left "stranded and give rise to the widespread creation of ghost towns" (UAW Automation Committee 1954: 4) through deindustrialization, but with the program, "Instead of closing one plant to shift production elsewhere, concerns can give proper weight to the great human cost imposed on the community that would be abandoned" (CIO 1953: 78). Management would therefore be motivated to consider the social consequences of automation and outsourcing since they bear additional costs from layoffs. They would be more likely to implement technological change that minimizes disruptions (Steigerwald 2010: 436).

Though the originally proposed policy was not adopted, supplemental unemployment benefits first appeared in Big Three contracts in 1955, eventually reaching 95 percent of a worker's regular pay over a year (Steigerwald 2010: 437). The program paid out $86 million within its first three years. Yet, it did not eliminate technological displacement, as Reuther attested in 1961 stating that "instability has by no means disappeared" (Steigerwald 2010: 437). Nevertheless, the GAW represented a corporatist policy aimed at influencing management decision-making and shifting the costs of automation and layoffs from workers to employers (see Cutler 1998: 223–224).

Beyond contractual battles, the UAW also engaged politically by advocating for national policies to manage automation and increase economic prosperity. Here, the UAW's ambivalence complicated their efforts because they appeared to support both the structuralist *and* expansionist interpretation of automation (see Woirol 1996). The *structuralist* position holds that the high unemployment between 1955 to 1965 was attributable to *structural unemployment*, i.e., "unemployment caused by a mismatch between available jobs and the skills and abilities of available workers" (Steigerwald 2010: 440). In light of the hundreds of thousands of autoworkers displaced by automation and the above average unemployment in Detroit, the UAW had sympathy with this view, as evidenced by their advocacy for the GAW and the rank-and-file 30 for 40 movement to address technological displacement (Abner 1963: 8). The UAW did, for example, influence the passing of the Manpower Development Training Act of 1962 that formed national vocational and retraining programs that retrained tens of thousands of workers (Steigerwald 2010: 442).

At the same time, the UAW also at times espoused the *expansionist* view that Keynesian policies that encourage economic growth could solve the automation problem if growth creates more jobs than automation destroys. As Walter Reuther put it in 1954, "Automation is more of a social and political than a trade-union problem. As long as the economy keeps expanding, the immediate problems of automation will work themselves out" (Cutler 1998: 328). He also expressed how the union changed from seeing automation as a bargaining table issue to a problem that "demanded an expansive social democracy" in response (Steigerwald 2010: 439). To this end, the UAW supported policies like increasing the minimum wage, improved unemployment compensation, early retirement benefits, and stimulating consumer demand (Cutler 1998:

350; Steigerwald 2010: 445). As UAW Automation Committee member Nat Weinberg stated, "A high level of demand would serve both to minimize the magnitude of adjustment problems arising from technological change, and to facilitate the adjustment process" (Steigerwald 2010: 442). Therefore, the union leadership favored both expansionist and structuralist policies to attack the issue of technological displacement and unemployment from multiple angles (see Reuther 1962). Though the Kennedy and Johnson administrations both passed Keynesian growth policies that the UAW championed, this increasingly came at the expense of structuralist policies as the mainstream discourse came to embrace the thesis of *creative destruction* that technology may be disruptive and displace workers but always creates more jobs than it destroys (see Woirol 1996: 77–127; Schumpeter 2003 [1942]). The UAW leadership was ambivalent about this too because the union-approved expansionist policies were being adopted, but the structuralist concerns of automation were being disregarded (Steigerwald 2010: 444–445).

American worker attitudes toward automation were internally conflicted. There was a tension between wanting more goods, but also the desire to cushion the shocks of technological displacement. Supplemental insurance cushions against technological displacement, but to the extent it discourages new technology deployment, then the annual improvement factor is decreased and the broader societal benefits from more output may be foregone. Workers also want new machines to relieve physical drudgery, but not to the point that jobs are eliminated. Thus, workers are necessarily conflicted because of their structural position and multiple contradictory interests that cannot be simultaneously fulfilled. Nevertheless, some structuralist and expansionist policies were adopted between the 1950s and 1960s, with the UAW accomplishing some of their bargaining and policy goals.

Workers and management have many opposing interests, but they share an interest in the successful flow of capital as value in motion. Workers have an interest in the flow of value because workers expend labor time to self-valorize and have an interest in increased production to aid realization for consumers. In their *dual role* as workers and consumers, they have a general interest in the capitalist flow of value, even if they also have special interests in their individual valorization. Management also needs worker valorization to generate the purchasing power needed for realization. Yet, there is still the management specific interest in accumulating surplus value, and automation aids this by increasing the rate of relative surplus value (Marx 1976 [1867]). Automation transforms work processes and saves costs through reducing direct labor requirements. The contradiction between the *common* and *special interests* of both sides are exemplified in the famous anecdote about Walter Reuther in an automated factory. As Reuther tells the story,

> Several years ago, when I went to the Ford-Cleveland engine plant where they had fully automated the production of engines, and I looked over the acres and acres of automated machinery, I was asked by a management person how I liked the situation, and I told him I was very much impressed, and he says, 'Well, you won't be able to collect dues from all these automated machines,' and I said, 'you know, that is not what is bothering me. What is bothering me is, how are you going to sell cars to all these machines?' And you know, we can make a great progress in the production of automated equipment, electronics and all that, but we're still going to have to make the consumers the old-fashioned way. (Murrow 1957: 9)

Tensions arose as both parties recognized how automation can negatively affect their interests in valorization *and* realization, i.e., how automation can eliminate opportunities for valorization that may subsequently limit opportunities for realization, thus endangering the entire system of capital as value in motion. The expansionist solution to this dilemma was to rely on economic growth to offset lost jobs and increase both profits and wages (see Piketty 2014). In the context of oligopolistic competition and high growth rates, relying on growth to counter automation concerns was plausible. Indeed, when Vietnam war defense spending and the absorption of young men into the military began in the mid-1960s, economic expansion made growth the "watchword of economic policy" so that "automation as a key issue was abandoned" (Woirol 1996; Steigerwald 2010: 442). Therefore, growth became the 'solution' to the automation question at this time.

Yet workers also have interests beyond capital. Workers do not only act on their instrumental rationality but also based on value rationality, i.e., values pursued for their own sake apart from cost-benefit analysis (see Weber 2013 [1922]). Asher (1995) describes how US autoworkers balance their instrumental and value rationality stating,

> In the broadest sense, auto workers had a more complex moral code than their employers. Auto workers believed that management had only one value: efficiency. Most auto workers, like other wage earners, were not opposed to efficiency per se. They understood that if their employers did not make a profit, there would be no jobs. Auto workers invariably felt that their managers and company executives were grossly overpaid, and were unfairly rewarded, even when they had failed to meet earnings targets. They realized that all foremen and managers were under pressure to make their plants or work areas profitable, under pain of dismissal or demotion. But production workers' moral sensibilities told them that

> human values had to be factored into decisions about what constituted a fair day's labor effort. Women and men had to be protected against injury, against a debilitating and enervating work pace, and against arbitrary dismissal if they protested against specifically unfair treatment, or if they violated factory rules because the frustration of performing alienated labor made it impossible to contain their anger and aggressive impulses. (132)

Labor versus management struggle is therefore not just about value distribution in the capitalist sense, but about human values such as dignity, fairness, health, and safety. Recognition of this is missing from the typical management perspective. Assuming managers are correct that union policies such as 30 for 40 or the GAW would decrease the productivity of the industry, workers *may accept this trade off*, not based on financial cost-benefit calculation but based on humanist or social justice criteria not taken seriously by management. As UAW representative Nat Weinberg (1974) explained,

> To workers, job satisfaction is *an end in itself* even if it should result in somewhat *lower* productivity. When the UAW won increased relief time for assembly line and certain other workers, it compelled the auto industry to hire literally thousands of additional workers to get out the same volume of production. That, obviously meant lower productivity, but what was wrong about it? (10; emphasis in original)

This also demonstrated the *ambivalence of labor toward productivity*, being in favor of general societal productivity, but against productivity pressures that push beyond human limits or against human values.

In the postwar decades when the United States was the largest industrial superpower, collective bargaining gains primarily improved the standard of living and added fringe benefits such as increased pensions, holidays, health insurance, and supplemental unemployment insurance. The lack of codetermination limited the opportunity to realize humanistic values at auto factories so long as the Taylorist split of management control and worker subservience remained central to American industrial relations. Nevertheless, note how the success and oligopolistic conditions of the auto industry were *preconditions* to making such gains. With the auto oligopoly, a booming domestic market, the relative lack of foreign competition, *and the efforts at staying on the technological and productivity forefront*, such concessions—although nothing is conceded without tough collective bargaining—were possible in part thanks to these favorable conditions.

3.2 *German Workers Codetermine Automation*

The debate surrounding the social and economic effects of automation was international. In Germany, the automation discourse took on a different character due to the unique circumstances of the German value-regime. The perceived need to adopt modern technology was wrapped up with the 'American Challenge' and competing with the United States at the global level (Servan-Schreiber 1968; Hilger 2003). During the *Wirtschaftswunder,* there was rapid expansion of production capacity, while the swift adoption of new technologies both increased employment *and* caused technological displacement. However, because of decades of nearly uninterrupted growth in the auto industry, there were few reports of *external* worker displacement. Yet the *internal* transfer of workers from job to job within the same company became so intense that in 1968 the landmark *Rationalisierungsabkommen* (Rationalization agreement) was enacted to address these issues.[7] This agreement codified the procedures for transfers and technological displacement, and it represented the aim of IG Metall and the works councils to reach a satisfactory compromise with management on the implementation of rationalization measures. Such corporatist policies reflected the different priorities and structural possibilities enabled by the codetermination system in Germany and the cooperative relationship between capital and labor. However, even as the policies differed, the ideological framing of automation between the US and Germany also had many similarities. The following explores the automation debate in Germany and the major policies enacted during this period.

For German workers, the starting point of the discussion surrounding automation was codetermination. In the early postwar years, IG Metall was most concerned with "achieving and securing the right of codetermination … starting with the individual company up to the highest positions in the central economic organization" (IG Metall 1954: 20; translation mine).[8] Besides exercising codetermination to gain higher wages and secure employment, their intention was for rationalization measures to be implemented with the active involvement and participation of the workforce (IG Metall 1952: 176; IG Metall 1956: 108). The union saw this codetermination of rationalization as necessary because of how automation was restructuring the economy (IG Metall 1958: 13).

---

7 The full title of the agreement was the *Abkommen zum Schutze der Arbeitnehmer (Lohnempfänger und Angestellte) vor Folgen der Rationalisierung* or the "Agreement to Protect Workers (wage and salaried workers) from the Consequences of Rationalization."

8 Original German text: "Erringung und Sicherung des Mitbestimmungsrechtes … beginnend beim Einzelbetrieb bis zu den höchsten Stellen der zentralen Wirtschaftsorganisation" (IG Metall 1953: 20).

Shared between US and German labor was the sense of ambivalence toward automation (see Brumlop and Jürgens 1983: 22–23). For IG Metall, automation supplied the "technical and productive preconditions for the final defeat of poverty in the world and for a high standard of living for all people" (IG Metall 1956: 39; translation mine).[9] They emphasized that they were willing to promote and support technical progress because they recognize how automation can be used to raise living standards (IG Metall 1958: 41). Yet, the union was also "aware of the economic and social risks bound up with the application of new manufacturing processes" (IG Metall 1958: 41; translation mine).[10] This ambivalence was echoed in the Volkswagen works council statement in 1982 on the introduction of industrial robots that there was "No general condemnation of the new technology, no obstruction of its introduction" but that there were demands for "the consideration of social consequences … and … for full codetermination by the affected employees in the planning and introduction of industrial robots as an essential prerequisite for the demand for social control" (Brumlop and Jürgens 1983: 23–24). Thanks to codetermination rights, worker intervention in the introduction and planning of technology was common.

For German workers in the 1950s and 1960s, with the memory of the Great Depression and WWII still fresh, labor's primary demand was for higher wages that rose in tandem with technical developments to drive the emerging mass consumer society (IG Metall 1953: 176–177; IG Metall 1962: 120). This demand made sense because, unlike in the United States, total employment in the metal industries continuously rose until the first postwar recession in 1966–1967 (IG Metall 1968: 75). IG Metall appreciated economic growth because "the introduction of new or improved technical processes do not appear to have adverse effects on the level of total employment as long as industrial production is growing" (IG Metall 1960: 51; translation mine).[11] Yet, as growth slowed in the late 1960s and early 1970s, decreasing employment in the metal industries due to automation became a concern. They identified automation and rationalization as the primary cause of the declining employment as the "labor saving effect of technical change can only be balanced through economic growth"

9 Original German text: "die produktionstechnischen Voraussetzungen für die endgültige Beseitigung der Armut auf dieser Welt und für einen hohen Lebensstandard für alle Menschen mit sich" (IG Metall 1956: 39).

10 Original German text: "Wir sind uns aber auch klar über die wirtschaftlichen und sozialen Risiken, die mit der Anwendung neuer Fertigungsverfahren verbunden sind" (IG Metall 1958: 41).

11 Original German text: "Generell ist festzustellen, dass die Einführung neuer oder verbesserter technischer Verfahren sich auf die Höhe der Gesamtbeschäftigung nicht ungünstig auszuwirken scheint, solange die industrielle Produktion wächst" (IG Metall 1960: 51).

(IG Metall 1974: 417; translation mine).[12] Achieving higher growth to ameliorate technological displacement was therefore an issue for IG Metall, especially for the auto industry during the oil crisis in 1973. However, the auto industry was among the healthiest metal industry in terms of employment, so the primary goal of German auto workers at this time was to develop procedures to regulate *internal* technological displacement and job transfers (IG Metall 1974).

Because of the continuous expansion for the auto industry, the combination of increased capacity and technical change did not typically lay off employees (*external* technological displacement) but transferred them into other production departments (*internal* technological displacement) (IG Metall 1958: 42). Such internal transfers affected hundreds or, in the case of Volkswagen, thousands of workers in the metal industries (IG Metall 1960: 52). Because technological changes did not result in layoffs, the auto firms frequently framed automation as an unproblematic socio-economic development. But IG Metall claimed such a characterization was misleading. Workers suffered through no fault of their own when they were forced to take on unfamiliar jobs due to new technology (IG Metall 1958: 42). There was the additional difficulty of finding jobs where the workers could earn their previous wages. According to IG Metall, management often took transfers as opportunities to suppress wages, especially when the new assigned tasks bore little in common with the previous tasks (IG Metall 1960: 52). Such problems formed the impetus for rationalization reforms targeting the issue of job transfers.

The calls for reform culminated in the Rationalization Agreement of 1968. Adopted in each auto company through negotiations with IG Metall, this agreement regulated rationalization processes in the industry. The opening statement expressed the ambivalence toward automation held by the workers,

> Rationalization, including mechanization and automation, as a constant process of economic and technical development, creates the necessary preconditions for economic growth and contributes to securing and improving the achieved standard of living ... However, rationalization measures can also have adverse consequences for employees. With this agreement, the parties to the collective agreement therefore strive to avoid or reduce such adverse consequences that arise from rationalization measures as much as possible. (Rationalization Agreement 1968: 1; translation mine)[13]

12 Original German text: "Der arbeitssparende Effekt des technischen Wandels kann nur durch Wirtschaftswachstum ausgeglichen werden" (IG Metall 1974: 417).

13 Original German text: "Die Rationalisierung unter Einschluss von Mechanisierung und Automatisierung als ein ständiger Prozess der wirtschaftlichen und Technischen

If technological or organizational changes are planned that could negatively affect workers, the works council was to be immediately informed about proposed changes, and management and the works council were required to reach an agreement regarding the possible personnel and social effects (Rationalization Agreement 1968: 2). The agreement stipulated that management is obligated to offer affected employees equivalent work through relocation or transfer, or if there is no equivalent work available, then the affected workers should have priority to equivalent work should it become available. If retraining is needed, then the costs of retraining are borne by the company, and the workers are entitled to receive their previous earnings for the duration of the retraining for up to six months (Rationalization Agreement 1968: 2–3). Finally, if rationalization causes layoffs, then the workers receive a severance package based on the time worked at the company (Rationalization Agreement 1968: 3–4). Overall, this agreement represented a corporatist means of regulating rationalization to benefit the workers so that they do not bear the disadvantages of technological progress, while employers enjoy its advantages.

Despite the extensive protections, reimbursements, and codetermination rights provided in this agreement, the focus remained on reducing the negative effects of automation rather than blocking technological change. This is partially because of the recognition that automation increases productivity and thus generates economic growth but also because of an awareness that improving productivity through new technology is necessary for the long-term survival of the company and therefore of jobs. In one IG Metall report, they state that negative employment effects from automation often occur in companies that *do not automate*, rather than ones that do (IG Metall 1958: 43). This is because "it is often the case that technically backward companies have difficulties with sales and have to make layoffs and, under certain circumstances, are even liquidated" (IG Metall 1958: 43 translation mine; see IG Metall 1961: 61).[14] This is how IG Metall explained the bankruptcy of the German automaker Borgward in 1961, where the firm laid off 19,000 workers because it could not

Entwicklung schafft notwendige Voraussetzungen für das wirtschaftliche Wachstum und soll dazu beitragen, den erreichten Lebensstandard zu sichern und zu verbessern … Durch die Rationalisierungsmaßnahmen können aber auch nachteilige Folgen für Werksangehörige entstehen. Die Tarifvertragsparteien streben deshalb mit diesem Abkommen an, solche nachteiligen Folgen, die durch Rationalisierungsmaßnahmen entstehen, nach Möglichkeit zu vermeiden oder zu mindern" (Rationalization Agreement 1968: 1).

14 Original German text: "… ist es oft der Fall, dass technisch rückständige Konkurrenzunternehmen in Absatzschwierigkeiten geraten und Entlassungen vornehmen und unter Umständen sogar liquidieren müssen" (IG Metall 1958: 43).

compete with its larger competitors such as Daimler-Benz and Volkswagen. They describe how,

> Even if different factors also played a role, it is certain that the lack of high levels of mechanization and automation contributed considerably to the collapse. In the long run, one cannot compete against automobile factories with modern equipment using manual methods. (IG Metall: 66; translation mine)[15]

In other words, the failure of Borgward to practice the *contemporary norms of socially necessary labor time* contributed to its collapse. This became even more important after the oil crisis when the Volkswagen works council agreed that rationalization processes aid in "securing the future of the firm through better products and improved productivity. It hopes that jobs can be maintained by means of an improved position in world market competition" (Brumlop and Jürgens 1983: 22). This is why the works council agreed to not obstruct automation, "because of international competition [condemning or obstructing new technology] would only lead to a redundancy scheme 'social plan' which would not be good for any of the affected workers" (Brumlop and Jürgens 1983: 23). Compared to American attitudes, it appeared that the cooperative stance between workers and management produced a heightened awareness of the role that automation played in securing the future of businesses and jobs.

Because Europe had to engage in technological catch up with the United States to meet the 'American Challenge,' it appeared obvious that the higher productivity attained through automation was necessary to compete with the United States. The US, meanwhile, did not take foreign competition into account when implementing technology and often used technology to weaken the union—a practice which did not appear in the IG Metall accounts (Reynolds 1989; Steigerwald 2010: 446). However, labor's conflicted attitude toward automation was common between the US and Germany, with the main difference lying in how structural differences in industrial relations enabled different policy achievements.

15 Original German text: "Wenn hier auch unterschiedliche Faktoren eine Rolle spielten, so steht doch fest, dass unterlassene Hochmechanisierung und Automatisierung wesentlich zum Zusammenbruch beigetragen haben. Man kann nicht auf die Dauer mit handwerklichen Methoden gegen modern ausgerüstete Automobilewerke konkurrieren" (IG Metall 1962: 66).

3.3 *Management Perspectives on Automation*

The following draws from public statements from management representatives in the United States and Germany to reconstruct the arguments used to promote, legitimate, and justify, corporate decisions to automate production. There are commonalities between the arguments made by automakers in both value-regimes. Their statements reveal how management ideologies closely align and aim at achieving optimal conditions for accumulating capital. To the extent that automation and technological progress achieved such ends, management was generally ready to defend automation.

Automakers framed their motivations for adopting automation as improving product quality, increasing production, and reducing labor costs, which thereby generated prosperity (Steigerwald 2010: 431). Heinrich Nordhoff stated in 1965 that automation had given a tremendous boost to productivity which offered a better product with better quality and a lower price then what was possible in 1953 (Wolfsburger Nachrichten 1965). The connection between prosperity, productivity, and mass production was clear for Nordhoff: "What remains is the fact, beyond any momentary differences of opinion, that productive power and productive performance is the foundation for prosperity and nothing else" (Nordhoff 1958b: 2; translation mine).[16] The chairman of the Board of Directors at Daimler-Benz echoed this when he stated that, "It will only be possible to achieve a higher standard of living for all if we produce more, better, and in a more rationalized way with our present labor force" (Könecke 1956a: 2). Praising technology was commonplace in the US because fascination with new technology had been part of American ideology since its founding (see Hounshell 1985; Flink 1988: 42–46). It is more noteworthy to see similar sentiments from German representatives considering how ambivalent the German attitude was toward productivity and adopting new technology in the first several decades of the 20th century (Bellon 1990; Stahlmann 1992; Hachtmann and von Saldern 2009). This reveals an ideological convergence around the importance of technology, automation, and high productivity in the US and Germany.

Unlike labor's conflicted views, management straightforwardly agreed with the expansionist view and disregarded the structuralist framing that automation was causing unemployment, which was also shared by conservative economists and many politicians and technocrats in the 1960s (see Woirol 1996; Knowles 2017: 118–143). As Henry Ford II declared to the President's Advisory

16 Original German text: "Bleiben wird die Tatsache über alle augenblicklichen Meinungsverschiedenheiten hinaus, dass immer die Produktionskraft und die Produktionsleistung die Grundlage für den Wohlstand sein wird und nichts anderes" (Nordhoff 1958b: 2).

Committee on Labor-Management Policy, "I disagree most emphatically with the effort to characterize automation and technological advance as a major cause of unemployment" (Ford II 1961: 1). When asked if automation was responsible for unemployment, General Motors president Harlow Curtice responded, "no, automation is what put 60 million men to work" (General Motors Heritage Center 1954: 2). Volkswagen's Nordhoff gave some credence to the notion that there may be some displacement, but denies automation is a source of dismissals: "naturally there can be a temporary overabundance of manpower during [automation's] practical implementation, but this is avoidable with proper planning. In not a single case has rationalization been a reason for layoffs" (Nordhoff 1958b: 3; translation mine).[17] Regardless of whether these they sincerely believed automation does not produce unemployment, they nevertheless argued against rhetorically connecting automation and unemployment.

Management claimed that automation triggered transformations of production that displaced direct labor and required more indirect labor. The common narrative was that while the composition of the workforce shifted from "sweepers" and "unskilled workers with monkey wrenches" to needing more "engineers, electricians, mechanics" etc., such shifts would not result in technological unemployment (Sullivan 1953: 13). As one Ford engineer stated in 1955, "the future of automation, we think, is encouraging. We believe that automation will create more, not less, jobs and industry" such as higher skilled jobs in electronics and machine tool building (Murie 1955: 17). From management's viewpoint, technological displacement will occur, but this outcome is inconsequential if new jobs replace old jobs, which, according to the expansionist view, is assured if automation generates economic growth. The new jobs, it is argued, typically required intellectual rather than physical skills. Nordhoff argued that automation makes this necessary because, while the worker who does physical work loses value every day, the machines can do what the worker can do better and without fatigue (Die Presse 1965). But even as automation replaced workers, automation has also provided better, cleaner, more fulfilling, and better paid jobs (Wolfsburger Nachrichten 1965). Filling in such jobs meant that millions of workers will have to retrain (Die Presse 1965), and this was perhaps easier in Germany than in the US given their differences in vocational education and apprenticeship (see Jürgens, Malsh, and Dohse 1993; Lüdtke 2009).

17 Original German text: "Natürlich kann es bei der praktischen Durchführung einmal zu zeitweiligem Überhäng an Arbeitskräften kommen, was aber bei richtiger Planung sehr wohl vermeidbar ist. In keinem einzigen Fall ist aber bisher die Rationalisierung Anlass zu Entlassungen gewesen" (Nordhoff 1958b: 3).

Nevertheless, management in both countries touted skill upgrading and more job opportunities as a promising outcome of automation.

For management, technological displacement was not cause for alarm or something to be controlled because the 'free market' in tandem with technological progress was understood to 'naturally' reallocate labor and increase the standard of living. As one American management spokesman put it, "I don't think we are consciously trying to ease the burden of our workers nor consciously trying to improve their standard of living. These things take care of themselves. They have a feedback of their own" (Conway 1955: 1). Automation does not warrant political intervention because, as one Ford engineer argued,

> the growth of Automation will be evolutionary, it should have no abrupt or harsh impact upon our working population—no more then the gradual shifting of employment from dying industries into new industries, to which we are thoroughly accustomed. And let's all remember that the willingness to make shifts is essential to the dynamic of the American Economy. (Murie 1955: 17–18)

Daimler-Benz Chairman Könecke echoes this belief that "the introduction of automatic production processes—also called transfer lines—really represents a gradual trend which moreover only affects a part of industry" (Könecke 1956a: 1). He goes on to argue that, considering the labor scarcity in the German labor market, "the task of accelerating the process of automation is an urgent one" (Könecke 1956a: 2). Such statements aim to assuage fears of automation by downplaying potential disruptive consequences.

However, other accounts frame this disruption as a virtue, crediting *creative destruction as the source of prosperity*. Henry Ford II advocated for a cultural embrace of the displacement and disruption of technological progress: "Obsolescence is the very hallmark of progress. The faster we obsolete products, machines, and antiquated costly ways of working, the faster we raise our living standards and our national wealth" (Ford II 1955: 12–13). He further argued that rapid obsolescence should be made palatable to Americans to "sell people on the flexible, dynamic, risk-taking economy" (Ford II 1955: 13). To this end, in a 1959 speech, Henry Ford II rejects,

> an attack by all elements of our society on the existing barriers to increasing productivity in industry … Let's try harder to get rid of the old world craft Guild psychology that has no place in our dynamic, fast changing economy—the psychology that locks people into marginal jobs and obsolescent skills. (Ford II: 1959 15–16)

Ford II contended that technology deployment without limit or restraint generates a vigorous economy that rapidly improves living standards, so long as people "put up with the sporadic irritations and upsets that go along with the free competitive system" (Ford II 1955: 13). This connection was also emphasized in Germany, as Könecke (1956) argued that, because automation should increase buying power and expand markets, "We should therefore approach the problems of automation not with fear and doubts but with confidence and optimism. If we continue to be guided by the ideal of an enlightened free enterprise economy and see to it that everybody benefits from technical progress" (3). Therefore, technological change should be embraced, and the 'market' should be trusted to deliver the best possible outcomes given this change.

There is a contradiction in this position because, on the one hand, it is argued that automation is gradual and evolutionary and *does not create* disruptions that warrant political intervention, yet, on the other hand, it is also argued that technological change and displacement *are* powerful drivers of economic growth that should be not just tolerated but *embraced or even accelerated* (see Rosa 2015). This is contradictory because technological change cannot simultaneously be *evolutionary* with no abrupt impacts and *revolutionary* with accelerating obsolescence that requires flexibility, dynamism, and risk-taking. One characterization implies slow change and the other implies rapid change, but both cannot be true at the same time.

Automakers claimed automation was needed to compete, but the competitive landscape differed between the US and Germany. According to Steigerwald (2010), American companies claimed automation was needed to gain "competitive advantage in a dog-eat-dog industry" (431). This was apparent for US independents which struggled to compete with the Big Three and were 'forced' into mergers to survive, but the main competition during the 1950s was for market share among the Big Three engaged in oligopolistic competition (Steigerwald 2010: 446). Under such conditions, high magnitudes of capital were accumulated in each firm, but each corporation was obligated to respond to the strategic actions of the fellow oligopolists, including investments in automation. Yet, competition, foreign or otherwise, did not appear as a consistent theme in the US. According to Steigerwald (2010: 446), there was no evidence that foreign competition factored into the implementation of new technology before 1970. This made sense considering the high percentage of the US and world market that American manufacturers held during this period (see Womack et al. 2007 [1990]: 42–43). There were alternative reasons to automate, e.g., cost savings, increased profit, or using technological prowess as a selling point, but competition, whether foreign or domestic, did not appear as a commonly stated motivation from Ford and GM representatives.

Weakening the UAW though automation may have been an unspoken motivation of the American automakers (see Reynolds 1989; Cutler 1998; Hounshell 2000; Meyer 2002; 2004; Steigerwald 2010). For example, Meyer (2002) recounts one Big Three manager stating in an interview that "Automation ... is any operation that removes a man from production," but then backtracks, stating, "Don't pin my name on that. We have a labor problem to think of" (71). Unionization made labor power more expensive, which prompted industry to engage in rationalization and automation to offset the increased labor costs through higher productivity (Cutler 1998: 277). But beyond valorization considerations were concerns over leverage and power (Cutler 1998; 2004). Pattern bargaining won many financial concessions and increased employment security, while automation and decentralization undermined the union's bargaining strength. As Steigerwald (2010) argues,

> If there is no smoking-gun evidence that the automakers saw automation as a means for ridding themselves of the UAW, there is cause for suspicion ... the first of the new transfer machines were installed in Buick plants soon after the great strike of 1945–46 was settled. In the absence of any serious external factors such as international competition, it could not have been coincidental that aggressive technological change corresponded to the high point of union strength. (431–432)

Though the stated motivation of automating was increasing productivity, the negative effects on the union appeared as a tacitly welcomed side effect by US management.

In Germany, competition was more important. This was because German automakers relied heavily on exports for their success and therefore their products had to compete globally. German corporations were also surrounded by competition from all sides, from rivals in France and Great Britain to American owned domestic competition from Ford and Opel. For these reasons, Daimler-Benz made their competitive orientation clear in a press release, "Daimler-Benz is deliberately taking the path of rationalization and far-reaching modernization, to meet the keen competition on the commercial vehicle markets" (The Digital Archives of Mercedes-Benz Classic 1969: 1). In a letter from chairman Könecke to Daimler-Benz employees, he explained the importance of rationalization saying, "the price reductions for our products which make us competitive among the rest of the large German and foreign motor companies and in this way directly secure your jobs are due only to the rationalization of our production" (Könecke 1956b: 2). Nordhoff claimed Volkswagen experienced similar competitive pressures: "From the point of view of the company there is a constant pressure from the market and wage agreements on the cost structure of the company, which results in a compulsion to continuously increase productivity (Nordhoff 1958a: 2; translation mine).[18] Such statements illustrate the competitive pressures German companies faced and how such pressures motivated automation.

Comparing the debates between capital and labor in both countries, there was agreement that new technologies and automation were desirable to stay at the forefront of productivity. This had been the consensus in the US for decades but was also becoming the consensus in Germany. This may be attributed as the German response to the 'American Challenge' or as an ideology legitimating the *Wirtschaftswunder*. It is important to note both the apparent consensus, but also *what positions are left unsaid*. There were no statements from labor *or* management *against increasing productivity or directly against automation*. At best, labor organizations were ambivalent about automation, i.e., they wanted to harness the positives of higher productivity but also wanted to mitigate any negative consequences that resulted from new technology. Pure Luddism, however, was never spoken. Luddism may have partially animated the spirit of line workers committing sabotage, but the main purpose was to protest alienating working conditions rather than reject technology and its benefits. This speaks to the 'common sense' that can be formed among social systems that delimit acceptable communications within and between social systems. Though there may be no true 'collective consciousness,' (Luhmann 2012 [1997], 2013 [1997]) social systems can nevertheless communicate with other social systems to generate *apparent agreement* about certain issues and release communications that fall within the parameters of that 'consensus.'

To the extent that all sides agreed that automation and increased productivity was beneficial, they consented to the *changing norms of social necessity* and thereby consented to the technological displacement and transformations of work that result from changing productive norms. The need to increase productivity therefore became the baseline, the unmoving foundation of decision-making, while the political question became how to best deal with the consequences of automation. Accepting the need to increase productivity, paradoxically, renders social domination both *visible and invisible*. Social domination is *invisible* to the extent that the desire and need for higher productivity is universally accepted. It is difficult to recognize the domination

18 Original German text: "Von der Sicht des Unternehmens her betrachtet ergibt sich, in den einzelnen Produktionszweigen unterschiedlich, durch einen permanented Druck des Marktes und der Lohntarife auf die Kostengestaltung des Betriebes ein Zwang zur kontinuierlichen Steigerung der Produktivität" (Nordhoff 1958a: 2).

of productive norms when one agrees that adherence to these norms and increasing productivity further is desirable. To the extent that social systems as *value-systems* accept and support capital as value in motion, the more they frame methods that speed up or improve the flow of value in motion as worthwhile. To the extent social systems agree it is important to increase productivity, social domination does not appear as domination at all, as the logic of capital is thereby accepted and integrated into decision-making (Postone 2015: 15). Social domination becomes *visible* in moments such as when American independents or Borgward decline or when workers rebel against speed-up. In other words, social domination appears when social systems face the consequences for failing to adhere to socially necessary productive norms or when such norms conflict too sharply with human values. In either case, the need to continually increase productivity, whether consensual or not, is an expression of social domination.

4 Pursuing Competitive Advantage: Combative vs Cooperative Industrial Relations

The postwar boom was not sustainable in the long-term. In Germany, saturation of the domestic and European markets by the early 1970s signaled the end of high growth and a shift away from first time car buyers. For Volkswagen, saturation demonstrated the weakness of the single model policy just as it had for Ford and the Model T decades earlier. The decline of this policy put the codetermination system to the test as the cooperative industrial relations assumed continuous growth to satisfy the demands of workers and management alike. The response to the crisis demonstrates the German manner of conflict resolution and restructuring under the pressure of rationalization.

The 'Treaty of Detroit' that enabled 'labor peace' through high wages and benefits was also put under strain as foreign competition, the Beetle above all, became a threat to the postwar prosperity. US industrial relations also were built upon the assumption that growth allows for high profits and improved wages and benefits for workers, but foreign competition could disrupt growth if left unchecked. In this way, the European response to the 'American Challenge' was successful, as European automakers became viable competitors. By the 1970s, competition prompted the Big Three to seek out every advantage possible—including increased automation—to have the edge over foreign competition and maintain their relative place in the global and domestic market. This strained the industrial relations of the American value-regime not just because of the increased competition but due to the combativeness of the system. The rise of wildcat strikes, sabotage, and grievances illustrate how tensions were boiling over (Norsworthy and Zabala 1985; Zabala 1995). Discussing these conflicts illuminates the differences in how the value-regimes deal with conflict and the pressure to rationalize.

4.1 *Beetle Invasion and the New Competition*

Before the late 1950s, it was not conceivable that foreign automakers could make headway in the American market. For over half a century, the US had clear technological and productive superiority, and the Big Three were among the largest and most profitable corporations in the world. With such a successful productive system and extensive capital and resources, it was assumed the Big Three could continue to accumulate capital indefinitely. This status quo was first disrupted by ambitious European carmakers, especially Beetle imports in the late 1950s and 1960s.

The Germans meanwhile finally had the means and motivation to challenge American global market dominance. Their growth model relied upon exports, and the US was an obvious candidate for export because it was the world's largest auto market (see Baccaro and Pontusson 2016). The American method of corporate globalization was emulated as German companies like Volkswagen and Daimler-Benz expanded manufacturing operations into countries like Brazil and Mexico in the 1950s and 1960s (Hilger 2003: 8; Flink 1988: 324). The precondition for expansion was the highly automated industrial system in Germany that was finally comparable to the standards of productivity, volume, and quality set by the United States. Exporting to the US forever disrupted the status quo and the assumption of continuous growth in the oligopolistic US value-regime.

Volkswagen's US exports started slowly with only 330 Beetles arriving in 1950. By 1956, VW was exporting 43,000 Beetles and 6,700 Volkswagen vans. The exports then exploded, reaching over 330,000 Volkswagens imported by 1964, making VW the highest selling foreign automaker in the US (Ewing 2017: 33–35). This influx shifted the balance of imports to exports in the US, as by 1967 the US went from a net exporter to a net importer of automotive products (Flink 1988: 293). Volkswagen sales in the US peaked at 570,000 units in 1970, which represented about one third of Volkswagen's total production. However, this fell to 487,000 exports in 1972 and would continue to fall as the Beetle became seen as technologically outmoded and lost popularity, resulting in the decline and end of the single model strategy in Germany (Ewing 2017: 36). Other European imports began to take ground as well. 60,000 European cars were sold in 1955 in the US, which rose to 700,000 cars by 1960 (Rooke 2008: 5). The total market share for imports rose from 7 percent in 1960 to 13 percent in

1970 (Klier and Rubenstein 2020: 56). Import market share continued to climb in subsequent decades.

The popularity of European imports was not only due to highly productive manufacturing, but in setting themselves apart from the mammoth cars with chrome and tailfins that the Big Three were selling (see Flink 1988: 279–287). Small European cars appealed to consumers who disdained the American consumerism and the military industrial complex that Detroit represented (Ewing 2017: 35; see Hoitt 2012). The Beetle represented a return of the 'reasonable' automobile that simply met transportation needs rather than display (horse)power, wealth, or social status (Schmidt 2007). European imports were appealing to the needs, wants, and desires of a sizable market segment that the Big Three had ignored, providing a market opening for imports.

Automobile competition in the 1950s and 1960s revolved around the realm of realization and marketing appeals rather than productive power. With productivity and automation levels at similarly high rates in the US and Germany, clear production advantages could not preclude competition as it had in the first half of the 20th century. There was no obvious means of increasing productivity that could lower the value of US cars enough to make cost the decisive factor for realization in competition against imports. Instead, car size, cultural appeal, and marketing—the domain of realization—were driving the sales of imports. Though most American drivers bought large Detroit manufactured cars, the Beetle and compacts revealed a previously underserved market segment. US automakers worked to regain lost market share through introducing their own compact models, e.g., the Chevrolet Corvair, that served this new market segment (Flink 1988: 287; see Whyte 2020: 100–106). The Big Three thereby shifted resources into producing compact cars that appealed to the wants, needs, and desires of these potential customers because they aimed at maximal capital accumulation in all possible markets and did not want imports to siphon surplus value from them. Therefore, different product and profit strategies were pursued to address this deficit.

This represented a shift in the profit strategies of automakers from pursuing production-based advantages to product, marketing, and realization-based advantages (see Boyer and Freyssenet 2002). Therefore, production supremacy is not always the most important competitive consideration, and competition based on product, marketing, and other factors remain important. Nevertheless, the relative parity of productivity and efficiency served as the *precondition and foundation upon which* competition based on other factors played out. In other words, only when productivity is relatively equalized and converges around limited acceptable arrangements of labor and capital with the requisite speeds and control over production time, then competition based on other criteria, such as horsepower, styling, or countercultural appeals, can take place. In this way, the technological catch up of European automakers and the capability to approach, match, or exceed the norms of socially necessary labor time were an important prerequisite for tackling the 'American Challenge' and presenting an import threat to American producers.

The rise of imports disrupted the status quo and was the first sign of weakness that ultimately culminated in a gradual long-term decline of American firms in the domestic and world market. Before this point, the high productivity and productive capacity of US industry insulated it from competition as the Big Three dominated the domestic market and expanded with little difficulty around the globe. This was also fortunate for the US value-regime, as the UAW could demand a larger and larger share of a continuously growing economic pie. The arrival of *competitively viable* imports threatened the prosperity of the Big Three and eventually affect domestic jobs and the willingness or ability of the corporations to reward labor as generously as in the past. The merits of the productive model, strategies, and technological development of each value-regime were placed into direct confrontation. Which value-regime was more sustainable for long-term economic development? Once they possessed similar mass production capabilities, competition intensified and the search for competitive advantages based on the development path and strength of each country was put to the test. Their merits can be observed in the ways each dealt with conflict, especially in response to productivity pressure, rationalization, and production problems.

4.2 *Combative Industrial Relations and the Blue Collar Blues*

The Treaty of Detroit was premised on increasing shared prosperity for the workers in exchange for 'labor peace' regulated through the grievance system with authorized strikes limited to production issues. Though it set the rules and limits of industrial relations, it only *contained* the acrimonious relationship between management and labor and compensated for it monetarily rather than building genuine cooperation. The sources of grievance were numerous such as the repetitive monotony of work, Taylorist alienation from shaping work processes, foremen pushing for speed-up, and safety issues. These issues culminated in a widespread distrust of management and a general sense of alienation and malaise (see Meyer 2004). However, without worker influence over production standards, like German workers enjoyed, the only legitimate option for the average worker was to handle complaints within the multistep grievance system. Both management and the union had incentives to keep worker grievances within that system and discourage and discipline illegal shopfloor action (Asher and Edsforth 1995: 13).

However, the system did not eliminate unauthorized action entirely. Each company experienced numerous wildcat strikes in the early 1950s, with GM experiencing 0.42 average man hours per employee lost to wildcats in 1950–1954, around 1.5–2.2 man hours for Ford and 18.6 man hours lost for Chrysler (Asher 1995: 148). These strikes were typically small and short lived but nevertheless represented the struggles faced by US workers and demonstrated workers' willingness to engage in shopfloor action regardless of the wishes of the UAW or management (Asher 1995: 148–149). As competition from imports applied *productivity pressure* to gain productive advantages, increasing work intensity further escalated tensions. As Thompson (1995) describes the situation in the early 1970s,

> life on the shopfloor had become more intolerable as more speedups and poorer working conditions, took their toll. To all observers, it appeared that Detroit's automobile factories were in a crisis. Shopfloor violence was commonplace, and wildcat strikes occurred with alarming frequency in many of the Big Three plants. The problems were still most severe in Chrysler's aging plants. (191)

Illegal wildcats were often initiated to express worker anger outside the grievance system.

Chrysler's industrial relations were especially contentious. According to Thompson (1995: 185), Chrysler was nearly bankrupted during the 1958–1959 recession and was a "tinderbox waiting to explode" by the late 1960s due to managerial aggression, long work hours, and dangerous working conditions. As the smallest oligopolist, Chrysler struggled to make investments in expanding or updating its facilities compared to Ford and GM. Therefore, to keep productivity levels high enough to adequately compete, Chrysler compensated for outdated equipment by increasing work intensity. As Thompson (1995) explains, "The prosperity that Chrysler enjoyed, however, was largely due to an intense speedup. Rather than investing in, or expanding and updating its facilities, as Ford and GM attempted to do, Chrysler tried to squeeze more out of the workers themselves" (Thompson 1995: 191–192). These conditions resulted in Chrysler having one of the most militant workforces and some of the most violent and costly wildcat strikes of the period (Asher 1995: 148; Thompson 1995).

Chrysler's example illustrates another aspect of social domination. If the norms of socially necessary labor time cannot be met via the methods used by the productivity leaders, such as investments in Detroit automation, then there is pressure to implement *alternative means of increasing productivity*. Here, Chrysler's tactics attempt to approximate the norms of social necessity via speed-up rather than automation, with negative consequences for the workers. However, for a profit oriented company, the 'choice' to speed-up can become a "damned if you do, damned if you don't" situation. Ending the speed-up may be more humane but hurts the ability to compete, whereas the speed-up may help Chrysler compete, but also risks of militant responses like wildcat strikes that offset or nullify the productivity gains of speed-up. In this way, both the company and the workers face the consequences of failing to meet the norms of socially necessary labor time.

Even at the comparatively 'peaceful' GM, industrial relations tensions were being pushed to the limit. GM experienced a rapid increase in grievances between 1952–1957, and another long-term climb in grievances between 1961 and 1969 occurred, with 1973 and 1979 being the top two highest years for grievances between 1947 and 1980. At GM's Van Nuys plant, for example, workers filed 3,489 grievances in 1970, which rose to a peak of 19,876 in 1979 (Zabala 1995: 216). Even with the increase in grievance bargaining, there were workers who were unsatisfied with the formal system and rejected the postwar consensus in favor of returning to the direct shopfloor bargaining of the late 1930s. These groups of radical workers "felt that the union's insistence on adhering to the postwar collective bargaining system, with its prohibition of unauthorized strikes, prevented workers from having any real power when it came to dealing with management" (Thompson 1995: 188). This presented a dilemma for the UAW because they had the contractual obligation to prevent illegal shopfloor activities.

Worker dissatisfaction was also expressed via workplace sabotage. By purposefully damaging commodities or equipment, workers both engaged in protest and engaged in indirect effort-wage bargaining by intentionally restricting output and constraining the administration of production (Zabala 1995: 210). The union is supposed to oppose such actions, but according to Zabala's (1995: 211–212) case study at Van Nuys, the local UAW often defended workers accused of sabotage, making sabotage a *supplement* to grievance bargaining rather than an *alternative*. The problem of workplace sabotage demonstrates many workers' preference for acceptable working conditions and a *slower pace of work over productivity* or product quality. As one saboteur expressed their antipathy, "Management don't give a damn about us, we shouldn't worry about their cars" (Zabala 1995: 220). While UAW leaders like Walter Reuther encouraged higher productivity for the sake of national growth and prosperity, from the worker's perspective, intense and repetitive work is often not worth promises of company or national prosperity that are not perceptible to individual experience. This makes direct shopfloor action like sabotage attractive to alleviate the immediate and intimate difficulties of work on the line.

The link between behavior that disrupts valorization and decreases productivity, the relative health of the firm, and the relative prosperity of the country is perhaps too mediated and obscure to be part of the decision-making process of a worker under extremely alienating and degrading working conditions (see Zabala 1995: 225).

Workers' antipathy toward their working conditions also influenced the productivity and costs of the US auto industry. In their quantitative analysis of the effects of worker attitudes on productivity and production costs, Norsworthy and Zabala (1985) indexed worker behavior, combining variables including grievances, unauthorized strikes, and quits from plant level data. From 1959–1976, these behaviors increased around 30 percent (Norsworthy and Zabala 1985: 556). For the period, a 10 percent increase of the index resulted in a 2.4 percent increase in the unit cost of production, signifying that more worker grievances, quits, and unauthorized strikes "increases production costs and reduces productivity" (Norsworthy and Zabala 1985: 554). They also calculated that if working conditions hypothetically changed so that the worker behavior index decreased by 10 percent, then billions of dollars would have been saved by improved productivity and lower costs. In the peak year of 1976, a 10 percent decrease would have resulted in savings of around $4.8 billion in production costs across the industry, nearly 5 percent of the total production costs (Norsworthy and Zabala 1985: 556; Zabala 1995: 211). In addition, Zabala (1995) argues that sabotage incurs "significant economic costs," and that "the effects of such sabotage on production costs and product quality were substantial" (211; 224).

These studies demonstrate the costs to productivity and production incurred due to grievances, quits, and unauthorized strikes, but the authors warn that this should not be interpreted as condemning workers. Rather, they argue that labor and management bear responsibility in cooperatively generating improved working conditions that would decrease the number of grievances and unauthorized strikes (Norsworthy and Zabala 1985: 557). This proved to be difficult as the US auto industry has a long history of management pursuing their production prerogatives at the expense of labor, structurally separating the interests of labor and management, and instituting an industrial relations system based on *managing grievance* rather than *alleviating the source of grievance*. They also resisted developing a codetermination system that would construct work standards acceptable to both management and labor. This path dependent trajectory has plagued the American value-regime to varying degrees up to the present (see Helper and Henderson 2014).

The legendary Lordstown, Ohio strike of 1972 exemplifies these issues. Opened in 1966, GM's Lordstown facility was framed as the 'plant of the future,' equipped with state-of-the-art technology including 26 multipurpose and programmable Unimate robots—one of the first deployments of industrial robots (Flink 1988: 244; Thompson 1995: 200). The combination of robots and single purpose welding machines in the body shop performed a total of 3,900 spot welds, resulting in and automation level of 95 percent, while much of the older American plants were averaging between 20 to 40 percent automation (Flink 1988: 244; Jürgens 2023: 190). Computer and IT systems that performed quality control, line balancing, and product mix scheduling were used for the first time here (Jürgens 2023: 189–190). The new breakthroughs in automation complemented the assembly line cycle time of 31 seconds. This unprecedented line speed produced 101 cars per hour, whereas most plants produced at a rate of 50–60 cars per hour (Thompson 1995: 201). Even though assembly speed was the highest in the world, workers were equipped with power tools, and an easy to manufacture car design helped reduce worker effort on the line (Thompson 1995: 201; Rooke 2008: 5). The intention of all this was to produce a small and inexpensive car, the Chevrolet Vega, at a new higher level of productivity and efficiency (Meyer 2004: 9). It was framed as an "import fighter" to compete with the small car imports that were gradually eroding GM's market share (Jürgens 2023: 189–190).

When the workers of Local 1112 initiated an authorized strike in March 1972, the media framed the strike as a young "hippie" workforce "bucking authority and rejecting industrial progress" (Thompson 1995: 200). The term 'Lordstown Syndrome' described workers who had grown up in the postwar period and were supposedly not prepared assembly line work (Jürgens 2023: 190–192). However, this interpretation is misleading. In the first few years of the plant, grievances were not primarily about labor intensity. Only after GM ordered a restructuring of the plant from Fisher Body and Chevrolet to the General Motors Assembly Division (GMAD) did serious problems arise. GMAD reduced the workforce from 8,500 to 7,700 without reducing the line speed. GMAD then changed work standards from three to two workers per job and insisted that all previous agreements with Local 1112 be renegotiated. The company assumed these changes would be tolerated because "GM believed the union would be fearful of wholesale job losses" if foreign imports were not dampened due to the success of the Vega (Thompson 1995: 201–203).

On the contrary, these changes angered workers because the job cuts and work standards changes put more pressure on each individual worker. As the local union president stated, "we could care how fast the line goes as long as there were enough people to do the job and still be able to blow [our] nose without being three car lengths in the hole" (Thompson 1995: 202). Because of these changes, tensions between workers and management spiraled out of control. Over 5,000 grievances were filed shortly after the changes (Flink 1988: 244). Chaotic working conditions led to more quality problems and incidents of sabotage were reported, resulting in an overflow of the 2,000-space repair lot (Thompson 1995: 203). Disciplinary layoffs were issued to nearly 1,400 workers, many of whom refused to do the work previously done by two or three workers, which further exacerbated the lack of manpower (Thompson 1995: 203). Therefore, exercising unilateral management control against the terms of the union contract pushed the workers to strike rather than the technology or the line speed *per se* (see Thompson 1994: 205–206; Jürgens 2023: 192). Backed by the national UAW, the twenty-two-day strike victory resulted in a reversal of the layoffs, resolved the pending grievances, and erased the disciplinary layoffs with back pay.

Lordstown encapsulates how the contentious American industrial relations system hampers the ability of the US value-regime to harness the full potential of new technology and automation. The productive potential at Lordstown was perhaps the highest in the world *if* the factory was sufficiently staffed with cooperative workers, but GM management pushed for production standards and staffing levels below what was tolerable for the union and against the contract rules. Therefore, the *push for higher productivity backfired* and instead resulted in increased worker tensions, quality issues, sabotage, and ultimately a strike.

Acrimonious interactions between capital and labor in the United States appears fundamental to US industrial relations. Examining the Lordstown case, the "anti-worker exceptionalism" (Greenhouse 2019: 8) of American capital may help explain the inability for the US auto industry to prevent losing ground to imports and harness the productive power of new technology. The industrial relations weaknesses of the US system were less apparent and more tolerable *for capital accumulation* when the industry experienced high growth and maintained technological and productive dominance. However, once competitors with equally or more productive systems and cooperative industrial relations appeared, the combative industrial relations became a *threat to the long-term stability* of the US value-regime (see Helper and Henderson 2014).

4.3 *Cooperative Industrial Relations Reckon with the Decline of the Single Model Policy*

Volkswagen experienced high growth and prosperity for over two decades due primarily to the success of its single model policy. The combination of high standardization, productivity, and appealing design made the Beetle one of the highest selling automobiles of all time, surpassing the Model T's record of 15,007,034 cars in February 1972 (Ewing 2017: 36). However, Volkswagen experienced a crisis like what Ford faced in the 1920s: relying on a single model alone, though advantageous for production, becomes disadvantageous when consumer expectations change, thus making realization the problematic factor. How Volkswagen, IG Metall, the works council, and the governments of Lower Saxony and the Federal Republic responded to the decline of the Beetle exemplifies how the value-regime cooperatively copes with crisis to satisfy the interests of all parties.

The trouble began with the end of domestic growth driven by first time car buyers. For the first time in the postwar period, car sales in Germany failed to grow in 1966, indicating that the German domestic market was reaching its saturation point (Tolliday 1995b: 112). Like the Model T, while the Beetle was a useful entry vehicle for an unmotorized society, Germans were going beyond the Fordist demand for basic transportation into the Sloanist phase of demanding a variety and diversity of models (see Boyer and Freyssenet 2002). With increasing domestic competition, VW's market share fell from 45 percent in 1960 to 33 percent in 1968 and 26 percent in 1972. The drop in domestic market share made VW more dependent on export sales, exporting 70 percent of its output in 1968, with 40 percent going to the US (Tolliday 1195b: 112–113). However, relying on American exports was problematic because US sales were also deteriorating. Volkswagen's share of total US imports fell from 62.6 percent in 1966 to 24.4 percent in 1974, showing how other imports had become more prominent in the US (Kemezis 1975). Volkswagen experienced problems due to rising German labor costs, competition from US compacts and Japanese imports, the devaluation of the dollar, and increased import tariffs. This combination caused the Beetle to be overpriced compared to American models, e.g., a Beetle had a sticker price of $2,849 compared to the $2,442 cost of the Ford Pinto (Flink 1988: 324–325). Tolliday (1995b: 114) summarizes the dire situation for Volkswagen in the US this way,

> Volkswagen sales in the United States fell from 570,000 in 1970 (35% of all VW sales) to 334,000 in 1974 and 203,234 in 1976 (16% of total sales). Sales of the Beetle melted away from 354,000 to 27,000. Largely as a result of the disasters in the USA, Volkswagen's global output fell from 1.6 million vehicles in 1971 to 1 million in 1975.

Volkswagen lost ground in its most important markets and struggled to develop an alternative to the Beetle.

The serious development of a new model policy did not commence until it was too late to replace the Beetle with equally successful models without incurring losses (Tolliday 1995a: 339). New models, the Golf, Passat, and Polo, were released between 1973–1975, but it took time before they fully replaced the sales volume of the Beetle (Jürgens 1998: 283–287). The 1973 oil crisis also depressed sales, which resulted in 40 percent of the German plant capacity and workforce being idled (Jürgens 1994: 95; Kemezis 1975). The gap between the decline of the Beetle and before the rise of the new models resulted in Volkswagen's first recorded losses, including 807 million Deutschmarks in 1974 and 157 million Deutschmarks in 1975 (Tolliday 1995b: 114). The situation was serious as Jürgens (1994) explains, "if a successor model for the Beetle could not be developed, the end of the company could be foreseen" (95). Resolving this crisis required coordination between Volkswagen, the works council, union, and government.

In German industrial relations, close cooperation between state, business, and labor systems is paramount. According to Brumlop and Jürgens (1983), the German industrial relations system rests on "highly formalized procedural forms prescribed by law" and "on a high degree of consensus on the role of management and labor as social partners" (11). The works council serves as the arbiter for the workers, and there exists essentially no tradition of rank-and-file autonomous shopfloor action or politics apart from the activities of the union and works council, unlike the split between the rank-and-file and the national union leadership in the United States (Brumlop and Jürgens 1983: 11–12; see Cutler 1998, 2004). Volkswagen CEO Carl Hahn, who served from 1982–1993, summarized the relationship as,

> The social peace in this firm, which is based on long readiness to cooperate and mutual respect, is one of the pillars on which the future of the VW firm rests. It is the result of the traditional good cooperation between management and the representatives of the employees. (Brumlop and Jürgens 1983: 13)

Ultimately, the negotiations between the systems produced an agreement amenable to both labor and management.

Despite the dire financial situation and employment threats, no strike or mass worker action occurred during the mid-70s crisis. At Volkswagen, although workers have the collective bargaining right to strike to win demands, there were no official strikes at Volkswagen from the 1950s–1970s. Reports of informal strikes or walkouts were also exceedingly rare. Instead, the typical form of collective protest is to take the grievance *en masse* to the works council which thereby halts work (Brumlop and Jürgens 1983: 10). Most labor relations conflicts involved increasing pay, and management almost always opted to "buy off" the group of workers (Jürgens 1998: 282). This system, where most conflicts are settled without major disruptions to production, saved production costs because it ensured the continuous flow of value and maintained high efficiency (see Norsworthy and Zabala 1985). However, the consequences of acceding to labor demands with increased pay was that "management had only a loose grip on wage costs. Wage drift was high" (Jürgens 1998: 282). This was not necessarily a problem in the Keynesian sense because distributing more value to workers stimulates demand throughout the economy, and if the company was growing sufficiently and increasing productivity, then higher labor costs were partly offset.

The crisis made it difficult to reach an agreement in the 1974 bargaining round. The leader of IG Metall, Eugene Loderer, urged the federal chancellor Helmut Schmidt to encourage Volkswagen management to work cooperatively with the workers to ameliorate the crisis. This ultimately resulted in the German government obtaining the replacement of VW CEO Rudolf Leiding with Tony Schmücker, who was known for his good relationship with IG Metall (Tolliday 1995b; Jürgens 1998: 284). The leadership change facilitated the process of cooperative crisis management and illustrates the political sway of unions in Germany. With the sharp decline in sales, Volkswagen wanted to eliminate 25 percent of the workforce, but the firm needed the consent of the union. IG Metall accepted that employment levels should be "dictated by the needs of the market," but stressed that redundancies should be kept to the minimum level "consistent with 'economic reality'" (Tolliday 1995b: 121–122).

The compromise resulted in a loss of 33,000 workers between 1973–1975 (Jürgens 1998: 288; Grieger and Lupa 2015: 121–125). The distribution of job losses favored native German workers who were "well protected by contracts, seniority, and the interest representation of the works council" (Tolliday 1995b: 122). Nearly 40 percent, or 13,000, of the effected workers were foreigners, which reduced the percentage of foreign workers from 16 percent to 7 percent of the total workforce (Brumlop and Jürgens 1983: 29–30). Older men and young women were also a high proportion of the redundancies (Tolliday 1995b: 122). This skewed distribution unveils the *de facto* two-tier employment system at VW with mostly skilled German workers at the top and unskilled foreign workers at the bottom. As Tolliday (1995b) describes,

> In this crisis the continuity of 'solidaristic' union policies was made possible, and confrontation avoided, by the fact that under the banner of 'no special protection' a large part of the workforce found itself *de facto* outside the protection of the union. (122; emphasis in original)

This stratification throws doubt on whether the German system fully lived up to its claims of solidarity and social justice.

However, no workers, whether foreign or native, were forced to leave the company, instead relying on voluntary quits or severance packages. Many found work in other auto companies who were not hit as hard as VW or were able to rejoin VW as the firm recovered, though for many foreign workers, the severance contracts were hard to refuse (Tolliday 1995b: 122; Jürgens 1998: 288). Volkswagen also initiated an early retirement plan where employees aged 59 could voluntarily retire until they entered the social security system at age 60 (Jürgens 1998: 288). These workers were paid partly through the state unemployment insurance, and the rest of their old wage was supplemented by the company until they reached age 60, thus shifting personnel adjustment costs to the public welfare system (Brumlop and Jürgens 1983: 31–32). Finally, a hiring freeze allowed the 'natural attrition' of retirements and voluntary departures to take their course to reduce the workforce (Jürgens 1998: 288). Overall, the agreement was "praised by both sides" as an exemplar of the effectiveness of the German industrial relations system to cope with change through cooperation (Jürgens 1994: 95). Compared to the US where agreements are often settled by strikes or grievance management, the consensus in Germany was reached without involuntary layoffs or strikes.

Despite the mutually satisfactory resolution, the Beetle crisis signaled the end of the rapid growth of core German production. While the Volkswagen Group, including both domestic and foreign production as well as acquired brands like Audi, grew over the decades, the core of Volkswagen in Germany fluctuated in size but never substantially surpassed the levels of production and employment reached in the peak year of 1971. The peak of production of over 1.7 million autos and over 114,000 production workers in 1971 for Volkswagen AG was never surpassed (Grieger and Lupa 2015). According to Jürgens (1998), this lack of employment and production growth signified that "from this time on, employment issues became 'zero sum games' within a stagnating organization" (284). The decline of the Beetle signaled the end of the postwar boom and the period of high growth for the core of Volkswagen within the German value-regime.

These examples of conflict resolution demonstrate how variable outcomes are possible with different systemic arrangements grounded in historical experience and cultural attitudes. Divergence in industrial relations and conflict resolution played a vital role in the following decades as both German and US value-regimes faced increasing competition and periodic crisis.

5 Convergent Automation, Divergent Industrial Relations

The remarkable growth and prosperity of the postwar years appeared to 'crack the code' of modernization, i.e., that a 'universal' modernization path could be taken regardless of socio-historic circumstances (see Rostow 1990 [1960];

Piketty 2014). According to the 'consensus,' Fordist mass production and Keynesian full employment policies enabled perpetual growth (Woirol 1996; Steigerwald 2010). Automation drove production growth and was understood as beneficial by labor and management leaders in both countries. German firms confronted the 'American Challenge' by embracing Fordist mass production and American style globalization (Hilger 2003; Hachtmann and von Saldern 2009). There was apparent convergence around the US precedent, including productive norms and technological development.

Yet divergent tendencies remained in industrial relations between the combative system in the US and the cooperative German system. Statements from labor and management in both value-regimes conveyed the importance of maintaining high productivity, and automation was understood as a necessary component of this. Yet, how high productivity was maintained and how technological displacement and other social effects of automation were managed differed. Therefore, even in this era of 'consensus,' a variety of systemic arrangements were possible that proved to generate high growth and capital accumulation.

The development of automation during this period has important implications for the analysis of *social domination* and *productivity as a social imperative*. On the one hand, transfer machines offered important gains in productivity that—even if productivity gains did not meet expectations due to breakdown and inflexibility issues—could not be ignored by automotive companies. Socially necessary labor time in the auto industry *adjusted to the speed of the transfer line*, producing more output per hour, and eliminating many semi-skilled direct production workers. On the other hand, transfer machines required substantial capital investment that smaller companies such as Studebaker, Packard, Nash and Hudson in the US and Borgward in Germany could not afford. For this reason, many companies that could not make the necessary investments either merged, e.g., Studebaker and Packard in 1954, or went out of business (IG Metall 1962; Hounshell 2000: 119). The pressure to acquire transfer machines to compete with the productivity of the bigger companies was acutely experienced by the independents as one commentator explained,

> As for the other independents, they will almost certainly be *forced to get in on automation as the price for survival*. Since the initial costs are high, however the independents may have to merge in order to afford it. Indeed, the automation expectations could be the clue to the recent decision of Nash and Hudson to link their destinies. (Hounshell 2000: 120; emphasis added)

This "force" to adopt automation that is the "price for survival" is best described as *social domination*. For these independents, the choice to invest or not invest in automation is hardly a choice at all when opting out only hastens bankruptcy. This "force" cannot be directly identified with the Big Three, Volkswagen, or other social systems, as they are not directing these mergers or bankruptcies. Rather, the "force" comes from the *reestablishment of productivity norms around the speed of the transfer machine*, i.e., that the expected valorization of the automobile commodity during the 1950s and 1960s can only be achieved at productivity thresholds possible with transfer machines. Therefore, the *pressure to automate* and the necessity of mergers to afford the proper investments are not *genuinely autonomous choices* but are influenced by a socio-historically determined *heteronomy* that operates outside all participating systems.

Labor leaders also understood the consequences of failing to automate, as IG Metall (1962: 66) diagnosed the bankruptcy of Borgward in these terms. Local 600 President Carl Stellato diagnosed the struggle of the US independents in similar terms,

> I want to point out … that where Studebaker and Kaiser … are not advanced or where they don't have as much automation … the workers in Studebaker, Packard, Kaiser and the rest of them can work for nothing—they don't have to take a fifty cent wage cut. They could work for nothing and they still wouldn't put the Studebaker Corporation in competition with Ford, General Motors, Chrysler and some of those that do have automation and do have the money to spend on automation. (Cutler 1998: 357)

His comments covered wage parity, suggesting that reducing wages may not be sufficient to accumulate capital if value-systems fall too far behind the socially necessary productive norms. While lowering wages is one means of reducing costs, it is not always enough to secure competitive advantage or even parity if the productivity gap between competitors is too large. If Stellato is correct, then deploying automation to maintain productivity standards was genuinely *necessary* for American independents.

Productivity pressure is experienced by the Big Three and large German automakers in different ways. Though part of an oligopoly, GM, Ford, and Chrysler understood the need to approximate one another in production technology and productivity to maintain their relative market position. Opting out of deploying transfer machines was not seriously considered. Transfer line technology was pursued because it increased productivity, and they had the potential for even higher productivity if issues of downtime prevention and flexibility were addressed. Absent union codetermination to influence technology deployment and production standards, management prerogative to accumulate capital was well served by automation. In Germany, the race to expand capacity to meet booming demand made automation indispensable, and many companies that did not invest fast enough folded as the German industry became increasingly concentrated (Tolliday 1995a: 334–335). For Volkswagen, automation enabled the company to achieve similar production levels and capacity as the Big Three, making VW the fourth largest automaker in the world.

Automation and also served *social-communicative* purposes. Big Three press releases referred to automation and technology to promote the *superiority of their production methods and products* and how automation creates a wealthier society. For example, Louis G. Seaton, vice president of Personnel Staff at GM, said in 1959 that,

> The soundest solution to unemployment is employment—more job opportunities through economic growth and technological progress … Insofar as our business is concerned this means providing attractive, high-quality products that people want and will buy. The only way we know to accomplish this is through … an efficient, well-trained cooperative work force. And our people are provided with the best, the most modern and the most efficient tools and facilities that can be obtained. (General Motors Heritage Center 1959: 1)

Here, GM linked employment and economic growth to technological progress and acquiring modern and efficient tools and facilities. For Ford during the early 1950s, press releases frequently promoted their new facilities as technical achievements. For example, the Cleveland Engine Plant was claimed to be the "most modern in the industry," and technical and productive achievements were cited positively, such as how automation at the Buffalo stamping plant reduced "manual handling of materials to a minimum" (Ford Motor Company Archives 1953b). In another release, it was claimed that automation represented a fundamental improvement to the assembly line stating, "even the moving assembly line that Henry Ford conceived as an automotive pioneer has taken an new stride forward at the engine plant," and that automation decreased work strain and created a safer working environment: "Throughout the plant, lessened employee fatigue and greater safety provide for greater efficiency and a better product" (Ford Motor Company Archives 1952c: 2). Automation and technological change were linked to numerous positive benefits for customers and workers, and rhetorical connections were made between automation and higher productivity, on the one hand, and 'progress' and 'modernity,' on the other.

German firms made similar statements. Daimler-Benz, for example, in a description of automation at Untertürkheim in 1956, bemoaned how time was "irretrievably lost" in manually shifting parts from single purpose machines, but that automation ensured precision and "reduces physical effort to a minimum" (Woltereck 1956b: 2–3). Heinrich Nordhoff stated in 1965 that automation was a 'tremendous impulse' (*ungeheuren Impuls*) that contributed to productivity and a better product, producing higher volumes with fewer mistakes and at a lower price (Die Presse 1965). Considering German workers also wanted to exercise their skills on automated equipment, the proliferation of automation mutually benefited firms, consumers, and workers (see Kern and Schumann 1987).

Automation and new technology supported the firm's self-description as 'progressive' and 'modern' businesses. These press releases act as communications that aim to "convince" other social systems of the firm's self-description of having 'advanced' and 'modern' production techniques that translate into superior products. Such narratives promote the overarching flow of value in motion and capital accumulation. Sufficient control over time and leading with high productivity thus becomes the *material-processual basis* to ground specific communications designed to promote the value-system's self-descriptions and aid in realization processes. In other words, *productivity is imbued with social meaning* and hierarchies of high and low productivity shape the distribution of value, social esteem, and power in modern society in multifaceted ways, i.e., *not* just economically but *socially*.

The link between high productivity and 'progress' or 'modernity' served not just the interests of companies but the *nation-state as value-regime*. Just as industry in the United States became ideologically framed as the 'arsenal of democracy' during WWII, the same productive system served similar ideological purposes during the Cold War. As Hounshell (2000) explains,

> During the crises of the Cold War—say, during the Korean war, at the time of the Sputnik launches in 1957, or even during the Cuban Missile Crisis of 1962—'Detroit automation' represented a beacon of hope for the United States, as productivity figures for US plants using transfer machines were far, far greater than those for automated plants in the Soviet Union. (101)

In the ideological battle between American capitalism and Soviet communism, productivity statistics served as a battleground of competition between value-regimes. The higher production and productivity numbers of the US, Germany, and allied countries compared to the Soviets demonstrated both the superior productive capacity of capitalism, but also how characteristics of capitalist value-regimes, such as the 'free market' and profit incentives generated superior outcomes compared to command economies. In this way, the power of productivity norms rewards highly productive systems not just economically, but socially, geo-politically, and ideologically.

Henry Ford II noted this theme in a 1964 speech, "For generations, our technology has been the most advanced and progressive in the world. It is the basis of our standard of living, of our national security, of our position in the community of nations" (Ford II 1964: 2). According to Henry Ford II, having the "most advanced and progressive" technology is given credit for the United States possessing the highest living standards and its position as a capitalist superpower. Therefore, keeping the Ford Motor Company on the technological forefront was not just about battling for market share against domestic and foreign competitors, but maintaining the productive superiority of the US value-regime to win the ideological war against communism in the Cold War. John S. Bugas, Ford vice president of industrial relations, echoed this sentiment,

> The fact that there is more output of goods and services and products of all kinds in the United States per man hour than in any other locality on the globe has really accounted for the difference in strength and influence between the United States and the rest of the nations of the world. In a very real sense the position of leadership in which our nation finds itself may be attributed very directly to the progress we have made in productivity. (Ford Motor Company Archives 1954: 8)

In this way, technological leadership is understood as a *national imperative*, linking US productivity to national geopolitical power. In this context, losing market share to imports is not just an economic threat. It is also a national threat imbued with a fear of insecurity and humiliation in addition to fears of job loss or lower profits. Meanwhile, the *Wirtschaftswunder* connected achieving mass production with Germany successfully responding to the 'American Challenge' and rising like a phoenix from the ashes from its dark past (Tolliday 1995a: 288; Hilger 2003).

Therefore, possessing the highest productivity, whether in the form of the firm, state, or value-regime, is not a mere socio-technical fact, but is loaded with *specific social consequences and meanings*. Possessing the highest productivity legitimates self-descriptive claims to 'modernity' and 'progress' while those who lag in productivity become framed as 'laggards' and 'backward.' The higher productivity of the United States legitimated among many social systems the claim that American capitalism possessed the superior productive system, and, by extension, the superior *social system* compared to Soviet communism. The 'truth' of these claims is not self-evident but are legitimated within the context of an overarching social system that values productivity and capital accumulation. In other words, the social domination of productive norms only takes effect in societies where *high productivity is rewarded economically, socially, ideologically, and even geopolitically*. Linking these seemingly disparate elements back to the root of productivity and control over time reveals the social power—and social domination—that productivity norms hold over modern social life.

The consequences of this domination extend from global politics to the life histories of individual workers. For the sake of higher productivity and capital accumulation, the installation of transfer lines displaced thousands of machine workers. Though many were reabsorbed into other parts of the auto industry due to industry growth, there is no doubt that technological change transformed the work of both skilled and unskilled workers as well as rendered some jobs and skills superfluous. At the same time, other skills became more necessary—though a general skill upgrading did not appear to be true for most workers (Bright 1958). What is important is how labor transformations made certain skills superfluous and others more desired. Detroit automation thereby displaced workers and disrupted skill and labor structures in both the US and Germany during the postwar decades. Considering the overwhelming economic *and* social imperative to increase productivity, the question for both value-regimes was never how to *prevent* technological displacement, but how to best *manage* automation's effects. Ideological narratives of national success may appear separated from the fate of technologically displaced workers, but this critical theory reveals the underlying social imperative that connects them.

That automation and high productivity was a priority at Volkswagen reveals how codetermination, strong labor systems, and full or partial state ownership do not *necessarily* result in worse economic or social outcomes—as market fundamentalists claim (e.g., Hayek 1944; Friedman 2002 [1962]). The so-called 'Red firm' embraced Fordist mass production and automation, which quickly grew the company and was not stopped by labor or the government (Brumlop and Jürgens 1983: 5–6; Tolliday 1995b: 120). The private US firms guided by the 'free market' lost market share to the 'Red firm,' making it difficult to claim strong labor systems or state ownership hurt the ability of VW to compete. In fact, the cooperative industrial relations made smoother work processes substantially less disrupted by labor-management conflict, which is associated with lower production costs (see Norsworthy and Zabala 1985). Therefore, Volkswagen's industrial relations system perhaps had the latent capacity and flexibility necessary to productively surpass the American firms if they oriented toward increasing productivity. However, German automakers generally pursued quality over productivity in the 1970s and 1980s, taking a characteristically German path toward diversified quality production (Kern and Schumann 1984; Sorge and Streeck 2016).

The divergent industrial relations represented different ways of coping with the interests of labor and management. They attempted to balance the interests of the workers in their self-valorization *and* interest in norms and values such as health and stress, and the interests of management to accumulate sufficient capital to continue the flow of value in motion through valorization, realization, distribution, and reinvestment processes which benefited both management and the workers. Tense industrial relations in the US increased production costs and decreased productivity, as well as disrupted the possible productivity and quality improvements of new technology and automation as seen at Lordstown (see Norsworthy and Zabala 1985; Thompson 1995). If Norsworthy and Zabala (1985) are correct that less industrial conflict results in higher productivity and lower production costs, then the German system of codetermination and cooperation likely contributed to the success of Volkswagen during the postwar years. Even if the accumulation of surplus value was partially offset by wage concessions, the uninterrupted speed of the automated machinery paired with the largely skilled workforce created the volume and quality of automobiles at sufficient value to sell millions domestically and abroad.

In this period, both American and German corporations mastered mass production and stayed on a similar technological and productivity level with their adoption of transfer lines and other automation. The critical factors for success, therefore, relied more on their *differences* such as their industrial relations systems and their ability to cope with change and increasing competition. In other words, the long-term stability of cooperative versus combative labor relationships can be compared once large differences in productivity are no longer the decisive factor explaining the divergence in relative size and accumulated capital.

Although the American industrial relations system was more acrimonious from the start, the negative effects of industrial conflict were not enough to reduce the overall dominance of the US auto industry in the first half of the 20th century. This was maintained for decades without any serious threat as long as there was no foreign competitor who could match the productive prowess of the US system. The oligopoly of the Big Three and the labor monopoly of the UAW also helped regulate and at times lessen the effects of tense industrial relations, at least if one compares the late 1950s and early 1960s to the 1970s (see Norsworthy and Zabala 1985). However, once mass production was no longer exclusive to the US—and was regulated more cooperatively and peacefully in other value-regimes like Germany—then the industrial conflict in the US went from an unfortunate but tolerable status quo to a significant liability and systemic weakness. Valorization advantages accrue to productive systems that better control time with as few interruptions as possible, so cooperative value-regimes like Germany can develop productivity advantages over American firms that result in long-term advantages in accumulating capital. This is precisely what emerged in the 1970s and 1980s, but instead of Germany gaining the decisive advantage over the US, Japanese auto companies gained productivity advantages that had serious long-term consequences for the American auto industry and the viability of its value-regime. Here emerges the link between the cumulative effect of industrial conflict and the ability to control production time from micro-level shop floor disputes to macro-level international competition.

CHAPTER 4

Productivity Gaps as Competitive Crisis: between Automation, Quality, and Lean Production in the 1970s–1990s

1 Tripartite Competition in a Stagnant Era

The 1973 Oil Crisis marked a transition point for the auto industry as the dramatic rise in global oil prices decreased car sales and consumers responded by purchasing smaller, more fuel-efficient cars (Flink 1988: 390–391). However, the oil shock only exacerbated evident trends in the world auto industry, namely that the high growth postwar period was over. After jumping from 5 million autos produced in 1949 to 11 million in 1965, US domestic production averaged around that figure between 1971 and 2007 (Klier and Rubenstein 2020: 51). Total sales, however, increased from around 11 million in 1965 to 15 million in 1985 and 17 million in 2000, which demonstrated the relatively slow increase in total sales though increased sales were not being met by domestic production but by imports (Klier and Rubenstein 2020: 46). With only 83 percent of American households owning a car by 1970 and 95 percent of US domestic sales being for replacement vehicles by 1980, the room for growth in the domestic market diminished as the nation reached a postwar saturation point (Flink 1988: 359).

In Germany, the curve of domestic production began to flatten in the early 1970s (The Digital Archives of Mercedes-Benz Classic 1978: 12–13). Volkswagen and its German subsidiaries experienced stagnant domestic production ranging from around 1.4 to 1.8 million units in domestic production between 1970 and 1996, about half of which was exported, even as its foreign production expanded (Jürgens 1998: 308; Grieger and Lupa 2015). The German market had matured, and exports were necessary to maintain domestic production. This became a problem because exports to the United States fell from over 740,000 exports in 1970 to 465,000 in 1977 (The Digital Archives of Mercedes-Benz Classic 1978: 8). Total German auto exports remained around 1.9 million between 1970 and 1977 due to a rise in exports to Western Europe that compensated for the lost US sales (The Digital Archives of Mercedes-Benz Classic 1978: 8). The 1980s saw modest growth as the total industry had increased total production and employment from approximately 25 percent from 1970 levels by the mid-1980s (Jürgens, Malsch, and Dohse 1993: 35). Even so markets were

 | DOI:10.1163/9789004736719_006

no longer expanding at the same rate as the postwar decades, which intensified competition for revenue and market share.

In mature markets like the United States and Western Europe, the auto industry experienced low growth, while the rest of the world, such as the Communist East or the Global South, would not or could not buy US or European automobiles *en masse*, because autos were still products produced in the capitalist core aimed primarily at consumers in core countries (see Wallerstein 2004). At the end of the 1980s, the US, Western Europe, and Japan were the three major regions of auto production, with each producing around 13 million cars annually, or 84 percent of total world production (Jürgens, Malsch, and Dohse 1993: 38). In this context, *any productive advantage could make a substantial competitive difference* in penetrating competitors' markets.

This is precisely what happened in the US domestic market—and to a lesser extent in the European market—with Japanese automakers such as Toyota, Honda, and Nissan. Japan's auto industry expanded rapidly during the 70s and 80s, surpassing Germany to become the second largest auto producer in 1967 and passing the United States as the world's largest auto producer in 1980 (Flink 1988: 327; Klier and Rubenstein 2020: 51). By the early 1970s, the Japanese market approached maturity, so the industry shifted from domestic sales to exports, exporting over 50 percent of its passenger cars by 1976 (Flink 1988: 328–329). Exports reached a high of 7 million units in 1985 (Heim 2020: 206).

In the United States, Japanese imports increased from 7,500 in 1963 to 182,000 by 1968. Sales then exploded in the 1970s from 1.37 million in 1976 to 2.4 million in 1980 (Flink 1988: 339–340). By 1980, 26 percent of total US sales were imports, most of which were from Japanese rather than German imports (Klier and Rubenstein 2020: 49). The Big Three had much to lose from the influx of imports. For the first time in over half a century of American dominance over the domestic and international auto market, the United States no longer represented a challenge to the world but *was itself being challenged*.

What allowed Japanese automakers to challenge the Big Three? Though there were various factors that contributed to Japanese success, the following discusses the role of *higher productivity of the Japanese production system*. Simply put, Japanese producers developed a system of *industrial organization, production technology*, and *industrial relations* that had a higher overall productivity than both American and German automakers (see Ohno 1988; Krafcik 1988; Womack et al. 2007 [1990]; Liker 2021). This system, popularized as *lean production*, allowed Japanese competitors to produce cars cheaper and with fewer defects than the Americans or Germans (Krafcik 1988; Womack et al. 2007 [1990]). In the context of mature markets and few growth opportunities, such productive advantages placed *productivity pressure* on US automakers to adapt or face decline.

The rapidly changing competitive landscape triggered a global productivity race. Companies, workers, and social scientists alike paid attention to productivity developments, and performance rankings among plants and between companies became of special interest as low productivity could spell doom in the long run (Krafcik 1988; Jürgens et al. 1993; Womack et al. 2007 [1990]). The US no longer held technological *or* productive dominance, but attempts were made to regain this lead by adapting elements of lean production and/or attempting to surpass Japanese producers by "leapfrogging" through deploying new technology (Finkelstein 2003). However, the struggles between management and labor that characterized the US value-regime hobbled attempts to catch up with Japan, so that the following narrative mostly recounts failed attempts to stop and reverse this slow decline (see Helper and Henderson 2014).

Japanese competition in Europe was not as serious. In 1985, the Japanese sold roughly 3.5 million cars in the US compared to only 1.2 million in Western Europe (Heim 2020: 223). German automakers remained strong domestic producers and exporters, but their growth in both arenas was slow compared to the enormous growth of Japanese production and exports (The Digital Archives of Mercedes-Benz Classic 197: 8; Heim 2020: 205–207). German automakers pursued alternative strategies to stay competitive worldwide.

In the 1970s and 1980s, a distinctly German production model emerged that emphasized the strengths of German engineers and skilled workers. Three movements are discussed that characterized the industry during this period: diversified quality production (DQP), new production concepts (NPC), and the humanization of work. Diversified quality production is a product and production strategy aimed at delivering a variety of products that appeal to consumers based on quality rather than price (Sorge and Streeck 2016). New production concepts refer to productive developments focused on high-tech automation steered by highly skilled operators to foster a *re-professionalization of production workers* amenable to the desires of the highly skilled German workforce (Kern and Schumann 1984; 1987). This harmonizes with efforts to humanize work by making production jobs more ergonomic and improved from the standpoint of human health, safety, and longevity.

These movements were path dependent developments of automation and skilled work in the postwar era and from continuous labor-management cooperation to push the frontiers of ergonomics, job integration, and product strategy. Germans developed "high road" production focused on manufacturing high-quality products with high-skilled workers, which were framed as an alternative means to compete with the Japanese (see Jürgens 1998: 295). This strategy appeared to be successful as, while output at VW's German operations stagnated, total revenue rose due to an increase in upmarket sales credited to the increased diversity of products (Jürgens 1998: 308). However, the entire German industry entered a crisis in the early 1990s rooted in the high costs, low profits, and comparatively inefficient production (Jürgens 1998: 296–299; Jürgens, Malsch, and Dohse 1993: 37; Jürgens 2004: 416; Tolliday 1995b). There is, therefore, an "ambiguity of [the] success" of this German model (Jürgens 1998: 296; see Tolliday 1995b).

The rise of Japan is the most impactful development in the world auto industry from the 1970s to the early 1990s. For this reason, an excursus explores Japan's ascension and explains lean production. This is important context for the discussion of productivity development in the US and Germany during this period. To understand the reactions to the "Japanese threat" (Jürgens, Malsch, and Dohse 1993: 37) it is necessary to understand *why* lean production challenged American and German mass production. The subsequent examination details the US and German response to Japan through the evolution of their production systems to explain the outcomes of a competitive struggle between "capitalisms" (see Albert 1993; Hall and Soskice 2003 [2001]).

2 Lean Production as Japanese Challenge

This excursus examines how the *lean production system* contributed to Japanese success (see Krafcik 1988; Womack, Jones, and Roos 2007 [1990]). The penetration of Japanese automakers into the North American and European markets shocked the industry and alerted analysts who wanted to understand what enabled Japanese automakers to disrupt the status quo so effectively. The 1970s oil shocks were a boon to Japanese automakers which, because Japan imported all its oil, were adept at building small fuel-efficient cars (Heim 2020: 206). Though Americans preferred larger vehicles (see Flink 1988; Klier and Rubenstein 2020), high gas prices convinced many Americans to buy small fuel-efficient Japanese cars. Because the Big Three had difficulties reorienting production toward small cars, the Japanese filled this competitive gap (Heim 2020: 206). Changes in needs, wants, and desires affected sales as American "gas-guzzlers" had a harder time realizing their value when fuel was costly.

While gas prices played a role in the Japanese ascension, productivity differences between the *lean production system* and the *mass production systems* in the US and Germany were also important, with the Japanese producing cars at lower cost and higher quality than competitors (Krafcik 1988; Womack, Jones,

Roos 2007 [1990]). With this development, foreign competitors no longer faced productivity pressure to catch up with American productive standards. Rather, Japanese manufacturers surpassed European *and* American automakers so that *Japan became the new benchmark*, which radically altered the production, sales, and profit-making landscape in the global automobile industry.

2.1 *Establishing the Productivity Gap*

Discourse surrounding Japanese competitive strength rose in tandem with Japanese imports (Jürgens, Malsch, and Dohse 1993: 40). However, the origins and extent of the competitive advantage remained unclear until studies from the businesses, unions, governments, and social scientists first appeared in the late 1970s (e.g., Clark 1979; Abernathy, Clark, and Kantrow 1983; Monden 1983; Krafcik 1988). Interest in understanding Japan was most pronounced in the US, but comparative studies were also undertaken in Germany (see Brumlop and Jürgens 1983: 15–16; Jürgens et al. 1993: 41; Jürgens 2021: 5).

Early studies revealed that differences in exchange rate or wages alone did not explain the gap, but that *cost advantages of higher productivity* resulting from socio-technical-organizational differences were apparent. For example, a UAW study in 1985 found that higher efficiency in direct production and assembly explained 38 percent of the Japanese cost advantage, wage differences accounted for 20 percent, 24 percent by the exchange rate, and 18 percent from tax advantages (Jürgens et al. 1993: 42). The MIT International Motor Vehicle Program (IMVP) conducted the most comprehensive studies on the productivity and quality differences between automobile assembly plants (see Krafcik 1988; MacDuffie and Pil (1995); Womack, Jones, and Roos 2007 [1990]). The most famous of these studies was *The Machine that Changed the World* (Womack et al. 2007 [1990]), which argued that Japanese lean production represented the highest form of manufacturing progress. The researchers described the purpose of their study this way:

> In every country and every company ... we have found an intense, even desperate, desire to know the answer to two simple questions: "Where do we stand?" and "What must we do to match the new competitive level required by lean production?" (Womack et al. 2007 [1990]: 77)

Clearly, the desire to understand this system was incredibly high.

The IMVP World Assembly Plant Survey of 1989 surveyed nearly 100 auto assembly plants in Japan, North America, Europe, Brazil, Taiwan, and Korea, among others (Womack, et al. 2007 [1990]: 85). The research team examined the hours required to assemble a standard vehicle and for quality in terms of number of assembly defects (Womack, et al. 2007 [1990]: 80–81). The first surprise was that there was a wide range of performance among plants and that not all Japanese plants were superior to US plants and European plants (Krafcik 1988: 1).

The survey revealed that the most productive plant for assembly hours per vehicle was Japanese (13.2 hours) and that the weighted average of Japanese plants (16.8 hours) was superior to American (24.9) and European plants (35.5). However, the best plants in the US (18.6 hours) and Europe (22.8) had superior performance to the worst performing Japanese plant (25.9). (Womack et al. 2007 [1990]: 85). The researchers concluded it was not accurate to consider all Japanese automakers "lean," or that all other plants were low performers (Womack et al. 2007 [1990]: 87–88).

European producers were on average further behind than American. The weighted average for Europe was 35.5 hours, twice as high as the average for Japan at 16.8, and the worst performing plant in Europe assembled a vehicle in 55.7 hours (Womack et al. 2007 [1990]: 85). A similar pattern was found in the Luxury Car Assembly Plant Survey which found that Japan could produce a luxury car in 16.9 hours, while Cadillac and Lincoln assembled at an average 35.7 hours, and the weighted average for European automakers stood at 57 hours—110.7 hours for the worst performing plant (Womack et al. 2007 [1990]: 89). The researchers theorized that *competitive pressure from Japanese imports and transplants in North America drove the impetus for productivity improvement*, while Europe, by not facing the same competitive threat "has not yet begun to close the competitive gap" (Womack et al. 2007 [1990]: 87).

Surveying assembly plants for quality defects revealed a similar pattern. Measured in defects per 100 vehicles, Japanese producers had a clear edge over American and European automakers with a weighted average of 52.1 defects for Japanese automakers in Japan, 78.4 for the US, and 76.4 for Europe (Womack et al. 2007 [1990]: 86). European producers fared better than American producers on average, and the worst US plant sat at 168.6 defects, the worst European plant had 123.8, while the worst Japanese plant had 88.4 defects (Womack et al. 2007 [1990]: 86). According to Flink (1988: 340), during the 1970s and 1980s, Japanese cars "established a reputation as the best built in the world," rating higher than American autos in a 1979 consumer survey and between Japanese, German, and American cars in a 1980 survey of American automotive engineers. It appeared that for most American and European plants, there was a *tradeoff between productivity and quality*. High productivity could be achieved at the cost of quality or vice versa, but both could not be achieved at the same time. However, for the Japanese, high productivity and high quality *were complementary* and did not require a tradeoff (Womack et al. 2007 [1990]: 93).

The higher productivity of most Japanese automakers often translated into costs. One MIT report from the mid-1980s estimated that the cost difference for small cars averaged $1,500 between Japan and the US, and a smaller cost gap existed between Japanese and European cars (Flink 1988: 335). According to GM's own estimates, in 1994, GM had a $1,500–2,500 cost disadvantage to Japanese cars attributed to differences in productivity and currency exchange (General Motors Heritage Center 1994: 4). Volkswagen's comparative study from 1980 revealed a cost differential of 3,000 Deutschmarks between comparable Japanese and German middle-class vehicles (Brumlop and Jürgens 1983: 16). This difference amounted to 30 percent of the total costs of the automobile (Jürgens et al. 1993: 41). Productivity advantages contributed to cost differentials, which aided penetration into North American and European markets.

The culmination of Japanese competitive advantage was also reflected in their profits. Japanese automakers made "dazzling profits almost without exception" from 1970 to 1985, with profitability developing "so much more favorably that of the [United States, Germany, and Great Britain]" (Jürgens et al. 1993: 39). In the US, the oil crisis of 1979 and the subsequent recession caused Chrysler's profit rate to fall to −18.5 percent or a 1.8 billion dollar loss, necessitating a plan by the federal government, the banks, and the UAW to save the company (Jürgens et al. 1993: 28–29; Flink 1988: 393–397). Ford also lost $1.5 billion and teetered on collapse, while only GM remained profitable but also experienced financial setbacks (Jürgens et al. 1993: 28–29; Helper and Henderson 2014: 50). In Germany, Volkswagen hit a high of profitability of approximately 8 percent in the early 70s during the final years of the Beetle craze but sharply fell to below −4 percent net profit in 1974, an over $300 million dollar loss (Jürgens et al. 1993: 37; Kemezis 1975). Thereafter, profitability returned, but remained at a low level, staying typically between 0 and 2 percent throughout the late 70s to the mid-1980s (Jürgens et al. 1993: 37). Productivity alone by no means determines the profit rate, yet there is no doubt that efficient production contributes to it. Considering the competitive advantages and growth of the Japanese industry during this period, only Japanese producers and GM as world leader maintained profitability throughout the 1970s and 1980s.

As productivity and quality advantages were revealed, governments, companies, and unions realized in both countries that measures were needed to close the productivity gap and narrow the competitive imbalance. As one report summarized the situation,

> Because the present competitive gap between the best Japanese producers and the weakest Western producers is so great, and because the process of adjustment by its nature will require many years to complete, it

> is evident that the potential for dramatic shifts in share among national auto industries and for disaster for individual producers will persist for many years. To make matters worse, the adjustment process will proceed in a macroeconomic environment that is likely to be only marginally better than that of the period since 1973. (Flink 1988: 407–408)

In mature markets and in a period of stagnant growth, the production advantages of Japanese automakers were *exerting productivity pressure* onto their American and European competitors. Because these advantages aided in accumulating capital, the *norms of socially necessary labor time adjusted to the productivity standards set by the Japanese lean producers*. After achieving comparable productivity to the United States in the 1950s and 1960s, European producers again fell behind as the 'Japanese Challenge' replaced the 'American Challenge.' For US manufacturers, productivity leadership changed hands for the first time since the Ford Motor Company developed the Fordist mass production system in 1914. Therefore, the Big Three were no longer setting the productivity norms that others were compelled to follow but were for the first time *compelled to catch up to the productivity norms* of other automakers. The economic imperative to increase productivity was especially acute in the United States because Japanese imports were proliferating in the American market. However, there are also alternative means to addressing competitive and cost differentials, such as decreasing worker valorization and implementing trade barriers. The next section explores how the US and Europe regulated trade to address the competitive imbalances.

2.2 *Trade Barriers, Transplants, and Productivity Pressure*

The world auto industry during this period was primarily a tripartite split between North America, Europe, and Japan. While respective domestic automakers generated the most production and sales, there was also considerable trade between the regions, with 4.2 million autos exchanged in 1985 (Jürgens et al. 1993: 38). However, by the mid-1970s, much of this trade (around 80 percent) were exports *from* Japan *to* Western Europe and the United States, with only 1 percent being imported into Japan (Jürgens, et al. 1993: 38). With such a large trade deficit, especially between the US and Japan, the Reagan administration applied "intense pressure" on the Japanese government to implement "voluntary import restraints" (VER) on the Japanese auto industry. This limited the import of Japanese autos from around 1.5 to 2.5 million autos from 1981–1994 (Flink 1988: 342; Benjamin 1999).

The VER program was designed to give US manufacturers "respite from Japanese competition while they retooled to produce small, fuel-efficient cars,"

(Flink 1988: 342) while not erecting tariffs, which would have "complicated negotiations over the massive and politically crucial economy-wide tax cuts the administration was proposing at the same time" (Benjamin: 1999: 2). Tariffs would have been the most straightforward policy, but the American affinity for "free markets," especially in the ascendent neoliberal ideology of the Reagan administration, was an ideological barrier (see Brown 2015; Jouet 2017: 175–179). The Japanese government also wanted to avoid tariffs, as one analysis estimated that tariffs would have cost Japanese automakers $11.2 billion (Berry, Levinsohn, and Pakes 1999: 422).

The regulations appeared to generate their intended effects as the profits of the US auto companies were estimated to have risen by $10.2 billion over the period, and the Federal Trade Commission estimated that the import restrictions saved 44,000 American jobs (Berry, Levinsohn, and Pakes 1999: 421; Flink 1988; 343). Without any trade restrictions, it was estimated in 1984 that "Japanese producers would have been able to sell one million more cars in the United States than they did, thereby reducing the sales of American firms by 10 to 15 percent" (Quinn 1988: 45). Thus, the VER did have a positive impact on the domestic US auto industry (Benjamin 1999: 2). It did, however, hurt American consumers as the price of a Japanese car in the US rose by around $1,200 (14 percent higher) and the price of an American-made car rose by around $600 (Benjamin 1999: 1; Flink 1988: 343). Price sensitive car buyers were therefore choosing domestic vehicles over Japanese cars, driving the increase in domestic profits (Benjamin 1999: 2). The restrictions convinced Japanese firms to establish transplants in the US.[1]

Honda established the first Japanese transplant in 1982 in Marysville, Ohio, followed by Nissan in Smyrna, Tennessee plant in 1983 (Flink 1988: 340–341; Klier and Rubenstein 2020: 52). Smaller Japanese producers also established transplants in the late 1980s, such as Mitsubishi (1987), Mazda (1987) and Subaru (1989) (Klier and Rubenstein 2020: 52). Eleven Japanese assembly

1 Volkswagen was the first US foreign transplant, establishing an assembly plant in Westmoreland, Pennsylvania in 1978 (Klier and Rubenstein 2020: 52). They aimed to reinvigorate US sales in the post-Beetle era and profit from American production though favorable exchange rates and lower labor costs (McKenney 2018: 100–103). However, the plant was also beset with troubles including "production setbacks, management shakeups, economic crises, and labor unrest" (McKenney 2018: 138). This occurred, in part, because *no attempt was made to transplant the cooperative German system to the plant*, so the combative relations typical of the US value-regime appeared at Westmoreland (Jürgens 1994: 96). In addition, Japanese competition was so intense that sales decreased from 177 thousand in 1980 to 53 thousand by 1987. It was then that Volkswagen decided to close the plant by 1989, blaming Japanese competition for the decline (Flink 1988: 326).

plants were established in North America by 1995 (Howes 1995: 167). Toyota established a joint venture in 1984 with General Motors called the New United Motors Manufacturing Inc. (NUMMI) by repurposing a shutdown GM plant in Fremont, California (Klier and Rubenstein 2020: 52). The plant was both unionized and implemented the lean production, which required establishing a UAW contract unlike any other in the US to facilitate the lean system (Ruben 1985). Because of this, NUMMI received considerable attention from social scientists wanting to learn about lean production and to observe its compatibility with unionized US workers (e.g., Krafcik 1988; Adler 1993a, 1993b; Berggren 1994; Womack et al. 2007 [1990]). The success of NUMMI, it was claimed, demonstrated that lean production could be successfully transferred to other countries with unionized workers (Adler 1993a, 1993b).

However, while Japanese transplants provided Americans jobs and were more preferable for the US economy than imports, the transplants had important implications for the Big Three and the American value-regime. First, transplants shifted the geography of production as many Japanese plants were located in the South (Klier and Rubenstein 2020: 52–53). These locations did not have a history of unionization and/or had right-to-work laws that hurt unionization efforts, thus most Japanese plants, with the exceptions of the joint ventures such as NUMMI, Ford-Mazda, and Chrysler-Mitsubishi, were not unionized by the UAW (see Ruben 1985; Babson 1993, 1995a). Transplant workers earned wages close to their Big Three counterparts but had less generous fringe benefits such as pension and health coverage (Howes 1995: 169–175). Transplants *de facto ended the labor monopoly* held by the UAW in the United States, hurt the pattern bargaining system established in the 1930s, and pressured the UAW to accept wage and benefit concessions (Howes 1995: 157).

These transplants did not transfer an integrated production system using American labor and American parts but limited local production to final assembly and the acquisition of US made parts. Thus, the contribution to the American economy was "little better than that of imports" (Howes 1995: 157). Processes such as design and engineering, and the manufacture of major components such as the engine, transmission, and electronic controls were confined to Japan, meaning numerous important jobs remained in Japan rather than the US (Howes 1995: 167). Profits from these ventures were also repatriated to Japan. Japanese imports and transplants, to the extent that they poached sales from the Big Three, weakened the US value-regime centered around the Big Three and the UAW. There essentially existed two sets of industrial relations in the US value-regime, one based on the Big Three and the UAW, and the other based on the mostly nonunion Japanese transplants. This had important implications for the financial health of the domestic automakers and the fate of the UAW workers.

The situation was more favorable in Europe. While tariffs on automobiles decreased generally in the three major regions since the 1950s, there were considerable non-tariff barriers imposed on Japanese imports. Import quotas were issued on Japanese automakers in many European auto-producing countries to "prevent the further penetration of markets" (Flink 1988: 294). Germany benefitted from such voluntary export restrictions, keeping Japanese market share in Europe to around 12 percent, although the European VER was rescinded in 2000 (Donnelly, Mellahi, and Morris 2002: 31). In addition, assembly transplants emerged in Europe starting with Nissan in the UK in 1984, and Toyota in the UK and France in the 1990s, practicing new productivity benchmarks on European soil (Rehder and Thompson 1994; Donnelly, Mellahi, and Morris 2002: 31). Thus, Japanese competition was more contained in Europe, partially explaining why Europe faced the 'Japanese Challenge' with less urgency.

Import restrictions and tariffs attempt to equalize the cost differences gained through higher productivity or other cost advantages. This can reduce the need or urgency to raise the domestic producers' productivity and therefore *reduces the productivity pressure of social domination.* If commodities produced at a lower speed and more expensive production process can successfully compete and accumulate capital because of government intervention in trade restrictions and tariffs, then the pressures to conform to standards of socially necessary labor time are effectively nullified by the government. Such trade restrictions represent one strategy of coping with social domination *apart from* increasing productivity in the domestic firms. Tariffs *directly counter productivity pressures* and the ability to use productive advantages to penetrate markets and accumulate capital. Such restrictions are therefore tools to defend value-regimes from competition and social domination.

2.3 *Lean Production Improves Productivity*

The following provides a schematized description of lean production, relying primarily on the writings of the system's originator, Taiichi Ohno, equivalent to Frederick Winslow Taylor or Henry Ford in terms of being the primary figure behind a comprehensive system of mass manufacturing (Jürgens et al. 1993: 43). The foundational premise of lean production is the *total elimination of waste* (Ohno 1988: 4). Ohno (1988) defines waste as "all elements of production that only increase cost without adding value—for example, excess people, inventory, and equipment. Too many workers, equipment, and products only increase the cost and cause secondary waste" (54). There are multiple types of waste that increase costs, from the waste of overproduction which can lead to the waste of surplus inventory, to the waste of excess movement of workers on the line or machines that make waste by producing defective parts (Ohno 1988:

19–20). Since waste increases cost, the purpose of reducing waste is to improve efficiency to reduce costs, which is achieved when the firm starts "producing only things we need using minimal manpower" (Ohno 1988: 18). As Ohno (1988) puts it,

> In the Toyota production system, we think of economy in terms of manpower reduction and cost reduction. The relationship between these two elements is clearer if we consider a manpower reduction policy as a means of realizing cost reduction, the most critical condition for businesses survival and growth. Manpower reduction at Toyota is a company-wide activity whose purpose is cost reduction. Therefore, all considerations and improvement ideas, when boiled down, must be tied to cost reduction. Saying this in reverse, the criterion of all decisions is whether cost reduction can be achieved. (Ohno 1988: 53)

Boyer and Freyssenet (2002) in their typology of productive models characterize this as a model focused on achieving *continuous cost reductions*. The other principles of LP flow from this all-encompassing priority.

Ohno describes two pillars that support the goal of eliminating waste: *just-in-time* and *autonomation*, or automation with a human touch. Just-in-time is a system of material flow that emphasizes acquiring necessary parts "at the right time they are needed and only in the amount needed (Ohno 1988: 4). This requires a total rearrangement of how materials flow through production processes. Instead of parts being produced in one process that are then *pushed* onto the next process, as in Fordism, the needed materials are *pulled* to final assembly backward from previous processes through a synchronized ordering and flow chain organized via an information conveyance tool called *kanban* (Ohno 1988: 5–6). Inspired by American supermarkets, the kanban system informs each production step what is needed, at the time it is needed, and in the amount needed, and thus facilitates just-in-time delivery of necessary parts (Ohno 1988: 25–30). The underlying objective of achieving smooth flow through production processes remains the same in both Fordism and lean production, but flow is achieved differently in a *pull* rather than a *push* system.

The better just-in-time flow is facilitated, the less inventory is necessary to house and maintain parts, with the ideal system requiring zero inventory (Ohno 1988: 4). This is desirable because, for Ohno (1988: 54), excess inventory is considered "The greatest waste of all." This is because inventories require storage space, warehouses, workers who haul materials, and transportation equipment (Ohno 1988: 54–55). These activities entail costs, but do not directly contribute to transforming the materials that constitute the automobile and are therefore considered indirect non-value-added work. Maintaining inventory for any length of time represents a *break in the flow of value in motion.* In an ideal frictionless process of value in motion, value always stays in motion with no inventory or wait times, flowing from valorization to realization to distribution and reinvestment in a continuous movement. Parts in storage are neither valorizing nor realizing their value and neither their value nor use value is being utilized while in storage. In fact, to the extent that inventory degrades physically (e.g., rusts) the use value and value of inventory likewise degrades, and additional costs must be applied to manage and maintain the inventory (e.g., rust prevention). To the degree just-in-time reduces the size of inventories, it avoids these costs. With this system, Ohno implemented a way to achieve more seamless flow of value in motion, which *set new productivity norms* while decreasing both capital and labor costs needed for storage space. According to the IMVP World Assembly Plant Survey, in 1989, the average Japanese plant had 0.2 days' worth of inventory for eight sampled parts compared to 2.9 days of inventory in North American plants and 2.0 days for European plants (Womack et al. 2007 [1990]: 92). In this way, lean producers had lower costs and a competitive advantage by understanding the importance of improving flow and how inventory is antithetical to the goal of keeping value in motion.

The second pillar is *autonomation or automation with a human touch.* Autonomation states that individual units of production should have the ability and autonomy to shut themselves down if there is any abnormality. For example, for automatic machines, defective parts can emerge if any irregularity, such as a piece of scrap falling into the machine, is not detected, stopped, and fixed to prevent future mistakes. To enable this, machines are equipped to make distinctions between normal and abnormal operations and countermeasures are taken to prevent recurrence. The emphasis lies in eliminating the wastes of machine breakdown time, the time wasted in producing and fixing defective parts, and the waste of overproduction, which can lead to the wastes of inventory (Ohno 1988: 6–8). Indeed, a 1983 study of Japanese and American manufacturing determined that the longer and consistent equipment run times possible through autonomation was the most important factor for explaining the Japanese productivity advantage (Abernathy et al. 1983).

This principle also extended to production workers, with implications for skill development. In lean production, workers also have the responsibility to stop the assembly line when a problem emerges (Ohno 1988: 7). This is facilitated with the *Andon cord* that hangs above each production worker that, when pulled, stops the line and immediately starts the process of problem solving (Ohno 1988: 21–23). The worker and fellow team members are tasked with asking the "five whys" to solve the problem, i.e., asking why the problem occurred continuously until the root of the aberration is found and corrected (Ohno 1988: 17). If implemented well, both machines and workers can detect and solve problems as soon as they occur, thus *minimizing the time* used to fix machine breakdown or other issues as fast as possible. Ohno compares this production philosophy to the fable of the tortoise and the hare. LP is like a tortoise that runs continuously without disruption, albeit usually *not* at the maximum speed possible to avoid overproduction and the risk of machine breakdown. By contrast, Fordist mass production is like the hare that runs at high speeds, but the *hypothetical advantage* of those high speeds is *negated* when long breakdowns occur (see Ohno 62–63; Liker 2021: 91–108). Ohno's philosophy aligns with David Harvey's (2017: 4–13) assertion that maintaining the consistency of value in motion is the most advantageous condition for capital accumulation.

To ensure flow and eliminate waste, workers must be equipped with the skills to perform a variety of jobs and fix a variety of problems, i.e., workers are *multiskilled* to address potential production problems (Adler 1993b: 3). Arranging workers in teams and frequent job rotation helps build the necessary multiskilled workforce (Ohno 1988: 23–34). Multiskilling equips workers to do as much value-added work as possible and reduces non-value-added repair personnel by giving production workers the responsibility to perform maintenance (Ohno 1988: 57–58). This entails skill upgrading compared to the unskilled or semi-skilled workers of "classical" Fordism and lessens the need for indirect skilled workers. However, in the name of eliminating waste, each job is *standardized as much as possible*, thereby resulting in workers who are multiskilled in a variety of repetitive and standardized jobs (Ohno 1988: 21–23). In addition, waste is constantly removed from production processes by the workers themselves through a process called *kaizen*. Continuous improvement, i.e., kaizen, means eliminating waste is a *never-ending pursuit*. To achieve this, workers are encouraged to make suggestions on how to improve productivity. Most accepted suggestions explicitly aim at eliminating waste, although improved ergonomics or other changes may be accepted if they also eliminate waste (Liker 2021). This makes direct production workers, rather than Taylorist industrial engineers, responsible for improving production processes.

Quality and productivity go hand in hand in LP. High productivity at the expense of quality *disguises waste* because either the manufacturer wastes time fixing the issue, or it is instead externalized to the customer. If quality issues are externalized then it is a kind of "cheating" where production appears efficient, but burdens the time of customers instead, which can have its own social-communication effects and harm realization. Therefore, quality production is "built in" through autonomation and multiskilled direct workers (Liker 2021: 129–144). This is how both high quality and high productivity are achieved simultaneously.

Automation plays a nuanced role in lean production. Womack et al. (2007 [1990]: 94) found that automation accounted for about one-third of the total difference in productivity, with more automated plants having higher productivity, but there was also a considerable difference in productivity between highly automated lean and non-lean plants. One explanation for this is that some highly automated plants, especially in Europe, are "improperly organized" so that nearly as many indirect maintenance and repair workers are added as unskilled direct workers are eliminated. Secondly, non-lean plants tend to have worse machine breakdown to operating time ratios, leading the analysts to conclude that lean organization and autonomation is necessary for optimizing automation (Womack et al. 2007 [1990]: 94–95). However, Toyota, the leading Japanese firm, has a somewhat cautious approach to adopting new technologies. LP aims to produce only what is demanded and flexibly respond to demand fluctuations. Therefore, large investments in inflexible machinery can be problematic if demand falls. Toyota typically delayed acquiring the latest technology until there was confidence the technology will improve efficiency (Liker 2021: 159–160). Therefore, while Toyota today utilizes hundreds of robots, automated machines, and even supercomputers, the company is not prone to invest in unproven technologies (Liker 2021: 160; see Jürgens 2023: 199–236).

All these practices were supported by a reward structure that fostered worker commitment to the system and identification with the goals of eliminating waste. In Japan, this was cultivated by practices such as lifetime employment guarantees for the core workforce, a monoculture that fosters corporate socialization, profit sharing and conditional "merit" based pay, and "enterprise" unions closely aligned with corporate interests (Babson 1995c: 238–242). With these practices, Wittrock (2015: 33) argues that LP in Japan was best understood as a "lean, long-term and loyal" orientation rather than simply "lean" focusing exclusively on cost-cutting. These practices fostered commitment and cooperative relations understood as necessary for LP but did not directly improve productivity themselves. Thus, these practices, though considered essential in the "wholistic" conception of LP (see Womack et al. 2007 [1990]), were rarely implemented or heavily modified in attempts to adapt LP to different value-regimes (Covarrubias and Ramírez Perez 2020b: 8).

Lean production is a system oriented toward continuously increasing productivity through eliminating wasted time in all production processes. It can also be considered a kind of technology (Harvey 2017: 9). It is a *type of scientific management* that has key differences from Taylorism but nevertheless shares the same optimization goals. Unlike Fordist mass production where production standards are updated with each model change, *lean production codifies continuous improvement as a daily task and imperative.* In this way, there is constant pressure to redefine productivity standards. By removing extraneous movement, time, workers, and equipment, the production treadmill accelerates so activities that *actively move value* make up as much production time as possible. LP is dedicated to strict control over time to achieve, not just optimized, but *continuously re-optimized flows of value in motion.* Therefore, it appears lean production more strongly embodies the logic of capital as value in motion than other production systems (Harvey 2017).

3 Automation 'Leapfrog' and Productivity Strategies in the US

When *The Machine that Changed the World* (Womack et al. 2007 [1990]) was released in 1990, it verified what had been understood in the American auto industry for nearly two decades: Japanese competition was producing higher quality automobiles at lower costs thanks to the productivity advantages of their lean productive system. The Big Three especially wanted to understand the causes of the Japanese advantage because they suffered the most from stagnating domestic auto sales that were increasingly eaten into by Japanese imports and transplants (Klier and Rubenstein 2020: 49). GM was losing market share at approximately 10 percent per decade since the 1970s (Helper and Henderson 2014: 50; Finkelstein 2003: 19). Ford also suffered from market share decline and financial losses during the early 1980s, while Chrysler became so precarious that it required a federally backed $1.5 billion loan guarantee in 1979 to save it from bankruptcy (Flink 1988: 393–397). Though Chrysler and Ford bounced back to profitability by the mid-1980s through union concessions, plant closures, and restructuring, the experience demonstrated the perils of a low growth, high competition market (Jürgens et al. 1993: 29; Flink 1988: 393–397).

Therefore, the pressure to match the "lean" productivity norms became increasingly urgent to halt or reverse the decline. The discussion details the attempts to prevent the long-term decline of the Big Three's productive system. One factor was government supported import restrictions, which benefited the US auto industry and saved jobs (Benjamin 1999; Berry et al. 1999). There were also attempts to implement aspects of lean production into American plants (Jürgens et al. 1993; Adler, Kochan, MacDuffie, and Pil 1997). New investments in technology, especially at General Motors, were made to surpass Japanese productivity norms through cutting edge production technology and automation (Finkelstein 2003; Helper and Henderson 2014). The purported wage differences between American and Japanese companies supplied ammo for management to pressure the UAW to accept wage and benefit concessions (Yates 1992). The UAW resisted, however, while union leadership acceded to some concessions, rank-and-file discontent was expressed via a critique of lean production, reframing it as "management by stress" (Parker and Slaughter 1988, 1995; Williams, Haslam, Williams, Cutler, Adcroft, and Johal (1992); Babson 1993; 1995a). The path dependent legacy of contentious relations between management and labor contributed to the failure of the US industry to stem the tide of competition by reaching the productive standards set by lean production (Helper and Henderson 2014; Lam et al. 1991). The US industry since the 1970s attempted to reverse industrial decline through these strategies.

3.1 *Automation and Adaptation to Answer the Japanese Challenge*

The 1970s and 1980s were a time of experimentation to implement elements of LP and coming up with "home-grown" solutions to counter the Japanese advantages (Jürgens et al. 1993: 386–390). The alternatives to lean production developed in the United States and Germany both centered around automation and new technology, albeit with different emphases. American corporations were also more willing to adopt lean practices than Germans, partly because of the urgency of addressing Japanese competition in the US market.

Technology had driven productivity gains in the auto industry since the advent of Fordism. In the postwar decades, Detroit automation defined the technological frontier and was associated with the United States as world productivity leader (Hounshell 2000). When it was recognized that productivity leadership was lost to the Japanese, a "fundamental break with past practices" in the Big Three became necessary for long-term survival (Jürgens et al. 1993: 377). Initially, it was believed that robots and automation were a primary cause of the Japanese productive advantage (Jürgens 2023: 188–189). Therefore, the Big Three invested heavily in cutting edge technology to "leapfrog" the Japanese (Yates 1992: 131; Finkelstein 2003). Billions of dollars were invested in new technology during the 1980s, including microelectronics, computers, and robots, which were supposed to commence a revolution in automobile production.

This revolution seemed inevitable as forecasts about the exploding power of technology abounded. For example, there were predictions that by 1990 robots would be able to approximate human capabilities in assembly, with 37 percent of employment in the world auto industry predicted to be automated by 2000 (Flink 1988: 401; Jürgens 2021: 3). These predictions did not materialize, but nevertheless, American automakers were convinced investments in assembly automation may single-handedly determine the future competitive landscape. Therefore, investments were needed immediately to reap these long-term benefits. As GM CEO Roger Smith explained in 1987, "Any automaker who didn't invest [in automation] a few years ago will be struggling tomorrow to compete" (General Motors Heritage Center 1987: 3). In a 1982 address on "Meeting the Japanese Auto Challenge," a Ford corporate projects director concurred that an "auto revolution" was sweeping Ford's plants, estimating that confronting Japan required retooling dozens of assembly lines where "hardly a machine tool or part will remain the same" (Barnes 1982: 11). Even as initial results disappointed, Smith maintained that early investment was beneficial because all firms will eventually have to make similar investments to stay competitive,

> Our competitors are going to have to shut down their plants, spend money on engineering, and they're going to have to do the things we've done to stay in the race. In some respects we've gone through the swamps and crossed the river and we're up on the high ground now … The competition will come. They've got their own little swamps and rivers to go through. (Behr 1986)

Among the Big Three, GM's Smith held the strongest conviction that "technology would restore GM's dominance" (Behr 1986).

This was reflected in GM's unprecedented $45 billion in acquisitions and automation between 1980 and 1985 (Helper and Henderson 2014: 53). For example, GM acquired Electronic Data Systems Corp. for its computers and software and partnered with Fujitsu Fanuc Ltd. of Japan to manufacture and sell robotics (General Motors Heritage Center 1982; Behr 1986). Ford formed a Manufacturing Technology Applications Department in 1981 to help "incorporate the latest cost-effective state-of-the-art techniques" such as robots and microprocessors to "[increase] productivity with a potential for substantial cost savings and additional assurances that our products remain competitive with those built anywhere in the world" (Ford Motor Company Archives 1981: 1–2). GM automated aggressively, typically retooling with all new technology all at once, while Ford applied new technology gradually and focused on rationalizing labor deployment and encouraging employee involvement (Jürgens et al. 1993: 197, 336–339). In either case, billions in investments were made to secure long-term productive advantages.

The technological basis for the "auto revolution" was the rise of computers and flexible robotics. Advances in computers allowed computer-aided design to complement computer-integrated manufacturing to move beyond the limits of Detroit automation (Flink 1988: 399). The main advantage was that computers could steer, synchronize, and program robots, whereas Detroit automation were purely mechanical devices (Jürgens 2023: 188). American company Unimation began the robotics industry in 1961, with some of the first industrial robots appearing at GM's Lordstown factory in 1969 (Association for Advancing Automation 2023). By the 1980s, robot capabilities advanced significantly. The first generation of robots were controlled by sequence-controlled devices with low flexibility, but the second generation could be freely programmed. The third generation integrated sensors and reacted to environmental changes (Jürgens 2023: 188). The high flexibility of the third generation was claimed to possess the highest automation potential because flexibility limitations were why final assembly remained so labor intensive (less than 10 percent of assembly was automated) while most other production areas were between 50–95 percent automated by 1990 (Jürgens 2021: 6). Transfer machines were sufficient for standardized processes, but final assembly was difficult to automate due to the necessary flexibility requirements (Jürgens et al. 1993: 67; Hounshell 2000; Jürgens and Meißner 2005: 42). Flexible robots promised to reconcile Fordism and Sloanism, i.e., the struggle between standardization and flexibility, because "robots can perform routine tasks much more cheaply than can human beings" (Flink 1988: 401; Jürgens 1993: 66–67). By 1987, half of all robot sales in the US were in the auto industry, with 26,000 robots operating in final assembly (Flink 1988: 401; Jürgens 2023: 188–189). There were also efforts to streamline production, reduce parts, and develop common platforms for different models to reduce complexity, save costs, and aid robot assembly (Yates 1992: 131; Jürgens et al. 1993: 53–59). Automatic guided vehicle (AGV) systems aimed to further automate materials handling as they "automatically carried parts from one workstation to the next on platforms guided by magnetic strips embedded in the floor" (Adler et al. 1997: 78; Jürgens 2023: 189–190). Machines and IT systems were networked to realize computer-integrated manufacturing (Jürgens 2021; Jürgens 2023: 189). Together, the technologies of the 1980s promised major advances in productivity and quality in auto production.

Despite the high expectations and massive investment, the gains in productivity and quality were lower than expected (Adler et al. 1997: 79). Internal GM reports found that despite the investments in automation, the Japanese cost advantage had not narrowed between 1981–1985 (Finkelstein 2003: 21). While industry efficiency on average improved 2.8 percent per year, GM's performance relative to Toyota's fell between 1984 to 1991, indicating the productivity gap was growing (Lieberman and Dhawan 2005: 1072). Therefore, productivity was increasing faster at Toyota than at GM despite the latter's heavy investments. This was partially due to problems with the technology. Robots often failed to work as expected, e.g., misplacing welds, crashing into each other, and installing the wrong parts on the wrong model (Ingrassia and White 1994: 111; Adler et al. 1997: 78; Jürgens 2023: 191). The AGVs frequently malfunctioned, e.g., veering off and roaming the halls, or staying frozen in place due to software errors (Adler et al. 1997: 78; Ingrassia 2011: 91; Jürgens 2023: 191–192). At some plants, the operation times for the high-tech areas were often below 50 percent (Jürgens et al. 1993: 189). As Ingrassia (2011) describes, the "factories of the future were becoming industrial houses of horror—and expensive ones at that" (91).

One notable example of these problems was GM's Hamtramck plant. Opened in 1985, the factory utilized state-of-the-art robots and AGVs. Its mission was to reduce GM's cost per vehicle by $2000 to match Toyota's prices (Ingrassia and White 1994: 78; Jürgens 2023: 193). It would accomplish this by applying ambitious new technologies as Ingrassia and White (1994) describe,

> Parts would arrive "just in time," and be toted by … AGV's … to the right spot on the line. Engines would be ferried to the car bodies by AGV's too. Robot arms would do all the painting … Massive welding machines called robo-gates would stitch together car bodies in seconds. Millions of dollars-worth of computers would test each car's electrical systems for malfunctions. (79)

However, Hamtramck failed to meet these expectations. Problems often emerged with the new tech that had to be fixed by the robot manufacturers. Undertrained workers stood helplessly by the complicated software-controlled technology. At times, all activities in the factory stopped due to major malfunctions (Ingrassia and White 1994; Jürgens 2023: 193). As the debacle unfolded it,

> turned into a Waterloo for Smith and his automation campaign. Hamtramck was a fantastically expensive and inefficient parody of Toyota's system. The plant had hundreds of robots, but it also had 5,000 workers on the payroll, just like an old-style GM factory. (Ingrassia and White 1994: 111)

With a factory full of robots *and* workers, automation at Hamtramck even failed at saving labor costs, defeating the purpose of automation (Jürgens 2023: 193). With these misfires, what was supposed to enable faster and smoother flows of value in motion instead stopped the flow of value and incurred additional repair costs. Although there were still productivity improvements in American plants during the 1980s, the automation "leapfrog" failed to close the productivity gap with Japanese lean producers (Jürgens et al. 1993: 282–286; Womack et al. 2007 [1990]).

Why did the automation strategy fare so poorly? The first issue stemmed from inflated expectations of immature technology. Even contemporary flexible robotics and computers are not flexible and fast enough to match the reliable flexibility of "lean" human teams on the assembly line (see Boudette 2018; Jürgens 2023: 194–197). It appeared GM adopted the "latest fad without really understanding the underlying processes and inter-relationships" (Finkelstein 2003: 22). Second, the secret of Japanese productivity was *misrecognized as a technological superiority* (Helper and Henderson 2014). Lean production was not based on the advanced "hardware" of computer-integrated manufacturing systems, but on the "software" of shop floor organization, teamwork, and management-labor relations (Ohno 1988; Degan 2011: 20). As Womack et al. (2007 [1990]: 94–95) observed, automation was most productive at lean plants, signifying that "software" and "hardware" must complement one another to achieve system optimization.

This was difficult to achieve at US plants due to labor-management conflict. The new equipment required skilled workers to maintain and repair the robots, but decades of skilled worker repression and automation resulted in a lack of competent skilled workers (see Reynolds 1989; Meyer 2004; Crumm 2010). This was a path dependent result of past automation that deskilled workers that created an "alarming" deficit of problem-solving competence and training among skilled workers (Jürgens et al. 1993; 187; see Bainbridge 1983; Weyer 1997). Unlike Germany, with its overabundance of skilled workers who enthusiastically pursued qualifications, the United States lacked skilled workers because of the decline of vocational training. It is also a cultural orientation as "the attitude … is that if you went into a trade, it's because you failed to get into college. People tend to look down on you and your job" (Harbour 2017; see Crumm 2010). Without extensive company-based training to make up for this deficit, American workers were ill equipped to handle the new technology. Finally, the tradition of strict job classifications in the US, which is absent in Germany, became a source of industrial relations conflict in the US, with confusion as to which skilled trades oversaw the new technology (Jürgens et al. 1993: 185–190). Thus, the characteristics of the US value-regime, with its conflictual industrial relations and devaluation of vocational training, hurt the ability of the Big Three to optimize new technology, precluding the possibility of an "automation leapfrog" (see Helper and Henderson 2014).

Adopting disparate elements of lean production before it was understood as a wholistic program was difficult because it was not clear what aspects of Japanese production processes were responsible for the productivity advantage. The adaptability of LP outside of Japan's socio-cultural context was also questioned (Wittrock 2015; Jürgens et al. 1993: 386). Nevertheless, American firms experimented with Japanese production methods as best they understood them, by implementing quality circles, work teams, just-in-time delivery, and making job demarcations resemble job structure in Japan. As Lam, Norsworthy, and Zabala (1991) put it, "Anything in Japanese management connected with productivity or product quality quickly obtains the attention of American business" (430). After the apparent failure of the "automation leapfrog," closely copying Japan became especially popular in the US during the 1990s after the publication of *The Machine that Changed the World* codified the popular understanding of LP outside Japan (Womack et al. 2007 [1990]). Automation thus fell out of favor with the Big Three, and the task of adopting lean production became the focus since the 1990s.

In the late 1970s and early 1980s, Ford and GM established branded programs designed to mimic Japanese practices as they were understood at the time. GM's program was called Quality of Work-Life (QWL), and Ford termed their program Employee Involvement (EI). Developed by management but endorsed by the UAW, by 1984 Ford had eighty-six EI programs and GM established QWL at 151 factories (Jürgens et al. 1993: 82–83). These programs entailed what Jürgens, Malsch, and Dohse (1993) term *new work and motivation* concepts aimed at improving the cooperation and communication between workers and management to achieve higher productivity. The goal was to approach the Japanese level of quality and productivity by motivating workers to actively prevent and solve production problems. As Henry Ford II (1982: 13–14) explained, the program was to forge a "new spirit of cooperation between the company's management and its union" that "has laid the groundwork for continued quality improvement and an all-out effort to achieve cost competitiveness." The programs signaled that management and union were willing to "do whatever was necessary to meet the Japanese competition," even if this meant trying to "beat the Japanese with their own weapons, 'to out-Japanese Japan'" (Jürgens et al. 1993: 322).

Improving worker motivation in the US was sorely needed due to decades of Taylorist division of labor, speed-up, and a buildup of grievances that made workers discontented and distrustful of management (see Norsworthy and Zabala 1985; Helper and Henderson 2014). In fact, it was illustrated empirically by Lam, Norsworthy, and Zabala (1991) that US firms had higher costs than Japanese firms stemming from negative workers' attitudes. Unlike the contentious American system, Japanese industrial relations were characterized by "non-adversarial collective bargaining, with lower grievance rates, fewer unresolved grievances, fewer strikes, and higher end process quality audits" (Lam, Norsworthy, and Zabala 1991: 431). The problems also stemmed from the American management approach that privileged fast over high quality production—which fomented workers discontent over speed-up—and an engineering tradition that favored producing parts with minimum instead of maximum perfection of tolerance (Meyer 2009: 160). All of this contributed to the low-quality reputation that American automobiles were garnering among disaffected US consumers. Their lack of ability to control time in production generated negative communications about their quality, leading to a reputation that hurt the realization possibilities of US autos (Flink 1988: 340; Meyer 2009: 160).

The new work and motivation programs were designed to address these problems. GM's QWL program reduced hierarchy and allowed a "greater degree of self-regulation in the jobs carried out" through establishing semi-autonomous work groups. Quality circles were permanent groups where workers were encouraged to meet regularly, receive problem solving training, and recommend improvements or implement their own decisions (Jürgens et al. 1993: 83). The success of the NUMMI joint venture with Toyota helped further spread the "team concept" in the late 1980s (Jürgens et al. 1993: 85). Beginning in 1979, Ford's EI program intended to implement "definite measures supporting worker participation in identifying and solving work-related problems," to increase "employee identification with the company," and to strengthen "the elements of 'jointness' between management and the union" (Jürgens et al. 1993: 88). This program did not entail formation of work groups in the spirit of autonomation but aligned closer with the Japanese goal of continuous improvement through kaizen, taking steps to cooperatively solve production problems. To this end, joint EI union and management steering committees were established to organize quality circles and problem-solving groups (Jürgens et al. 1993: 90). As Henry Ford II (1982: 14) described, the EI efforts made it so "production employees are now actively participating in decisions about their jobs and our products."

In both companies, the programs were aimed at low-skill assembly line workers, what Jürgens Malsch, and Dohse (1993: 325) describe as a qualification strategy "from below," as opposed to the German strategy of prioritizing high-skilled workers. Giving such workers more autonomy and control allowed them to fix problems with their on-the-ground knowledge of production processes. For example, one worker gave an example of mismanagement fueled by ignorance that cost the company money, "I knew that I would ruin the press if I did what the foremen had told me to do. The foreman said ... do it like I told you. What happened, was that the press actually was ruined and a lot of money went down the drain" (Jürgens et al. 1993: 323). The new work and motivation programs were designed to prevent such occurrences by breaking down the Taylorist division between workers and management and moving toward management union cooperation.

These efforts to copy Japan in the 1970s and 1980s represented small movements toward the LP model. However, by the early 1990s, the homegrown programs were largely discontinued and replaced by "Modern Operating Agreements" that implemented lean principles into the plant contract (Babson 1995c: 232–235). The EI and QWL programs added quality circles and participation *onto* the structure of work rules and shopfloor authority that prevailed in American plants, whereas these new agreements sought to fundamentally change work structure and industrial relations to align closely with Japanese practices (Babson 1995c: 233). These programs declined because being lean "required more than adding Quality Circles to existing work relations," as they ultimately did little to change work processes. The training costs and time away from the job often cost the companies more than measurable productivity improvements, making them a disappointment for both workers and management (Babson 1995c: 235).

The just-in-time inventory system were not yet widely practiced in either the US or Germany during the 1980s (Jürgens et al. 1993: 65). The American inventory system was best described as a "just-in-case" system where large inventories were kept to guard against mechanical failures, and there was little incentive to fix the source of breakdowns when they occur (Caplan 1983; Parker and Slaughter 1988: 3). This attitude toward inventory management largely continued until later pushes for lean production in the 1990s (see Adler et al. 1997).

A combination of both the automation and imitation strategy appeared in GM's Saturn project. The first new General Motors brand in 70 years, Saturn was a line of small cars built in a new facility in Spring Hill, Tennessee, beginning in 1990. It was described by Roger Smith as having the potential to "overcome our present-day inefficiencies and to become truly competitive with producers of small cars everywhere and anywhere in the world" (General Motors Heritage Center 1984: 1). This was accomplished by taking the lessons learned from the NUMMI joint venture combined with high-tech manufacturing and automation to "leapfrog the rest of the industry" (Ingrassia 2011: 117; see Flink 1988: 401–403). GM and the UAW reached an agreement in 1985 that Saturn was exempted from the master contract and framed the project as a union-company partnership. The new contract resembled the Japanese model with only six job classifications, self-directed teams, just-in-time inventories, and continuous improvement (Adler et al. 1997: 62–63; Ingrassia 2011: 118–119). The contract also provided for more democracy in the workplace with management and union representatives making consensus decisions on production issues, which went beyond the cooperative structure of lean firms (Adler et al. 1997: 63; Ingrassia 2011: 120). Overall, The Saturn system was a synthesis of Japanese lean production and a "European sociotechnical approach" entailing workplace democracy and worker-management consensus building (Berggren 1994; Babson 1995c: 254–255; Adler et al. 1997: 63–64; Ingrassia 2011: 127). Although Saturn was somewhat successful in the early 1990s, neither GM management nor the UAW committed to spreading the "Saturn system" to the entire company. UAW president Steve Yokich was expressly against the tradeoffs detailed in the Saturn contract (Adler et al. 1997: 64–65; Ingrassia 2011: 126–128). With neither side enthusiastic about the project, Saturn remained a half-hearted experiment that had little influence on GM. The Saturn plant was shut down, and the brand was discontinued after the 2009 GM bankruptcy.

The UAW was ambivalent about the implementation of the Japanese "recipes" for higher quality and productivity. As market share declined, workers became increasingly afraid of plant closures and losing their jobs and so were motivated to implement changes if it meant maintaining their valorization (Reinhart 1999; Rothstein 2008). Some proposals, such as more participation in the workplace, were attractive to workers, similar to how establishing corporatist control of the workplace was attempted by Walter Reuther decades earlier (Jürgens et al. 1993: 322; see Cutler 1998). For example, in a UAW document "Towards a Union Perspective on QWL," MacLeod (n.d.: 1) argues that workers should welcome efforts by management to include them in decision-making "if employers have finally realized that better treatment of the workforce is necessary in modern times, they should be welcomed to the union's effort." He argued that if the Taylorist division of labor and work practices result in inefficiencies, then QWL has the potential to partially return the shopfloor to when workers had autonomy over their work (Macleod n.d.: 7). If the program was well implemented, then "QWL can improve product quality and increase productivity ... not through speed-up, but by working smarter, increasing skills in the workforce, reducing absenteeism, reducing scrap, and so forth" (Macleod n.d.: 6). There were voices in the UAW speaking in favor of QWL not just for the sake of jobs and long-term company survival, but of the potential for such programs to empower workers.

However, other changes were not welcomed by the UAW. For example, efforts to combine direct and indirect tasks or decrease the number of job classifications, which were designed to limit job flexibility—the antithesis of the Japanese multiskilled worker—were resisted by the UAW (Degan 2011: 18; Russo 1984; Parker and Slaughter 1988: 5). The degree of local UAW reception to change appeared to correspond with management's willingness to cooperate and honestly engage with the workers (see Adler et al. 1997). Womack et al. (2007 [1990]: 100) described a paradox they observed in the IMVP study. In many Ford plants, the contract remained essentially as it had been since 1937, and yet workers were *de facto* implementing teamwork and collectively solving problems even when it went against the technical details of the contract. By contrast, many GM plants updated the contract with all the formal stipulations of lean production, yet very little of the contract was implemented in practice and morale remained low.

The foundational problem was the *entrenched antagonism between labor and management* in many plants, which was difficult to change through new programs despite the expressed commitment from the union and management. According to one GM executive, the issue was that "there was no change in the culture. Workers and managers continued their old antagonistic ways" (Helper and Henderson 2014: 64). This executive also gave an example of the botched execution of LP methods, "In some of the factories where they installed the Andon cord, workers got yelled at when they pulled it" (Helper and Henderson 2014: 64). The issue was mutual distrust, with managers believing workers pulled the Andon cord out of laziness rather than a genuine attempt to fix a production problem, or that the low skilled workers were incapable of problem solving or continuous improvement. While management was intent on "making workers and the UAW their allies in the struggle to restore industry competitiveness," attempts to push for teamwork and joint decision-making rang hollow in the context of demands for "equality of sacrifice" through concessions and numerous plant closings (Yates 1992: 131). Therefore, efforts to cooperatively catch up to Japanese productivity were troubled from the start.

3.2 *The UAW Resists Productivity Pressure*

The "leapfrog" automation and imitation plans were productivity-oriented strategies to overcome the productivity pressure imposed by Japanese competitive advantage. Lowering labor costs, concessions, and reducing production capacity was another means to achieve the same goal. Plant closures due to lower sales and market share instilled fears of job loss (Yates 1992: 131; Perl 1984). This compelled the weakened UAW to engage in concession bargaining where "new contracts conceded the hardly won benefits of previous years" (Meyer 2009: 162). They believed that if they did not accept concessions that the Big Three could "face possible bankruptcy, thus threatening the jobs of autoworkers and leading to a decline in union membership" (Yates 1992: 132). UAW leadership thought a strategy of cooperation with management would help the company ensure jobs for the future.

Chrysler's 1980 bailout was coupled with over $450 million in UAW concessions, about $10,000 per worker, and twenty plant closings. This restructuring lowered Chrysler's breakeven point from 2.4 to 1.1 million cars, which led to a bounce back of $2.38 billion in profits by 1984. Ford similarly recovered from billions in losses in the early 80s to attain record profits of 2.9 billion by 1984. To accomplish this, the firm closed seven plants and laid off 44,000 production workers, to reduce its breakeven point to 2.5 million vehicles (Flink 1988: 394–395). Even GM, which lost $763 million in 1981, swiftly restructured, with GM workers conceding $5,500 in deferred wages, a wage freeze, and less paid holidays (Ingrassia 2011; 80; Russo 1984: 62; Flink 1988: 396). Moreover, despite GM earing record profits of 5.3 billion by 1984, a leaked memo revealed that GM planned to eliminate around 100,000 jobs from 1984 to 1986, eliminate cost-of-living-adjustments and the annual improvement factor, and expand subcontracting to force parts makers to compete and be "disciplined by the marketplace" (Russo 1984: 64). By 1984, the UAW had given $5 billion in concessions during the slump, approximately 250,000 autoworkers were laid off from 1979 to 1982, and autoworker unemployment was estimated at 24 percent. The automakers claimed that concessions that "hold the line on labor costs" are necessary "if they are to compete against foreign auto makers for the rest of the century" (Perl 1984).

These changes in value distribution improved the financial health of the Big Three, but at great expense to the workers and communities. With their labor monopoly broken by nonunion transplants, declining membership, and fears of more layoffs, plant closings, and technological displacement, the UAW leadership worked with management to enact concessions and nominally approved of the team concept and automation if they promised to secure jobs for the future (Yates 1992: 137–138). As Parker and Slaughter (1988) describe,

> UAW leaders, anxious to preserve jobs, advocate the team concept as a way to increase companies' productivity. That relates to job security: management has often used the threat of job loss to induce workers to accept team concept. GM workers in Van Nuys, Calif., for example, voted in team concept (by a narrow margin) when the company threatened to close either their plant or one in Ohio. But for all the public talk about the job security the team concept was supposed to provide, interviews with NUMMI workers reveal that fear of plant closings is still uppermost in their minds. (5)

There were, however, structural changes that improved job security. For example, the firms established Jobs Banks in 1984. This program paid technologically displaced workers 95 percent of their salary after 48 weeks of unemployment and supplementary unemployment insurance are exhausted until the company found the worker a new job (Babson 1995c: 247; Schoenberger 2009; Ingrassia 2011: 87–88). This program, however, was not enough to inspire broad confidence in job security.

With the turn to neoliberalism and the nationwide attack on unions in the 1980s (see Nicholson 2004; Brown 2015; Greenhouse 2019) the Big Three felt empowered to maintain concessions even during the recovery of the mid-to-late 1980s (Perl 1984; Yates 1992). The UAW typically took an oppositional stance against the corporations to improve workers' living standards, but the economic turbulence of the 1980s convinced UAW leadership that adopting a more cooperative stance was the best long-term option (Yates 1992). Because the UAW built into their contracts that the union prospers when the company does—based on the assumptions of high growth of the postwar decades—it was difficult to demand more when the companies faced financial trouble. The corporate logic was that if workers benefited from company growth, then there ought to be an "equality of sacrifice" when the company performed poorly (Yates 1992: 138). The Big Three also pointed to transplants as a reason for concessions because nonunion transplant workers had less generous benefit packages (Howes 1995). However, it was also well known that wage and benefit differences were not the most important factor in explaining the Japanese competitive edge. Rather, their productivity advantages produced a large share of the cost advantage gap. Therefore, it could not be claimed that reducing wages and benefits to the lowest common denominator would be enough to compete with the Japanese.

Ultimately, concessions were used as a lever to partially address the cost advantages produced by the productivity gap but were not a sufficient long-term solution. The Big Three and the UAW were caught in a paradox. On the one hand, unlike Taylorist-Fordist mass production where the productivity norms were enforced by a strict division of labor with no need for committed workers to solve production problems, achieving the higher productivity levels of LP supposedly required high worker commitment and motivation which was supported through strengthened job security for the core workforce even during economic downturns (Ohno 1988; Babson 1995c; Womack et al. 2007 [1990]; Liker 2021). Therefore, the QWL and EI programs as well as job guarantee programs such as the Jobs Bank, were steps toward ensuring the necessary worker commitment to reach the socially necessary levels of productivity. On the other hand, with intense foreign competition, declined sales, and idled plant capacity, layoffs and restructuring that appeared "inevitable," hurt the emergence of the necessary commitment, or at least *commitment from positive inducement rather than fear*. In addition, lean production's philosophy of eliminating waste claimed that such layoffs and plant closings were "wastes" that needed to be eliminated to foster a lean enterprise. LP works best in high growth environments where worker commitment and cooperation are fostered by job guarantees and any displacement from eliminating waste is offset by internal job transfers. This was possible for major Japanese producers who experienced nearly uninterrupted growth until the 1990s, but impossible for the Big Three who built up decades plant, equipment, and a large workforce that the lean production ethos considered "waste."

The discontent with concessions was exacerbated because management rarely made sacrifices of their own. For example, GM made a "historic blunder" wherein the same day that concessions were agreed to in 1981, a new pay plan was released that made it easier to get bigger bonuses for GM executives. The UAW was outraged by this, and according to Ingrassia (2011), "in decades to come, General Motors would pay for this blunder many times over in combative labor relations" (80). Even when the companies were making record profits in the mid-to-late 1980s due to restructuring, concessions, trade barriers, and productivity improvements, the need for continued sacrifice from the workers was emphasized with little change in the benefits accruing to management and shareholders (see Russo 1984; Flink 1988; Keller 1993). Top management demanded austerity for the UAW for the sake of the future of the company but were not willing to make sacrifices themselves, solidifying the reputation of Big Three management as an 'old boys club' that was insular, self-serving, and disconnected from workers' concerns (see Keller 1993; Ingrassia 2011).

To foster the commitment and cooperation necessary to implement productivity improvements, perhaps management should have been the first to take pay cuts, since the productivity of shopfloor workers is the root of the productivity gap problem. It may have been more beneficial in the long-term for the Big Three to eschew concessions or even to increase wages in exchange for higher moral and genuine cooperation to reach the prevailing productivity norms. The UAW would have had to compromise on the necessary changes to work organization to achieve this, but it is plausible that substantive job guarantees and no concessions could have switched the mindset of the UAW from a defensive position of fear that cooperation would kill their jobs to one that sought to improve productivity (Russo 1984; Perl 1984). This may have ensured capital accumulation for the company and jobs for the workers in the long run. The contradictory strategy of requesting cooperation, in a reverse course from decades of combativeness, while simultaneously undermining the conditions that could foster cooperation proved to be unsuccessful.

The UAW leaders formally endorsed the idea that new automation and implementing Japanese methods could help ensure autoworkers' jobs. Leadership was, however, split on the efficacy of this approach as Yates (1992) describes,

> Although some UAW leaders remain suspicious of the benefits of this work organization and of concessions, their fear of foreign competition and strong identification with the American auto companies prevented them from seriously considering an alternate no-concessions strategy. Other UAW leaders were more enthusiastic about the changes accompanying restructuring and wholeheartedly accepted the corporate discourse of joint decision-making and teamwork. (Yates 1992: 138)

Despite the hesitancy, the official position supported the "team concept." However, the rank-and-file were more split on the question of automation and imitating Japan, and many expressed their discontent against union leadership's position—exposing another split between leadership and the rank-and-file. One local union official put it this way, "It used to be 'us versus them,' the union against the company ... But now, it's become 'us versus them and them,' like it's the auto worker against the company and the union" (Perl 1984). Just as in the debates over automation in the 1950s and 1960s, the renewed wave of automation and push for Japanese production methods during the 1980s exacerbated the split between the direction of leadership and the desires of the rank-and-file (Yates 1992).

Labor's ambivalence toward technology persisted into the 1980s. As Jürgens, Malsch, and Dohse (1993) describes for the US and Germany,

> In all companies and countries we investigated the unions had a basically positive attitude toward the modernization and the introduction of technology in the production processes. But this was accompanied by a large degree of uncertainty with regard to the thrusts in the introduction of technology which were actually taking place. From what was largely a defensive stance the unions were trying—with different degrees of success or failure depending on the country and the economic situation—to cushion as much as possible the negative consequences of technological developments for the employees, especially redundancies and downgrading. As to the question of replacing work with technology there was no basic union counter-position. indeed, the substitution effect was accepted in principle, although the unions tried to attenuate the redundancy and reassignment effects with agreements for wage and employment security. In this respect they were quite successful in West

> Germany, but the pressure on employees and their representatives was much, much greater in the USA and Great Britain—if only because of the economic situation. (175)

Thus, while worker attitudes were similar, German workers had more influence on technological development thanks to codetermination. But in the US, the "pressure" of the "economic situation" signified the social domination to rapidly apply technology to fight against more productive competition.

Nevertheless, American workers did resist unilateral management control. For example, rank-and-file activist Mike Westfall led a movement at UAW Local 598 to raise awareness about the dangers and opportunities of new automation, stating that new technology should benefit workers in terms of early retirement, job guarantees, a shorter workweek, and eliminating undesirable work (Westfall 1981: 10). He argued that, while workers do not want to move backwards technologically and "no one here is against the companies making a reasonable profit" to retain jobs, "we must not allow the use of technology for speed-ups, breaking of work rules, union busting, robot like control over workers or technological unemployment" (Westfall 1981: 10–12). Furthermore, technology should be "subject to bargaining" and "developed in a democratic direction and by democratic process" to prevent job loss and deskilling or hurt collective bargaining (Westfall 1981: 13–15). Westfall's writings embodied the rank-and-file desire for corporatist control and syndicalist leverage over the Big Three's automation push.

Despite rank-and-file fervor for a radically different direction, productivity pressure and a precarious bargaining position convinced UAW leadership to be deferential to management's automation campaign (Yates 1992: 138; Jürgens et al. 1993: 175). Management was also not inclined to compromise with the UAW, as Roger Smith's attitude was "every time you ask for another dollar in wages, a thousand more robots start looking more practical" (Finkelstein 2003: 23). With concessions, automation, and foreign competition bearing down on GM workers, many had poor morale and "a fatalistic sense that many plants were doomed anyway," thus dampening the chances of efficacious rank-and-file action (Womack et al. 2007 [1990]: 100).

There were, however, rank-and-file groups that fought against these circumstances. Organizations such as the New Directions movement and Locals Opposed to Concessions called for the abandonment of the cooperative relationship between management and labor and a return to the confrontational style of collective bargaining (Russo 1984: 67; Babson 1995c: 249; Yates 1992; Ingrassia 2011: 122–129). The New Directions movement gained some traction in attacking labor-management cooperation, especially against Saturn and its promoter UAW Vice-President Don Ephlin who was "forced" into early retirement in 1989 due to pressure from the New Directions campaign (Serrin 1985; Babson 1995c: 249; Ingrassia 2011: 122). The philosophy of New Directions, beyond taking a militant stand against concessions and cooperation, reframed lean production as "management by stress," as developed by *Labor Notes* researchers Mike Parker and Jane Slaughter (1988; 1995).

Management by stress is a reinterpretation of lean production from the union workers' point of view, emphasizing how LP entails high labor intensity and speed-up, high physical and mental costs, and threatens the independence of unions. This represents one side of a split in the discourse that asks whether lean production *empowers* or *exploits* workers (see Eaton 1995: 70–71). For proponents, (e.g., Ohno 1988; Womack et al. 2007 [1990]; Adler 1993a) multiskilling and relying on worker input and cooperation for the success of the system empowers workers. In the management by stress view, tight buffers result in work intensification, which can cause exhaustion and repetitive stress injuries (Eaton 1995: 70–71). The claim that lean systems were beneficial because they expanded worker responsibility and the exercise of intellectual skills was dismissed because these efforts were aimed almost exclusively "in the service of management goals" (Eaton 1995: 71). In other words, if lean production was described as a form of "democratic Taylorism" according to Adler (1993b), then the empowerment school emphasized the *democratic* aspects of lean production while the management by stress school emphasized the *Taylorist* aspects of the system (Eaton 1995).

According to management by stress, the foundation of LP is to *constantly and purposefully* stress the system to expose weaknesses and waste that are then eliminated through work redesign. Stressing the assembly line is accomplished by "increasing line speed, cutting the number of people or machines, or giving workers more tasks" (Parker and Slaughter 1988: 2). Stressing the system may produce an apparatus that "optimizes itself" through identification and elimination of waste but is problematic because "human beings are the cogs in the system, not transistors, computers, and motors" (Parker and Slaughter 1988: 2). For example, when the Andon cord is pulled, there is pressure to find the source of the problem and get the line back in operation as soon as possible, and when the lines are constantly stressing workers to their limits "the only solution is to keep up, no matter what it takes" (Parker and Slaughter 1988: 4). Parker and Slaughter (1988) recount an anecdote of one Mazda worker who simply could not keep up with the pace of the assembly line,

> She had a hard time one day and pulled the stop cord several times. The next day management focused attention on her. Several management

> officials observed, and they set up a video camera to record her work. She found herself working further into the hole. She worked into the hole too far and fell off the end of the [two-foot] platform and injured her ankle. They told her it was her fault—she didn't pull the stop cord when she fell behind. (4)

Here, the "waste" was the worker who could not keep up with the speed of the line, rather than a malfunction of equipment or another issue. Likewise, the just-in-time system, by eliminating inventories that protect one department from problems in another, produces a *fragile* system that reveals inefficiencies to be corrected and puts additional pressure on the teams and low-level management to solve these problems (Parker and Slaughter 1988: 3).

Though the system of employee involvement and teamwork promises worker power to control and change working conditions, Parker and Slaughter (1988: 2) argue that this is impossible because management chooses the technology, production layout, and processes of the highly standardized jobs that are first designed by production engineers. The involvement of workers is limited to providing suggestions that 'kaizen' the efficiency of the standardized job, rather than suggestions workers would choose to improve working conditions (Parker and Slaughter 1988: 3). In other words, instead of relying upon industrial engineers to redesign jobs to achieve optimal efficiency, this is delegated to workers themselves who continuously improve their own jobs. Self-regulation and self-improvement do not *reduce control* but is "*a change in the form of control*" (Jürgens et al. 1993: 372; emphasis mine). While multiskilling promises skill upgrading, the management by stress view frames multiskilling as an attempt to expand management flexibility to assign jobs and dismantle job classifications. The multiple skills that workers learn do not require complex training or specialized knowledge but entailed multiple types of repetitive jobs that required "only manual dexterity, physical stamina, and the ability to follow instructions precisely" (Parker and Slaughter 1988: 5).

The lean approach to automation limited it to what is proven to increase productivity, avoided waste, and was not offset by requiring indirect workers (Liker 2021). According to management by stress, the high standardization of jobs made it easier to be automated, as routine tasks are more susceptible to automation (Parker and Slaughter 1988: 4; see Frey and Osborne 2013). This is admitted by proponents of lean production, as Womack et al. (2007 [1990]: 102) describes, "we believe that once lean-production principles are fully instituted, companies will be able to move rapidly in the 1990s to automate most of the remaining repetitive tasks in auto assembly—and more." In addition, many of the Japanese transplants during the 1980s boasted of having some of the most automated plants (Parker and Slaughter 1988: 4).

Through teams and employee involvement, lean production claimed to respect human dignity more than the Fordist-Taylorist system. However, the management by stress view argued that LP has a narrow definition of humanity, i.e., that "human fulfillment is achieved only by striving for management's goals," or, as one Mazda manual framed it, "If you are standing in front of your machine doing nothing, you yourself are not gaining respect as a human being" (Parker and Slaughter 1988: 5). The management by stress framework affirmed the assessment that lean production at its core aims at utilizing all available means to increase productivity, including motivating workers to facilitate continuous improvement. Autonomy, multiskilling, employee involvement, and teamwork are all oriented towards the *goals of productivity for the sake of capital accumulation*, not for *self-conscious direction of work processes chosen by the workers*. Therefore, Parker and Slaughter (1988: 5–6), advocated for the alternative production system found in Sweden's Volvo plants at Kalmar and Uddevalla. Here, the system was also based on teamwork and multiskilled workers, but the workers operated at stationary workstations with long cycle times and performed a variety of tasks at each station (Parker and Slaughter 1988: 5–6; see Berggren 1994, 1995). Such experiments were short lived, however, with the Uddevalla plant closing in 1993 and the Kalmar plant closing in 1994, just as lean production was gaining ascendency as the globally recognized "one best way" (Berggren 1995: 277–279).

In any case, Parker and Slaughter (1988) argued that the Big Three was adopting lean production because management believed it improved productivity and quality to increase profits, but also results in "great cost to a humane work environment" (6). The result of LP was therefore that "management reduces resources and staffing, while demanding increased output through appeals to pride, institutional loyalty—and fear of job loss" (Parker and Slaughter 1995: 45). Thus, management by stress illuminates the *dark side of lean production* from the point of view of the workers. It describes the human costs of the system often left out by proponents (e.g., Womack et al. 2007 [1990]; Adler 1993a, 1993b).

Even as the Big Three and the UAW leadership endorsed the team concept, many locals and rank-and-file workers resisted. As the president of the Lordstown Local 1112 advised workers: "If they eliminate jobs in your area and add the work to you, work at a normal pace and build quality and if you can't get it all, leave it go. We have to stick together to preserve our jobs and work pace" (Russo 1984: 63). Decades of shopfloor tradition, stint, and job structure were on the line, and thus many workers resisted the new management demands

(Helper and Henderson 2014). Even as rank-and-file workers were encouraged to resist, others felt the fear of job loss as a more compelling reason to comply. The high rates of sabotage during the 1960s and 1970s decreased after 1983, in part due to fear of job losses which "seem to reflect workers' fears that the plant would be closed if product quality were not maintained" (Zabala 1995: 225). Many workers, therefore, became more attentive to quality and amenable to quality circles and work teams (Zabala 1995: 224–225). This can be understood as an effect of social domination. When productivity/quality concerns become urgent due to competition and a productivity/quality gap, some workers reacted by improving their quality and productivity when they might otherwise commit sabotage if they did not feel the pressure to improve performance for the sake of their jobs. In addition, because the UAW endorsed these changes, they also disciplined workers to comply with them, often foreclosing the possibility of organized militant action against lean production (Yates 1992: 142). Worker discontent was instead expressed via votes against local contracts that endorsed teams, with many only narrowly passing (Yates 1992: 138).

Management by stress and the empowerment versus exploitation discourse (Adler 1993a; Eaton 1995) raises the distinction between *fulfilling human values* versus the *requirements of capital.* LP opponents advocate for human wellbeing beyond mere tolerance of harsh working conditions toward workers' control over working conditions and overcoming the Taylorist-Fordist division of labor and degradation of work (see Parker and Slaughter 1988; Eaton 1995; Meyer 2004; Jürgens et al. 1993). Yet, as the decades long decline of the Big Three demonstrated, *productivity gaps exert productivity pressure to reach the socially generalizing standard of productivity*, which at this time were the lean producers. Workers found themselves in a dilemma as their goal was both to control and humanize work and to maintain jobs—which requires the company to succeed in the capitalist market. Therefore, while management by stress critics may be correct that LP required worker commitment and cooperation to aid in capital accumulation while simultaneously submitting workers to alienation and continuous stress that may be morally condemnable, this critique does not address the problem of *social domination.*

Regardless of the specific socio-cultural-historic circumstances that allowed the Toyota production system to emerge (see Ohno 1988; Wittrock 2015), the unavoidable fact was that a *higher level of productivity was achieved* within this system that was both *sustainable*—even if there were high costs for the workers—and was *accumulating capital,* including by poaching sales that might otherwise go to the Big Three. Even if alienation was high, LP was effective at pushing forward the flow of value in motion and setting new productivity standards in the auto industry—including kaizen processes that continuously push for productivity improvements. In the *capitalist* world-system, possessing the highest existing productivity standard is *rewarded socially* because of the *social value placed on higher productivity* (e.g., leanness represents industrial progress). It also aids in *capital accumulation* because productivity leadership is a competitive advantage as the productivity leader defines the temporal valorization standards that competitors are compelled to follow (Postone 1993: 290). Because American auto firms lost productivity leadership, questions of more humanization and worker control were not possibilities that were *only* being avoided out of avarice, greed, or anti-union sentiment—although this likely contributed—but were increasingly difficult to achieve unless the proposed changes *simultaneously close the productivity gap*, or political intervention protected less productive value-systems from social domination. In this way, social domination is expressed as a *restriction on viable responses to competition*, e.g., limiting the focus to means of closing the productivity gap.

This dilemma was grasped by many critics of LP, though not diagnosed at the level of historical dynamics and social domination. Howes (1995) argues that Japanese transplants were harmful for the domestic US industry because the Japanese companies were not establishing a full production system in the US that relied on US jobs, expertise, and resources to the same degree as the Big Three. She warns that the way for American companies to avoid hundreds of thousands of displaced workers is to find,

> An alternative approach to restoring competitiveness … one that marshals trade and industrial policies to create a market for US motor vehicles, protects them from excessive competition over the next decade, and provides micro-level institutions that *assist and require US firms to adopt production and organizational techniques that will make them sufficiently competitive by world standards*. (Howes 1995: 177; emphasis mine)

With the failure of the "leapfrog" automation strategy or the domestic development of an alternative program of matching or surpassing LP, what else could enable the Big Three to become "sufficiently competitive by world standards" other than adopting the techniques of LP which constituted the global productivity standard?

Berggren (1994; 1995) points toward Volvo's Uddevalla plant as an alternative to lean production, with its long cycle times, teamwork, and worker autonomy. However, he does not argue that the Uddevalla plant's humanistic qualities alone made it a desirable alternative. Rather, because Uddevalla was *improving productivity at a rapid rate*, including its own continuous improvement program, it may have been able to eventually match or surpass the lean production system if not for its closing in 1993 (Berggren 1995: 284–288). Proponents and critics alike understood that a humanistic critique of LP was not enough, and that a viable alternative required addressing the productivity problem. This dilemma was experienced as social domination that undergirded the decision-making of these value-systems for the sake of long-term survival. In this sense, adopting LP or establishing an equally productive alternative was not a fully autonomous choice, but was felt as *heteronomy*. Unless an alternative was developed that both humanized work and matched or exceeded the productivity of lean production, then it appeared that coping with "management by stress" was the only viable option.

3.3 *Consequences of Losing Productive Leadership*

Without an alternative means to close the productivity gap, management failure to foster the cooperation and trust of the workers, and labor's resistance to change contributed to the slow decline of the domestic US industry (Helper and Henderson 2014). American auto manufacturing had higher costs due to higher frequency of strikes, grievances, and sabotage (Lam et al. 1991; Zabala 1995). The UAW leadership and rank-and-file split on the question of either embracing or resisting the "team concept" for the sake of long-term job security, with many conflicts emerging on the local level (Perl 1984; Russo 1984; Yates 1992; Jürgens et al. 1993: 324). The companies used internal benchmarking between plants and external benchmarking to the lean productivity standard to compel plants to change, which exacerbated the fear of closures (Jürgens et al. 1993: 372). Regardless of whether the grievances and reasons for distrust were justified, the lack of genuine collaboration to implement LP or an approximately productive alternative contributed to the decline.

Helper and Henderson (2014) describe three reasons why GM, the largest of the Big Three with the most to lose, gradually lost sales and market share. First, GM's enormous success led them to "deny the threat posed by foreign competition for over a decade" (Helper and Henderson 2014: 67). Whether through management arrogance or the "ossifying effect of decades of market power," concerted efforts to address the productivity challenge did not appear until the mid-1980s (Helper and Henderson 2014: 67). Second, once GM recognized that its position was threatened, it took time to understand what LP entailed, with publications such as Ohno (1988) and Womack et al. (2007 [1990]) only clarifying lean production for English speakers in the late 1980s (Helper and Henderson 2014: 67). Third, once LP was understood, it remained difficult to enact an "effective relational contract" that put LP principles into practice. As the authors explain,

> GM's history of adversarial relations with its blue collar workers and suppliers, its reliance on an operating model that assumed there was very little need to exchange knowledge across either firm or functional boundaries, and its muddled and unaccountable internal processes made it difficult to build the credibility fundamental to effective long-term relationships. Moreover even after the firm had recognized the importance of adopting techniques like continuous improvement and cross-functional communication, it took some years to understand the nature of the relational contracts that would be needed to diffuse them within the organization. Managers accustomed to governing by fiat appear to have found it difficult to understand the potential benefits of discussion and collaboration. Even after the techniques had been widely diffused and problems of clarity seemed to have been overcome, problems of credibility continued to arise. (Helper and Henderson 2014: 67)

Similar problems existed at Ford and Chrysler as combative industrial relations characterized the American value-regime (see Norsworthy and Zabala 1985; Adler et al. 1997; Kochan, Lansbury, and MacDuffie 1997: 311).

The consequences of the decline can be observed through job losses and plant closings. Such losses may have originated from increased automation, implementation of LP, or from declining market share resulting in excess capacity, but all were *influenced by the productivity pressure exerted by more productive Japanese competition.* There were financial troubles during the recessions in the early 1980s and early 1990s with a period of prosperity in the mid-to-late 1980s when import restrictions were at their most effective (Benjamin 1999; Ingrassia 2011: 96–97). The employment decline was striking. GM's hourly employment grew until its peak in 1979 at 468,000 workers, declined sharply to a decade low of 313,000 workers in 1982, recovered to 397,000 by 1985, but again declined reaching 226,000 by 1994 (Yettaw 1994: 5; General Motors Heritage Center 1994). Ford's hourly employment also reached a peak in 1979 at 204,000, fell to a low of 106,000 in 1982, recovered to 116000 by 1985, then resumed a slow decline reaching 104,000 by 1993. Chrysler's peak was reached in 1973 with 113,000 hourly workers, but then dropped to a low of 39,000 workers by 1982, which recovered to 72,000 by 1988, but again fell to only 56,000 by 1993. Overall, production worker employment at the Big Three fell from a peak of 767,000 in 1979, to a low of 459,000 in 1982, recovered to 574,000 by 1985, and then declined to 396,000 by 1993 (Yettaw 1994: 5). During Roger Smith's tenure from 1981–1990, GM's market share fell from 48 to 36 percent (Finkelstein 2003: 19). In response, GM went through multiple rounds of closures and layoffs throughout the 1980s and 1990s. For example, in December 1991, GM announced 21 factory closings and 74,000 layoffs in what would be known as the "Christmas Massacre" (Special to People's World 2024 [1991]). The ostensible goal of these moves was to streamline operations due to the slump in sales (Masci 2000: 27). From 1978–1993, 134 total facilities, including parts plants, parts depots, foundries, and assembly plants were closed from the Big Three resulting in the loss of 168,234 jobs from plant closings alone (Yettaw 1994: 5). Some workers may have been internally transferred or used the Jobs Bank, but there was nevertheless a net loss of valorization opportunities.

The decline can be partially explained via the same logic that IG Metall used in 1962 to explain the bankruptcy of the German automaker Borgward (IG Metall 1962: 62). It is *not* the companies that automate or eliminate waste through LP that decline in capacity and personnel, but the ones that do not. Companies that do not conform to socially general productive norms experience productivity pressure to conform or face challenges in the market. The key distinction here is that it is not a special property of automation equipment *per se* that gives a competitive advantage, but the *total productive activity and control over time* within the production system—with its definite labor power, capital equipment, and organization—that operate together to establish the productivity norm. As one Ford executive argued in 1982: "The reason we have such deplorably high unemployment in the auto industry today is not because of automation and robots, but because somewhere along the line the American auto industry lost its competitive edge" (Poling 1982: 22). In the 1970s to the early 1990s, there were multiple attempts to close the productivity gap between the Big Three and lean producers such as homegrown interpretations of lean processes and "leapfrog" automation, but these attempts did not close the productivity gap enough to counter the continued penetration into the American market. Even though US firms were improving productivity, (see Jürgens et al. 1993: 281–305) the Japanese were engaging in their own activities to continuously improve their own production at the same time (Abolhassani, Harner, and Jaridi 2018). Thus, Big Three remained *comparatively* less productive than the Japanese lean producers. Having the *second* highest productivity rate is still problematic when capital favors the highest productive systems at the expense of less productive systems.

In sum, Japanese competition created an urgent need for change in the American value-regime. The Big Three needed to either adopt Japanese methods or create a superior system of their own. However, the "automation push" failed and it ultimately took decades to generalize lean processes in the American companies. Ingrassia (2011) describes the problem this way,

> Between 1980 and 1992 GM, Ford, and Chrysler had tried robots, reorganization, diversification, Japanese joint ventures, and more. They had gone from record losses to record profits and back to record losses. Detroit's quality had improved but it still trailed the Japanese, who weren't standing still. (97)

After the apparent failures of the automation strategy in the 1980s, adopting the lean production system was seen as the only viable strategy and the industry became disillusioned with the disappointment of industrial robots. Automation did not disappear entirely but became less prominent than organizational changes such as just-in-time delivery and teamwork (see Jürgens 2023: 194–197). Despite the weaknesses of 1980s automation, much of automobile production was and continued to remain automated (see Krzywdzinski 2020a). The rise of lean production *did not* end efforts to automate production or dismantle the already very high levels of automation in certain production areas like the body shop or engine construction. However, attempts to aggressively implement automation in previously un-automated areas such as assembly were shelved in the United States (Krzywdzinski 2020a). The diminishment of automation as a driving force of productivity development should not be exaggerated to conclude that automation and technology was no longer central to the productive power of the industry overall. Since the 1990s, however, becoming lean was the focus of the Big Three as they struggled for survival into the new millennium.

4 The Rise and Fall of the German Quality Production System

Recovered from the oil crisis, the mid 1970s to the early 1990s were characterized by the forging of a German model distinguished from the American and Japanese systems. This model was built to accommodate the *mutual interests of both labor and management* in the pursuit of job security, high wages, and codetermination in working conditions on the one hand, and market success and financial return on the other. In other words, the system flowed from the structure and power dynamics of the cooperative system to fulfill the desires of both capital and labor. The compromise entailed three main components: diversified quality production (DQP), new production concepts (NPC), and the humanization of work. Each aspect is discussed in detail with close attention to productivity and automation development.

The success of this model in the 1970s and 1980s stemmed from the growth of export sales in a mature European market that was partially protected from

Japanese competition, along with rising sales in foreign subsidiaries in emerging markets, including for Volkswagen the addition of new subsidiaries such as SEAT in Spain in 1986, Škoda in the Czech Republic in 1991, and a joint venture in China in 1983 (Tolliday 1995b: 129; Grieger and Lupa 2015: 156, 168). However, just as the mid-70s crisis ushered in this new phase of development, another crisis of profitability in the mid-1990s brought this phase to an end. Both the merits and weaknesses of the system are assessed to explain how automation contributed to the successes and failures of the German industrial path.

4.1 *Diversified Quality Production: Alternative to Raising Productivity?*

Since the 1920s, Sloanism codified market segmentation from basic transportation at a low cost to complex luxury vehicles at a high cost. Premium German automakers, such as Daimler-Benz and BMW, had always focused on selling a variety of high priced, high quality autos in the luxury car segment (see Bellon 1990; Stahlmann 1992), but even Volkswagen and the American-owned German companies had framed their mass market vehicles as beneficiaries of "German quality work" encapsulated by the "Made in Germany" label (Lüdtke 2009). Quality-based product strategies blossomed after the mid-1970s as the Beetle crisis pushed Volkswagen to establish a more diverse product range to replace the Beetle. Selling cars based on quality became a business ethos known as *diversified quality production* (DQP) (Streeck 1991).

While Japan and the United States competed based on low costs, with lean production's systematic elimination of waste being well suited for cost-based competition, DQP allowed Germany to remain competitive by *reframing the competitive criteria* from price to diversity and quality. DQP constitutes an ideal type of business strategy that combines a diverse model range and customization options with high quality that can extract high prices, which in turn supports the highly skilled and highly paid workers capable of manufacturing these products (Sorge and Streeck 2016: 1). By pursuing diversity, the productive system flexibly responds to frequently changing customer demands, which was a common occurrence in the overcrowded markets of the 1970s and 1980s in the tripartite regions (Jürgens 1994: 98; Sorge and Streeck 2016: 1). In the shift from a sellers' to a buyers' market, it was important to fulfill customer tastes in terms of body types, models, and equipment variations to maximize realization potential (Jürgens et al. 1993: 59). From 1971 to 1985, the number of car models and variations offered by BMW and Daimler-Benz doubled and more than tripled at Volkswagen, going from 13 to 44 variants by 1985. The American owned companies Ford and Opel also increased model variants but at a modest rate, going from 18 variants for both companies in 1971 to 25 and 24 respectively in 1985 (Jürgens et al. 1993: 61). In addition, specializing in certain automotive technologies such as diesel engines was believed to give a competitive advantage and reach customers wanting to reduce carbon dioxide emissions (Pries and Wäcken 2020: 98). The push for diversity was especially aimed at wealthier consumers who were willing to pay more for customization rather than accept the "reasonable" automobile that meets basic transportation needs, as exemplified by the Beetle (see Schmidt 2007 [2005]).

Quality here refers to producing products based both on the "superior use value rooted in durability and reliability" and their ability to meet the qualitative criteria of customer preferences in terms of the "intrinsic value of the product, including the symbolic and status-enhancing value of its brand" (Sorge and Streeck 2016: 4). In other words, with exceptional design and strict quality control, the corporations could extract high prices and maximize profit through disseminating self-descriptions that their autos had excellent quality compared to the non-German competition (Streeck 1991; Lüdtke 2009: 185). Purchasing based on quality rather than price meant that the firms gained high profit margins per vehicle rather than maximizing cost advantages to sell at a low price, which reduced profit margins for the sake of higher volume (Sorge and Streeck 2016: 5). Turnover data illustrated an increase in average turnover per vehicle at Volkswagen from 1971 to 1986 at 11 percent per year or from 6,300 DM to 16,900 DM, and an even larger increase for BMW of 20 percent per year or from 22,600 DM in 1971 to 48,100 DM in 1985 (Jürgens et al. 1993: 59). This did not mean, however, that attention to quality decreased production volume. Rather, the point of DQP was the *mass production of premium products*. In other words, DQP was "meant to achieve mass production and at the same time to accommodate quality standards of premium products" (Lüdtke 2009: 185). Ultimately, DQP aimed to "obtain superior competitiveness in world markets" through "a diversified product range, and non-price competitive marketing strategies, combining all these with high wages, skilled labor, and a flexible, non-Taylorist organization of work" (Streeck 1991: 25).

DQP thus defined the industrial logic of a "German model" that appeared as a viable alternative to the "low-cost strategy of catching up with the Japanese" (Jürgens 1998: 295). Its relative success in the 1970s and 1980s appeared to validate the competitiveness of Germany's social partnership system (Tolliday 1995b: 125). In fact, Streeck (1991) claimed that the German "institutional constraints and opportunities" were what generated the conditions for this "virtuous circle of upmarket restructuring" (54). The DQP strategy had "elective affinities" or "complementarities" with the specific social, economic, and political conditions of Germany that enabled the viability of this model (Sorge and Streeck 2016: 5). Non-economic social institutions supported by national laws generated the conditions for high wages, low economic inequality, and workplace participation (Streeck 1991: 31). Simply put, DQP was possible in Germany thanks to the characteristics of its value-regime, and was practiced in a variety of industries from textiles and machine tools, to food processing (Jürgens 2004: 415). This opposed the liberal view that regulatory constraints create worse economic outcomes (e.g., Friedman 2002 [1962]). Instead, Sorge and Streeck (2016) argue that a country that fosters this strategy represents a

> non-liberal version of capitalism, defined by socially imposed limits to market pressures and a political capacity of workers (and governments) to shape managerial decisions, in order to safeguard non-capitalist interests in addition to and alongside capitalist interests. (10; see Hall and Soskice 2003 [2001])

In this sense, constraints are not only restrictive in a purely negative sense but can also be *productive* as new forms of work, products, and business strategies such as DQP *emerge from constraints*, not despite them. For the system to work, capitalist and non-capitalist interests need to be balanced to simultaneously fulfill the interests of both management and labor. This is best fostered when it is mutually supported by business, labor, and government through laws, cooperative relations, customs, and expectations.

The pursuit of DQP was mutually beneficial and structurally necessary in the 1970s and 1980s. It was structurally necessary because, as one Daimler-Benz executive described, the low growth in car sales in Europe and beyond meant that absorbing increasing costs through quantitative growth was no longer viable (Zahn 1978: 2). Upscaling products and introducing product variants avoided the need to cut costs by appealing to market segments that were less price sensitive (Jürgens et al. 1993: 61). If enough consumers were willing to pay for the higher priced product, then DQP appeared to benefit all parties simultaneously—the customers, the firm, the union, and the workforce (Jürgens 1994: 99).

The strategy was considered "obviously very attractive from a union point of view," because high priced goods allowed for large profit margins that could both sustain the firm and pay the high skill workers well (Jürgens et al. 1993: 61; Jürgens 2004: 413). Because government regulations and collective bargaining ensured strong employment security, it was difficult for management to adjust the workforce and "commits them to the path of internal flexibility through transfers and training" (Jürgens 1994: 98). In other words, with job security essentially guaranteed for the core German workforce, it was more advantageous for management to train and flexibly deploy their abundance of human capital to manufacture a diverse range of high quality products compatible with the skills of that workforce then aim to cut costs or eliminate the "waste" of extra workers. These "redundant capacities" or a "surplus of competencies" are precisely what is needed to respond to the "uncertainty of existing and evolving demand" (Sorge and Streeck 2016: 4). The success of this model appeared to show that high wages, strong unions, and high skilled labor were "not incompatible with commercial success and economic competitiveness," and were suitable for the "ingrained social and productive principles" of Germany (Jürgens 1998: 295; Jürgens 2004: 412).

DQP also placed new demands on production, making automobile production more complex as production processes had to flexibly adapt to construct a variety of models with more customization and higher quality (Jürgens et al. 1993: 59). The demand for more variety made the "classical" Fordist aim of standardization difficult. Thus, the cost advantages of economies of scale could not be utilized to the same extent, which constituted another source of rising costs (Jürgens et al. 1993: 59; see Piore and Sabel 1984). Like the introduction of the yearly model change (see Reynolds 1989), the increased diversity also challenged the workers and required new production technology. Highly flexible machines steered by qualified workers were needed to realize DQP (Jürgens 1994: 98). The increased flexibility also increased equipment costs, but product upgrading helped compensate for this (Jürgens et al. 1993: 59). This amounted to a system of *flexible specialization* (see Piore and Sabel 1984) that synergized with the new production concepts that emerged during the same period (Kern and Schumann 1987).

Though these strategic decisions were detectable in many German industries in the 1970s and 1980s, DQP was never an explicit strategy of any company, nor a model that can explain everything about the German auto industry's structure, performance, and trajectory (Jürgens 2004: 412). Rather, it is best understood as an ideal type (Weber 2012) of a business logic exercised to varying degrees in the German auto industry during this period. There was some doubt about the long-term viability of this strategy, such as one Daimler-Benz executive who was doubtful that the "belief in superior quality" would make "every increase in cost manageable" (Zahn 1978: 5; translation mine).[2] In addition, Jürgens, Malsch, and Dohse (1993) found that all the managers they interviewed stated that the *cost penalty from the DQP strategy* with its "demands on the flexibility of production and personnel" were one of their most serious concerns (61). Nevertheless, the 1970s and 1980s represented the height of the

2 Original German text: "Das gibt auch Anlaß, sich darüber klar zu werden, daß keineswegs—etwa im Glauben an überlegene Qualität—jeder Kostenzuwachs verkraftbar wäre" (Zahn 1978: 5).

DQP strategy, applying it to achieve market success without competing directly with the Japanese or Americans.

This avoidance of competition is an attempt to *escape from productivity pressure and social domination*. By forming "socially imposed limits to market pressures" (Sorge and Streeck 2016: 10), the compulsion to increase productivity to match the norms of socially necessary labor time is partially nullified. By not competing for all customers but specifically aiming for a less price sensitive clientele, the need to increase productivity to reduce costs is softened. Profits can instead be earned via higher profit margins per vehicle extracted through a price premium rather than through the lower costs achieved through highly efficient production.

There is, however, a balance that must be struck. Productivity cannot be totally disregarded, as DQP entails the *mass* production of premium commodities, rather than a return to low volume craft production. This is one reason why new production concepts were needed to facilitate the desired diversification and high output. Productivity was not overlooked but rendered tertiary in priority compared to the demands for diversity and quality. As long as there existed a customer base willing to pay a price premium that offsets the increased personnel and capital costs and the foregone cost reductions through increased productivity, then both workers and firms could satisfy their interests without the need for extensive rationalization—at least not along the lines of the lean production. Indeed, the German industry did pursue a rationalization plan to both facilitate the DQP strategy and increase productivity through a unique combination of a high skilled workforce and flexible production technology.

4.2 *Humanization of Work*

In the 1970s, the alienating working conditions of the assembly line increasingly scrutinized from workers in the United States and Europe (Meyer 2004; Jürgens 2023: 280). The speed-up strike in Lordstown became a symbol of worker discontent against assembly line work, and the "Lordstown syndrome" was a disease that demanded a cure (see Thompson 1995; Jürgens 2023: 189–192). Passive resistance, as expressed in absenteeism, fluctuations, and recruitment problems were accelerating, and active resistance such as strikes, protests and sabotage fomented in the US and Europe (Albers et al. 1971; Jürgens 2023: 280–281). Surveys in the late 1970s revealed that Volkswagen workers were also concerned with monotony, high physical and mental stress, low chances of advancement, and the risk of deskilling. The assembly line was particularly problematic for VW workers as four-fifths of them were not willing to work on the assembly line, and a third of line workers intended to resign because it was seen as a haven of degraded low skilled labor (Jürgens 2023: 280–281). As IG Metall (1974) described, "The long-term goal is the elimination of all inhumane jobs such as assembly line work, other lopsided repetitive work processes, and dirty, dangerous, physically difficult or mentally stressful jobs" (418; translation mine).[3] Rampant dissatisfaction intensified the calls to humanize work.

Volvo's Kalmar and Uddevalla factories were the most famous examples of humanized workplaces as these Swedish plants abolished assembly lines and replaced them with stationary workstations where work teams assembled vehicles in long work cycles at their chosen pace (Berggren 1994, 1995). American workers also desired more humanized working conditions, but the UAW lacked the codetermination rights to pressure for systematic implementation, and defending against concessions, Japanese competition, and productivity pressure became the priority (Weinberg 1974; Jürgens et al. 1993: 377). In other words, the productivity pressure exerted in the US meant that humanization efforts were largely foregone to address the competitive threat posed by the Japanese. In addition, many American humanization efforts such as the work motivation programs were spearheaded by management and therefore were often met with distrust and resistance from the rank-and-file (Weinberg 1974; Parker and Slaughter 1988, 1995; Babson 1995a: 233–234). Although German automakers never went as far as Volvo, concerted efforts to humanize work occurred in the 1970s and 1980s.

German workers were motivated and enabled to achieve humanization measures thanks to the strengthening of the codetermination laws in 1972 and 1976. The federal government also implemented a program which promoted projects throughout German industry to humanize work and develop alternative design approaches (Jürgens 2023: 281). Because foreign workers were no longer a sizeable contingent of the workforce to staff the low skill assembly line jobs after the mid-70s oil crisis, the remaining German workers were motivated to "enrich" the repetitive low-status assembly jobs (Brumlop and Jürgens 1983; Jürgens et al. 1993: 116–123). To ameliorate the relatively high (7–9 percent) unemployment rate in Germany, the German government encouraged German firms to train additional apprentices regardless of company need (Jürgens et al. 1993: 122; Jürgens 1995: 296). With Germany's cultural orientation toward qualifications (Lüdtke 2009), German automakers soon found themselves with an overabundance of technically trained workers who they

3 Original German text: "Als Fernziel geht es um die Beseitigung aller menschenunwürdigen Arbeitsplatze wie Fließbänder, andere sich einseitig wiederholende Arbeitsvorgänge sowie schmutzige, gefährliche, körperlich schwere oder psychisch belastende Arbeitsplätze" (IG Metall 1974: 418).

could not all employ in the jobs they trained for. Therefore, many of these skilled workers worked directly on the assembly line. This was both disadvantageous for the skilled workers who wanted to exercise their skills and for companies who recognized that unused skills degraded quickly when not exercised (Jürgens et al. 1993: 123). The solution satisfactory to both management and labor was to "enrich" production work to utilize these workers' skills. This situation motivated humanization efforts and promoted the development of new production concepts (Jürgens et al. 1993: 123; Kern and Schumann 1987). For these reasons, humanization was supported by German government, management, and labor—especially by IG Metall and the works councils (IG Metall 1974). Thus, unlike the US where humanization was initiated from the top down and aimed at achieving corporate productivity goals (see Jürgens et al. 1993: 103–110), humanization efforts in Germany emerged from the *bottom up and top down simultaneously* as they were forcefully advocated for by IG Metall and works councils with the support of the government that supplied incentives for management (Jürgens et al. 1993: 118).

Central to this was labor's willingness to accept new technologies if workers played a role in their implementation and shaped their social consequences. In a reaffirmation of labor's ambivalent stance, the deputy chairman of the general works council at Volkswagen stated that, "We at IG Metall and the employee representatives are not against technical progress. We only want to make it socially manageable" (Autogramm 1984: 3; translation mine).[4] Towards this end, IG Metall and the works councils worked to achieve extended codetermination rights in the implementation of new technologies and regulations outlining wage and transfer rights for technologically displaced workers beyond the 1968 rationalization agreement. By the early 1980s, the Volkswagen works council was usually informed about new rationalization measures before they were implemented but did not have codetermination rights to shape their implementation (Brumlop and Jürgens 1983: 24). However, by 1987, a new rationalization agreement formed between IG Metall and the auto companies that explicitly gave the works councils extensive information rights and to participate in the planning and implementation of new technology throughout the entire process (Rationalization Agreement 1987: 3–4). Another stipulation was that new technology or organizational changes must abide by the principles of a "human design of work" (*Menschengerechte Gestaltung der Arbeit*) and "securing and expanding qualifications" (*Sicherung und Erweiterung der Qualifikation*) which satisfied the workers' desires for more training and the

4 Original German text: "Wir IG Metaller und Arbeitnehmervertreter sind nicht gegen den technischen Fortschritt. Wir wollen ihn nur sozial beherrschbar machen" (Autogramm 1984: 3).

humanization of work (Rationalization Agreement 1987: 3). The agreement also extended protections for workers from dismissal and regulated transfers.

Influencing the planning phase is important because otherwise new technological development may improve productivity at the expense of humanization. Management's interest in improving productivity and automating production must be balanced with labor's interest in improving working conditions and humanization. As IG Metall explained,

> Humanization must be understood as a design task, and humanization requirements must be included in the planning of technical and organizational changes. As a result, the works council must have a right of co-determination right from the planning stage … As long as it is solely within the employer's discretion to determine what is produced under which working conditions, the employer's interest in rationalization will prevail. Humanization then only takes place to the extent that it promotes rationalization. (IG Metall 1983: 425; translation mine)[5]

Under lean production, humanization *only* occurs when such measures *also fulfill the goal of eliminating waste*. This approach is rejected here, as IG Metall explicitly pursued humanization *for its own sake* and implemented measures beyond those that improve both productivity and humanization simultaneously. At Volkswagen, the "tandem principle" (*Tandemprinzip*) became policy, which postulated that goals of humanization and rationalization must be considered as equal priority and systematically accounted for when making decisions about rationalization projects (Jürgens 2023: 289–290). As Jürgens (2021) explains,

> when Volkswagen began to introduce industrial robots, a kind of "tit for tat" rule was established: for each robot installation aiming primarily at improving efficiency, another installation should be introduced primarily with the aim to ergonomically improve working conditions. This rule is still followed today. (4)

5 Original German text: "… muss Humanisierung als Gestaltungsaufgabe begriffen werden, und Humanisierungsforderungen müssen schon in die Planung von technisch- organisatorischen Umstellungen einfließen. Daraus folgt: Schon bei der Planung muss dem Betriebstrat ein Mitbestimmungsrecht zustehen … Solange es allein in der Verfügungsgewalt der Arbeitgeber liegt, zu bestimmen, was unter welchen Arbeitsbedingungen produziert wird, wird das Rationalisierungsinteresse der Arbeitgeber obsiegen. Humanisierung findet dann nur insoweit statt, wie sie die Rationalisierung fördert" (IG Metall 1982: 425).

The goals of improving productivity and improving working conditions became a balancing act where both are explicit goals that may be at cross purposes but must nevertheless be pursued and negotiated between management and labor.

The tensions are also alleviated through applying new production concepts, where skilled workers are motivated to improve the productivity potential of highly mechanized production processes through increased humanization. As Kern and Schumann explain, through re-professionalization and enrichment of production work,

> The increased attractiveness of the remaining work offers better opportunities for coming to terms with rationalization. At the same time in the greater weight accorded human labor within the production process there is a possibility of alleviating the pressure on work conditions, including work safety. Since industrialists need the workers' cooperation in modernization, they have to offer something in return. Employees and their representatives can therefore demand their price. (Kern and Schumann 1987: 164)

Thus, humanization incentivizes the skilled workers who facilitate the productivity improvements of automated technology, which should result in net productivity gains and improved working conditions. This demonstrates how humanization and new production concepts are synergistic developments.

Improving ergonomics was a major humanization goal. Even though the works councils did not have extensive influence on new technology implementation until the 1987 rationalization agreement, supplementary plant agreements typically allowed works councils to intervene in decision-making to improve the "ergonomic design of the environment of the workplace" (Brumlop and Jürgens 1983: 28). By 1990, codetermination laws determined that works councils had the right to mediate technological and organizational change, especially when workers referenced the findings of ergonomic science. Unsurprisingly, therefore, Jürgens, Malsh, and Dohse (1993: 119) found in their comparative study of the US, British, and German industries that both German management and labor took ergonomic considerations seriously. Influenced by new production concepts, most ergonomic solutions involved finding technological solutions to improve ergonomics, safety, and working conditions. As Tolliday (1995b: 126) explained, the aim was on "utilizing institutionalized labor/management cooperation to operate a 'humanized' Taylorism, running at reasonable speeds, and relying on technology-oriented solutions to production problems." Thus, humanization improved *through* new technology, not despite it.

A second goal was the reduction of stress and strain through reduced work time. The aim was not to decrease work intensity *per se*, but to compensate for the stress and strain of monotonous labor through frequent breaks and less time on the job (Brumlop and Jürgens 1983: 40). Intensity was decreased through longer work cycles, as the typical one minute work cycles in the US and Japan were elongated to between two to five minutes in Germany (Jürgens 1995: 297). Throughout the 1970s and 1980s, IG Metall used Volkswagen as the pacesetter for demanding "extended break times, shorter working leave, educational leave, and time-off in exchange for overtime" (Tolliday 1995b: 127). For example, the 1979 collective agreement implemented a five-minute recreation break for every hour of work, in addition to a three-minute break for personal needs (Brumlop and Jürgens 1983: 38). This measure alone was estimated in 1981 to have protected 4,000–4,500 jobs from technological displacement (Brumlop and Jürgens 1983: 38–39). Weekly working hours had been decreasing since the 1950s, with 48 being the standard in 1950 which was lowered to 40 hours by 1967 to 38.5 by 1984 and was scheduled to reach 35 hours by 1995—although the crisis of the early 90s made the weekly working hours even lower (Jürgens et al. 1993: 121). IG Metall claimed that its worktime bargaining strategy saved 500,000 jobs from rationalization via the syndicalist withdrawal of labor power (Edsforth and Asher 1995: 178). Thereby, both humanization and syndicalist goals of job preservation and increasing labor market power were advanced. This also demonstrates that corporatist and syndicalist goals can be achieved simultaneously with enough leverage from powerful labor organizations (see Cutler 1998). Overall, when comparing a typical American and German factory, Jürgens, Malsch, and Dohse (1993: 120–121) found that with breaks, working hours, vacations, and holidays, the workers at the German plant worked 16 percent fewer hours than US workers. Such measures were cost intensive for the companies but nevertheless were agreed upon through management and labor cooperation (Brumlop and Jürgens 1983: 40). Though Germany retained the assembly line and did not go as far as Sweden, the German auto industry was innovative in its approach of humanizing Fordism through improved ergonomics and work time reductions.

4.3 *Automation, New Production Concepts, and the Subjectivity of Labor*

Influenced both by flexibility demands on product strategy and humanization efforts, new production concepts (NPC) constituted the emerging industrial ethos in Germany during the 1970s and 1980s. With changes in the labor market and structural conditions such as the removal of foreign workers to perform low skilled jobs and German workers' pursuit of qualifications, new possibilities of work structure and labor deployment were explored. At the same time, new technologies such as industrial robots, microelectronics, and computers were framed as means to aggressively automate production, including in assembly which heretofore remained nearly untouched by mechanization. In this context, NPC provoked new combinations of technology, work organization, training, and deployment of direct production workers. The aim was to increase productivity and utilize the skilled workforce to achieve the degree of flexibility necessary for the DQP strategy. Flexible specialization was the goal rather than the mere mass production of standardized products (Piore and Sabel 1984). By contrast, lean production was not considered a viable alternative because it was seen as a form of speed-up that German workers would not accept and NPC was considered an alternative means to increase productivity and lower costs (Tolliday 1995b: 125–126).

NPC was theorized by industrial sociologists Horst Kern and Michael Schumann who derived their concept from intensive studies of the auto, machine tool, and chemical industries from the 1960s to the 1980s (Kern and Schumann 1984, 1987). The following frames NPC as an ideal type of industrial production derived primarily from their framework. Next, Volkswagen's application of new forms of work and technology are explored, especially in the automation of the assembly line at Volkswagen's famous Halle 54 in Wolfsburg. Like lean production, NPC deviated from "classical" Fordism, and developed similar goals and solutions to production challenges. Yet, they also constitute distinct production philosophies with different means of utilizing labor and technology to improve productivity.

According to Kern and Schumann (1984, 1987: 154–155), mass production from the late 19th century, especially in the United States, was based on a capitalist rationality that held that work should be mechanized as much as possible to increase productivity and that workers who could not be substituted by machines were sources of potential disturbance, and therefore should be subject to Taylorist control. However, Kern and Schumann (1987) found in their studies of the German auto, machine tool, and chemical industries that new technologies were not maximally automating human labor but were subject to comprehensive job planning that opened new opportunities for production workers. In the auto industry, they observed the "Forceful utilization of the new technologies—especially in the assembly sector" and a "leap in mechanization to partly automated single aggregates and machine systems" (Kern and Schumann 1987: 161). In contrast to Braverman's (1998 [1974]) deskilling thesis, task integration and a *reskilling* of the direct production workers occurred in these highly automated areas. In these departments, the deskilled machine-feeding jobs were declining and replaced with "re-professionalized" direct workers with technical qualifications (Kern and Schumann 1987: 161;

Jürgens 2004: 411). Industries pursuing NPC were aggressively pursuing automation aligned with a "technology strategy" designed for skilled workers called *Facharbeiter* rather than Taylorized unskilled workers (Tolliday 1995b: 125).

The core of new production concepts are the new means of employing skilled labor and advanced technologies. Though these new technologies still automate labor and therefore the "social scandal of unemployment" remains a social problem, NPC places *more* significance on the workers who remain. Kern and Schumann (1987) explain this as a paradox,

> precisely at the historical moment in which technical possibilities for substituting human labor are explosively expanding, consciousness of the qualitative significance of human work performance, the appreciation of the special qualities of human labor, is at the same time increasing. (160)

They argue that this is *not paradoxical* because NPC claims that reducing human labor to the lowest residual and unskilled level places *limits on productivity gains* that can only be rectified by qualified skilled workers. Therefore, "enlightened" treatment and respect for labor as well as the fostering of technical skills for direct workers is *necessary for higher productivity* (Kern and Schumann 1987: 160–162). For example, workers can improve productivity by applying their skills to minimize machine downtimes (Jürgens 2023: 282–284). The lean approach and NPC philosophy both agree that skilled direct production workers were important to increase efficiency, but they disagree on the *types* of skills and *how* those skills should be deployed (see Springer 1999). Instead of multiskilled workers working on highly standardized jobs, production of a diverse range of high quality products required workers to have the skills necessary to flexibly respond to challenges inherent to flexible mass production (Reynolds 1989; Springer 1999: 136). Both systems departed from Taylorism in returning responsibility to direct production workers but differed in what that responsibility entailed.

The qualification offensive promoted by government and labor organizations created an overabundance of professionally trained skilled workers who were deployed in direct production jobs (Jürgens et al. 1993: 122–125; Jürgens 1995: 296–297). High skilled indirect workers such as maintenance and repair workers typically worked flexibly and with high autonomy, but these workers remained a relatively small labor elite at roughly 10 percent of the total production workforce in both American and German automakers. With the plethora of skilled workers, between 25 to 50 percent of direct production workers were skilled workers at Ford, Opel, and Volkswagen (Jürgens et al. 1993:

122). Through their vocational training, these workers possessed knowledge of "physical-technical functional problems concerning modern production installations" and a competence to quickly react to breakdowns, improvise, and take preventive action (Kern and Schumann 1987: 163).

The more automated production became, the more important the automated systems controller (*Anlagenführer*) became in controlling machine processes. The ideal of NPC was for skilled human labor to act as *subjects* that dominate the machines as *objects* (Springer 1999: 135). This appealed to the longstanding German desire for autonomy, job enrichment, and quality work (Springer 1999: 120; Hachtmann and von Saldern 2009; Lüdtke 2009). While NPC emphasized making workers the subjects of optimization, LP makes workers both *subjects and objects* of optimization by eliminating waste from standardized movements and encouraging workers to kaizen their jobs (Springer 1999: 135). Yet, NPC expected flexibility and improvisation to become the norm rather than standardization (Kern and Schumann 1987: 162–163). NPC appealed to German workers sensibilities, not just in terms of higher pay that comes with job enrichment but as an opportunity to exercise skills, perform quality work, and have more autonomous control over working conditions.

Like GM's Roger Smith, Volkswagen CEO from 1982–1991, Carl Hahn, introduced new automation as the "principal route to increase productivity and lower costs" (Tolliday 1995b: 125–126). VW established its own robot production department so it could develop new automation in-house (Jürgens 2023: 288–289). Robot deployment in the early 80s was primarily in welding and painting with 942 robots in the eight German plants by 1983 (Brumlop and Jürgens 1983: 19–20). This grew to around 4,000 robots by 1991, with 900 deployed in Wolfsburg (Jürgens 2023: 288–291). Between 1975 and 1985, many trades experienced automation leaps, e.g., mechanical production (70 to 90 percent automated), engine assembly (30 to 60 percent), and the paint shop (30 to 50 percent). The press and body shops moved from 80 to 85 percent and 60 to 70 percent automation respectively (Granel 1986: 16–19; Jürgens 2023: 305). But most notable was the rise in assembly automation from 5 percent to 25 percent (Jürgens et al. 1993: 71; Jürgens 1998: 291).

Volkswagen was the first in the world to pursue extensive assembly automation. Halle 54, the robotized assembly area in Wolfsburg, became a site of pilgrimage for technological planners around the world who frequently called it "innovative, brilliant, and futuristic" (Keller 1993: 175; Jürgens 1998: 291). The system involved worker-led module assembly of components that would feed into the two parallel mechanized lines at the "technical center" (Jürgens 2023: 295). Before and after the technical center were four conventional assembly lines with around 3,500 workers each to perform the remaining assembly

(Jürgens et al. 1993: 356). On the automated line, there were buffer zones so workers could respond to breakdowns without shutting down the whole line, allowing between one to two hours of downtime before the assembly line "crashed" and idled thousands of workers (Jürgens et al. 1993: 358; Jürgens 2023: 297). The mechanized lines performed ten operations within strict 20 second cycles at speeds which were impossible to achieve manually (Jürgens 1998: 292; Jürgens 2023: 298). The robots performed what previously involved overhead work and heavy lifting, so there was a humanization element as well (Jürgens et al. 1993: 356). The robots were computer controlled, but there were maintenance personnel on standby and around thirty workers dedicated to each line (Jürgens et al. 1993: 356). When operating efficiently, Halle 54 assembled 3,000 units of the VW Golf and its variants per day, and shortened assembly time by two hours in the mechanized areas and one hour in manual assembly (Jürgens 1998: 292; Jürgens 2023: 302–303). Therefore, higher productivity and quality was achieved with the new automation. Though around one thousand workers were displaced from the lines, the remaining work was humanized through the reduction of overhead work. However, capacity increases, increased capital requirements, and product changes caused overall personnel numbers to rise—as did VW's break-even point (Jürgens 1998: 292; Jürgens 2023: 302–303).

NPC reached its height during the 1980s at the same time as the diversity quality production strategy and the humanization movement. New technology paired with skilled workers complemented the demands for diversity and quality. Automation often increased both humanization and productivity. Workers were willing to be flexibly deployed if they could exercise their skills on the shopfloor and be guaranteed employment security, full pay protection in job transfers, and retraining rights (Brumlop and Jürgens 1983; Tolliday 1995b: 126–127). Through cooperation, the interests of management, workers, and customers were satisfied simultaneously. With the structural conditions of the value-regime, a "high road" path was achieved in Germany. Unlike the US in its struggle to imitate the Japanese, Germany forged its own path with little interest in emulating lean production. However, confidence in the German model soon faltered by the early 1990s.

4.4 *The German System in Crisis: Productivity, Costs, and Profitability*

Executing the diversified quality production strategy through new production concepts while improving productivity and humanization required the German value-regime to balance high cost production, products, and labor while still reaping profits. Balance was sustained during the 1980s but became unbalanced by the early 1990s. The issues included wage drift, "grossly increased personnel requirements in the indirect areas," high capital costs, and a high breakeven point, which were not compensated for by productivity gains from the automation strategy (Jürgens 1995: 297; Jürgens 2023: 303–305). A second problem was that the high-quality low-competition segment of the German DQP strategy eroded as American and Japanese competition were achieving higher quality at lower costs (Tolliday 1995b: 129; Herrigel 1996; Womack et al. 2007 [1990]: 88–91). Japanese automakers were attaining quality and diversity at lower costs, throwing doubt on the German assumption that there was a tradeoff between high quality and high productivity (Tolliday 1995b: 129; Jürgens 2004: 415). Thus, by the early 1990s it was ambiguous whether the "German model" was successful, as Tolliday (1995b: 130) describes,

> the linkages between the success and the model are not straightforward. In certain respects, broader market, product and cyclical changes provided conditions in which the "model" could thrive for a time despite serious shortcomings which were later to be exposed.

This discussion below describes these shortcomings and how they resulted in a crisis.

The first issue was that, while productivity increases from automation did occur, they were not as high as expected, not enough to counter rising costs, and did not close the productivity gap with lean producers. Though VW's technology strategy fared better than GM's, "cost and manpower savings targets were not achieved by assembly automation" (Tolliday 1995b: 128; Jürgens 1998: 293). At VW's Halle 54, the technology's flexibility was more limited than expected and minor changes in product design "cause major problems of readjusting the technology" (Jürgens 1998: 293). Despite the utilization of skilled *Anlagenführer* and *Facharbeiter*, machine breakdowns were frequent, with 100 million Deutschmark losses due to breakdowns in the mid-1980s (Jürgens et al. 1993: 358–360; Jürgens 2004: 414). Breakdowns were mitigated by large buffer areas, but these absorbed capital and floor space, and encouraged a "firefighting" approach to solving production problems rather than ameliorating them permanently (Jürgens 1995: 297; Jürgens 1998: 293). Productivity researcher Ron Harbour (2017) describes the automation orientation that contributed to these results,

> When it comes to what functions to automate, we've seen differing philosophies. The manufacturers we saw as most competitive—the Japanese, the Koreans—needed a business case for automation. Whereas automakers in Western Europe and even the United States went more aggressively

> towards automating things, even when that didn't pay off. We've seen examples of companies installing automation that required more people, with higher skills, than were required before. They did it just to display their technological prowess. (2)

This characterization describes how automation benefited the overflow of skilled workers, but only a limited benefit for accumulating capital—a lack of pay off. This shows how automation can serve multiple interests depending on how it is deployed. It does not have to entail deskilling but rather can be oriented toward skilled workers. It also does not always minimize the time of production for maximum surplus value gain and can be slower than lean but manual manufacturing processes.

The diversified quality production strategy "promoted an orientation towards quality control which relied on separate groups of workers for quality control inspection and for repairs" (Jürgens et al. 1993: 126–172; Jürgens 2004: 414). This arrangement provided skilled jobs but also dramatically increased indirect personnel requirements (Jürgens 1995: 297). As Womack, Jones, and Roos (2007 [1990]) described Wolfsburg in the late-1980s,

> At the end of the assembly line was an enormous rework and rectification area where armies of technicians in white laboratory jackets labored to bring the finished vehicles up to the company's fabled quality standard. We found that a third of the total effort involved in assembly occurred in this area. (91)

According to these "craftsmen" workers, the enormous rework areas were "proof of our company's dedication to quality," but Womack, Jones, and Roos (2007 [1990]: 91) argue that these indirect workers were the same as fitters from the early 20th century, adjusting parts and rectifying mistakes—many of which were caused by the robots (see Keller 1993: 175). Because of this, VW's production system was deemed the "fattest production system in the world" with large buffers, large rework areas, and parking lots of unfinished vehicles "wasting both real estate and capital" (Tolliday 1995b: 128; Ewing 2017: 51).

There was a gap between the ideal and actual performance of the German system and a gap between German productivity and the *socially necessary standard* set by lean producers (Krafcik 1988; Womack et al. 2007 [1990]). The same productivity, flexibility, and quality problems were being addressed by US and Japanese firms, but lean automakers executed methods that combined "high efficiencies and low costs with high quality and market related flexibility" (Jürgens 1994: 99). LP demonstrated that the supposed tradeoff between high productivity and high quality was illusory, which allowed them to encroach upon the DQP-oriented market segment German producers occupied (Herrigel 1996). While it was assumed large rework areas with skilled workers were necessary for high quality, the lean manufacturers proved that a cheaper solution was to give direct responsibility for quality to direct production workers (Ohno 1988; Jürgens 2004: 414). Instead of relying on the improvisation of skilled workers to tackle production problems (Kern and Schumann 1987), LP illustrated how it was possible to "standardize work sequences even in high variety production" to achieve both high productivity and flexibility (Springer 1999: 129). In LP, production problems are solved at their source and kaizen improved processes, but in Germany there were "no systematic efforts to alleviate production problems, either in the form of incremental improvement activities on the shopfloor or in the early stages of product development," instead relying on technological solutions monitored by skilled workers (Jürgens 2004: 414). Thus, the German model was neither "fragile-lean," i.e., sensitive to breakdown but svelte, nor "robust-buffered," i.e., protected from breakdown but bloated, but was "fragile-buffered," i.e., sensitive to breakdown and bloated by excess of all kinds—the worst of both worlds for productivity and costs (Jürgens 1995: 297). Thus, the productivity gap of around 20 to 40 percent between Japan and Germany is explained both by the strengths of LP and the *comparative* weaknesses of the German model (Krafcik 1988; Jürgens 2004: 416; Womack et al. 2007 [1990]).

By 1993, costs rose so that the breakeven point at VW was 105 percent of production capacity (Jürgens 2004: 416; Ewing 2017: 48). This stemmed from the high capital investment, wage drift, and maintaining a large workforce, which was not compensated for by productivity-based cost reductions (Jürgens 1994: 99). High average wages stemmed from both the high proportion of skilled workers and struggles between labor and management over wages, often granting workers higher wages in exchange for labor flexibility (Brumlop and Jürgens 1983; Jürgens 1998: 289–291). While the workforce grew by 18 percent between 1983 and 1992, personnel costs grew by 68 percent (Jürgens 1994: 105). The works council could block job cuts, so it was difficult to reduce the workforce in any circumstance (Ewing 2017: 48). This was advantageous for the DQP and NPC strategies, but when combined with high fixed capital investment, it became difficult to lower any costs without extraordinary measures.

Profitability in the German auto industry had historically been low since the mid-1970s but had worsened from the 1980s into the 1990s (Jürgens et al. 1993: 37). While turnover at VW increased 113 percent and production by 65 percent from 1983–1993, profits declined by 110 percent (Jürgens 1994: 105). As Ewing (2017: 48) describes, "Because of high labor costs and inefficient factories, the company made practically no money on the cars it did sell." This was exacerbated in the 1991–1992 "profitless prosperity" when the high costs resulted in a 770 million Deutschmark loss for VW despite record output and a 1.8 billion loss for Daimler-Benz (Tolliday 1995b: 129; Herrigel 1996: 37). Even the IG Metall chairman, who was also on Volkswagen's supervisory board, demanded higher profit rates (Jürgens 1998: 297). The question was how to achieve higher profitability while satisfying workers and management to maintain the cooperative consensus? Laying off workers was not only legally and contractually restricted but could also hurt the high morale and worker cooperation necessary according to both German and Japanese models. Therefore, a solution that was agreeable to both sides was the only viable path forward.

With estimates that 30,000 jobs needed to be shed, a cooperative agreement was reached between IG Metall and Volkswagen to reach this target (Jürgens 1998: 305). 20,000 jobs that would otherwise be eliminated were saved by reducing working hours from 36 to 28.8 hours per week. 10,000 workers were released but received either early retirement or were incentivized by voluntary dismissal packages (Jürgens 1998: 305). The remaining workforce took a 20 percent pay cut and agreed to increased working time and labor flexibility (Grieger and Lupa 2015: 184; Ewing 2017: 55–56). Experiencing similar crises, in 1993 Daimler-Benz announced it would shed over 20,000 jobs, with Ford eliminating 10,000, and Opel eliminated thousands of jobs at its Bochum and Russelsheim facilities (Donnelly et al. 2002: 32). In total, a 20 percent reduction of the German industry workforce occurred, from 824,324 in 1990 to 661,826 by 1994 (Herrigel 1996; Jürgens 2004: 416). This drop would have been more severe if not for the work time reduction measures, which effectively amounted to a job sharing program (Jürgens 2004: 416). Thus, through corporatist codetermination, syndicalist job sharing proved effective in blunting the social impacts of the crisis (see Cutler 1998; 2004).

After the crisis, German carmakers distanced themselves from the previous automation strategy and NPC (Tolliday 1995b: 129; Jürgens 2004: 416). The orientation shifted toward Japan, though not in a straightforward adoption process (see Springer 1999; Krzywdzinski 2020b). Unlike the US, Germany had abundant skills and cooperative relations that would likely have allowed Germany to adopt LP at any time, yet DQP, NPC, and humanization were pursued as uniquely German strategies to fulfill the interests of workers and management (see Herrigel and Sabel 1999). This was sustainable from the mid-1970s to the early-1990s but ultimately proved unsustainable in the long run. In the context of limited markets and increasing competition, new solutions to close the productivity and cost gap or means to evade productivity pressure were needed. Otherwise, the German industry faced social domination from unsustainable costs and competition from more efficient production systems (see Herrigel 1996). Thus, the German model could not afford to be static but required new solutions to production problems (Jürgens 2004).

5 Productivity Trumps Automation

Most striking about this period was how "hard" automation was no longer the primary driver of productivity. The most productive "lean" systems were less automated than GM and Volkswagen, and automation investments proved costly and contributed to later crises. "Soft" technologies, i.e., organizational arrangements, succeeded where "hard" technology failed (Degan 2011). Understanding how value-regimes shaped the flow of value in motion helps explain these surprising results.

In the German value-regime, codetermination mediated rationalization not through capital-labor conflict, but by *capital and labor working together*—not against automation and rationalization—but toward rationalization with "socially acceptable concessions" for the sake of both profitability and the interests of (high skill) workers. Protected by trade barriers in a low growth environment, the German industry nevertheless prospered from the mid-1970s to the early-1990s. Despite generally lower productivity, the diversified quality production strategy mitigated productivity pressure by designing niche products that emphasized quality over price. The Germans did not sell "cars" but *Mercedes-Benz*, *BMW*, and *Volkswagen*, distancing themselves from the expectation of conforming to the socially necessary value of standard autos and toward establishing a monopoly on the socially necessary value *for their* products. Flexible specialization, e.g., expertise in diesel passenger cars, set Germans apart (Piore and Sabel 1984; Ewing 2017; Pries and Wäcken 2020: 98).

Such distinctions helped German automobiles realize their value in a crowded international market, but how high quality was achieved was nevertheless inefficient. As Keller (1993) argues in her critique of Volkswagen's automation strategy, "The company didn't seem to grasp that quality had to exist in the context of other values. There was no question one could build a perfect car by hand, but it hardly suited the modern demand for mass production at low costs (175)." Keller identifies the *social demand* for low-cost mass production, but it is inaccurate to claim that VW did not balance quality with other values. VW's values were to humanize work, diversify products, and employ skilled labor operating technologically sophisticated machines. Their values were *not* to increase productivity and lower costs by all available means. The German "high road" system increased productivity *through* high paid skilled workers, high-cost automation, and high-cost cars, not despite them. Efforts to humanize work or increase wages in ways that decrease productivity and profits were valid cooperative choices as there is no determinist reason value cannot be distributed broadly within value-systems. There is also no reason why the German model could not prove sustainable at the mezzo level of the value-regime. Yet, developments at the macro level signified that, while high automation requiring skilled workers satisfied both labor and management interests, it also created a *comparatively* slow production process that was high cost and sensitive to crisis.

The early-1990s crisis was partially caused by cost imbalances within the value-regime, but it also originated from *social domination at the macro level.* As Herrigel (1996) explains, "the problem confronting ... German industry ... is that they are being challenged by an alternative system of flexible manufacturing that is superior to their own" (33). Lean production was not only adept at producing low-cost standard products but also flexibly and cheaply produced high quality specialized products better than German manufacturers. Lean production demonstrated the quality/productivity and specialized/standardized tradeoff was unnecessary, collapsing the distinction between high quality niche and low-quality volume products. Thus, Japanese competitors entered German high-quality markets by providing necessary quality *and* higher productivity at lower costs (Herrigel 1996: 34–35). Social domination exerted on German automakers by (Japanese) developments outside their value-regime set productivity and quality standards that redefined socially necessary labor time to levels below what Germans achieved with their "fragile-buffered" production system (Jürgens 1995: 297).

Springer (1999: 122–123) argues that humanization efforts in the 1970s and 1980s were supported by weak competition in the product market and strong labor market competition, yet after the 1990s crisis, product competition became strong and labor market competition became weak, making humanization no longer a priority to satisfy skilled workers. The question then became whether to move away from the German model or not? Would German workers accept LP if humanization is lost and workers experience "management by stress?" Can German automakers survive without such changes? Herrigel (1996) describes the stakes,

> If ... the entrenched interest in the old departments of management and among the various skilled groupings on the shop-floor succeed in

> blocking movements in this direction, it is difficult to imagine, given the dramatic productivity and cost differentials currently separating German producers from their major competitors, how the decentralized industrial order can continue to reproduce itself in the form which it had adopted in the 1980s. (48)

The industry faced a similar dilemma as in the first half of the 20th century. Could less productive but humanized German systems survive in the long-term, or was adaptation to the globally dominant standard necessary? If change was necessary, how could this be managed cooperatively? The transition to Fordism occurred under the Nazis, but any transition from German mass production to LP must be freely chosen and negotiated through codetermination.

The US dominated as the largest mass producer in the world because it was at the top of the technological and productive hierarchy for decades (Herrigel and Sabel 1999: 7). But when the norms of socially necessary labor time reset to the temporality of Japanese lean producers, the entire American industry felt *macro-level productivity pressure for the first time* since the advent of Fordism. Despite inefficiencies from labor-capital conflict (Norsworthy and Zabala 1985; Zabala 1995; Helper and Henderson 2014), US productive superiority enabled the accumulation of vast sums of capital while *managing* its internal contradictions. The battle between management and labor was not for survival but over distributing the fruits of prosperity. By the 1980s, the discussion shifted from how to distribute prosperity to how to survive, as the status of productivity leader was lost to the lean producers. As one GM representative described the problem to a UAW audience in 1988,

> I am here to tell you that our competitive health is not good at this time. It is not good for three reasons. First, our competition has gotten better. Secondly, there are more competitors, and finally we have not responded as we can and as we must. To be a productive organization, the value of what we produce must be greater than the cost of what we produce. This is our problem today. We are having to price our products below what they are costing us. (Selvala 1988: 6)

The social domination of value is evident as GM recognized it was out of step with the socially necessary value set by its competitors (Postone 1993).

For the American industry, Japanese competition was an "economic Pearl Harbour" that prompted the need for change in the value-systems (Holweg 2008: 5). The Big Three needed to either adopt LP or create a superior system of their own. However, the "automation leapfrog" failed and LP took decades to generalize (Kochan et al. 1997; Helper and Henderson 2014). As Hounshell (2000) describes, by the late 1980s "Detroit automation" had "become an epithet, shorthand for outmoded, inefficient, and inflexible American methods that contrasted sharply with the idealized 'lean production' methods of Japanese automakers" (101). Automation investments were made to improve the flow of value in motion, but this is not guaranteed. GM believed aggressively automating would regain productivity leadership, but this did not materialize (Finkelstein 2003). This was partially due to the immature technology and because of the combative industrial relations and lack of training that worsened performance (Jürgens et al. 1993; Ingrassia 2011; Helper and Henderson 2014). The contingent choice to invest in high automation had long-term consequences as such large investments carve path dependent developments in cost-structure, workforce training, and organization. It is time consuming and costly to deploy and maintain automation. If the time savings from the machines disappoint their potential and/or fail to meet the macro level socially necessary standard, then automation can become a costly mistake, especially when *assessed against the socially necessary standard.*

Distrust between management and labor hurt implementation of both the automation strategy and LP (Finkelstein 2003; Helper and Henderson 2014). Both labor and management were at fault—at times misunderstanding or undermining organizational change. Many in management wanted to maintain Taylorism or thought workers would abuse the added responsibility (Helper and Henderson 2014: 64). Workers did not want to eliminate stint or experience "management by stress," and did not trust management to uphold their responsibilities either (Parker and Slaughter 1988; Helper and Henderson 2014: 64). Thus, mutual distrust and resistance hobbled the adoption of LP and prevented new automation from reaching its potential.

While the official UAW position was to accept the "team concept" and some concessions, the leadership and rank-and-file were split and stuck in a dilemma. The wages and benefits won through hard bargaining were at stake, just as the work rules, seniority, and job classification system that benefited workers were framed as fetters on improving productivity. Management, paradoxically, needed high worker commitment to achieve LP, yet commitment was difficult to foster considering the legacy of labor-management conflict, especially when labor is asked to radically change their production system and accept concessions and layoffs. Commitment in LP resembles what Brown (2015) describes as the *neoliberal character structure* where competitiveness, meeting benchmarks, and a sense of responsibility are internalized drives. This clashed with UAW values of a "fair day's work for a fair day's pay," autonomy, and freedom outside of work (Asher 1995; Cutler 2004; Meyer 2004). Workers were being asked to identify with management productivity goals to maintain jobs, but job cuts, radical contract redesign, and concessions all worked against such internalization. Programs such as the Jobs Bank, Quality of Work Life, and Employee Involvement aimed to ensure job security and foster commitment, but these did not fully ameliorate the fear of plant closings and layoffs (Russo 1984). The cooperative stance from UAW leadership and declining grievances derived largely from fear, not from the internalized commitment (Yates 1992; Zabala 1995).

There was also the "management by stress" discourse that encouraged the UAW to resist implementation of LP as it degraded work and aimed to eliminate "waste" that workers benefitted from (Parker and Slaughter 1988, 1995; Babson 1995a; Meyer 2004). Though whether LP was empowering or exploitative was debated (see Adler 1993a; Eaton 1995), the management by stress analysis may be correct while lacking a viable alternative. Assuming management by stress is a justified characterization of LP and the intensified alienation is morally condemnable; the problem remains that *moral critiques do not address social domination*. Because lean producers were accumulating capital and penetrating US markets, the productivity standards of LP exerted a *gravitational pull* to compel the US value-systems to achieve similar levels of quality and productivity or face further decline. Even though the human costs may be high, the system was *effective from the view of value in motion*—which is what matters most in modern capitalist societies. That value in motion matters most is not solved by asserting humanist values against capitalist values because the latter values are rooted *structurally* in modern capitalist societies based on value. Livelihoods and businesses reproduce via value and are compelled to do what it takes to keep value in motion within their own systems. Maintaining an "inferior" but "humane" system is difficult, as German and Swedish automakers discovered (see Berggren 1995). LP is not *objectively* "superior," and the US and German systems are *not objectively* "inferior," but only *from the point of view of capital*. When someone claims lean production is "superior" the speaker implicitly buys into and supports modern capitalist ideology that obscures or ignores the human costs of LP. Yet, the claim to "superiority" is *not baseless* as lean producers did rapidly accumulate capital while non-lean firms lost ground. Thus, the discussion of LP "superiority" is not simply a rhetorical game, but a socio-communicative reflection of the *temporal-productive realities of different value-systems*.

Preventing management by stress *and* corporate decline could not be done through rhetoric or moral appeals but required either government protection, corporate willingness to dimmish profit over time, or developing a productive system that was somehow both comparably productive and humanist. Yet government protection ended in the mid-90s, the Big Three were unwilling to attenuate their pursuit of profit in the search for alternatives, and such an alternative that was *both* highly productive and humanist never appeared. The first two options also had their own problems. The VER restrictions helped the industry but hurt the consumer who had less access to cheaper Japanese transportation for the benefit of large American corporations. Lowering profits to shareholders and bonuses for managers would have certainly helped but reach their limits when a lack of profits affects the long-term investments necessary to improve productivity in the future. In addition, when the UAW resisted concessions, they implicitly also fought for less income polarization between management and labor and for lower profits for the Big Three. Accepting lower profit rates and a more equitable value distribution was always a possibility, but without sufficient bargaining leverage or codetermination, this was difficult to achieve, especially in the American value-regime where businesses are especially profit oriented (see Sloan 1964; Jouet 2017). What ultimately occurred was a slow and disjointed adoption of LP over decades that failed to prevent GM and Chrysler's bankruptcies. That these were the most viable choices demonstrates *the heteronomy of social domination*. In other words, the "choice" to improve productivity in particular ways was not experienced as truly optional for the industry, as any other choice was liable to hasten decline rather than ensure survival.

Three productive systems appear here. The Japanese system combined cooperative relations with highly motivated multiskilled workers and low-inventory lean processes to become the productivity leaders (Ohno 1988; Womack et al. 2007 [1990]). The American system aimed to become more productive but encountered difficulties due to its conflictual relations, investments in immature technology, and undertrained workforce (Jürgens et al. 1993; Finkelstein 2003; Helper and Henderson 2014). The German system had cooperative relations ideal for achieving high productivity but eschewed imitating the Japanese in favor of their own path focused on high quality, flexibility, and humanization at high costs and at the expense of productivity (Jürgens et al. 1993; Jürgens 2004). According to Postone (1993: 290–291) competition should compel the American and German firms to reach the level of productivity set by the Japanese. These technological-organizational developments are only one part of an underlying capitalist historical dynamic that perpetually pushes productivity forward. This is partially why lean producers were so successful as kaizen activities *consciously and continuously* search for ways to improve productivity. As should be expected if Postone's (1993) analysis is correct, the productive system that most purposefully pushed value in motion forward became the rising star. If the social domination thesis is correct, then convergence around lean principles as the *productive basis* for auto production should occur (see Pries 2003; Weyer 2011).

The cleavage is *not* between productive and unproductive systems. Both the US and German industries held enormous productive capacity with large assemblages of capital and labor which produced millions of commodities a year. Even though all three systems are among the most productive to ever exist, the social domination thesis holds that the *most productive system* has certain advantages in accumulating capital that are felt as disadvantages to the second or third most productive system. Thus, *comparison* is vital for understanding social domination.

Comparison can illuminate why the automation strategies in the US and Germany "failed." In the US, lack of training and conflictual relations hurt the strategy, but even Germany suffered from limitations in flexibility and immature technologies (Jürgens et al. 1993). Yet, the Japanese were also highly automated, including being nearly as automated as Volkswagen in all areas except for assembly (Jürgens 2021: 6). As Womack, Jones, and Roos (2007 [1990]: 94–95) found, automation did aid productivity, but lean organization plus automation produced the best results in terms of hours per vehicle. Thus, assessing the "failure" of automation must occur in two ways. First, automation was a "failure" to the extent it did not meet expectations within the context of its own system, e.g., downtimes, errors etc., which both value-regimes experienced (Jürgens et al. 1993; Ingrassia 2011). Second, both were also "failures" because they did not improve productivity to the point of becoming productivity leader—meaning the full significance of failure or success *requires outside reference to the prevailing productive standard* beyond the control of US or German automakers. In this way, social domination shapes categories like success/failure. Though it appeared self-evident for decades that the most automated system would be the most productive, the "failure" of the automation strategies demonstrated how this was not always true and that combinations of labor and capital that were less automated but more productive via other means can win out against the most automated systems.

The value-systems constantly observed other systems and compared the productivity of different plants. GM maintained efficiency by implementing intra-company competition among their brands and factories, while Ford observed and compared their plants to Japanese standards since the late 1970s (Jürgens et al. 1993: 262–272). Volkswagen focused less on comparison during the 1980s, but both German and US firms became increasingly focused on benchmarking and comparison with Japan when the *Machine that Changed the World* (Womack et al. 2007 [1990]) was published (Jürgens et al. 1993: 277–278). This put productivity pressure on workers to meet benchmarks with the threat of plant closing or other punishments if production goals were not met (Russo 1984; Jürgens et al. 1993: 372).

This reveals some differences between how Fordism generalized versus lean production. Fordism generalized in the US both through economic competition and through academic and industry publications (Arnold and Faurote 1915; Hounshell 1985). It took decades to generalize Fordism in Germany because of the economic conditions and ambivalence among companies and workers until the fascist state-led modernization program of the 1930s (Hachtmann and von Saldern 2009). With lean production, lack of study, clear understanding, and a language and cultural barrier hurt the social-communicative spread of LP, though the economic and productivity pressures remained acute (Jürgens et al. 1993: 40–44; Helper and Henderson 2014; Wittrock 2015). By the late 1980s, interest in closing the competitive gap inspired international research projects and translations of Japanese texts to aid in understanding LP (e.g., Krafcik 1988; Ohno 1988; Adler 1993a; Womack et al. 2007 [1990]). Quantitative productivity comparisons were especially useful because they detailed in precise hours per vehicle the socially necessary temporal norm and the gap between company performance and the benchmark. Socially necessary labor time became *knowable, measurable, comparable, and assigned importance and meaning* across the global industry. The book *The Machine that Changed the World* (Womack et al. 2007 [1990]) itself changed the world through communicating to business, labor, and governmental social systems the parameters, stakes, and importance of improving productivity to meet lean standards. Through its forceful message of lean productive "superiority" and data to validate its claims, such studies contributed to the *social* domination of global automakers. Recognizing this explains how the logic of capital is reinforced socially through communication. The socially necessary temporal norms asserted themselves through economic outcomes whether they are consciously understood and quantified or not, but rigorous study, comparison, and communicative dissemination aided in the generalization process.

This is exemplified by the controversial "one best way" discourse. After the publication of the IMVP research, debate exploded about whether the Japanese had discovered the "one best way" to produce automobiles or if there were several viable productive models (see Jürgens et al. 1993; Boyer and Freyssenet 1995, 2002; Pulignano 2020; Covarrubias and Ramírez Perez 2020b). Researchers claimed that it was possible to be profitable by pursuing alternative productive arrangements and strategies such as the DQP strategy or focusing on product innovation. Setting aside the merits for or against it, the primary issue with the "one best way" concept is the implication that any productive system could remain the "best" method forever without being replaced—resembling an "end of history" narrative. To claim this is to miss the underlying historical dynamic of capitalism that continually pushes productivity forward, making even the most productive system at any given time *contingent, fragile, and subject to change* (Postone 1993). LP was only the "one best way" insofar as the leanest producers possessed the highest standards of productivity that existed at that time. Just as Fordist mass production replaced craft production, and whether through evolutionary means (kaizen) or Schumpeterian creative destruction, there is no static state of what constitutes the most productive means to produce a commodity.

Nevertheless, the fact that there was a "one best way" debate at all engendered a social-communicative effect on concrete production processes. The notion that LP was the "one best way" persuaded value-systems to change in specific directions, eliminating waste and transforming labor processes in the US and Germany. Thus, there is *social* power in the idea of "one best way." As William I. Thomas stated in his Thomas Theorem, "If [human beings] define situations as real, they are real in their consequences" (Thomas and Thomas 1928: 571–572). Therefore, LP both *is* and *is not* the "one best way" depending on how it is perceived within social systems—a social construction of reality. After the publication of the IMVP research, the data and the "one best way" narrative contributed to reforming entire production systems. Thus, the "one best way" narrative existed as a sociological fact with concrete effects, even if it was conceptually problematic. This too expresses *social* domination, i.e., that efforts to approach the "one best way" represented a *social* compulsion to achieve higher productivity levels.

In this period of low growth and limited markets, capitalism remained a *struggle for survival*, the terms of which were *constantly changing* and not determined by any single social system or locus of power. High automation in all three countries was rendered socially necessary in some production areas where it proved to be faster, cheaper, sufficiently flexible, and aided in accumulating capital (Krzywdzinski 2020a; Jürgens 2021: 6). Yet, *productivity as a social imperative trumps automation*. New technologies that do not sufficiently improve the flow of value in motion or do not meet the socially necessary standard may hurt capital accumulation. A linear path from less to more automation is therefore not inevitable, as the value of any given technology *for capital* is not self-evident, but only to the degree it facilitates capital as value in motion. Even an improving and/or increasingly automated system is "devalued" if a competitor's system sets the worldwide industry standard (Harvey 2017: 72–93). The task set before the American and German industry at the turn of the 21st century was how to respond to these challenges to prevent crisis and further decline without assuming automation was the solution.

CHAPTER 5

Globalization and the Race for Productivity

1 Productivity Pressure in the Age of Globalization

By the mid-1990s, the situation for the German and American auto industry was not encouraging. The German industry found success during the decade and a half between the first oil crisis in the mid-1970s to the early 1990s with its diverse and quality focused product strategy and its simultaneously humanized and highly mechanized production processes. Yet, the structural weaknesses in the production system, its cost structure, and the increased competition led to a crisis that prompted the need to rethink the merits of the new production concepts and reappraise the value of lean production (Springer 1999). The domestic US industry suffered from decades of market share losses and was feverishly struggling to close factories, elicit concessions from the UAW, and implement productivity measures to close the productivity and quality gap with the Japanese who continued to set up transplants in the US (Ingrassia 2011; Helper and Henderson 2014). Meanwhile, the Japanese industry, led by Nissan, Honda, and Toyota, made further inroads in the US and European markets. In fact, Toyota grew to surpass GM as the largest automaker in the world in 2009, a title GM held for over seven decades, after GM filed for bankruptcy (Ingrassia 2011; Liker 2021).

In some respects, the development of the German and US auto industry from the mid-1990s to the 2020s was a reaction and continuation of the trends observed in the 1970s and 1980s, with lean producers in ascendency as Womack, Jones, and Roos (2007 [1990]) predicted. Yet in other ways, the fall of the Soviets and the rise of 'peripheral' countries (Wallerstein 2004) such as China and India completely restructured the global competitive landscape. The collapse of the Iron Curtain, the reunification of East and West Germany, and access to Eastern Europe was a boon to the German auto industry. Eastern European markets with few automobiles were avenues to sell cheap models, and the cheap labor in Eastern Europe incentivized outsourcing to lower cost production sites for German manufacturers (Jürgens 2008; Jürgens and Krzywdzinski 2009; Sturgeon, Memedovic, Biesebroeck, and Gereffi 2009). The North American Free Trade Agreement (NAFTA) made Mexico an attractive investment for outsourcing production in the US (Covarrubias 2020). The rise of automobility in China was also fortuitous for both the US and German industry as joint venture opportunities gave companies, especially

 | DOI:10.1163/9789004736719_007

Volkswagen and GM, access to a nearly untouched market that grew explosively (Wenten 2020). The opening of previously closed markets provided new growth outlets for exports and transplants. While the mature markets in Germany, the US, and Japan grew slowly, stagnated, or even declined, new growth outlets abroad assuaged problems faced by auto companies at home (Sturgeon et al. 2009: 11).

The competitive struggle was no longer narrowed to market share competition within mature markets but became a scramble to enter new growth regions. In the rush to capitalize on the emerging opportunities, eliminate smaller competitors, and consolidate global capacity, new joint ventures (JV), acquisitions, mergers, and alliances appeared (Donnelly et al. 2002; Holweg 2008: 7; Sturgeon et al. 2009: 9). For example, Volkswagen acquired multiple European companies, Chrysler merged with Daimler-Benz, Italy's Fiat, and finally an American-European conglomerate called Stellantis, and Nissan and French producer Renault forged an alliance in 1999 (see, Howell and Hsu 2002; Sturgeon, Memedovic, Biesebroeck, and Gereffi 2009; Covarrubias and Ramírez Perez 2020). Thus, the size and scope of the already enormous auto companies ratcheted to a further level of transnationalization, making it questionable whether national origin still mattered (see Robinson 2004, 2014; Holweg 2008: 8).

Globalization was the watchword in the 1990s and 2000s as, from the opening of Eastern Europe, China and Mexico, a transnational capitalism dominated by transnational corporations emerged (see Robinson 2004, 2014; Wallerstein 2004). A global middle class in countries like China and India materialized (Milanović 2016) and economic inequality within countries became more prominent than inequality between countries (Piketty 2014, 2020). These developments convinced transnational corporations to place less importance on the US, Japan, and Europe as the three major economic regions of the world and to instead adopt a global focus (Robinson 2004; 2014).

Global vehicle production more than doubled between 1975 and 2007, from 33 to nearly 73 million and increased to nearly 100 million by 2018 (Sturgeon et al. 2009: 10; Statista. 2021a: 9). Covarrubias and Ramírez Perez (2020b) describe the enormous size of the contemporary auto industry stating,

> Global auto industry revenues reached $3.8 trillion in 2018 after growing at an annual rate of 3.3% for the last five years. This means that if auto manufacturing were a country, it would be the fifth largest economy in the world, after the United States (with a GDP of $20.4 trillion), China (14), Japan (5.1), and Germany (4.2). The 11 largest auto makers ... appear in the top 100 of the 2018 Fortune Global 500, namely Toyota (ranked 6th), VW (7th), Daimler (16th), GM (21st), Ford (22nd), Honda (30th), SAIC (36th),

> BMW (51st), Nissan (54th), Dongfeng Motor (65th), and Hyundai (78th) … These auto corporations manage more resources than most of the world's economies. Toyota's and VW's revenues are only next to the wealth of the world's top 16 economies. Put differently, their economic reach is greater than that of 169 nations (3).

Globalization, corporate consolidation, and emerging automobility in peripheral countries made this possible.

This explosive growth is partially due to China becoming an increasingly important market and auto producer. Thanks to production in China through JVs with tripartite companies such as GM, Volkswagen, and Toyota, China became the largest auto producing country in the world by 2009, producing over 25.7 million vehicles by 2019, more than the domestic production of Japan, the United States, and Germany combined (Klier and Rubenstein 2020: 51; OICA 2023). Through these joint ventures, the transnational auto companies were among the primary beneficiaries of Chinese growth (Wenten 2020). In this arrangement, corporations from core countries benefited from producing in a semi-peripheral country, with mixed results for production and workers in the home country (see Wallerstein 2004). This started to change, however, by the 2020s when non-Chinese automakers began to lose favor in China at the same time Chinese automakers started exporting their cars, especially electric vehicles, abroad (Ou, Lin, He, Przesmitzki, Wu, Zheng, Lv, and Qi 2020; Webster 2024).

With the dramatic globalization of world markets, Womack, Jones, and Roos's (2007 [1990]) prediction that the fate and fortunes of auto companies would be dependent on their ability to adopt lean production appeared wrong (see Boyer and Freyssenet 2002). The emergence of new markets meant that there was no 'end of history' either in terms of the production system development or growth opportunities. The MIT researchers' attempt to declare a 'one best way' based on the total package of lean production practices was premature, partially because some of the practices—such as the door to door car selling popular in Japan (Womack et al. 2007 [1990]: 173–195)—were specific to Japanese culture and had no advantage or relevance for other firms or countries (see Wittrock 2015). In addition, the value-regimes of each country and value-systems of each firm had their own sets of resources, regulations, and industrial relations that meant implementing lean production would necessarily be hybridized.

However, the International Motor Vehicle Program scholars were correct that elements of lean production and the general orientation toward eliminating waste and cutting costs became a major preoccupation of auto companies around the world, with Toyota constituting the global productivity benchmark (Holweg 2008; Weyer 2011; Liker 2021; Krzywdzinski 2020b). And the benefits of being productivity leader speak for themselves, as Toyota went from being around half the size of GM in 1990 to surpassing GM to become the world's largest automaker in 2009. Toyota also enjoyed a high profitability rate—with a total net income from 2004 to 2018 at $179.7 billion, more than the total net income of Ford ($46.9 billion), Volkswagen ($37.3 billion), and Honda (75.4 billion) combined (Womack et al. 2007 [1990]; Liker 2021: 3–4). Even with new growth outlets, the crises of the early 1990s in the United States and Germany meant that increasing productivity was a priority. The following details how lean principles, particularly those aimed at improving productivity, were adapted to US and German conditions—just as Fordism generalized after WWII. The analysis provides the opportunity to observe similarities and differences between how LP generalized in both countries. This is also a narrative of how globalization radically changed the competitive conditions of the world auto industry.

In the United States, the long decline of the Big Three continued through the 1990s into the 2000s, coming to a head in the 2008 financial crisis and bankruptcy of both GM and Chrysler in 2009 (Ingrassia 2011; Helper and Henderson 2014). From over 30 percent of the domestic market share in the mid-1990s for GM and around 10 percent for Toyota, by 2017 GM had only 17.5 percent market share, a mere 2.8 percentage points more than Ford and 3.3 percentage points higher than Toyota at 14.2 percent (Helper and Henderson 2014: 50; Klier and Rubenstein 2020: 47). Thus, GM was no longer dominant even in its home market. Besides Fiat-Chrysler at 11.9 percent, the other large companies were Japanese or South Korean with Honda at 9.6 percent, Nissan at 9.3, and Hyundai at 7.4 (Klier and Rubenstein 2020: 47). Meanwhile, German producers struggled to maintain a sizeable presence in the United States, despite many attempts to penetrate the market (see Hoitt 2012; Ewing 2017). Volkswagen only held 3.3 percent of the US market, 2.1 percent for BMW and 2.2 percent for Daimler-Benz (Klier and Rubenstein 2020: 47). Production in the US value-regime became increasingly comprised of nonunion transplants with the Big Three accounting for 87 percent of production in 1990 being reduced to 78 percent in 2000, 55 percent in 2010, and a slim majority of 52 percent in 2017 (Klier and Rubenstein 2020: 51). The US can now be characterized as a heterogeneous value-regime with the social contract based on the 'Treaty of Detroit' fractured through the growth of nonunion transplants and decades of concession bargaining (see Yates 1992; Howell 1995).

The Big Three scrambled to improve their productivity while simultaneously demanding concessions and reducing capacity. The implementation of lean production was haphazard and differed between plants and firms, but the struggle for survival prompted the need to improve productivity and reduce costs (see Adler, Kochan, MacDuffie, Pil, and Rubinstein 1997; Ingrassia 2011). With the emergence of consultant agencies such as the Harbour Report that systematically measured and reported productivity levels of US plants—both Big Three and transplants—benchmarking and competition for achieving the highest levels of productivity and quality possible were widely promoted (e.g., Vasilash 1997; DeMarines 2000; Winter 2003; Africa Wire 2008; Harbour 2017). The productivity race was on as the US became an intense battleground of competition between the domestic producers and the importers and transplants.

In Germany, recovery from the 1990s crisis signaled the need to reevaluate their production system and cost structure. The main issue was how to adapt lean productivity improvements while maintaining the spirit of cooperation that animated the German auto industry for decades? Integrating LP in this context was difficult, met resistance and setbacks, and required compromise, yet it appeared that the German system could integrate some lean elements while keeping the skilled Facharbeiter and codetermination system intact (Jürgens 1995, 1997, 2021; Krzywdzinski 2020b). The diversified quality production strategy and pursuit of new production concepts were modified through the move toward lean production (Springer 1999; Sorge and Streeck 2016).

The urgency for productivity improvement was somewhat muted by the fact that German companies were particularly successful in taking advantage of new growth opportunities. The opening of Eastern Europe allowed for both low-cost production and new sales opportunities to emerge just east of Germany (Jürgens and Krzywdzinski 2009). In addition, Volkswagen's JV in China beginning in the 1980s made VW profit from the rise of China, and Daimler-Benz and BMW also profited from their status as German luxury brands to service the emergent Chinese elite (Wenten 2020; Bormann et al. 2018; MacDougall 2020: 4). The arrival of new export and transplant opportunities made it so the 'high road' of domestic German production was subsidized through sales abroad and foreign transplants with significantly cheaper labor and lacking the same systems of codetermination present in Germany (Jürgens 2008; Jürgens and Krzywdzinski 2009; McKenney 2018). Volkswagen's growth during the 2000s and 2010s, driven by China, was so explosive that the Volkswagen Group, with all its brands such as Volkswagen, Audi, and Škoda, either surpassed or were close behind Toyota in terms of total worldwide sales of over 10 million each per year from 2014–2019 (Statista 2021a: 31; Statista 2021b: 12). Thus, after GM's bankruptcy in 2009, both Volkswagen and Toyota have at times claimed the status of world's largest automobile producer, and it is debatable to determine—via a variety of metrics—which company is truly the world's dominant carmaker after GM was dethroned.

Finally, future trends and challenges facing the automobile industry are discussed including Industry 4.0 and the electric vehicle transition. Overall, the auto industry since the 1990s has engaged in a productivity race to achieve the high benchmark set by the leanest producer Toyota which has risen to be one of the largest and most profitable automakers in the world, as well as race to secure sales in new markets around the world.

2 Productivity Convergence and Divergence in the 21st Century

By the mid-1990s US and German automakers were convinced that change was needed. The question was, what form would this take? In both value-regimes, it seemed obvious that more automation was not the answer, and influential works such as Womack, Jones and Roos (2007 [1990]) in *The Machine That Changed the World*, made the case that wholehearted adoption of lean production was the most evident solution to productive, competitive, and profitability problems. Even with ready-made guides that described LP, implementing it was not easy. Radical change in practice and orientation of both management and labor was required for its implementation. There were also socio-legal systems within each value-regime that meant that LP, as described by Womack, et al. (2007 [1990]), could not be applied wholesale. Thus, productivity development since the late-1990s is primarily defined by trial and error in adapting lean principles to different production systems. In the wake of crises and increasing competitive pressure from imports and foreign transplants, increasing efficiency to close the productivity gap and reduce costs became an imperative.

2.1 *Productivity Improvement before and after the Bankruptcy Crisis*

The domestic American auto industry from the mid-1990s to the 2009 bankruptcies were in a struggle against decline. The market share of the Big Three continued to erode, while the Japanese, Koreans, and Germans established transplants and benefited from no import restraints (Berry et al. 1999; Helper and Henderson 2014: 50; Klier and Rubenstein 2020). Labor-management relations were slow to change as declining share prompted concession bargaining resisted by the UAW, and with the characteristically American combative industrial relations, it was difficult to establish the relational contracts and cooperative culture needed to implement lean principles (Ingrassia 2011; Helper and Henderson 2014). In the 1980s, there was still confusion about what the Japanese advantage was and how it could be implemented, but by the 1990s, with trial-and-error experimentation, transplant experience, and various publications (e.g., Womack et al. 2007 [1990]), the details became well known. Therefore, its implementation became a matter of will for labor and management to reform the work structure and culture.

The generalization of lean principles in US domestic firms took a complicated course to achieve higher productivity and quality and lower costs. This was spurred on by productivity research, e.g., the Harbour Report, which documented progress in productivity via assessments of how many hours it takes to build a vehicle in each plant. This discourse prompted a competitive productivity race between companies and between plants. The discussion then turns to the late 2000s crisis, which triggered the bankruptcy and government bailout of Chrysler and GM and the near collapse of Ford (Ingrassia 2011). The bankruptcies occurred despite continuous improvements and reform efforts because of an unsustainable sharp dip in auto sales that exacerbated the weaknesses of the firms (Ingrassia 2011; Cutcher-Gershenfeld, Brooks, and Mulloy 2015). The discussion concludes with the post-bankruptcy recovery in the 2010s and 2020s.

In the 1980s, American firms experimented with Japanese methods in a few plants such as Saturn and NUMMI. Once a consensus emerged around what lean production constituted thanks to publications like *The Machine that Changed The World* (Womack et al. 2007 [1990]), the Big Three's task was how to implement these practices plant by plant, contract by contract (Kochan et al. 1997; Adler et al. 1997; Holmes 2004). As Roger Smith's tenure ended in 1990, the focus at GM shifted from automation to lean, with CEO Robert Stempel stating in 1992 that the company was "accelerating the implementation of lean production" through "eliminating waste … to reduce operating expenses, inventories, lead times, and floor-space requirements, while increasing quality and throughput" (General Motors Heritage Center 1992: 1–2). Despite intentions, there was little diffusion of lean production between 1989 and 1994 beyond the individual plant experiments, as GM aggressively downsized and Ford and Chrysler incrementally implemented lean practices (Kochan et al. 1997: 311).

Adler, Kochan, MacDuffie, Pil and Rubinstein (1997: 83) describe how the smoothness of the transition depended on factors such as plant age, local-level union-management relations, and the "extent to which they have been retrofitted with new technologies and/or product lines." For example, Chrysler's Jefferson North plant in Detroit was a new facility with an older workforce that positively responded to work teams but was less adept at implementing continuous improvement and active problem solving (Adler et al. 1997: 74–78). At GM's Wilmington Delaware plant, after a 1992 announcement that the plant would close by 1996, management and the UAW cooperated to improve productivity through just-in-time process flow to shrink inventories and remove buffers. However, teams and job rotation were not introduced, and kaizen activities remained low. As a result, productivity was among the highest within GM, but quality lagged below average. The authors conclude that *plant-specific characteristics and history* contributed to how lean principles were received and implemented (Adler et al. 1997: 78–83). This plant by plant approach was necessitated by the decentralized structure of UAW local bargaining units, which was advantageous for the companies as fragmented collective bargaining allowed for 'whipsawing' with plants competing to improve productivity to prevent plant closings (Jürgens 1993: 262–278; Holmes 2004: 12; Rothstein 2006: 71). 'Cooperative' plants that agreed to renegotiate the plant agreement in alignment with lean principles were generally more likely to stay open or receive new work than plants that resisted (Babson 1995c: 246; Rothstein 2008: 66). Thus, by the late 1990s, the Big Three plants existed on a spectrum from mass to lean production, exhibiting "the widest range of practices found anywhere in the world" (Kochan et al. 1997: 311).

This resulted in "piecemeal rather than systematic learning" at varying speeds within Big Three plants (Cutcher-Gershenfeld et al. 2015: 22). While improvements did occur, the approach was problematic because LP required "deeply integrated organization learning principles" based on distributing knowledge across the workforce (Cutcher-Gershenfeld et al. 2015: 22; Liker 2021: 255–291). As Liker (2021: xxvi) describes, lean should not be applied "mechanistically" from the top down like a toolbox of solutions to production problems but cooperatively implemented "organically," requiring both organizational and cultural change. Without mutual management-labor consent, the results may disappoint, as happened in plants where lean principles were formally listed in the contract but hardly practiced (Womack et al. 2007 [1990]: 100; Helper and Henderson 2014: 64). As Helper and Henderson (2014: 56) recounts from one worker, the attitudes of the "old days" such as "Slow down, don't work so fast," or "Every now and then, throw a monkey wrench into the whole thing so the equipment breaks down—the repair people will have to come in and we'll be able to sit around and drink coffee" needed to be changed for LP to work. Likewise, management attitudes like "Kick ass and take names. The dumb bastards don't know what they're doing," and "If you don't do it my way I'll fire you and put somebody in who will" needed to be excised (Helper and Henderson 2014: 56). This century-long legacy in the US value-regime erected barriers to lean implementation that partially explain the numerous 'false starts' in Big Three plants (see Rubinstein and Kochan 2001; Cutcher-Gershenfeld et al. 2015: 23).

Adoption of LP accelerated in the 2000s as the continued market share decline and the continued growth of Japanese firms signaled the "increasing recognition of the need for transformation" (Cutcher-Gershenfeld et al. 2015: 10). As Cutcher-Gershenfeld, Brooks, and Mulloy (2015: 23) explain, although "learning could have been faster, particularly during the 1990s when the lessons were increasingly clear, important progress has been made throughout the 2000s." For example, in the 2003 UAW-Ford bargaining agreement, Quality Operating System Coordinators were designated to take responsibility for "driving standardized work processes and joining with team leaders to generate continuous improvement suggestions from work teams" which helped Ford reach lean benchmark quality by 2010 (Cutcher-Gershenfeld et al. 2015: 5). The quality gains resulted in $1.2 billion savings in warranty costs by 2008 (Cutcher-Gershenfeld et al. 2015: 6). The detailed system of job classifications and work rules were modified to allow greater flexibility of work assignments through teamwork, with many plants increasing production from two to up to six products on one line (Cutcher-Gershenfeld et al. 2015: 16). In 2006, the implementation of thirty "competitive operating agreements" that included "far-ranging" work rule changes generated efficiency improvements estimated at $500 million at Ford (Cutcher-Gershenfeld et al. 2015: 7). At GM, the "General Motors production system" based on Toyota's practices and a more effective relational contract with the UAW was gradually diffused, spearheaded by managers who were trained at NUMMI and Saturn (Helper and Henderson 2014: 66). Thus, more systematic company-wide efforts at diffusing LP were made in the 2000s.

Though organizational changes were the focus of productivity improvements, technology and automation remained important. Despite the failure of the aggressive automation 'leapfrog' in the 1980s (Finkelstein 2003), the firms still publicized technological progress to aid in value realization. For example, a 2015 Ford press release advertised the acquisition of 500 new body shop robots that produce a "tougher, more durable truck," and increased paint shop automation for more "durable paint application" (Ford Motor Company Archives 2015a: 2). Another release noted quality inspections were done by robots with cameras to "ensure the highest quality standards are met" and that robots were installing roofs and door panels (Ford Motor Company Archives 2015b: 2). Thus, despite the disappointments of the 1980s, new technologies kept their socio-communicative relevance and importance in the self-descriptions of value-systems.

Improvements in robotics made them a staple throughout auto factories. The stock of robots and robot density (robot stock per 1000 blue-collar workers) in both the US and German auto industry rose from around 10,000–30,000 in the early 1990s to over 100,000 by 2018 (Krzywdzinski 2020a: 31). However, the increase in robots did not generate new leaps in automation and efforts to automate assembly in the US were discontinued after the 1980s. As one Ford manager described, the American attitude was that it was best to be a "cautious adopter of new technology, but ... a fast second adopter" (Krzywdzinski 2020a: 25). Even so, many areas of production—such as press shops, body shops and mechanical processing—remained near full automation in the US, Germany, and Japan since the early 1990s (Krzywdzinski 2020a: 49–50). New machines typically replaced old machines rather than workers, which is why automation levels did not change much. In fact, automation levels in body shops were so high—between 90–100 percent—that the German industry magazine *Automobil Produktion* stopped quantifying the level of automation around 2010 forward (Krzywdzinski 2020a: 18–19). As a GM employee manual described, robots were ubiquitous in the body shop for welding the body "in a time frame and with a degree of accuracy no human workers could ever approach" (General Motors Heritage Center 2019: 36). In the paint shop, robots spray painted vehicles programmed to apply the exact amounts of paint in precise areas for just the right length of time. Robots did perform limited assembly tasks that required heavy lifting such as the marriage of the car body onto the chassis (Cutcher-Gershenfeld 2015: 24; General Motors Heritage Center 2019: 37–39).

Computer hardware and software improvements made increasingly sophisticated robots that generally became more complex with higher precision and greater flexibility (Krzywdzinski 2020a: 50). For example, since the mid-2000s, multi-robot cells where robots work together to grip, process parts, and check quality, were deployed in body construction. Although such robots could work at inhumanly fast speeds, they were not the only source of productivity gains. Rather, productivity increased primarily through improving design manufacturability and standardization that aided both robotic and human assemblers (Krzywdzinski 2020a: 20–21; Jürgens 2023). In the engineering departments, advances in computer software and "simultaneous engineering" inspired from lean design philosophies enabled rapid product development and enhanced manufacturability (Cutcher-Gershenfeld 2015: 24–25; Krzywdzinski 2020a: 22–30). In addition, lean production worked synergistically with new technologies to reorganize processes to optimize material flows (Liker 2021: 159–180; Krzywdzinski 2020a: 19).

There were also differences in technological approach. Germany maintained higher assembly automation levels and has led in innovative in new manufacturing technologies (Krzywdzinski 2020a: 20; Jürgens 2021: 1–7; Jürgens 2023). The Big Three focused more on new product development, e.g., electric vehicles and driverless cars in partnership with Silicon Valley and tech startups, than on pushing the frontiers of manufacturing technology (Albert 2019; Klier and Rubenstein 2020: 43–45; Krzywdzinski 2020a: 30, 40). In Japan, deploying flexible workers and technologies remained top priority (Liker 2021; Krzywdzinski 2020a: 32). Though there were differences in emphasis and path dependent developments, there remained convergence around high automation in most areas of auto production except assembly (Krzywdzinski 2020a: 18–19, 49–50; Jürgens 2021: 6–7, 17; Jürgens 2023). This suggests that near full automation has become *socially necessary* for many areas of auto production especially as increasingly sophisticated software systems and robots improve their flexibility to satisfy everchanging consumer demands.

The Big Three's productivity improvement efforts were documented through the rise of productivity research agencies. After the importance of lean production was made clear, organizations designed to quantify, benchmark, and compare plant performance emerged which promoted a 'productivity race' among all auto plants in the United States (Womack et al. 2007 [1990]; Harbour 2017). These publications made socially necessary labor time measurable, quantified, and meticulously documented so that productivity benchmarks could be recognized and consciously pursued. The most influential of these publications was the Harbour Report which published yearly on the productivity of auto plants across the US since the 1980s (Statler 2004; Lutz and Walsh 2014).

Vasilash (1997) explains the importance of the Harbour Report stating that companies were "interested in the study because it allows them to know what the benchmarks are and what they have to do to get as competitive as the benchmarks." The reports were often dismissed by the Big Three at first but became increasingly important in the 1990s as the Big Three's market share continued to shrink (Winter 1992; Salter 2004: 78). The report eventually became the primary benchmark for US auto industry manufacturing productivity, was covered extensively by automotive journalists yearly, and high ranking plants would celebrate and publicize their achievement (Walsh and Lutz 2014). The hours per vehicle (HPV) numbers often became the basis for management bonuses and targets for operational management (Weyer 2011; Jürgens 2023: 352). Company executives and Wall Street put stock in the Harbour Report as well, making it an important way the industry disseminates self-descriptions about its 'industrial progress' (McCracken 2003). Thus, the socio-communicative aspect of competition became increasingly important as the Harbour Report and similar publications were polycontexturally observed by numerous social systems and influenced their decision-making.

Starting in the mid-1990s, the Nissan plant in Smyrna, Tennessee was considered the benchmark for hours per vehicle (HPV) in the United States

(Business Wire 1995; Vasilash 1997). Based on the gap between HPV and the benchmark and assuming labor costs per hour, the Harbour Report estimated the cost penalty competitors experienced compared to the benchmark and how many 'excess' workers would need to be excised to meet the benchmark. For example, with Nissan's HPV at 28.32 at Smyrna in 1997, GM's HPV of 44.59 meant that it cost GM $700 more per car than Nissan, and GM had an 'excess' of 43,610 workers to the benchmark (Vasilash 1997). By 2001, Nissan's benchmark was at 27.63 HPV while GM's HPV remained at 40.52, which meant GM still had over 38,288 'excess' workers (Ward's Auto World 2001). With such a wide gap, Jim Harbour warned that "Those plants that aren't competitive are going to die," and that the choice is either to improve productivity and quality or "they won't have a decision. They won't be around" (Vasilash 1997). Considering the report's importance, it may have influenced decisions on plant closings or workforce downsizing. Thus, productivity pressure was experienced through economic outcomes *and* reinforced socially through the communications of observant social systems.

Manufacturing reforms paid off as GM's productivity jumped by 8.8 percent in 2000, and GM and Chrysler increased 7.4 and 8.3 percent respectively from 2001–2002, as their transition to lean production accelerated productivity growth faster than their competitors who already implemented lean methods (DeMarines 2000; Winter 2003; Weyer 2011). The cost per vehicle gap between the Big Three and Japanese rivals fell by 1997–2003 from around $400–700 to $300–400 (Vasilash 1997; Winter 2003). The HPV gap between the least and most productive producers narrowed rapidly, as the 17.17 HPV gap in 1998 was reduced to 9.08 in 2004, 7.33 in 2005, to only 5.17 HPV in 2007 (PR Newswire 2006; Just-auto.com 2007). Ron Harbour praised this development as every automaker continued to improve. The productivity numbers were closer to parity and the differences between the most productive and least productive plants were shrinking (Ward's Auto World 2006). American automakers thus became competitive globally, being ahead of most other regions in productivity and only narrowly behind Japan (RP news wires 2007). However, since the US market stagnated while Japanese firms took increasing market share, the Big Three continuously shed volume. Harbour estimated that Toyota gained an equivalent of one assembly plant per year in new market share (Ward's Auto World 2006).

Overall, productivity in the auto industry increased enormously, with Harbour estimating that personnel requirements to produce the same number of vehicles fell by one third between 1990 and 2008. In 2008, Harbour credited serious productivity improvements for why the Big Three were not forced into bankruptcy yet even as the productivity gap closed there were other problems plaguing the Big Three (Africa Wire 2008). For example, in March 2009 Jim Harbour argued that GM and Ford were on par with Toyota in terms of manufacturing efficiency but they still suffered from a legacy of poor quality that caused them to offer thousands of dollars in rebates to offset lingering perception problem (Automotive News 2009). The Big Three used aggressive rebates and low interest financing to make sales, reduce overproduction, and avoid further declines in market share. However, this often caused vehicles to sell at a loss, which contributed to the billions in losses in the mid-2000s (see PR Newswire 2006; Ingrassia 2011: 193; Cutcher-Gershenfeld et al. 2015: 7). By 2007, GM had over one million unsold cars that were aggressively pushed onto dealers whose showrooms were also full of unsold vehicles (Ingrassia 2011: 193). Thus, a blockage in the flow of value in motion—a devaluation of unsold cars—also contributed to financial decline (see Harvey 2017: 72–93). Thus, realization is not just a matter of *present* costs and quality but has a socio-communicative element where *past inefficiency and poor quality* affects the chances of present value realization. The 2008 financial crisis and the drastic drop in demand further hurt realization, leading to a terminal crisis for GM and Chrysler.

The specific circumstances leading to the bankruptcy crisis of 2009 were complex. The imminent cause was the dramatic drop in auto sales from a projected 17 million in 2006 to under 11 million in 2008 due to the financial crisis, which exacerbated the decades of downsizing and billions of recent losses (Ingrassia 2011: 211–212; Cutcher-Gershenfeld et al. 2015: 10). Some blamed the crisis on so-called 'legacy costs,' i.e., fringe benefits, cost-of-living-adjustments (COLA), the Jobs Bank, pensions, and health care coverage (e.g., Wall Street Journal 2008; Ingrassia 2011). If the Big Three were not 'burdened' with these legacy costs, they would have a competitive cost structure compared to Japanese competition, so it was claimed. While it was true the Big Three had more generous benefits then transplants, this was not a "conspiracy to be uncompetitive" but a "product of business success and a determination to share the gains across multiple generations of the workforce" (Cutcher-Gershenfeld 2015: 13; Greenhouse 2019: 94–106). Founded on the Treaty of Detroit and decades of collective bargaining, similar benefits were sidestepped by foreign transplants because they mostly stayed nonunion and located in right-to-work states outside the Midwest (Howell 1995; Holmes 2004; Klier and Rubenstein 2020). Maintaining a labor monopoly from the 1930s through the 1970s kept wages and benefits both high and at parity through pattern bargaining, while breaking this monopoly through nonunion transplants put pressure for concessions as the higher labor costs became a competitive disadvantage (Howell 1995; Holmes 2004; Rothstein 2006; Ingrassia 2011). Rather than engage in 'race to the bottom' concession bargaining, there is no reason why unionization of the transplants could not have given all American autoworkers similarly high benefits and prevented the increasing heterogeneity of the value-regime.

Efforts to unionize transplants, however, were difficult. The UAW tried to "sow the seeds of unionism" at the Japanese, Korean, and German transplants for years, but management worked vigorously to prevent unionization, from settling in states with little union tradition to human resource strategies "designed to convince workers they do not need the protection of a union" (Rothstein 2006: 73). The transplants warned their workforces that "the decline of the Big Three is evidence of the failure of unionism" (Rothstein 2006: 73). From the 1980s to the 2010s, multiple UAW organizing drives and union votes were made at the transplants, but all union certification elections were either lost or withdrawn due to lack of support (Rothstein 2006: 69; McKenney 2018). Thus, while the number of nonunionized autoworkers grew to around 100,000 between 1983 and 2008, the Big Three shed nearly 500,000 jobs through downsizing and restructuring (Rothstein 2008: 67). In 1983, there were 996,000 jobs in the motor vehicle and motor vehicle equipment sector with 586,000 of those being unionized. By 2023, the overall industry grew to over 1.4 million jobs but with only 213,000 union members (Hirsch, Macpherson, and Even 2024). The entry of foreign automakers and nonunion suppliers made this stark decline possible. Not only was the UAW bleeding membership in companies it had worked with for decades but was unable to secure unionization at these new entrants as the overall sector grew. Rothstein (2006: 73) argued that regaining the labor monopoly was paramount for the UAW to regain the leverage to stop concessions and blunt the speed-up of lean reforms, stating, "there is no other way forward" for the UAW. Yet within the first quarter of the 21st century, only one foreign transplant was successfully unionized, severely blunting the UAW's ability to bargain against concessions or work reforms (Klier and Rubenstein 2020: 53).

The UAW did achieve one historic victory, however, when the Volkswagen plant in Chattanooga, Tennessee voted to join the UAW in April 2024. This was significant in part because the UAW lost unionization votes at VW Chattanooga in 2014 and 2019, and because this was the first successful union vote at a Southern plant, besides the Big Three, and at a foreign transplant (see McKenney 2018; Brooks 2019; Krisher and Hall 2024). There was anticipation that this may be the first in a string of victories that may restore union power. However, the next major union vote at the Alabama Mercedes-Benz plants in May 2024 was a failure, signifying that the UAW was still fighting an uphill battle (Boudette 2024). Considering the UAW leadership's endorsement of Kamala Harris over Donald Trump, it is unclear how much success the UAW will achieve in industry unionization under the second Trump administration (Isidore 2024).

The Big Three possessing the highest productivity for decades and dominating global markets were the conditions in which most union benefits were negotiated and won. Securing union wins increased membership and laid the organizing foundation and momentum for future victories. The emergence of more productive competition ate away at market share and sales, which made keeping such benefits difficult to justify, much less expanding them. Thus, the large productivity gap contributed to lower economic performance, making both 'legacy costs' *and* inefficiency sources of competitive disadvantage. Perhaps if the Big Three responded rapidly to the Japanese productivity challenge that threatened their market share, then competition may not have occurred so destructively and the 'race to the bottom' would not have occurred. In this hypothetical, instead of cutting 'legacy costs' to close the cost gap, the UAW may have been better equipped to reclaim the labor monopoly rather than face a decline that mirrored the Big Three. Yet, the lack of cooperative relations and active resistance made such flexible and rapid responses unlikely. Ultimately, waves of concessions and layoffs coincided with gradual productivity improvement through adaptation of lean production (Helper and Henderson 2014). While contingencies and alternative paths were open, the history and structure of the value-regime made the American industry particularly ill-equipped to work out a compromise to prevent decline and bankruptcy.

The relationship between the UAW and the Big Three was not statically acrimonious, however. When the president of the UAW, Ron Gettelfinger, testified before Congress in 2008, he supplied evidence that the UAW was responsive to the challenges facing the Big Three and committed to enabling their success (Cutcher-Gerschenfeld et al. 2015: 8). Part of this was from the UAW's increasing willingness to improve productivity through reforms to work rules and adoption of LP through effective relational contracts (Kochan et al. 1997; Helper and Henderson 2014; Cutcher-Gershenfeld et al. 2015). There were even examples of workers finding the reorganization to LP empowering, showing how the debate between whether lean is more empowering or exploitative cannot be decided conclusively (Adler 1993a; Eaton 1995; Adler et al. 1997; Cutcher-Gershenfeld et al. 2015: 5–8). One GM executive explained in advance of the 2003 contract negotiations that management's relationship with the UAW had improved and that the union understood the importance of productivity to the whole company (Tribune Business News 2003). Closing the productivity gap in the 2000s required more constructive relations between labor and management.

However, it is doubtful that the cooperative turn was due to genuine enthusiasm for lean reforms and a cooperative spirit aligned with corporate interests. Rather, it was motivated by a mixture of fear and a lack of leverage to resist. "Union defeat bred leadership timidity [and] an ideology of 'jointness' between labor and management" according to Lichtenstein (2024: 49). Decades of downsizing made fears of job loss unavoidable, and this was exploited by managements that "forced local union leaders to concede work rules or risk losing their assembly lines to plants with more amenable labor relations" (Rothstein 2006: 71). These 'whipsawing' practices gave the "impression among local unions that a refusal to relinquish control over the shop floor might cost jobs, while an embrace of labor management 'cooperation' might save them" (Rothstein 2008: 66). Thus, outwardly cooperative behavior that narrowed the productivity gap appeared under duress, despite the insistence by lean proponents that LP required a loyal and committed workforce (Womack et al. 2007 [1990]). Rinehart (1999) explains this paradox stating,

> That efficiencies can be realized in the absence of even the most genuinely progressive human resource practices is no mystery … there are functional alternatives to commitment, alternatives that produce behaviors similar to those exhibited by committed workers. These *compliant* behaviors arise from the more coercive sources of 'motivation,' such as high unemployment, higher underemployment, job insecurity, etc. (27; emphasis in original)

Thus, the US experience demonstrated that successful lean reforms were possible when *motivated by fear* rather than loyalty or positive incentives. Individual plant and company analyses demonstrated that local union motivations varied between combinations of fear and resistance and cooperativeness and openness to change, so no one single attitude can define the Big Three-UAW experience (Jürgens et al. 1993; Adler et al. 1997; Kochan et al. 1997; Cutcher-Gershenfeld et al. 2015).

As the financial trouble worsened in the mid-2000s, compromises to reduce benefits and wages were negotiated (Ingrassia 2011). For example, in 2007, healthcare benefits were reorganized, and a two-tier wage system was introduced where 20 percent of the workforce took 40 percent less pay (Rothstein 2008; Ingrassia 2011: 202; Cutcher-Gershenfeld et al. 2015: 4). These concessions exacerbated income inequality and removed favorable valorization opportunities for many Americans. As Robert Reich explained after the crisis, "Even if some manufacturing jobs return, those jobs are not the same sort of high-wage, high-benefit jobs we used to have in manufacturing" (quoted in Katel 2011: 606). This was also reflected in the decline of UAW membership from its peak of 1.5 million members in 1970 to 370,000 by 2023 (Shepardson 2024). After the bankruptcy and industry bailout, the wage and benefit gap between Ford and the transplants fell from $20.55 in 2005 to $6 in 2010 (Cutcher-Gershenfeld et al. 2015: 4). Each round of negotiations and periodic job cuts were contentious, but compromises were eventually reached (see Doran 2005; Rothstein 2006; Maynard 2007; Rothstein 2008; Ingrassia 2011). Thus, the UAW was not intransigent, and management was not draconian as "there was a capacity to adjust wages and benefits to new competitive realities, but it was a negotiated process of adjustment rather than a unilateral cut" (Cutcher-Gershenfeld et al. 2015: 12). Post-crisis, the change in the UAW-Big Three relationship was described as,

> For the UAW, the shift in operating assumptions is still ongoing and no less central to its operations. Historically, unions have derived power from the threat of withholding labor. However, there is a shift underway whereby the UAW is learning to derive power by enabling work … This is evident in the expertise the union now brings to discussions of quality, safety, predictive and preventative maintenance, workforce development, team-based operations, and other such topics. (Cutcher-Gershenfeld et al. 2015: 23–24)

Thus, while the structure of the value-regime remains the same and the legacy of contentious relations still has a bearing, recovering from the financial crisis left management-union relations functionally more cooperative—even if begrudgingly so due to the weakened UAW position.

This decades-long relationship pattern abruptly ended, however, in 2023 with the election of Shawn Fain as president of the UAW. Fain is unique as the first UAW president to be directly elected by union members. In the previous system in place since the Walter Reuther era, UAW leadership was chosen by local union officials and select union convention delegates which made it so that "Reuther and his successors were elected and re-elected by upward of 99 percent of the vote" (Lichtenstein 2024: 50). However, by 2021, reforms demanded by the rank-and-file allowed membership to hold direct elections for union officials, with outsider Shawn Fain winning the presidency in 2023 (Lichtenstein 2024: 50–51). With this victory, Fain and his staff of labor militants sought to put "the movement back in the labor movement" and demanded "No Corruption, No Concessions, No Tiers" from the Big Three (Lichtenstein 2024: 51). By the eve of the 2023 contract negotiations, decades of concessions and lean reforms had weakened union power substantially and placed workers under 'management by stress.' Workers at the Big Three reported issues of speed-up, 10-to-12-hour mandatory shifts without overtime, and a plethora of repetitive motion injuries. The two-tier compensation system made it so workers hired after the bankruptcy crisis did not even enjoy the high wages, healthcare, and pensions that made auto work acceptable to American workers since the five-dollar day (Brown 2023: 8–9). With new leadership, the expectations were high for the UAW to disrupt this status quo.

Breaking from traditional pattern bargaining, the UAW began a "stand-up strike" where the union "hit selected, high-profit plants at all three Detroit-based companies, ratcheting up the number of parts depots on strike according to the progress—or lack of progress—in negotiations" (Lichtenstein 2024: 52). This new strategy worked well as the companies were taken by surprise and forced to guess where would be struck next, and gradually adding strike locations kept the negotiations in the news cycle. The resulting labor-management contract was an unambiguous victory for workers. The union did not accept any concessions while the Big Three restored COLA, which was removed after the bankruptcy crisis, granted a 25 percent wage increase over the four-and-a-half year contract, and eliminated the two-tier wage system (Lichtenstein 2024: 53). These recent events signify a return to labor militancy and combative industrial relations that were relatively muted over the last several decades. The contract was not a step toward codetermination but was a revival of the 'Treaty of Detroit' spirit of financially compensating for the alienating and repetitive auto jobs. Even though direct gains were limited to the Big Three and the UAW, it was no coincidence that many transplants announced raises like those won by UAW workers soon after the strike (Lichtenstein 2024: 54). Thus, while the American value-regime remained heterogeneous, the 2023 "stand-up strike" brought labor–management relations closer to the pattern experienced through most of the 20th century. Such gains were enabled by the post-bankruptcy recovery, but it is impossible to predict how the shifting competitive landscape with the rise of China and EVs may change the bargaining conditions when the UAW contract expires in 2028.

After the bankruptcy and bailout of GM and Chrysler, the economic recovery allowed a somewhat smaller US domestic industry to rebound. Becoming lean over the 1990s and 2000s was not enough to prevent the crisis, but it did set up the industry to be nearly on par with Japanese transplants so that the productivity gap was no longer a pressing competitive disadvantage (Automotive News 2009; Weyer 2011; Abolhassani et al. 2018: 146). As Cutcher-Gershenfeld, Brooks, and Mulloy (2015: 23, 3) explain, lean principles became pervasive in the US domestic industry, which has been "revitalized in recent years through a commitment to quality, innovative production and management techniques, a constructive relationship between management and labor, and improved relations with suppliers." Employment rebounded with the total US industry, including foreign transplants and suppliers, falling from 1.3 million workers in 2000 to 660,000 in 2009, to recovering to around 1 million by 2018 (Krzywdzinski 2020a: 34). Profits also returned in the 2010s, though GM and Ford fell behind Toyota, Volkswagen, and other companies on various metrics including revenues, sales, and profits (Cutcher-Gershenfeld 2015: 3; Statista 2021c, 2021d).

The rebound was not enough to reclaim lost market share however, with GM and Ford holding less than 20 percent of the American market each, and Chrysler fell below Toyota by 2017. The Big Three that had dominated with 95 percent US market share in the 1950s possessed only 45 percent by 2010 (Klier and Rubenstein 2017: 47–48). In 2021, for the first time in American history, a foreign automaker, Toyota, surpassed GM to become the bestselling automaker in the US with 2.3 million sold versus 2.2 million from GM (Wayland 2022). Compare these sales to a prosperous year like 1985 where GM sold over 6.4 million vehicles in the US (General Motors Heritage Center 1985). GM, one of the largest corporations in the history of the world, was a shell of its former self as it continued to downsize. For example, GM sold Opel and abandoned the European market in 2017 (The Economist 2017). Rather than operating as a transnational giants, GM and Ford may come to be largely confined to the American and Chinese market, e.g., around 54 percent of Ford's sales and 77 percent of GM's sales were from either the US or China in 2019 (General Motors 2020: 2; Ford Motor Company 2021: 5). This is not necessarily problematic as domestic automakers, suppliers, and transplants all keep value in motion within the American value-regime to the benefit of American workers. Yet, it does speak to how the US has declined relatively as a world power in this global industry. What is important to note here is the role of productivity leadership, or lack thereof, contributed to both the rise and fall.

Thus, while the US value-regime survived the crisis, it has radically transformed. The oligopolistic conditions of the US auto industry have given way to highly competitive struggles among domestic and foreign firms. The labor configuration has become highly heterogeneous as the labor monopoly has broken and union representation has declined. In addition, waves of concessions have decreased the wages and benefits of auto workers, gutting the original purpose of the Treaty of Detroit. Only very recently have these concessions partially been reversed thanks to the "stand-up strike," and it is unclear whether these wins are durable or precarious. Though issues of realization, strategic blunders, product trends, and contentious industrial relations all contributed to this outcome, productivity pressure from the persistent productivity gap since the 1970s also played an important role. Not only did higher productivity, quality, and control over time allow lean producers to gain cost advantages which drove the economic decline of their competitors, the socio-communicative discourse around the lower productivity and quality of Big Three vehicles added *socially based productivity pressures*.

The US industry was under social domination to 'fix' its products and production processes to conform to the standard of socially necessary labor time set by their competitors. The process of change was not straightforward as patterns of implementation reflected plant history and had varying degrees of acceptance and success (Adler et al. 1997). The 'adoption' of LP is best thought of as an *adaptation* and *hybridization* of lean production principles rather than the acceptance of a 'model' as Womack, Jones, and Roos (2007 [1990]) insist (see Pries 2003). The structures and patterns of the US value-regime were still present but nevertheless adapted certain production principles and coalesced around general combinations of capital and labor to bring production performance in line with socially necessary production standards. This is how convergence on certain levels of automation and productive practices and divergence in industrial relations and other value-regime characteristics can coexist if productivity targets are met. The common denominator is the constant struggle to overcome productivity pressure, close the efficiency gap, and secure new productive advantages to advance capital accumulation.

2.2 *Maintaining the German Path through Hybridization*

By the late 1980s, the disappointing performance of automation and rising labor costs generated dissent in the German industry with management planners reconsidering ambitious automation goals (Tolliday 1995b: 129; Jürgens 2004: 416). As one VW plant manager described in 1991,

> We cannot and do not want to achieve our goals with still more capital expenditure on machines and equipment but rather with the help of the human potential in our factories. New management philosophies and restructuring of qualifications are the path forward. (Jürgens 2023: 316; translation mine)[1]

The industry became disillusioned with automation approaches derided as 'CIM [computer integrated manufacturing] ruins' (Jürgens et al. 1993: 72; Krzywdzinski 2020b: 511). The early 1990s crisis, partially instigated by high fixed capital expenditures, further confirmed the need for change. The European market was quasi-protected from Japanese competition via export restraint until 2000, so direct Japanese competition and market share loss was not the

1 Original German text: "Unsere Ziele können und wollen wir nicht mit noch mehr Kapitaleinsatz für Maschinen und Anlagen erreichen, sondern mit Hilfe des menschlichen Potentials in unseren Werken. Der Weg sind neue Managementphilosophien und die Neustrukturierung von Qualifizierungsinhalten" (Jürgens 2023: 316).

primary motivation (Donnelly, Mellahi, and Morris 2002: 31; Jürgens 2008: 52). Nevertheless, the crisis demonstrated that the German cost structure was unsustainable, whereas "not only were Japanese cars of high quality, but the time taken to build them was far shorter than in Europe ... so much so that their costs were considerably lower" (Donnelly, Mellahi, and Morris 2002: 31). The opening of low-wage countries in Eastern Europe and Asia added to the productivity pressure as superior efficiency was needed to keep German wages high and prevent outsourcing (Jürgens 2008; Jürgens and Krzywdzinski 2009; Krzywdzinski 2020b: 521). These concerns made the productivity imperative salient, as Springer (1999) described, "More than ever the question now is how to raise productivity and maintain it at a competitive level" (124). Adopting lean production appeared to be the most obvious path forward.

However, cooperative relations and codetermination mean that the most 'obvious' path is not always taken in Germany. For domestic German plants the attitude was "*Japan kapieren, nicht kopieren*," or *understand Japan, but do not copy it* (Kryzwdzinski 2020b: 507). This was because the companies and unions realized that direct adoption of Japanese 'models' would be difficult given the structure of the value-regime, such as the legally established rights of codetermination, the predominance of vocationally trained workers, and the legacies of new production concepts (NPC) and the humanizing work, with some lean concepts contrasting strongly with German practices and culture (Krzywdzinski 2020b: 507; Jürgens 2021: 8). In any case, Germans typically preferred domestically developed solutions as their attitude was that "we made it, so it must be the best" (Keller 1993: 175). Thus, the measures, even as they were influenced by LP, were nevertheless attuned to the special characteristics of the German model (Jürgens 2023: 316–319).

Just as in the US during the 1980s, even though lean production was framed as 'best practice,' there was not much clarity or agreement as to what it entailed (Jürgens 1995: 298). For example, it was assumed in the 1980s and early 1990s that 'lean' teamwork was an extension of the semi-autonomous and self-organizing teamwork system developed at Volvo as part of the new production concepts (NPC) (Springer 1999: 126–127). However, lean production's emphasis on standardization, short work cycles, and strict cycle times meant that lean teamwork was very different and often countered the humanization goals of NPC (Springer 1999: 126–127; Krzywdzinski 2020b: 515–516). Nevertheless, German automakers reoriented away from automation and NPC based on the Uddevalla example based on long cycle times and stationary assembly (Jürgens 1995: 302; 2004: 416; 2021: 4; Krzywdzinski 2020b: 513–514).

Experiments were first pursued in the early 1990s at new production sites made available after German reunification as they could be "planned without reference to the established structures and procedures at domestic production sites" (Jürgens 2008: 54). Two exemplars were Opel's Eisenach plant and Volkswagen's Mosel plant in the former East Germany. Eisenach was explicitly modeled on LP based on GM's experience with the Toyota-GM joint venture NUMMI, and Mosel also aimed to replicate NUMMI, with workers calling it the "NUMMI of Saxony" (Jürgens 1994: 104; 2004: 416; 2008: 54). In selecting upper management, preference was given to those who had worked at NUMMI, while Volkswagen recruited managers from Nissan's UK plant for their Martorell SEAT plant in Spain (Jürgens 1994: 104; 1995: 304). Even German luxury brands like Porsche understood that "Japanese auto manufacturers were more efficient and that, to survive, it needed to copy their methods" by importing former Toyota managers and engineers to implement LP (Ewing 2017: 52). Many lean principles were implemented at these plants, such as kanban regulated just-in-time systems, short cycle times, and teams tasked with quality responsibilities (Jürgens 1994: 104; 1995: 304). At Eisenach, Andon cords were installed to stop the assembly line when problems emerged—the first of its kind in Germany (Jürgens 1995: 304; Krzywdzinski 2020b: 512). The plants were also tasked with eliminating waste and implementing kaizen practices (Jürgens 1994: 104).

Some aspects of the German model were also present, such as the fact that nearly all production workers were *Facharbeiter*. Yet, their function was different at Eisenach because the extensive maintenance department typical of German plants was absent, and the direct production workers were expected to perform maintenance like multiskilled LP workers (Jürgens 1995: 304–305). This coincided with an emphasis on on-the-job multiskilling rather than the years long formal vocational training typical in Germany (Krzywdzinski 2020b: 512). Though codetermination was formally functional at both Eisenach and Mosel, these plants were considered independent as a matter of corporate law and therefore did not have company-wide board representation, and their works councils were not included in the company-wide works councils (Jürgens 1995: 305). Nevertheless, the Eisenach works council saw the lean orientation as a "valuable opportunity" and was more willing to compromise on issues such as performance regulation than works councils in West German plants (Krzywdzinski 2020b: 512). The lean experiments in new plants were the opposite approach from Japanese transplants, i.e., instead of the 'peripheral' transplants adapting and learning from the practices of the 'core,' the restructuring occurred first in the transplants that were then gradually transferred to the 'core' (Jürgens 1998: 304).

During the first half of the 1990s, West German plants attempted to combine lean principles with new production concepts, arguing that the failure of the automation strategy was the insufficient deployment of the potential of skilled work and task integration (Krzywdzinski 2020b: 512). Daimler-Benz stayed closest to the NPC model as they experimented with stationary work-stations with long cycle times (30 minutes) manned by groups who took responsibility for quality control (Krzywdzinski 2020b: 513). By contrast, BMW pursued a 'maximalist strategy' by radically restructuring and flattening the company hierarchy and introducing Japanese style U-shaped lines with work teams (Herrigel and Sabel 1999: 20–24). At Volkswagen, a new model launch was seen as an opportunity to reorient production processes toward LP. For example, just-in-time practices were put in place at the Salzgitter plant in 1991, and Wolfsburg restructured by decentralizing management, organizing work teams, and engaging in continuous improvement activities (Jürgens 1994: 104; Grieger and Lupa 2015: 175; Ewing 2017: 51).

German plants were most enthusiastic about adopting just-in-time, team organization, and on-the-job multiskilled training, but rejected increasing assembly line speeds, structuring teams to encourage peer pressure on performance or attendance, and mandating flexible overtime (Jürgens 1994: 106). In addition, highly automated areas maintained the focus on vocationally skilled workers, task integration, and worker self-organization, though manual assembly areas no longer favored skilled labor (Krzywdzinski 2020b: 512). Thus, LP implementation in the early 1990s was selective and not aimed at transferring LP as a 'model' (Jürgens 1994: 106). The pattern also demonstrates how German workers are open to change, but, when possible, used codetermination to select work changes understood as advantageous to them.

After the early 1990s crisis, experiments with stationary assembly were abandoned because they proved to be difficult to organize, prone to error, and failed to motivate workers or reduce absenteeism (Jürgens 1997b: 268–269; Krzywdzinski 2020b: 514). No further radical experiments in increasing assembly automation or humanized stationary group work were pursued, thus posing the question whether this signaled the 'end' of new production concepts (see Kern and Schumann 1998; Springer 1999). Instead, the discussion turned to whether Germany was experiencing a 'return to Taylorism' as the corporations moved to "standardized work with a strict zero-buffer, one-piece-flow orientation and short cycles of about a minute" (Jürgens 1997b; Krzywdzinski 2020b: 514). Just-in-time, built in quality, teamwork and kaizen eventually became standard in German companies, although they varied in their emphasis at the companies based on the path dependencies of their previous developments (Krzywdzinski 2020b: 515; Jürgens 2021: 8–9). Even Volkswagen's quality assurance department, which was heavily criticized by lean proponents (see Keller 1993: 175; Womack et al. 2007 [1990]: 90–91), was restructured with most of the 6,000 employees transferred to production to focus on building in quality rather than rework (Jürgens 2023: 277). Thus, it appeared lean production practices were eventually generalized in Germany.

However, even as "the spread of lean production swept away most earlier approaches based on 'new production concepts' and 'humanization of work,'" works councils still exercised their legal rights provided by the German Works Constitution Act and cooperative agreements to modify the lean methods (Kuhlmann, Sperling, and Balzert 2004; Krzywdzinski 2020b: 515). If German workers had to be the subject *and* object of optimization rather than the subject directing machine labor, then workers wanted to influence how they were to optimize their work (see Springer 1999). For example, instead of management choosing team leaders, German teams elected their own spokespersons, which made them more self-organizing (Krzywdzinski 2020b: 515). Though the teams were not autonomous in terms of self-regulation and task differentiation as in Swedish style group work (see Berggren 1994), they did have the freedom to hold team meetings within working hours and collectively decide on matters such as job rotation and scheduling (Krzywdzinski 2020b: 516). While the imperative to continuously improve work was accepted, many plant-level collective agreements stipulated that no employee shall be dismissed due to efficiency gains, which provided similar job security to past rationalization agreements (Rationalization Agreement 1968, 1987; Krzywdzinski 2020b: 515). Workers also wanted to avoid performance pressure from monetary incentives. The compromise was that companies and works councils worked together with teams to devise plant-level agreements that regulated performance targets and works councils mediated if conflicts arose (Krzywdzinski 2020b: 515–516). Therefore, implementing teamwork was a codetermined process with teams having influence on their regulation and on the setting and control of performance targets (Jürgens 1997a: 111; Krzywdzinski 2020b: 516).

Volkswagen's Auto5000 program was the most ambitious step toward mixing lean and German systems. It was framed by the company and works council as an alternative to the 'Toyota Way' (Schumann, Kuhlmann, Frauke, and Sperling 2006; Krzywdzinski 2020b: 516). From 1999–2009, Auto5000 existed as a separate unit within the Wolfsburg plant with a separate collective agreement (Grieger and Lupa 2015: 204). Weekly working time was seven hours longer, wages were twenty percent lower, and there was no distinction between skilled and semi-skilled workers. It emphasized team self-organization and direct team involvement with quality and productivity targets which was absent from Japanese lean production. The basic work processes involved the typical lean standardized work on short work cycles operated by multiskilled teams with frequent job rotation, but it also appealed to German sensibilities with an emphasis on vocational training, supportive rather than controlling supervision, and participation in designing process changes and optimizations (Schumann et al. 2006; Krzywdzinski 2020b: 516–517). The program was dissolved in 2009, however, because workers and IG Metall became unwilling to accept the lower compensation for Auto5000 workers. Nevertheless, many of the basic concepts from Auto5000 spread within VW (Krzywdzinski 2020b: 518).

Thus, not only did codetermination persist while adapting LP, in some respects it was strengthened (Jürgens 2021: 8). As Jürgens (1997a) describes

> It has become clear that codetermination was not an obstacle to the introduction of lean production … Rather, it provided a framework in which lean production practices could be maintained even in difficult situations. It has also become clear, however, that for it to support lean production, the union had its conditions. These conditions shaped the way lean production was implemented and the concepts and priorities that surrounded the process of change.

Even as there was some 'grumbling' about LP among IG Metall and the works councils, there was no opposition movement comparable to the New Directions Movement in the US (Jürgens 1995: 303). Thus, a form of LP was codified in Germany, albeit hybridized and influenced by labor-management compromises (Jürgens 2021: 9). After the weaknesses of the previous German system were revealed, the value-regime utilized its cooperative flexibility to generalize lean principles through terms agreeable to management and labor.

There were tensions, however. Part of the reason LP was pursued was because globalization trends put German high-wage systems in competition for production with low-wage locations such as Eastern Europe (Jürgens and Krzywdzinski 2009). This was partially addressed through the rise of temporary agency work during the 2000s. Employing more temporary workers increased flexibility and lowered labor costs in Germany because these workers were not covered by the IG Metall collective agreements (Krzywdzinski 2020b: 514; Jürgens 2021: 8; Jürgens 2023: 287). Nevertheless, there was a general concern among workers whether Germany would be able to maintain its high-wage, 'high-road' system or if it would be dismantled by 'competitive pressures' as some concessions and wage restructuring, such as more temporary workers, occurred in the 1990s–2020s (Weinthal 2003; Jürgens and Krzywdzinski 2006, 2009; IG Metall 2007: 114; Grieger and Lupa 2015: 222). Adapting LP ameliorated this by increasing productivity closer to competitive levels, and because works councils and IG Metall accepted lean reforms in exchange for increased employment security to maintain the workforce and not close plants. This decoupled the reforms from unemployment fears, making the workers more amenable to change (Jürgens 1997a: 115–116).

German automakers also adopted a platform strategy after the 1990s crisis to reduce costs and standardize manufacturing. Although platforms were used in the US for decades (Howell and Hsu 2002: 45), they were relatively new to the German industry (Grieger and Lupa 2015: 175; Ewing 2017: 53). By standardizing technologically demanding parts across multiple vehicles on the same platform, especially parts not visible to customers such as the engine and transmission, costs for development and design were greatly reduced (Sturgeon et al. 2009: 20). Although there are no industry-wide parts standards and platforms are generally exclusive to companies, Volkswagen's acquisitions in the 1990s and 2000s made it ideal for sharing platforms across multiple brands such as VW, Škoda, and SEAT (Sturgeon et al. 2009: 9; Jürgens 2009: 231). The vehicles made on VW's platforms rose from 50 percent in 1998 to 98 percent in 2004, as it consolidated its number of platforms from around sixteen to four and harmonized both within and between platforms for further savings (Jürgens 2009: 231–232; Grieger and Lupa 2015: 175). American, Japanese, and rival European carmakers were also working to build on increasingly consolidated platforms, but the strategy paid off especially at Volkswagen thanks to its multi-brand strategy (Donnelly et al. 2002: 35; Sturgeon et al. 2009: 20; Ewing 2017: 53). The platform standardization complemented lean processes, generating productivity increases superior to what would be possible by only applying one reform (Jürgens 2009: 232).

German companies in Germany remained at the forefront of automation development while the US and Japanese companies retreated from new automation since the early 1990s (Krzywdzinski 2020a: 14). Although automation levels were comparable in most production areas in all three countries (Krzywdzinski 2020a: 19; Jürgens 2021: 6–7), Germany was the only one experimenting with new assembly automation. For example, in 2009 Daimler-Benz converted its rear axle assembly from a manual process supported by two robots to a process with 45 robots and half the assembly workers. In 2019, Volkswagen celebrated how its Mosel plant had increased its assembly automation from 12 to 30 percent to build its new electric cars (Krzywdzinski 2020a: 15–16). Despite these advancements, assembly remained largely labor intensive with the highest level of automation at German plants rarely surpassing 30 percent—the same level it was in the early 1990s (Krzywdzinski 2020a: 16; Jürgens 2021: 9).

Jürgens (2023) details the recent state of automation in Wolfsburg, which is perhaps the most automated plant in the world but also not too dissimilar from most plants in many production areas. At Wolfsburg's foundry, over 100 industrial robots handle the molds and cores, and cameras check the cores for any deficiencies that robots can correct (Jürgens 2023: 324–326). The automation level is around 95 percent with around 50 workers primarily for monitoring and quality control. This is a far cry from the River Rouge foundry in the 1920s that required 10,000 workers (Hounshell 1985; Jürgens 2023: 327). Engine production at Wolfsburg involves robots and transfer machines working together to machine the cast part. Emphasis is placed on rapid convertibility of machining stations for flexibility and model variants. Sensors measuring temperature, vibrations, acceleration, and pressure are connected to a central computer to detect disturbances, and testing and measuring activities were performed at various points by workers or robots (Jürgens 2023: 327–328). This machining process was between 85 to 90 percent automated. Engine assembly, despite being an assembly task, was around 55 to 60 percent automated to accommodate variant flexibility. Thus, around 600 workers operated in engine production, with a total production time of around 2 hours—compared to the 23 hours to machine and assemble an engine at Highland Park in 1914 (Hounshell 1985; Jürgens 2023: 329–330).

In the press shop, efforts to remove manual material handling at individual presses using simple mechanical devices had already automated the press shop by the 1950s (Jürgens 2023: 330). The adoption of quick die-change techniques from lean production (see Ohno 1988: 39) and robots for inserting blanks and material handling further automated pressing processes. The individual presses with workers who insert and remove parts were replaced by large press systems, and the previously time consuming and labor-intensive press tool changeouts occur quickly and largely automatically. At Wolfsburg, the press line was around 80 percent automated (3,400 workers) in 1975 which increased to around 95 percent by 1997 (1645 workers) (Jürgens 2023: 330–334). Developments in body construction were heavily influenced by model changes, with lean principles, modularization, and flexibility requirements driving process changes (Jürgens 2023: 334–337). Such concerns made the automation level fluctuate since the 1990s while the number of robots increased fivefold between 1991 and 2012 from 536 to 2571. Body construction employment decreased around 50 percent (around 7,400 to 3,700) between 1975 and 2012 as the automation level rose from 60 to 93 percent and robot welders replaced human welders (Jürgens 2023: 338). Thus, body construction remained highly automated despite increasing demands on product diversity and flexibility. The Wolfsburg paint shop also automated rapidly from 30 percent in 1975 to around 80 percent in the 1990s as flexible robots coated car bodies and immersed them in paint baths. The number of paint shop workers also fell from 5,400 in 1985 to 1,900 by 2012 (Jürgens 2023: 339–341). Finally, Wolfsburg's assembly processes were the most highly automated in the world at around 30–37 percent, but most of the changes to assembly were influenced by lean methods, model changes, and modularization rather than increased automation (Jürgens 2023: 341–347). The automation level remained low compared to other production processes, even in Germany, due both to the growing number of models, variants, and equipment options and because assembly remains the most sensitive to disturbances—whether from delayed supplier deliveries or technical failures in upstream processes (Jürgens 2023: 346).

Overall, the repetitive alienating work of the assembly line remained (see Meyer 2004, Jürgens 1997b) but was largely eliminated in the highly automated areas, which in Germany were staffed by vocationally trained specialists (Jürgens 2023: 355). The perennial problem of having more vocationally trained workers than there were employment positions persisted, but new technologies also opened new training paths (Jürgens 2023: 358–362). New technical developments tended to replace less flexible machines with more flexible machines rather than machines replacing workers. New technologies became more competent in reckoning with the demands for increasingly sophisticated vehicles in diverse variants. To the extent these technologies handle these new demands, the less likely *the machines could be replaced by flexible workers*. Thus, realization concerns made *flexibility the key determinant of automation levels*, as model changes sometimes reintroduce workers into previously automated processes.

As Krzywdzinski (2020a) describes for the US, Japan, and Germany since the 1990s, assembly employment has been largely stable, yet,

> a slow decrease in manufacturing employment is evident in the occupations typical of highly automated areas, such as machine operation but also welding. This could be explained by the automation of the few remaining manual activities (e.g., the replacement of manual parts insertion by material handling robots), or by the increasing efficiency of digital process control techniques, which allow a smaller number of workers to operate ever bigger and more complex production processes. (49)

Automation undoubtedly played an important role in the history of automobile production, yet for decades automation has largely stayed near the same high level and has not made inroads into assembly as human flexibility remains socially necessary.

The combined platform strategy, lean methods, and high automation had many positive effects and brought the German auto industry closer to benchmarked standards. For example, between 1994 and 1996, productivity in the Volkswagen Group increased by 30 percent and "costs fell as a result of shorter production times" (Grieger and Lupa 2015: 176). By 1997, the HPV for producing the VW Polo decreased from 24 to 15 hours, and for the Passat from 31 to 22 hours (Grieger and Lupa 2015: 176). Profits also recovered as VW passed the breakeven point in 1994 and made a one billion deutschmark profit by 1997 (Ewing 2017: 55). Productivity increased across Europe as the productivity gap between the US, Japan, and Europe fell between 1989 and 2000. The average HPV gap between Japan and Europe fell from 18.7 in 1989 (16.8 vs 35.5 HPV) to 9 in 2000 (12.3 vs 21.3 HPV) (Holweg 2008: 28). Thus, the reforms appeared to pay off.

However, the productivity race had a different character in Europe. The Harbour Report has analyzed European automakers since 1996, but the results are not publicized and kept private for company use only (Weyer 2011: 3271). Nevertheless, in 2007 the results of the 2005 European Harbour report were leaked which revealed substantial HPV gaps between plants. Unsurprisingly, Japanese transplants were the most productive, e.g., 12.4 HPV for the Nissan plant in Sunderland, UK while the Audi, Neckarsulm plant took 101.1 HPV for its vehicles (Weyer 2011: 3271). Daimler-Benz and BMW plants refused to participate in the study because "they were afraid of the public impact" of the public knowing the results (Weyer 2011: 3272). The leaked report became a "violent scandal" at Volkswagen, as it revealed that Wolfsburg took 50 hours to produce the Golf, while its volume competitors typically took 25 hours or less (Jürgens 2008: 56–57). In response, Volkswagen has periodically reaffirmed its commitment to raising productivity with new programs and contract agreements that "align productivity, labor costs, and capacity utilization with the competition" (Grieger and Lupa 2015: 222, 226; see Ewing 2017: 108–112, 116–120). Since the report reflected poorly on German automakers, there has been little public reporting on the European Harbour Report (Jürgens 2023: 352). However, considering the VW Wolfsburg plant won an "Automotive Lean Production Award" from a European automotive consulting firm in 2018 due to its "exemplary pace of change" in greater productivity and efficiency, there may have been improvements in the HPV gap since 2005 (Just-auto.com 2018).

What explains the productivity gap even after lean principles were applied across the German industry? First, just as German automakers attempted to close the productivity gap, productivity leaders continued to push the productivity frontier forward as the HPV of Japanese producers also decreased over time, albeit at a slower rate (Holweg 2008: 28 Springer 1999: 127–128). Second, lean principles were hybridized through German codetermination, which may have stifled productivity gains. For example, the 'tandem principle' at Volkswagen where production changes that increase productivity are balanced with changes that improve ergonomics and humanization may have, in some instances, decreased productivity gains (see Jürgens 2021: 4). Third, the German unions and works councils and their power to "regulate performance and incentives meant that it was not possible to develop a form of lean production in Germany that relied on 'management by stress'" (Krzywdzinski 2020b: 520–521). Thus, while LP implementation improved productivity, codetermination kept labor intensity within limits acceptable to German workers. This may not affect efficiency improvements from just-in-time or autonomation, but it may raise HPV by slowing down the assembly line. Finally, the platform strategy and expanding the global value chain to low-wage locations in Eastern Europe provided alternative means to lower costs that did not rely on increasing productivity, which may have lessened the productivity pressure on German workers (see Jürgens and Krzywdzinski 2009; Ewing 2017: 53).

There did, however, appear to be a cost and profit penalty associated with these choices. In 2015, Volkswagen briefly surpassed Toyota as the number one bestselling automaker in the world, yet their profits stood at 6 percent versus Toyota's 10 percent. This occurred partially because, despite volume cars being half of sales revenue, the profit on these models was around 3 percent or less due to high manufacturing costs. The Volkswagen Group was also "dangerously dependent" on its luxury brands, e.g., Audi and Porsche, for its profits (Ewing 2017: 188–189). Since BMW and Daimler-Benz are also primarily luxury automakers, it appears the German auto industry relies on a reformulated DQP strategy for much of its profits (Sorge and Streeck 2016). Thus, the post-lean German model still requires a *balance between manufacturing costs and worker interests* as productivity has improved but within limits. This may mean German companies eschew potential profits that would be possible if factories further narrowed the HPV gap or met the benchmark, but this is manageable if other methods, such as the platform strategy, keep costs within tolerable limits. The lack of a crisis from the early 1990s through the 2010s indicated that the balance could be maintained for long periods and productivity has improved enough to satisfy both labor and management. The productivity imperative is still present, and the implementation of hybridized lean principles transformed production, but there is also room for codetermination and humanization if other factors balance out the costs of not meeting the productivity benchmark. Thus, German automakers continuously *attempt to avoid productivity pressure* to maintain high wages and humanized working conditions for German workers.

Productivity development in both value-regimes was primarily influenced by the adoption of lean production, improving manufacturability through platforms and computer aided design, and deploying highly automated and increasingly flexible technologies (Krzywdzinski 2020a). In both the US and

Germany, LP was adapted based on the characteristics of the value-regime. The productivity enhancing principles were adopted nearly universally even as they were hybridized (Pries 2003). The value-regime specific industrial relations remained, and the supposedly lean 'bundles' of human resources that fostered and supported LP in Japan were typically not adopted (Covarrubias and Ramírez Perez 2020b: 8). There were multiple ways to foster the necessary commitment to LP such as codetermination, fear, or determination to keep a plant open. Value-regime characteristics can be advantageous or disadvantageous for making productivity gains from LP. For example, the US had difficulty making effective relational contracts (Helper and Henderson 2014), while codetermination both enabled and restrained LP in Germany (Krzywdzinski 2020b). Nevertheless, by the 2010s, nearly all American and German firms accepted lean principles as desirable in theory even if they were not executed perfectly in practice (Pries 2003; Weyer 2011; Jürgens 2023).

3 Globalization and Opportunities for Growth

Even after a century of production, only 12 percent of the world population owned a car by 2000 (Howell and Hsu 2002: 43). While the US, Western Europe, and Japan were saturated markets, there was always latent growth potentials in untapped world markets. The reasons for this are many, including lack of consumer purchasing power outside the core, the politics of imports, tariffs, and transplants that made trade a sensitive issue, and logistical advantages when there is proximity between manufacturers and markets. Therefore, the global auto industry was primarily a *core* industry making *core* products for the *core* countries (Wallerstein 2004; Sturgeon et al. 2009; Covarrubias and Ramírez Perez 2020b, 2020c).

Since the 1990s, however, trade agreements and neoliberalization spearheaded by the World Trade Organization increased the flows of foreign direct investment (FDI) and cross border trade, which stimulated auto production and sales in previously unreached areas (Sturgeon et al. 2009: 9). In states like China and India, the growth of auto production coincided with the rise of gigantic domestic markets that no automaker could afford to ignore. In fact, most of the global industry's growth was driven by these new markets while the triad regions stagnated (Howell and Hsu 2002: 43–44; Sturgeon et al. 2009: 11; Wenton 2020). In these regions, industrialization fostered a *global* consumer middle class beyond the core countries (Milanović 2016). In other cases, such as Mexico for the US and Eastern Europe for Germany, cheap labor was the impetus for expanding operations to its neighbors. They provided cheap exports of components and vehicles for the American and Western European markets while the domestic market in these semi-peripheral areas grew modestly (Jürgens and Krzywdzinski 2009; Sturgeon, Memedovic, Biesebroeck, and Gereffi 2009: 9; Covarrubias 2020; Guzik, Domański, and Gwosdz 2020). Both automakers and suppliers increased FDI and integrated the value chains of their domestic industries to gain competitive cost advantages (Sturgeon et al. 2009: 12–14). This *regionalization* of the American and German auto industry signified that the dynamics of the value-regimes could not be fully grasped in a nation-state production and sales framework. Expanding cross-border relationships between core and semi-periphery regions and the transnationalization of auto corporations became more prominent with the recent wave of globalization (see Wallerstein 2004; Robinson 2004, 2014).

Tripartite companies maintained significance, e.g., in 2006 the top 12 firms from Japan, Germany and the US still accounted for 75 percent of world production (Sturgeon et al. 2009: 19). Yet, the pursuit of cheap foreign labor, the requirements to form joint ventures (JVs) in China, and other foreign transplants modified the emphasis on domestic production (Sturgeon et al. 2009: 9). This following discusses two developments in the globalization of the auto industry. First, how did the German and US industry globalize to form regional production systems? Second, how did American and German companies pursue JV production in China? Both developments reveal trends in the auto industry in terms of its production and employment with important implications for the workforces of the domestic industries.

3.1 *Regionalization and the Pursuit of Cheap Labor in Mexico*

American firms were the earliest globalizers since the 1910s (Patch 1932; Flink 1988: 252–254). While US companies maintained global connections and partnerships into the 21st century (Howell and Hsu 2002), their primary concern was defending the US domestic market share from erosion by imports and transplants. Transplants have increased in recent decades with the Big Three operating only 26 out of the 43 assembly plants in the US in 2018. Japanese manufacturers had 11 transplants, VW, BMW, and Daimler-Benz owned 1 each, with Korean Hyundai having 2 and Tesla operating 1 plant (Klier and Rubenstein 2020: 52). The American value-regime was being 'colonized' through FDI with parts of the value chain transplanted to the US utilizing nonunion workers with less wages and benefits (Howell 1995). Besides adopting lean methods, outsourcing production to Mexico was another strategy for the Big Three to achieve lower costs and become competitive against their foreign rivals (see Covarrubias 2020; Wenten 2020: 282).

Since the mid-20th century, production in the North American auto industry has shifted gradually from the northern Midwest of the US and Canada to the less unionized Southern States and Mexico (Klier and Rubenstein 2008; Cutcher-Gershenfeld et al. 2015: 4, 18–19; Klier and Rubenstein 2020: 52–53). The purpose of outsourcing to Mexico was to take advantage of its proximity to the US, the tariff free trade enabled by NAFTA since 1994, and cheap labor (Sturgeon et al. 2009: 14; Covarrubias 2020: 323, 331–334). Before NAFTA, the Mexican auto industry, with no domestic firms and exclusively relying on FDI, was miniscule (Covarrubias 2020: 324; 338). Mexican output has grown from 1.2 million vehicles in 1996 to 2 million by 2006 and 4 million by 2019, while US domestic production largely stagnated around 11 million units (Sturgeon et al. 2009: 11; Covarrubias 2020: 325; Statista 2022). NAFTA was intended to secure Mexico as the 'backyard' of the Big Three, with the 62.5 percent North American vehicle content rule meant to dissuade Japanese and European automakers from accessing the US through Mexico (Covarrubias 2020: 342; Klier and Rubenstein 2017). At first, this worked as intended, with over two thirds of Mexican production occurring in American owned factories. However, the declining market share of the Big Three and increased FDI from German and Japanese producers drove down the Big Three output share to 22 percent by 2016. After the 2008 financial crisis, foreign automakers chose Mexico over the US for new investment with 9 out of 11 new plants in North America being built in Mexico in the 2010s. The Big Three has apparently lost the NAFTA advantage just as they lost the lead in the Mexican market in terms of sales and production capacity in parallel with their displacement in the US domestic market (Covarrubias 2020: 319, 329, 342).

Besides free trade agreements that attract FDI, Mexico's cheap labor pools were especially alluring. Since NAFTA, the Mexican auto industry expanded from around 113,000 to 800,000 jobs in dozens of assembly and parts plants (see Cutcher-Gershenfeld 2015: 19; Covarrubias 2020: 338). This shifted North American auto sector employment from 8 percent Mexican and 83 percent American employment to Mexico having 42 percent of the jobs and the US reduced to 51 percent (Covarrubias 2020: 338). These hundreds of thousands of Mexican workers make far less than their American counterparts, whether unionized or not, with a mean hourly wage of $2.3 per hour or $2.9 in total compensation in 2016 compared to the US average hourly wage of $26.50 and $47 in total compensation. In addition, because of concessions in the US, average wages for American autoworkers have fallen since the enactment of NAFTA from $36 to $27, lending credence to the idea that Mexican labor is putting downward pressure on US wages. Potential outsourcing to Mexico has also been used to threaten plant relocation if concessions are not accepted (Covarrubias 2020: 333–335). Mexico's low wages are due to its state-led industrial relations aimed at "pleasing management and attracting international flows of capital" (Covarrubias 2020: 336). This value-regime is characterized by state-allied unions that "collectively bargain" with management to form "protection contracts," which give management considerable power to determine work rules with no viable means to counter the "race to the bottom" (Covarrubias 2020: 336). Corruption among unions and politicians has kept the Mexican labor movement in line and prevented efficacious political action to increase wages (Covarrubias 2020: 336). The Mexican state is actively involved in the suppression of workforce demands for higher wages for the sake of FDI. The low wages and free trade access that were originally meant to give a competitive advantage to the Big Three has instead come to benefit capital accumulation for both American and foreign firms alike at the expense of autoworker wages and job opportunities in the US and Mexico.

Low wages were not the only advantage, as the greenfield sites in Mexico were the perfect sites for implementing lean production with new workers who did not have to 'unlearn' Fordist methods like the UAW did (Dassbach 1994; Muller, Rehder, and Bannister 1998). Though hybridized within the Mexican value-regime, LP became the standard at new Big Three plants taking lessons from domestic plants such as at NUMMI as well as in in Mexican-Japanese transplants (Dassbach 1994; Muller, Rehder, and Bannister 1998; Covarrubias 2020: 326). The result was a kind of 'low-wage lean production' that, despite the low wages that may ordinarily dampen worker motivation, nevertheless generated a highly productive workforce (Dassbach 1994; Covarrubias 2020: 333). This demonstrates how, even when low wages effectively reduce costs, productivity concerns are still salient, and how LP was pursued as the global standard even in low-wage countries like Mexico.

The relationship between the US, Mexico, and foreign auto companies can be summarized like this,

> The problem facing American auto producers multiplied when Asian producers were able to outperform them in their own territory through better high production systems. They then moved to Mexico in the hope that the benefits gained from nearshoring and cheap, qualified labor would provide them the necessary leverage to beat international companies in the race for market share. Not only were the results to the contrary, but the impact of the process on the downgrading of labor has been overwhelming. Throughout the NAFTA era, wages in the [Mexican auto industry] were frozen and even decreased during the boom of the past

> ten years. Still, wages in the US auto sector decreased at a higher rate, dragging Canadian wages with them. The increasing US trade imbalance with Mexico is the inevitable outcome of this all. (Covarrubias 2020: 343)

Mexico thus became a site for low-wage production and represented a *regionalization* of the North American value-regime for both US value-systems and their foreign competitors. This also signified the global spread of LP and how free trade agreements and pools of cheap labor can be exploited by transnational corporations.

3.2 *Regionalization and the Pursuit of Cheap Labor in North America and Eastern Europe*

By the 1990s, European automakers were comparatively less globalized than their US or Japanese competitors, which contributed to Europe being perceived as the "weakest of the triad car producers," due to their "parochial" orientation centered on production "concentrated inside its frontiers and only a limited presence elsewhere" (Donnelly, Mellahi, and Morris 2002: 30). Apart from Volkswagen, which established production plants in North and South America as early as the 1950s and 1960s, German auto companies typically maintained the vast majority of their production in Germany (Donnelly, Mellahi, and Morris 2002; Grieger and Lupa 2015). This strategy kept jobs, skills, and capital in Germany, and formed the basis for the export based German growth model (Baccaro and Pontusson 2016). However, after the crisis of the early 1990s, it was clear that not only was there a domestic need to "reduce costs, shed labor, rationalize plants, raise productivity and improve their relationships with suppliers in attempts to boost efficiency" but to expand by opening plants near new markets (Donnelly, Mellahi, and Morris 2002: 30). Thanks to such efforts, it appeared that German automakers overcame many weaknesses through domestic production reform while maintaining core competencies and taking advantage of low cost production opportunities in other countries that supported the overall financial health of the corporations (Jürgens 2008). This included access to new markets and outsourcing opportunities directly to the East after the fall of the Soviet Union, transplants in North America, and Chinese joint ventures.

Part of this expansion included setting up new transplants in the US and Mexico to improve German standing in the US market. Volkswagen established a transplant in Mexico as early as 1967 and a short-lived transplant in the US in the 1970s and 1980s (see, Flink 1988: 324–326; Grieger and Lupa 2015: 92, 126; Covarrubias 2020: 326), but a ramping up of German production did not begin until the 1990s. VW gave US production a second chance by building a plant in Chattanooga, Tennessee which began production in 2011 (McKenney 2018). Transplants of the German premium brands appeared in the late 1990s, with Daimler-Benz building a plant in Tuscaloosa, Alabama and BMW in Spartanburg, South Carolina (see Pries 1999, 2003). Since the US is a major market for luxury automobiles, the German automakers recognized they needed to set up plants in the US to prevent market share loss from Japanese luxury brands that had US transplants (Donnelly et al. 2002: 36). Audi, Daimler-Benz, and BMW also opened new plants in Mexico in the 2010s (Covarrubias 2020: 326).

What is most relevant is whether these transplants transferred the German model to the US with its codetermination rights, new production concepts, and strong union representation, or did the transplants take another path? According to Pries (1999: 15, 2003) both BMW and Daimler-Benz saw production in the US as an opportunity for a clean slate to experiment with lean methods, including recruiting managers from Honda and Toyota to shape production processes (see Donnelly et al. 2002: 36). BMW's Spartanburg plant was more experimental, and aligned with Honda's emphasis on flexibility, while Daimler-Benz aimed to emulate the Toyota production system, with emphasis on standardization and continuous improvement (Pries 1999, 2003). Thus, each plant varied in approach, but nevertheless implemented the core lean principles such as work teams, just-in-time pull systems, built in quality processes, and reducing waste (Pries 1999: 22).

Contrary to the German tradition of strong unions in domestic factories, the three US plants were *nonunion with active efforts to prevent unionization* by BMW and Daimler-Benz, such as locating in right-to-work states in the South and paying higher wages to placate the workforce and prevent a union campaign (Pries 1999: 17, 2003). This also occurred at Volkswagen's Tennessee plant, though state intervention also played a role in the failure to unionize VW up until the 2024 victory following the 2023 "stand-up strike" wave (McKenney 2018; Krisher and Hall 2024). As Donnelly, Mellahi, and Morris (2002) describe, the aim was to recruit "young green labor, far removed from the influence of the powerful Union of Autoworkers and where labor costs were considerably lower than in Michigan" (36). This indicated that the German companies *did not intend* to transplant the German model to the US, especially considering how essential worker codetermination undergirded by strong worker organizations is central to the German system. There were other breaks from German norms, such as how skilled workers were not placed in direct production roles, which meant less task enrichment and less team self-organization then in Germany. With no union or works council, there was no codetermination of performance and work standards, leaving management to unilaterally control such matters (Krzywdzinski 2020b: 518). In this way, German automakers appeared content to retain the pro-worker policies of codetermination and strong worker representation in Germany only, while dropping the most distinctive cooperative and pro-worker aspects of the German productive model for the sake of lower costs and higher productivity in their foreign plants. It could be argued that the most 'German' aspect of the transplants were the German designed cars and parts imported from Germany. Otherwise, the production systems appeared to be a mixture of Japanese benchmark methods and American anti-union attitudes. As Pries (2003) describes, there was a hybridization of "German product, quality and technical standards [which] were merged with Japanese or 'transplanted Japanese' work organization mechanisms and US-style task-oriented management and jobs" (89). As in Germany, this was not wholesale adoption of a production model but an *application of lean production principles* that, according to Pries (1999: 22), were found "everywhere in all plants we studied" (see Pries 2003: 96–99).

A similar pattern appears with the opening of Eastern Europe after the fall of Soviet Communism in the early 1990s. Volkswagen worked most aggressively to set up production in these European peripheries. With the acquisition of the Spanish auto company SEAT in 1986, VW gained access to cheap labor and the opportunity to model new Spanish production facilities on lean systems (Donnelly et al. 2002: 33; Jürgens 2008: 53). VW also gained an early foothold in Eastern Europe through their acquisition of the Czech automaker Škoda in 1991 (Grieger and Lupa 2015: 168). By the 2010s, the Volkswagen Group operated 12 brands from across Europe, from the low priced Škoda and SEAT to the mid-range Volkswagen, to the luxury Lamborghini and Porsche (Grieger and Lupa 2015: 258–345). Within this automotive empire, the core Volkswagen AG in Germany grew slowly, but the parent company was supported by production sites and brands throughout Europe, some with high labor costs such as the German companies Audi, Porsche, and Volkswagen AG, and others with much lower labor costs such as SEAT and Škoda (Jürgens 2008: 57; Grieger and Lupa 2015). The VW works council found this arrangement acceptable as long as undesirable labor intensive production at the bottom range of models were shifted to low cost locations in Spain and Eastern Europe while higher value-added products stayed in Germany. In this arrangement, German jobs were maintained because complex German products were exported to these low-cost locations (Tolliday 1995b: 128).

Eastern regions that were isolated from the global capitalist economy for decades became integrated semi-peripheral zones linked with Western European production networks (Guzik et al. 2020: 393). Since the early 1990s, the Eastern European auto industry grew enormously, accounting for over 700,000 out of the 2.5 million automotive jobs in the EU. Similar to the relationship between the US and Mexico, Eastern European output roughly tripled between 2004 and 2017 with 3.7 million cars produced in 2017, whereas the output in Western European countries remained nearly the same (Guzik et al. 2020: 379–380). Much of the production is in automotive parts for export, with automotive suppliers from Western Europe, North America, South Korea, and Japan all operating in Eastern Europe (Guzik et al. 2020: 384). Such exports were crucial for the German auto industry as of the percentage of automotive parts imported from Eastern European into Germany rose from 9 percent to 37 percent between 1995 and 2005 (Jürgens and Krzywdzinski 2009: 32).

In some respects, Eastern European expansion represents a *regionalization of production* very similar to the relationship between Mexico and the US, taking advantage of proximity for just-in-time deliveries and cheap labor to lower overall production costs. The most obvious similarity is the pursuit of low wages as the primary reason behind the shift of manufacturing activity away from Western Europe to the East. In 2016, the full-time equivalent labor cost per hour in the automotive industry was 79 euros in Germany, 45.5 euros in Spain, 20.2 in the Czech Republic, 16.1 in Poland and 11.7 euros in Romania (Guzik et al. 2020: 387–388). The region is also like Mexico in that selling vehicles in Eastern Europe is not the main priority of the automakers, as the market remains limited, and imports of second-hand vehicles predominate (Guzik et al. 2020: 389). Therefore, it appears that these countries are being pursued for their cheap labor to export inexpensive vehicles and low-cost components for the benefit of Western European automakers.

Yet, there are also indications, unlike Mexico, that there is a gradual process of product upgrading and more high road production developing in these countries. Though Eastern Europe primarily built simple low value parts in the 1990s, by the mid-2000s, more high and medium value-added products and expanded product ranges began to be manufactured (Jürgens and Krzywdzinski 2009: 34; Guzik et al. 2020: 384). In addition, new modern facilities were equipped with state of the art technology and implemented principles of lean production such as teamwork, continuous improvement, and increased standardization (Jürgens and Krzywdzinski 2009: 33–34; Guzik et al. 2020: 392). For workers in these countries, there is usually union representation and a generally cooperative relationship with management, including in companies that avoided unionization in their American transplants, such as Volkswagen and Toyota. Though more temporary workers were deployed then in Germany, there was nevertheless a small core of employees in many firms that had strong job security (Jürgens and Krzywdzinski 2009: 36–38). The arrangement in the Eastern European industry can be interpreted, according to Jürgens and Krzywdzinski (2009), as a "limited high-road model" that bears some common features and attitudes toward skilled labor, training, and union cooperation as in Germany, but "at the same time sticks to low wages and a broad margin of precarious employment" (39). In other words, while there have been no attempts to transfer production wholesale into Eastern Europe, these countries represented opportunities to subsidize costs and expand low market production through a production system with some similarities to German industrial relations yet with much lower labor costs.

The German auto industry and its workers have primarily benefitted from this, as Eastern European production has "boosted the price competitiveness of German firms in comparison with their Western European competitors" and the total number of jobs in the German auto industry has not decreased overall despite the transfers (Jürgens and Krzywdzinski 2009: 32). However, transfer opportunities to cheaper locations have put pressure on German workers to accept concession bargaining such as accepting pay cuts and increasing labor time flexibility (Jürgens and Krzywdzinski 2006; Jürgens 2008: 67; Jürgens and Krzywdzinski 2009: 32). This is not too unusual as German workers have been willing to, at times and within limits, make sacrifices for the sake of company competitiveness if the interests of the core German workforce for job security and codetermination are maintained.

This can be interpreted as the reappearance of the *two-tier system* of core German and peripheral non-German workers within German auto production. However, now the non-German workers work the typically lower skill and lower paid jobs in factories in their home countries rather than in Germany. As Guzik, Domański, and Gwosdz (2020: 394) argue, the "Central European semi-periphery cannot be understood without its relationships with the Western European core, and in a static manner; it is dynamic and relational in nature" (see Wallerstein 2004). In this dynamic, the highly skilled *Facharbeiter* of the core German workforce can maintain job security and high wages if some lower-skilled activity is outsourced to lower cost countries. As Jürgens (2008) explains,

> the exploitation of cost structures in low-cost locations ... play a particularly important role for both German carmakers and component suppliers in maintaining their competitiveness on the market in spite of the high-cost situation in Germany. This has also safeguarded domestic jobs and relieved the pressure on wages and working conditions. (69)

This dynamic is more pronounced in the US and especially Mexico—where nearly all the characteristics of the German system are discarded in favor of cheap labor and management control over high valorization and codetermination (see Pries 1999, 2003; McKenney 2018; Covarrubias 2020; Krzywdzinski 2020b). It therefore appears that for the German 'high-road' system to work, foreign production outside the core domestic workforce must *not* adopt the 'high-road' German system—or protections are limited—and wages must be sufficiently low. This is not surprising considering the early 1990s crisis showed how the cost structure of the German system can become out of balance and lead to serious financial instability and job losses. Yet, the reliance of the core on the periphery for the sustainability of the transnational system reveals how the core German system appears to not be self-sufficient for accumulating capital. Rather, the success of the German auto industry in recent decades is predicated on a global tiered system of a hybridized LP with German codetermination within Germany, and lower wages, less worker representation and codetermination, and more rigorous implementation of LP for workers employed outside the German core.

3.3 *Globalization and the Precarious Reliance on Chinese Growth*

China under Mao produced around 3,000 vehicles per year for the party elites (Wenten 2020: 281). Over a decade after the 1978 political-economic reforms, China produced barely 600,000 cars by 1990 with over 1.6 million workers, making it one of the smallest and least efficient auto industries in the world (Womack et al. 2007 [1990]: 275). Three decades later, China was the largest global automobile producer, manufacturing over 25 million vehicles in 2019 (OICA 2023). How did this occur and how did it effect the German and American industries? While regionalization was important to gain 'competitiveness' through low-wage production, Chinese growth was also an important outlet for both auto industries.

To learn from established manufacturers in terms of technology, management techniques, and R&D, the Chinese government required any company selling in China to establish a joint venture (JV) with a Chinese state owned enterprise with a minimum of 50 percent Chinese ownership (Wenten 2020: 281). In the 1980s to the mid-1990s only Volkswagen had the strategic foresight to pursue a joint venture with Shanghai Automobile Industry Corporation (SAIC) in 1984, while most automakers only became interested in China after its ascension to the World Trade Organization in 2001 (Wenten 2020: 282–283). These policies made China attractive as a potential market, making JVs with global automakers popular around the turn of the 21st century. With this enthusiasm, the Chinese auto industry grew explosively with 1.2 million autos produced in 1996 more than doubling to 3.2 million by 2002 and then doubling again to 7.2 million by 2006, reaching over 25 million autos produced in 2019 (Sturgeon et al. 2009: 11; OICA 2023). Global passenger car sales rose by 55 percent between 2005 and 2018, but without China the increase would have only been 11 percent, demonstrating the extent to which China alone has driven global growth (Bormann 2018: 7).

Volkswagen was the first major global automaker to succeed in China through its JV with SAIC. The motivation was to offset productivity and sales problems troubling Volkswagen through opportunities in China. The JV produced simple models with outdated technology at a high profit margin in the 1980s and 1990s, and the lack of competition gave VW 54 percent of Chinese market share by 1996 (Wenten 2020: 282–283). This was reduced to 18 percent in 2005 due to the influx of joint ventures, but overall market growth more than offset this with Volkswagen China selling over 4 million vehicles by 2019 (Volkswagen Group 2019: 23; Wenten 2020: 283; Pries and Wäcken 2020: 94). This accounted for nearly 40 percent of the roughly 11 million vehicle sales and approximately 40 percent of the profit for the Volkswagen Group (Wenten 2020: 285). Therefore, a significant portion of the growth and success of Volkswagen in the last several decades can be attributed to an early wager on Chinese growth, a historical development that was impossible to predict when the JV began.

The German auto industry appears increasingly dependent on sales of cars built outside of Germany. While total automotive production in Germany remained static at around 5.5 million units from 2008 to 2016, vehicle production from German factories located abroad nearly doubled from 5.3 to 10.1 million units. From this foreign production, approximately 4.7 million sales were from China alone in 2016 (Bormann 2018: 7–8). With nearly all sales growth occurring in production facilities abroad and half of that occurring in China, it is beyond doubt that the German industry is dependent on foreign sales and Chinese growth for their success.

This has become problematic for German automakers as sales in China dropped in the 2020s. Before the Covid-19 pandemic, German companies collectively held 25 percent of the enormous Chinese market. By 2024, this had dropped to 15 percent (Chilton 2024). In the third quarter of 2024, BMW sales in China dropped by 30 percent, 19 percent for Porsche, 15 percent for Volkswagen, and 13 percent for Mercedes-Benz (Chilton 2024; Collis 2024). The decline is partially due to the rise of EVs over internal combustion engine (IC) vehicles in China, a segment where German automakers only hold 10 percent market share (Chilton 2024; Der Spiegel 2024). In addition, domestic Chinese manufacturers have improved their offerings through JV technology transfer, state subsidized R&D, and new digital features to offer comparable performance at cheaper prices than European competitors (Kennedy 2024; Chilton 2024). This competitive shift is a major concern for the German corporations, with

Mercedes-Benz council chief Ergun Lumali stating a continued decline in global sales could be "fatal" in the long-term (Collis 2024). The more dependent German industry becomes on China, the worse outcomes may emerge if Chinese growth stops, or the Chinese reject German products. Only time will tell if German companies can regain from these losses or if this represents a turning point where China can no longer be a growth outlet.

American automakers also benefited from JVs in China. Formed in the late 1990s, JVs with Ford and GM became profitable in the 2000s and 2010s with Ford selling around 600,000 and GM selling over three million in China in 2019 (Ford Motor Company 2021: 5; General Motors 2019: 2). GM especially took an "aggressive business position in China" which allowed it to nearly match VW's output despite later entry (Howell and Hsu 2002: 44). By 2015, nearly a third of GM's global sales were in China, indicating how crucial Chinese sales were for post-bankruptcy GM (Wenten 2020: 285). Citing increased focus on the US and Chinese markets, GM divested from Opel in Germany in 2017, indicating a shift in globalization strategy (The Economist 2017). Instead of seeking to regain global dominance, as they held through most of the 20th century, American firms invested in the largest and highest growth markets like the US and China and divested or deemphasized other global markets.

Chinese production also has other advantages for the transnational corporations. Just as in Mexico and Eastern Europe, Chinese workers have low wages by international standards, though high within the local context, with workers valorized between $5,000 and $10,000 depending on the national origin of the firm and the prevalence of temporary labor (Wenten 2020: 291–297). The cost advantage is partially offset by the shortage of skills and the lack of fixed capital that needed to be addressed through investment in machines and vocational education (Jürgens and Krzywdzinski 2015: 1207; Wenten 2020: 284). Nevertheless, both issues are being overcome as new sites implement state of the art technology, thereby gradually approaching the socially necessary productivity standards set by the US, European, and Japanese firms (Wenten 2020: 292). The automation rate in Chinese JVs is typically lower than in home countries. For example, automation in the body shop of one European JV was 27 percent for an older model, whereas body shop automation is typically upwards of 80–95 percent in most companies (Wenten 2020: 290). However, the Chinese aim to reach the global standard of automation levels as stated in the Chinese government's 'Made in China 2025' program that advocates for "progress in automation, innovation, quality and use of information technology" (Wenten 2020: 288). This is desirable because the productivity is higher at newer sites with higher automation rates (Lüthje, Luo, and Zhang 2013; Krzywdzinski 2020a; Wenten 2020: 290–291).

In addition to more automation, Chinese companies and JVs are implementing lean production in their plants. According to studies of German, Japanese, US, and Chinese auto firms in China, it was found unanimously that companies were implementing "standardized lean production systems broadly based on the Toyota Production System" (Jürgens and Krzywdzinski 2015: 1221–1222; Krzywdzinski and Jürgens 2015: 26). As one Chinese production manager stated,

> Our benchmark is Toyota. The top management including me has been for some time to Toyota to learn from them … We started to introduce the concept of lean production already in 2004 and 2005. From that time we promoted the concept throughout the plant. (Jürgens and Krzywdzinski 2015: 1220)

Lean principles such as just-in-time, multi-purpose flexible machinery and robotics, teamwork, and kanban appeared broadly in Chinese factories. Multiskilling, job rotation, and kaizen activities were present in Japanese JVs while tasks were limited and Taylorized in American and European JVs (Wenten 2020: 290). However, Chinese firms are working toward skill and competence upgrading, so the ideal of a multiskilled worker may yet become the standard in China (see Jürgens and Krzywdzinski 2015). Lean principles have hybridized with Chinese industrial culture, with state-aligned unions and Chinese vocational training and occupational certification idiosyncrasies persisting in these firms (Krzywdzinski and Jürgens 2015: 28; Wenten 2020: 293–294). Striving for the productivity standard through more automation and lean methods through hybridization with value-regime characteristics appears to be the pattern in China. In other words, there is convergence on productivity standards, but divergence as to how to manage and facilitate industrial upgrading within the Chinese national context.

The EV transition invites the opportunity for China to 'leapfrog' expertise in battery and EV manufacture without the need for JV technology transfer. Chinese dominance in battery technology has emerged as China accounts for 60 percent of the EV battery market (Wald 2024). Chinese EV battery facilities are also highly productive with "huge plants that are highly automated, which they claim translate into low error rates, improved quality, and rapid production" (Kennedy 2024). This has, in part, allowed for nearly two-thirds of available EVs in China to be cheaper than their combustion engine counterparts, which further fuels the transition (McKerracher 2024). These developments have major implications for the future of the global auto industry because, even if China may not have a productivity advantage in IC car manufacture, China may have established a productivity gap in the EV sector (see Webster 2024). Lower labor costs *and* a productivity edge may make competition with Chinese EVs difficult to counter without other sources of competitive advantage.

Major challenges face JVs and Chinese firms in the future as China aims to expand domestic producers and shift from growing the domestic market toward increasing global exports in the 2020s (Wenten 2020: 287–290). For example, Chinese EV exports exploded from around $1.5 billion in export value in 2020 to $34.1 billion by 2023 (Webster 2024). This reflects the Chinese industrial pattern of developing expertise in a product and then flooding the international market with that commodity through cheap exports rather than focusing on fostering domestic demand (Klein and Pettis 2020). This was not a plausible strategy for vehicle exports in the past due to the quality and productivity deficits in Chinese automobile manufacture for IC cars, but 'leapfrog' expertise in EV development may be the path forward to not only overcome these barriers but have a productivity and cost advantage over Western rivals. If Chinese EV exports continue to grow thanks in part to domestic Chinese firms achieving the same or superior productivity and quality standards as their JV partners, then this could have serious long-term consequences for the US and German auto industry (Jürgens and Krzywdzinski 2015: 1220; Webster 2024).

In addition, if Chinese growth 'cures all ills' then there is the question of what will happen when growth slows as China reaches a saturation point. The enormous size of the Chinese market is still a net benefit for the transnational corporations, but the end of high growth could signal a return to the highly competitive fights for market share within a largely stagnant or low growth market as in the 1970s to the 1990s, periods which were characterized by recurring industrial crisis. The early signs of this are already apparent as overcapacity, dozens of competitors and emerging start-ups, and an intense fight for market share has triggered a price war in the Chinese domestic market, with automakers racing to offer discounts and incentives to survive (Reuters 2025). The full ramifications of this price war in addition to a potential slowdown of global growth have yet to be reckoned with.

4 Electric Vehicles, Industry 4.0, and the Never-Ending Pursuit of Productivity

Even as lean production has generalized and built in quality, just-in-time logistics, and autonomation constitute the 'common sense' of auto production, historical examination indicates that the imperative to improve productivity is a never-ending process and that lean production is not the 'end of history' for production systems but is itself a manifestation of a larger capitalist historical dynamic (Postone 1993; 2015). This is not only true because LP practices continuous improvement, thus ensuring that the pursuit of further productivity is a *fundamental objective and daily task of the system*, but because developments both within and outside the industry have the potential to push the technological and productivity frontier even further. The discussion turns to two disruptive developments that are transforming the auto industry: electric vehicles and Industry 4.0.

4.1 *The Electric Vehicle Transition: Radical Product Change Meets Radical Production Change*

Due to increasing environmental concern, government policy to address climate change, and the improvement of batteries and other technologies, electric vehicles (EVs) have become an upcoming transportation technology that enables personal mobility with less environmental impact (International Energy Agency 2024a). Since the IC car won over battery power in the early 20th century (Flink 1988: 7–10), IC vehicles have been a major source of carbon emissions (McNeill and Engelke 2014: 120–122; International Energy Agency 2024a). The technical and range limitations of EVs have been largely overcome, thus making EVs an increasingly viable replacement for IC cars (Kumar and Alok 2020). In the late 1990s, part IC powered, part battery powered hybrid electric vehicles such as the Toyota Prius popularized the idea of electric vehicles for certain environmentally conscious consumers (Liker 2021: 327–328). However, only since around 2012 have fully electric vehicles made inroads in the global auto market (International Energy Agency 2024b). Government led global policies to fight climate change, special subsidies, and regulations have appeared to encourage EV adoption (Sierzchula, Bakker, Maat, and van Wee 2014; Bormann et al. 2018; Clinton and Steinberg 2019; Scheiber 2021). Thanks to these subsidies and incentives, EVs are rising in popularity, with important implications for the future of the auto industry, its workers, and its production processes. Just as EVs represent a shift in the automobile as a commodity, so too does it alter the production of that commodity.

The development and sale of EVs was spearheaded by American companies, with sales of over 200,000 in 2017 and around 765,000 autos in the US fleet—one-fourth of the total worldwide (Klier and Rubenstein 2020: 42). This was less than 1.2 percent of US vehicle sales and only 0.2 percent of vehicle stock, but EV sales had grown to nearly 10 percent of new sales and over 2 percent of the US car stock by 2023 (International Energy Agency 2024c). In addition, the distribution of EV sales is highly skewed among the states, with California being a clear leader with over 1.25 million EV registrations

(3.4 percent of total vehicles) versus states like Tennessee with less than 35 thousand registered EVs (0.5 percent of total vehicles) by September 2024 (Alternative Fuels Data Center 2024). By the mid-2020s, however, these sales numbers were far behind states like China, Germany, or Norway (International Energy Agency 2024c). This may be because of the relatively cheap price of oil and the over a century-long inertia of American wants, needs, and desires which may be mitigating demand (Klier and Rubenstein 2020: 43). However, the Biden administration aimed for EVs to comprise 50 percent of all new vehicle sales in the US by the 2030s, allocating tens of billions in investment and subsidies from the Inflation Reduction Act (IRA) for auto companies and other businesses and organizations to meet this ambitious goal (Scheiber 2021; White House 2022).

The US is also home to Tesla, the world's leading auto startup that exclusively sells—primarily luxury—EVs. Since purchasing the Fremont, California NUMMI plant after the 2009 GM Bankruptcy, Tesla has established facilities and factories in the US, China, and Germany (Tesla 2023). While Tesla's rise may help the US value-regime secure production and jobs for the future, Tesla remains a nonunion company. CEO Elon Musk has goaded the UAW to attempt to unionize Tesla, expecting an embarrassing failure, while the UAW claims Musk has engaged in antiunion tactics such as firing Tesla employees for organizing (Dias 2022). Thus, Tesla does not represent a revival of the US industrial relations system based on collective bargaining with the UAW but continues the heterogeneous fracturing of the US value-regime. Nevertheless, Tesla is the first new successful American automaker to emerge in decades, signifying how EVs are changing the competitive dynamics of the industry as newcomers threaten the old guard by establishing expertise in EVs rather than IC cars (see Perkins and Murmann 2018; McClean 2022).

The German auto industry has historically been skeptical of EVs, instead drawing upon decades of expertise in diesel engine technology (Pries and Wäcken 2020: 98). The environmental merit of diesel engines is mixed because while they do release less carbon dioxide, they emit nitrogen oxides that are harmful to human health and the environment (Ewing 2017: 2). In the 2000s–2010s, in a gambit to increase US market share, Volkswagen targeted would-be hybrid or EV buyers with an aggressive 'clean diesel' marketing campaign, selling VW cars equipped with nitrogen oxide reducing devices (Ewing 2017: 145–158). However, it was discovered in September 2015 that the device only worked properly when the car's computer detected that it was being tested for emissions. Thus, nitrogen oxides were emitted above the legal limit in normal driving conditions. This constituted a 'defeat device' which violated US vehicle emissions laws (Ewing 2017; Pries and Wäcken 2020: 97). The revelation of this deception triggered an international scandal which caused billions in losses for VW in addition to restitution to buyers in the US and Europe and ongoing litigation (Ewing 2017; Pries and Wäcken 2020: 97).

In the aftermath of this scandal, Volkswagen, BMW, and Daimler-Benz committed to a fundamental shift in strategy toward EVs (Bormann et al. 2018: 12–13; Pries and Wäcken 2020: 105). While Germany is behind Japan, the US, and China in battery production and technology, billions of Euros and tens of thousands of employees have been dedicated to R&D in this area and a plethora of new German EV models have been released, with more planned in the future (Ewing 2017; Pries and Wäcken 2020: 104–105). German sales of EVs were very low until 2020, but they have risen markedly since with around 30 percent new car sales being EVs in Germany in 2022 and over 5 percent of the vehicle stock being EVs in 2023 (International Energy Agency 2024c). The rate of EV adoption fell in 2024 to less than 13.5 percent of new car sales, however, in part due to legal budgetary constraints that prompted a withdrawal of EV purchase subsidies (Book, Demling, Fahrion, Giesen, Hage, and Hesse 2024; Anderson 2025). The German focus on exports over domestic demand and the unwillingness to exceed strict budgetary limits for the sake of necessary investments and infrastructural improvements may contribute to a slower EV transition in Germany and less attractive EV offerings in a fiercely competitive global EV market (see Klein and Pettis 2020).

The aggressive push for EVs and the gradual reduction of IC auto production will have profound effects on the workforce and production processes at all auto companies due to differences between EV and IC autos. The similar outward appearance belies very different systems under the hood. The powertrain systems for EVs are very simple compared to an IC while the battery is more complex than a fuel tank (McClean 2022). Nevertheless, in the net balance of complexity, EVs contain approximately 30 percent less parts than IC autos, which means EV production generally requires much less labor to manufacture (Scheiber 2021). As Bormann et al. (2018) explains,

> Compared to today's highly complex internal combustion engine, the electric engine is a relatively easy-to-grasp technology. Other complex components of the engine architecture associated with combustion, such as the transmission and exhaust systems, will no longer be necessary in a future of electric motors. (18)

EVs therefore simplify auto production through simplifying the commodity. This is a problem for workers and unions because employment in the auto industry has benefited greatly from the opposite trend of increasing complexity and product innovations, such as on board electronics, cameras, and added features and functionality (Jürgens and Meißner 2005: 42; Jürgens 2023: 320–321). Auto companies aimed to simplify the product for the sake of productivity and costs through the platform strategy, but realization demands for diversity, added features, and customization have meant that product trends for more complexity have generated positive employment pressures that mitigate efforts to eliminate waste (Jürgens and Meißner 2005: 42; Holweg 2008: 11). The increasing complexity of automobiles has also limited production automation, especially in assembly. The move to electric motors and batteries may reduce the complexity of the automobile to the point that automation of previously unautomated assembly processes becomes economically viable, with the potential of becoming the new productive benchmark (Krzywdzinski 2020a: 50–51). If increasing complexity has been an 'ally' to workers in the past, the rise of EVs represents a turning point in the opposite direction.

Even with billions of dollars of federal government investment, it is estimated that the US auto industry could lose a net 75,000 jobs in the transition to EVs (Scheiber 2021). This loss could be mitigated or even result in net job gains if more EV parts are manufactured in the US. This is because about 75 percent of the parts for the IC powertrain are manufactured in the US versus less than 50 percent for the EV powertrain (Scheiber 2021). The 2022 IRA promotes domestic production by offering tax credits of up to $7,500 for new electric vehicles that meet the necessary requirements including domestic sourcing of battery components and assembly in Canada, the US, or Mexico (U.S. Department of Energy 2024). Prospects could also improve if more domestically manufactured vehicles, both from the Big Three and from Japanese and German transplants, are sold in the US, whose market share currently stands at around 50 percent for the past decade (Scheiber 2021). One way this could be achieved is if the Big Three regained substantial market ground back from imports and transplant competitors—which has not occurred since the 1960s except for temporary upswings (see Whyte 2020: 109–115). Alternatively, if transplant manufactured vehicles increase their sales over imports without sourcing major components from their home country, then this would benefit US domestic manufacturing. The IRA tax credit system also encourages this because transplants are incentivized to source locally to be eligible to offer the maximum credit (U.S. Department of Energy 2024). However, this also conflicts with other incentives and objectives for building batteries and other EV components in their home country (e.g., Pries and Wäcken 2020: 104–105). Therefore, it appears that transnational corporations will have to strategically choose what subsidies and incentives to pursue in which markets and for what ends, and governments will have to weigh the costs and benefits to maintaining jobs and activity in the value-regime when considering potentially expensive and complex policy frameworks.

The EV transition also has implications for workers and the UAW as new battery and EV component plants open across the US. The Big Three and non-union suppliers wanted to undermine the UAW by establishing joint ventures to build EVs in new plants not covered by the UAW master contract in primarily southern right-to-work states, thus creating an 'EV tier' of workers with lower wages and benefits (Lichtenstein 2024: 52–53). A predicted hours per vehicle reduction of 30 percent and IC plant closures and relocations were also concerning for the UAW as the transition to EVs could threaten union jobs (UAWD 2023). Legislative compromise in the IRA made it so EV plants were not automatically unionized, but clear support from the Biden administration, e.g., Biden was the first sitting president to appear on a UAW picket line, helped pressure the Big Three. Ultimately, the "stand-up strike" of 2023 made it so GM and Stellantis battery plants would be covered under the UAW contract, and Ford agreed to card-check unionization of new EV facilities (Lichtenstein 2024: 53). Thus, the return to labor militancy appears to have thwarted the Big Three's attempt to establish an 'EV tier' to undermine the UAW. This prevented the American value-regime from falling further from its roots in the 'Treaty of Detroit,' and may halt a potential 'race to the bottom' for domestic EV development.

In Germany, the employment diagnosis is also concerning, as a seven to ten year transition to EV production threatens 600,000 German jobs with approximately a third of the value chain reduced by EV production (Bormann et al. 2018: 18; Pries and Wäcken 2020: 106). A rapid transition is necessary because failing to invest in the necessary infrastructure and workforce to catch up to the US and China in EV production "may also threaten jobs and mean that opportunities to create the jobs of the future are lost" (Bormann et al. 2018: 18). In addition to the billions of euros in investment, the auto companies negotiated with IG Metall and the works councils to devise plans for saving auto industry employment. The workers' organizations support the growth of EVs if battery production is in Germany, supporting domestic employment and reducing dependence on China. Furthermore, a 2018 collective agreement was made at VW that stated, "no workers will be dismissed for reasons of the shift to electric car production until 2028" (Pries and Wäcken 2020: 106). Overall, the attitude of German workers is that the EV transition, though starting later than other countries, is necessary because "employment has to be saved by innovation and not just resistance to change" (Pries and Wäcken 2020: 106). Thus, a balance must be struck between meeting climate targets and transforming the auto industry without sacrificing jobs (Bormann et al. 2018: 19).

However, falling sales in China and lower post-pandemic demand throughout Europe triggered a crisis in late 2024 (Chilton 2024; Collis 2024; Automotive News Europe 2024). In September 2024, Volkswagen announced that it was eliminating labor agreements that guaranteed jobs and was considering cutting up to 30,000 jobs as well as closing factories in Germany for the first time in the company's history. VW management argued this was necessary because it was failing to meet sales and profit targets and had lost around 500,000 in European sales, which is the equivalent of around two plants (Automotive News Europe 2024). The perennial productivity gap also appeared to be a problem as VW only had a 2 percent profit margin in the first 9 months of 2024 which induced management representatives to call for increasing efficiency and reducing costs (Jolly 2024). According to former Volkswagen Group CEO Herbert Diess, while it takes Tesla approximately 10 hours to produce an EV, it takes Volkswagen's factory in Zwickau three times longer to produce an EV, prompting him to also call for improved productivity in German factories (Eddy 2021). This demonstrates how productivity gaps persist in Germany, contributing to cost problems, and shows the sustained importance of recognizing and addressing those gaps in the switch from IC to EV production.

Despite the dire situation, after marathon negotiations with IG Metall and the works council, a 'Christmas miracle' was announced in December 2024 where 35,000 German jobs would be cut over time through 'socially responsible means,' but all factories would remain open. For workers, job security guarantees would run until 2030, but they would forgo bonuses, reduce permanent employment for trainees, and cut capacity at five factories by around 700,000 vehicles. At the same time, around 4,000 managers would also not receive bonuses and take a 10 percent pay cut (Mossalgue 2024). Other German automakers from Daimler-Benz to BMW to Ford Europe are also under pressure to cut jobs if sales do not improve, and the final rationalization plans and deals with the workforces at German automakers have not yet been decided at time of writing (Collis 2024; Deutsche Welle 2024). Nevertheless, in the tradition of labor-management codetermination, the German industry appeared prepared to cooperate to meet goals of meeting the EV transition without sacrificing employment in Germany, or at the very least handling any job losses through 'socially responsible' measures. Only time will tell if they succeed or if the simplification pressure on employment, flagging sales, or the head start of foreign competitors will make the dual goals difficult to keep in the coming years.

Finally, the rise of Chinese EV exports has prompted responses from the US and the EU. The United States *de facto* banned Chinese EVs in September 2024 by implementing a 100 percent tariff against Chinese EV imports as well as a 50 percent tariff on solar cells and a 25 percent tariff on steel, aluminum, EV batteries, and other key minerals (Lawder 2024). American officials claim Chinese EVs pose national security concerns such as user data going to the Chinese government or concerns over long-distance hacking (Hoppenstedt 2024). Canada likewise raised their Chinese EV tariff by 100 percent, and Mexico is being pressured by the US to halt Chinese FDI flows to prevent Chinese EVs from being built in Mexico and coming to the United States through this 'back-door' (Rabson 2024; Oré 2024). The situation mirrors the entry of more affordable Japanese cars in the 1970s and 1980s but differs in the response. Rather than implementing voluntary export restraints that only limited Japanese imports from entering the US market during the 1980s and early 1990s, these tariffs effectively block Chinese EVs entirely. This may protect domestic jobs and the Big Three, as one cannot lose market share to a competitor who is not in the local market. Yet, it also means there are less affordable EV options for Americans, less competition that could spur innovation, and ultimately slows the EV transition—which subsequently hampers one means to fight against climate change and reduce pollution (Rabson 2024).

The EU also implemented a tariff plan in late 2024, claiming that Chinese automakers benefitted from state subsidies that unfairly undercut EV prices (see Ou et al. 2020). The European tariff schema is granular with specific duties varying from company to company, such as an 18.8 percent tariff on Tesla rival BYD and a 35.5 percent tariff for Chinese state-owned SAIC. German automakers are against the tariffs as the head of the German auto industry association, Hildegard Müller, stated that these tariffs are a setback for free trade and preserving European jobs and growth (Cook 2024). The German industry's defense of China against the tariffs may be due to fears of retaliatory tariffs against German automakers in China and reflect a general desire to maintain partnership with China considering the industry's dependence on Chinese sales. Therefore, unlike decades earlier with the Japanese, the Chinese are targeting Europe instead of North America as one of their primary expansion outlets. How the influx of Chinese EVs worldwide, a 'Chinese Challenge,' will play out differently than the 'Japanese Challenge' or 'American Challenge' remains to be seen, but it is nevertheless the most pressing question of the contemporary auto industry and the global EV transition.

Thus, EVs represent a major shift in auto manufacture with implications for production processes, work structure, and employment. Early indications show how the differences in value-regimes and value-systems are navigating the issues of the decreasing valorization in the commodity which may decrease valorization opportunities for the workforce. The US has a head start over Germany, but disregarding worker interest in job security and maintaining wages and benefits may undermine productivity through increased worker discontent on the shopfloor (see Norsworthy and Zabala 1985; Zabala 1995). The EV transition may be another opportunity to undermine the UAW, working conditions, and worker power in the US, though the recent wave of labor militancy under Shawn Fain appears to have made domestic EV manufacturing on par with IC production (UAWD 2023; Lichtenstein 2024). The German industry may have had a late start in EV production and is currently struggling in China, but the Germans may utilize their highly skilled workforce to catch up and may even develop a new DQP strategy that keeps German EVs competitive. In any case, German workers may be better off then American workers by virtue of the commitment to cooperation and job preservation from the German companies. The response to the 'Chinese Challenge' in EVs during the 2020s and 2030s may be the biggest global challenge to the US and German industry since the rise of the Japanese. As of early 2025, it appears the response so far is an echo of past responses as the German industry plans for 'socially responsible' measures for rationalization and the American industry engages in heightened protectionism to prevent market share loss (Lawder 2024; Rabson 2024; Mossalgue 2024). Overall, the challenge at hand is that value-regimes and value-systems which can "successfully wage war on complexity" are better positioned to meet the challenges of the future (MacDuffie and Fujimoto 2010: 25).

4.2 *Industry 4.0: Hype or New Productivity Standard?*

By the 2010s, the fundamentals of lean production were well and many elements were adopted and adapted by auto companies around the world. Even though Toyota remains the global productivity leader, the productivity leap from integrating lean production has already occurred for most companies, and no further dramatic reductions in hours per vehicle should be expected from further implementing LP beyond the continuous improvements that constitute the core philosophy (Weyer 2011: 3279–3284). Yet, with the continuous pursuit of productive and competitive advantage to accumulate capital and goaded by the business press promoting an international productivity race (Harbour 2017), the search for the *next revolution in auto production* is an imperative for global automakers. A collection of technologies and production techniques called Industry 4.0 is touted as the next leap in automobile production (see Krzywdzinski 2020a; Jürgens 2021). Considered part of the so-called 'fourth industrial revolution' of emergent technological advances in areas such as artificial intelligence, robotics, 3D printing, quantum computing, and biotechnology (see Schwab 2016), Industry 4.0 refers to how these technologies are being implemented in the auto industry to improve efficiency. While industrial robots and computers have been used in auto production since the

1960s, modern software, computing, and internet connectivity have advanced considerably thanks to the exponential growth in misprocessing power (Brynjolfsson and McAfee 2011, 2014; Frey and Osborne 2013: 14; Knowles 2017: 31–32). In auto production, the focus has been primarily on implementing the 'Internet of Things,' i.e., the networking and connectivity of all technology in the factory, as well as using data collection and analysis to optimize production processes with real-time information exchange, machine learning, and big data (Rifkin 2014; Butollo et al. 2018; Krzywdzinski 2020a, 2020b: 519–520; Jürgens 2021). Unlike lean production, however, Industry 4.0 does not comprise a production philosophy or specify best practices for implementing these technologies beyond insisting that deploying these disparate technical developments should improve production performance as well as make improvements in ergonomics and working conditions (Butollo et al. 2018; Krzywdzinski 2020a: 10; Jürgens 2021: 10–11). Preliminary studies show that changes so far have been gradual, and that Industry 4.0 shares many continuities with LP (Krzywdzinski 2020b: 519; Jürgens 2021: 10).

For example, in internal logistics operations, 'smart' assistance systems instruct workers to pick certain parts via light signals or computer generated voices that are also capable of identifying errors. The goal is for workers to execute the preplanned optimized course of action. Production machines networked through the Internet of Things inform teams of maintenance specialists of problems in real-time, which can help coordinate maintenance workers, more efficiently utilize their time, and fix problems as fast as possible. In a pilot program at Audi, automated guided transport systems use data collected from the shopfloor to determine the most efficient path for assembly through decentralized assembly stations, skipping unnecessary steps and preventing a disruption at one station affecting the entire production flow (Jürgens 2021: 11–14). In some assembly areas, cameras have been installed to determine whether work is being performed correctly to "ensure that tasks are completed according to predefined standards" (Krzywdzinski 2020b: 519). These examples only scratch the surface of possible Industry 4.0 applications. The commonality is how machine and worker connectivity enable data collection and analysis that can be used to determine and enforce purportedly more efficient production processes.

Industry 4.0 shares some features with lean production, such as their orientation toward optimization and rationalization. Both emphasize standardized work, with Industry 4.0 promising data to further optimize the system and "allow mastery over increasing demands on quality, time-to-market and interdependencies in supply chains" (Krzywdzinski 2020b: 519). Information is important to both LP and Industry 4.0, but the difference between kanban and the mountains of data and analysis provided by Industry 4.0 is that kanban relies on the just-in-time principle of providing just the right information at just the right time, no more, no less (Ohno 1988: 25–30). By contrast, companies utilizing Industry 4.0 may become overwhelmed by the influx of data and fail to use it to substantially improve production processes (Liker 2021: 168–169). That is why combining Industry 4.0 and LP may synergistically work to improve productivity by putting the data from Industry 4.0 under the principle of just-in-time and using it to kaizen production processes, just as it was argued in the 1980s that the full capacity of new automation was best utilized under the lean system (Ohno 1988; Womack et al. 2007 [1990]).

Yet, there is a tension in combining the two because Industry 4.0 implements *technological* measuring of outcomes and data-based analyses for work process optimization rather than relying on *shopfloor knowledge* and worker suggestions for continuous improvements. How can preplanned computer-determined processes then be improved through worker experience and suggestions? As Jürgens (2021: 12) suggests, it is likely that "employees will tend to focus on the functioning of the assistance systems themselves, rather than the production process as such." This functionally reintroduces Taylorism in a different form. Instead of workers internalizing and exercising kaizen, Industry 4.0 *re-alienates* the responsibility for shopfloor problem solving and rationalization from the worker. However, instead of placing the responsibility in the hands of industrial engineers, it is instead given to cameras, computers, and data analytics. It also constitutes a new form of automation that deskills workers as shopfloor knowledge is rendered superfluous by Industry 4.0 (Krzywdzinski 2020b: 520).

This could become problematic because, as the problems with automation in the 1980s demonstrated, eliminating human experience can lead to a deficit of problem-solving competence if unexpected failures occur (Bainbridge 1983; Weyer 1997; Krzywdzinski 2020b: 520). In 1980s Germany, new automation 're-professionalized' skilled workers on the machines, including the enriched jobs of assembly work on the automated assembly lines (Kern and Schumann 1984; 1987; Jürgens et al. 1993). Yet with Industry 4.0, the potential re-professionalization of shopfloor workers is muted as the expertise and power over production flows back to engineers and data analysts. The Industry 4.0 discussion among German workers is less focused on hoping for further professionalization but resisting the danger of deskilling. Multiple German studies have detailed how the works councils are attempting to ameliorate or block the negative effects of Industry 4.0 technologies such as deskilling, increased technical surveillance, and performance control (Kuhlmann et al. 2018; Haipeter, Inger, and Gabi 2018; Krzywdzinski 2020b: 520). It is a question of how to prevent the transformation of 'good' work into precarious work with worse pay and downgraded skills (Bormann et al. 2018: 18). However, if the deskilling of shop-floor and maintenance workers results in more frequent and longer breakdown times, then Industry 4.0 might have negative productivity impacts and thereby *not* become the standard of socially necessary labor time. Only time will tell what potential benefits *and* drawbacks this technologically oriented approach to problem solving and production optimization may bring.

One recent experience at Tesla demonstrated the potential dangers of too much automation even with contemporary technology. In the mid-2010s, Tesla attempted to implement the most advanced assembly robots and newest technology into their production processes at their Fremont, California plant. Tesla's aim was to use its production line as a "laboratory for untested techniques" that was supposed to produce cheaper Tesla models at higher volumes (Boudette 2018). They also broke with standard procedure as fundamental changes to the line were made in the middle of the production run rather than focusing on establishing stability and then pursuing continuous improvement as lean production stipulates (Boudette 2018; Liker 2021: 332–336). Around $2 billion was spent on new technology but the result was a "manufacturing hell" according to Elon Musk (Boudette 2018). The recent example of Tesla is a cautionary tale that reconfirms the lessons of the 1980s, that *increased automation, new technology, and productivity improvement do not always coincide*, and that manual processes with higher productivity trump highly automated but less efficient processes in modern capitalism. Industry 4.0, or some of its technologies but not others, may become the industry standard but only if it succeeds where Tesla failed in *proving* that these technologies can improve the flow of value in motion and accumulate capital. Just as workers and their 'human capital' must prove themselves useful to capital to become 'socially necessary' so must new technologies, including electric vehicles and Industry 4.0 (see Knowles 2023a).

5 Global Generalization and General Globalization

In 1988, International Motor Vehicle Program scholar John Krafcik (1988) declared the 'triumph' of lean production. Was he correct or was this declaration premature? Lean production as a wholistic 'model' was not completely adopted by any value-system because no value-regime was identical to the Japanese conditions that gave rise to LP. 'Productive models' exist where different governance compromises and business strategies (e.g., diversity and quality) place importance on competitive arenas other than the continuous cost reduction (Boyer and Freyssenet 2002). However, globalization and the increasing importance of international benchmarking have made keeping pace with productivity development a concern for all value-systems. Thus, convergence around lean principles as the *productive basis* for auto production is apparent in the global auto industry (see Pries 2003; Weyer 2011). Productivity enhancing practices such as just-in-time, autonomation, and built-in quality appear nearly universal, even as their practical application adapted to the conditions of the value-regimes. In this narrow sense lean production appears to have 'triumphed.'

LP can be conceptualized as an organizational technology not based on fixed capital investment (Harvey 2017: 9). It is a type of scientific management that differs fundamentally from Taylorism. It exercises instrumental reason that is oriented toward eliminating waste from both machines and workers rather than the Fordist-Taylorist deskilling automation logic. Rather than pose Fordist and 'post-Fordist' lean logic as totally distinct, it is useful to identify their common denominator: their historic substantiation as one part of a capitalist historic dynamic characterized by continuous productivity increases (Postone 1993). Whether to 'automate at all costs' or 'aggressively eliminate waste' is not pursued for its own sake but is influenced by what will improve productivity and aid capital accumulation. Since the 1990s, the norms of socially necessary labor time readjusted to the speed of the just-in-time delivery and the standardized one minute cycle. To keep value in motion flowing at the socially necessary magnitude, adaptation of lean principles became the standard in the US and Germany.

In the US, the need for change became urgent as market share declined and overcapacities inclined. Lean implementation was incremental during the 1990s and accelerated in the 2000s, yet this was not enough to prevent bankruptcy for GM and Chrysler (Adler et al. 1997; Kochan et al. 1997; Cutcher-Gershenfeld et al. 2015). Cost cutting via outsourcing to nonunion suppliers or Mexico did not close the cost gap enough either, though they contributed to the degradation of UAW jobs and overall working conditions and pay in the US value-regime (Holmes 2004; Covarrubias 2020). The UAW tried to regain its labor monopoly by unionizing transplants but could not convince most transplant workers of the benefits of unionization, especially as the Big Three declined (Holmes 2004; Rothstein 2006). Combative relations contributed to the haphazard implementation of LP as the union was split about lean reforms that may secure jobs but required transforming work performance and job structure (Rinehart 1999; Rothstein 2006; Helper and Henderson 2014; Cutcher-Gershenfeld 2015). The post-bankruptcy US domestic industry reformed its cost structure and was thoroughly lean, but struggled within its domestic market, retreated from some international markets, and became increasingly dependent on cheap labor in Mexico and sales in China to make profits (Ingrassia 2011; Cutcher-Gershenfeld 2015; The Economist 2017; Covarrubias 2020; Wenten 2020). Thus, the US value-regime fractured into the unionized Big Three and nonunion transplants, making outsourcing and labor costs important sources of competitive advantage as the productivity gap narrowed and productive norms converged around lean production.

The decline of the Big Three is a case of social domination *par excellence*. The Big Three experienced intense productivity pressure from a productivity and quality gap *rooted in how the lean producers possessed more control over time*. The domination had both economic *and* social dimensions as lower productivity and quality hurt sales and market share as well as generated negative communications about the Big Three, e.g., they were inefficient, uncompetitive, low-quality etc. (e.g., Vasilash 1997; Hounshell 2000; Womack et al. 2007 [1990]; Harbour 2017). There were wage and benefit differences between transplants, imports, and domestic plants, but the cost differentials did not originate from labor costs alone. Even though productivity pressure is *not monocausal* in explaining the Big Three decline, it is a good example of how sustained productivity differences can contribute to decline and pressure convergence around the manufacturing practices of the productivity leaders.

For the UAW, the implementation of LP was more than just originating from management but was *pressured* by overarching productive norms deemed 'socially necessary' *because* of their successful implementation at Toyota and others. Therefore, while the 'management by stress' of the workers at Toyota came directly from Toyota management, it is incomplete to say that the work restructuring at Big Three factories were *only* a result of management fiat. Rather, work was transformed due to *social domination*, i.e., through pressure to conform to a new set of productive norms that received both economic power from lean producer's increasing market share, *and* social power through claims of productiveness, progress, and modernness. The decades it took to reform and close the productivity gap contributed to billions of dollars in losses in the 2000s and the bankruptcies. This does *not* mean each reform or concession in their specificity was 'inevitable,' as wage and benefits struggles are one but not the only means to make up for productivity related disadvantages and there was always the contingency that an equally or more productive alternative could emerge. The point is that productivity pressure is experienced as social domination *unless and until* the productivity gap sufficiently narrows or the pressures are assuaged via lower labor costs, growth outlets, outsourcing, or other means. There is always a choice in how to deal with the productivity problem, and the US and Germany did handle the problem differently, but nevertheless the productivity problem is unavoidable and must be addressed.

The German case demonstrated an example of both increasing productivity by transforming valorization processes while also balancing the overall cost structure with other cost reduction means to become 'competitive.' Rationalization required labor-management compromise that balanced both profitability and the interests of German workers. Like the US, German workers also faced pressures to improve productivity, outsource manufacturing, and make concessions, but codetermination made it so many of the changes most affected workers outside the German value-regime (Pries 2003; Jürgens 2008; Krzywdzinski and Jürgens 2009; Krzywdzinski 2020b). Despite these threats, adoption of lean principles, starting from experiments in new plants transferred into the core West German plants, was achieved *through codetermination*, not despite it (Jürgens 1994, 1995, 1997a; Krzywdzinski 2020b). The hybridized lean system was shaped by codetermination so that 'management by stress' was mitigated in most German plants. Short cycle times returned, standardization synergized with the platform strategy, and just-in-time flow emerged (Jürgens 1997b, 2009), but German workers codetermined limits to labor intensity and continued to pursue humanization when possible (Jürgens 2021; Krzywdzinski 2020b). However, this contributed to a persistent productivity gap that became a source of tension between management and labor (Weyer 2011; Grieger and Lupa 2015; Ewing 2017). Thus, contemporary German production represents a mix of 'best practices' and characteristically German compromises that do not appear to fully satisfy either workers' desires for humanization and new production concepts or managements' desires for profitability and optimization (Jürgens 2021).

Like American critiques of 'management by stress' (e.g., Parker and Slaughter 1988; Babson 1995a, 1995b; Reinhart 1999), German critics lamented that lean implementation made German companies turn away from NPC and automation in favor of a return to short cycle times and standardization (Kern and Schumann 1998; Springer 1999; Hachtmann and von Saldern 2009: 204–207). LP was criticized for not providing opportunities for re-professionalization or increasing vocational skills, which frustrated many ambitious high skill workers confined to the assembly line (Kern and Schumann 1998; Springer 1999: 133; Jürgens 2004: 415; Hachtmann and von Saldern 2009: 205). Springer (1999) criticized how worker participation was limited to making "the process of rationalization itself … the object of participation," and that "Participative rationalization is no alternative emancipatory act against the capitalist enterprise" because participation was limited to management objectives of optimization and eliminating waste (138–139). Kern and Schumann (1998: 10) argued that a return to NPC to realize the collective productive intelligence of the German skilled workforce was the best long-term strategy, despite weaknesses revealed by the early 1990s crisis. Thus, even as adoption of LP was shaped by codetermination, there was still a sense of loss that the German model pioneered in the 1980s was partially dismantled and reformed into lean production with German characteristics.

That the dominant 'logic' of rationalization changed from the predictions that NPC would re-professionalize and humanize work to a logic of 'management by stress' demonstrates how rationalization driven by the productivity pressure of a historical dynamic operates on a *non-human* logic. Rationalization in the auto industry has entailed deskilling and reskilling as well as increasing and decreasing automation—there is no 'master' pattern that characterizes the entire dynamic. Some trends, such as NPC, have combined rationalization with humanization, but the *most productive developments* have not always been *maximally humanized*. Many rationalization trends are only categorized and theorized in the short to medium term, but this misses the long-term historical dynamic that occurs through the *Longue Durée* (Braudel 2009 [1960]). There is no 'technological determinism,' especially since 'hard' technology as fixed capital is not always the most productive. What emerges to disrupt existing methods is contingent, as the history of Fordism and lean production show. Where new productive methods come from and under what conditions cannot be predicted beforehand. Nevertheless, it is useful to identify the historical dynamic and observe what technologies and work organizations take on the force of social domination by pushing the norms of socially necessary labor time forward.

American and German critiques of lean production emphasize how implementing lean reforms degrade working conditions and increases labor intensity, and they instead suggest developing productive systems that improve productivity and coincides with human values (Parker and Slaughter 1988; Kern and Schumann 1998). However, the *nonhuman logic of capital* exerts productivity pressure on agentive social systems to conform to the most productive system whether it is more *or* less humanist than possible alternatives. The logic is not necessarily *inhuman* either as many humanization reforms have restricted productivity gains while others enabled them. Social domination pressures toward the *most productive system regardless of whether that system is more or less humanist than the less productive systems*. Fulfilling human needs is not the central aim of capital accumulation, just as re-professionalization or humanization of work is not the central aim of improving productivity to increase capital accumulation (Knowles 2017: 189–191). Unions and businesses as value-systems can nevertheless respond to these productivity pressures differently, even as they shape and push the decision-making processes in certain directions.

Publications like the Harbour Report enforce productivity pressure via international benchmarking that measures and compares efficiency criteria but not humanization. Comparisons between factors such as work-in-process, defects, space utilization, amount of inventory, set-up times, and above all HPV, intensify the productivity race and pressure to conform to benchmarks (Reinhart 1999: 20; Weyer 2011). Even with the private Harbour Report in Europe, the hesitancy of BMW and Daimler-Benz to participate and the scandal at VW upon the release of the 2005 report indicate how even German automakers understand the *social stigma* attached to low productivity and try to avoid it (Weyer 2011: 3272; Jürgens 2023: 352). Therefore, the proliferation of social systems that closely observe and compare productivity parameters further increased productivity pressure in the global auto industry, which contributed to the convergence around lean principles.

Increasing globalization since the 1990s has been important for two reasons. First, global outsourcing in pursuit of low wages addressed cost control issues as a complement to productivity raising strategies. In both cases of Mexico and the US and Germany and Eastern Europe, costs were lowered to raise 'competitiveness' and increase profits. This outsourcing can be framed as 'dark value extraction' where the monopolistic position of buyers (the automakers) puts pressure on numerous suppliers in low-wage regions to maintain low wages and thin their margins to attract FDI and contracts. The extracted value is 'dark' in the sense that the valorization that would have otherwise gone to high-wage domestic workers in the core value-regime is unaccounted for—unseen—on the official books but nonetheless is extracted through lower labor costs and higher surplus value for the automakers. This benefits both corporations and customers through potentially higher profit margins and lower prices than what could be offered otherwise at the expense of workers in the peripheries (Clelland 2014). Through establishing these (dark) value chains, value in motion flows increasingly outside the core value-regime.

This *regionalization* obscures what it means to analyze a value-regime because the rough equating of the nation-state and its socio-economic-political arrangements are no longer adequate when an increasing portion of the value chain is outsourced to regions with different socio-economic-political arrangements. The value-systems of the firms and their suppliers are incomplete without reference to the dynamic relations of the entire region and multiple countries, and the high profits of transnational corporations cannot be understood without recognizing the larger portion of cheap labor undergirding it. China also plays a role, as even though its JV requirements prevent China from being a direct valorization boon for German and US workers, it nevertheless supports the financial health of the parent companies.

This holds especially for Volkswagen because balancing wage, humanization, and job control imperatives determined through codetermination with the productivity imperative has been a continuous struggle in Germany. After the release of Harbour data in 2005 comparing European productivity levels revealed that VW group took on average twice as many assembly hours per vehicle as its rivals, the CEO of the Volkswagen brand made a surprising but revealing statement: "The German part of Volkswagen now survives only because VW works abroad or subsidiaries with the help of cross-subsidies" (Jürgens 2008: 57). Although VW continues to improve productivity in Germany, this nevertheless indicates that the pressures for internal reform were partially dissipated through globalization, outsourcing, and strong foreign sales. In this way, German high-wage, high-road production appears *dependent* upon regionalization to low-wage countries to the East and the Chinese boom (Jürgens 2009: 234). While cooperation and 'codetermination' in a specific sense, i.e., kaizen, is necessary for high productivity, the *German tradition* of codetermination and humanization that renders productivity concerns secondary appears to be sustainable only if it is limited to a nationally based labor elite and *consciously not applied* to foreign subsidiaries with lower wages and unilateral management enforcement of benchmark lean practices. In other words, the German codetermination system can be conceptualized as one node in a *globalized two-tier system* whose persistence can only be understood with reference to its relationship to the other node of low-wage labor that does not get the full benefits of works councils, codetermination, or, in some instances, union representation.

On the surface, it appears German firms have partially avoided productivity pressure by maintaining humanized high-wage work in Germany despite a productivity gap, yet comparing German firms abroad versus domestically reveals how domestic humanization and high-wages are subsidized by 'management by stress' and lower wages abroad. Less productivity pressure for German workers required more productivity pressure and less valorization for foreign workers. Domestic work processes have also reorganized toward LP and pressures to make concessions were also present, but the decline of working conditions, wages, or worker power was far less in Germany than in the US or compared to German firms abroad (Pries 2003; Jürgens and Krzywdzinski 2009). Globalization represents a radical change in the distribution of value and job opportunities, yet German companies do not appear to be globalizing in a fundamentally different way from their competitors. That German firms do not purposefully transplant the labor empowering aspects or high wages of the German system to their foreign plants hints that German management does not operate on a 'humanized logic' fundamentally different from the 'logic of capital' but are legally and structurally constrained in Germany to work within cooperative systems that have produced humanized results within the value-regime *but not beyond it*.

This question of "how can German workers maintain more autonomy, higher wages, and more humanization" has remained a fundamental question in the German value-regime since the beginning. The answer has differed over time, e.g., maintain craft systems at the expense of increasing production, exploit foreign forced labor, recruit *Gastarbeiter* to do undesirable jobs, automate undesirable jobs and employ new production concepts, and aggressively globalize, but the answer almost always involved sacrifices for (usually) non-German workers. Thus, the 'humane' and 'cooperative' German model has always had a darker side. This does not mean codetermination is not desirable but invites contemplation of what conditions might allow codetermination to extend beyond the German labor elite. Although it may appear German firms have found ways to evade productivity pressure and social domination, the thorny questions of social domination and balancing costs across the transnational German auto industry has prevented German codetermination from spreading the same way Fordism and lean production has.

A survey of global production processes demonstrates the extent to which lean principles have become the global benchmark of productivity that is nearly universally implemented, albeit hybridized. This was seen in Mexico, Eastern European countries, and China, in addition to domestic American and German firms. Furthermore, the pursuit of LP as global manufacturing standard practice has been observed in other countries such as France (Fridenson 2009: 169; Pardi 2020: 122–124), Brazil (Marx, Marotti de Mello, and Ferreira de Lara 2020: 354), Italy (Calabrese 2020; Pulignano 2020), and Australia (Clibborn et al. 2020: 260–261). After decades of misrecognition, trial and error, and relational change between labor and management, the productivity enhancing core of LP has generalized across the auto industry worldwide, just as Fordism did in the decades after WWII. As Weyer (2011) assesses the global competition for productivity, he notes,

> In the past, [productivity increase] was more possible on their own than it is today by the implementation of lean production systems. Nowadays, these methods are known nearly everywhere and continue to be applied. However, they will usually not cause a leap in production. (3284)

"Stringent implementation of lean production principles no longer leads to success," because LP has been generalized to the extent that the productivity gap has narrowed enormously for most companies and therefore even if lean practices are "methodically pursued" they "no longer lead to a leap forward in production" (Weyer 2011: 3279; see Holweg 2008: 6–8). Therefore, even as Japanese producers remain the productivity leaders (Liker 2021), LP's generalization means that the productivity gap is no longer as influential in terms of competitive advantage as in the 1970s–1990s.

It should be unsurprising then that globalization and shifting production to low-wage areas has become a new source of competitive advantage to complement the pursuit of higher productivity. For most companies, the simultaneous pursuit of higher productivity in all locations and the search for low-wage production indicates that this is not a question of *either/or* but *both/and*. The opening of previously closed markets also meant that the relative fortunes of auto companies became more based on their strategic skill in entering markets and partnering to expand capacity in the right places for cheap labor and new sales. In this way, strategic maneuvering and foresight such as Volkswagen's early entry into China or the exploding popularity of SUVs in the United States are historical contingencies which have little relationship to relative productivity levels. Just as in the 1950s and 1960s when there was relative productivity parity for major producers, factors such as style, public image, or appeal to identity may be more important for realization than advantages derived from higher productivity. In such a situation, there is enough contingency and space in the global market for multiple transnational auto companies to find sales and profit around the world. This is one reason why the prediction by Womack, Jones, and Roos (2007 [1990]) that lean producers would overrun mass producers was wrong, not just because mass producers gradually came to adopt the core lean practices, but because the globalized world with millions or billions of unreached potential car buyers had enough space for firms around the world to profit from globalization simultaneously. Simply put, the globalization race is not as much a race for productivity as a race to enter markets, form effective partnerships, and exploit cheap labor—which requires a different set of strategic skills.

Nevertheless, this can only remain true so long as there are sources of growth that 'cures all ills' and creative destructive innovations in productivity do not appear to widen the productivity gap and make productivity pressure and social domination a renewed concern. The decades of growth in the 1950s and 1960s also appeared unstoppable but were ultimately followed by decades of low growth. Thus, it must be asked how long the current growth wave will be sustained or will global markets soon be saturated? The answer may depend on the political struggles that decide how social systems, especially states and businesses, address climate change or the development of new forms of mobility that may fundamentally change the production and business models of the global auto industry.

In making these decisions, struggles to promote *environmental values* such as reducing pollution and fighting climate change come into conflict with *the flow of value in motion*. The EV transition proposes a manufacturing revolution that may result in a net loss of jobs and/or a shifting of production locations both within and between countries. Because maintaining value in motion remains central to the decision-making of so many value-systems, including businesses, labor organizations, and governments, any push for green technologies cannot be done for environmental values alone, but must consider how any given move may disrupt, enable, or disable capital accumulation. This is especially high stakes considering China's growth in the EV sector, as it represents an opportunity for China to reset the global competitive landscape to a situation where Chinese expertise in green technology dwarfs that of legacy automakers in the US and Germany. Cheap Chinese labor and potential productivity advantages may cause Chinese firms to exert productivity pressure and put downward pressure on wages on the rest of the global industry. This makes geopolitics, environmental values, and economic concerns vital to the future of mobility and the EV transition.

It is unclear whether Industry 4.0 techniques and technologies will become the industry standard and whether companies will face productivity pressure and competitive disadvantage if they do not adopt Industry 4.0. With this uncertainty, some analysts recommend focusing on improving production processes through the proven lean methods rather than waiting for the "promised land" of Industry 4.0 (Rüttimann and Stöckli 2016: 499). Industry 4.0 should be thought of as "the topping on that cake. It makes Lean Production more flexible; whether it makes it faster, smoother, and more stable and more accurate has to be proven" (Rüttimann and Stöckli 2016: 500; Jürgens 2021: 10). The final point is crucial. That the goal of these new technologies is to make a faster, smoother, and more stable production process is not in doubt—especially in the context of the intense worldwide productivity race—but that new technologies and processes must *prove themselves* demonstrates how the implicit faith that increased automation and new technology always increases productivity has come under scrutiny.

While there is certainly 'hype' behind Industry 4.0, consider how promises of improved productivity and industrial progress allow certain value-systems to accumulate capital such as financial markets or machine tool manufacturers, but not necessarily enable the auto companies to accumulate more capital. In other words, new technology that disappoints automakers because they were 'overhyped' may still accumulate capital for machine tool manufacturers, tech companies, or venture finance firms. Therefore, there is always the danger of a gap arising between the discourse surrounding a product and its actual performance. Only substantiated performance can generate productivity pressure while hype without performance can be counterproductive. In this way, the theory posed here provides a framework to differentiate between empty techno-hype and change that pushes the productivity and the capitalist historical dynamic forward.

The discussion of Industry 4.0 falls within the recent wave of automation discourse in the 2010s and 2020s (e.g., Brynjolfsson and McAfee 2011, 2014; Frey and Osborne 2013; Ford 2015; Kaplan 2015; Frey 2019; Susskind 2020). Most of these publications take a broad look at the capability of new technologies and judge that they may have powerful disruptive effects on the economy, including predictions that new forms of automation such as improved robotization and Industry 4.0 may automate the routine work of assembly lines, welders, and other jobs central to auto production (see Frey and Osborne 2013). Although automation may be a real possibility in some industries, such predictions when applied to the auto industry fail to account for how highly automated the auto industry already is and how the remaining manual work is not due to its technical impossibility, but because continuously improving multiskilled workers stripped of 'waste' can perform at the level of speed and flexibility deemed socially necessary. What is deemed socially necessary is not just determined by achieving smooth production processes, but also the ability to flexibly react to consumer demands to better ensure value realization (see Krzywdzinski 2020a, 2020b; Jürgens 2023: 347–352). Even as the assembly line is automatable to some degree, as Volkswagen has demonstrated, the reality of needed flexibility has meant that humans on the assembly line are still the socially necessary standard *unless and until* a new generation of technologies *proves* to outdo humans at these tasks and generate more capital for value-systems that adopt these technologies. It is unclear whether Industry 4.0 or other new technologies will be capable of this (see Boudette 2018).

This critique of Industry 4.0 is not to argue that lean production really *is* the 'end of history,' rather, it is to reiterate that technological capabilities *in the abstract* do not generate productivity pressure and social domination. *Only when applied in capitalist production and proven to improve the flow of value in motion and capital accumulation can the technology take on the standard of socially necessary labor time.* Many technologies since the advent of Fordism have temporarily become socially necessary and were then replaced with new technologies that become the new socially necessary standard. Subsequently, automation remains very high in many production areas today (Krzywdzinski 2020a; Jürgens 2021; Jürgens 2023). The task set before the developers of Industry 4.0 technologies is to go beyond shallow *claims* of 'progress' and toward *enforcing* 'progress' on an industry by pushing forward socially necessary labor time and ultimately toward accumulating capital. If companies that adopt Industry 4.0 develop a substantial productivity gap with those that do not, then adopting Industry 4.0 takes on this enforcement power and generates productivity pressure. It is too soon to predict if this will become the case.

Nevertheless, the race for productivity goes on, and this impulse has only gotten stronger in the last few decades. Therefore, even if Industry 4.0 disappoints or even proves counterproductive, the continuous search for new productivity advantages pushes each firm to achieve not just incremental but even revolutionary advances over their competitors. Perhaps advancements in AI and improving the capabilities of robots to perform non-routine tasks will eventually generate adequate assembly robots, but this is likely decades away, if viable at all. Only time will tell if this struggle to set new standards of socially necessary labor time will result in a new wave of automation or if the flexibility and adaptability of human workers prevails in the coming decades.

CHAPTER 6

Productivity as Social Imperative—towards a Critical Theory of Automation, Technological Displacement, and Social Domination

1 The Drivers of History

Systemic arrangements of business, labor, and government are of vital importance in understanding how productivity development, automation, and technological displacement play out within value-regimes. The United States and Germany diverged based on the path dependent developments and characteristics of their value-regimes yet often converged in technological and organizational practices, *especially* when those practices increased productivity. By examining tendencies of divergence and convergence, a critical theory of automation and technological displacement can be outlined. Expanding upon existing theories, we conclude by critically analyzing the historical lessons to construct this critical theory.

The social, economic, and political impact of the automobile on modern society is nearly incalculable. Its proliferation has sped up the pace of life, forged new social norms, generated technical achievements in product and production technology, and formed gigantic transnational businesses that put millions of workers and machines to work. The industry's history was not purely contingent but shaped by omnipresent social domination that pressured all value-systems toward increasing productivity, which influenced the development of technical and organizational systems that ultimately eliminated humans from many production processes. Much has been written about the production changes and automation in the auto industry (e.g., Arnold and Faurote 1915; Hounshell 1985; Flink 1988; Jürgens et al. 1993; Womack et al. 2007 [1990]); Jürgens 2023), yet much has remained at the level of description, explaining 'what is the case.' This book has aimed beyond examining 'what is the case' to discover 'what lies behind it' (Luhmann 1994). The concepts theorized here—social domination, productivity pressure, productivity as social imperative etc.—are evidenced throughout the industrial history of both countries.

A *Longue Durée* examination reveals consistent themes. An awareness of, grappling with, and promotion of productivity remained continuously relevant. Maintaining or securing productivity leadership was a frequent goal

 DOI:10.1163/9789004736719_008

and benchmarking to the productivity leader became increasingly important for both economic survival and social image/self-description. Automation was often considered synonymous with productivity gains, but paradigm shifts in the 1980s demonstrated how *the most automated systems are not always the most productive*. These dynamics are explicit in statements within both countries.

Confronting the 'Japanese challenge' was urgent in 1990s Germany as Herrigel and Sabel (1999) describe, "Thousands of the finest industrial producers in Germany have all been struggling throughout the decade to make themselves cheaper, higher quality, and more flexible producers, or be competed into oblivion by those who can" (28). This UAW member interviewed on a 1957 Edward R. Murrow broadcast expressed labor's ambivalence on the social effects automation but ultimately accepted the importance of automation for maintaining American leadership,

> No, none of us, and I don't think our union, kicks about the introduction of automation. We welcome it because unless this country automates, it's going to be in rough shape in competition with other countries. The problem for us is who pays the cost of automation. The UAW is for automation. We're for progress, but we are not for the working people, who are the least able to afford it, to pay the total cost of automation, and in terms of human misery and suffering, that is exactly what is going on in Detroit and in the country. (Murrow 1957: 10)

This speech from a works council meeting at Benz in the 1920s conveyed the importance of improving productivity to manage costs—a perennial problem in the German industry,

> If we ask ourselves where our high manufacturing costs come from, this is based on that ... in the working time we expend to finish an automobile, we always have to reckon with a number of working hours that sometimes amounts to twice as much of what we know from foreign factories ... it is impossible for us to compete on the world market with such working hours ... We must urgently adapt to American manufacture, while always considering German quality. (Stahlmann 1992: 158–159; translation mine)[1]

1 Original German text: "Wenn wir uns fragen, woher unsere hohen Herstellungspriese kommen, so ist das damit begründet ... dass wir in der Arbeitszeit, die wir aufzuwenden haben, um ein Automobil fertig zu stellen, immer auch mit einer Arbeitsstundenzahl rechnen müssen, die teilweise das Doppelte von dem betragt, was wir von ausländischen Fabriken wissen ... mit solcher Arbeitsstundenzahl ist es uns unmöglich, auf dem Weltmarkt zu konkurrieren ...

According to a statement from vice chairman of GM John F. Smith in 1991, lean reforms were "forced by global competition" as the company sought,

> world class standards as the competitive benchmarks for our products and processes ... We're aiming for best-in-class products, as defined by the customer; lean organization and management, as measured against world competition, and low cost positions, so we can be price competitive. (General Motors Heritage Center 1991: 1–2)

Even as Kern and Schumann (1998) advised against Germany adopting lean production in favor of new production concepts, they argued that NPC advances productivity as an approach that, "centers on the further development of productivity and innovation resources and the struggle of technological leadership must rely on the cultivation and development of productive intelligence and creative human capacity" (13).[2] Henry Ford II (1955) framed accepting the creative destructive dynamism of capitalism as the best way to harness the productive potential of new technologies,

> Part of the price of progress may be the willingness to accept change in the time, place, and type of employment that is available. In order to reap the full advantage of the new technologies, we must avoid the fatal freezing of men, machines and methods into rigid patterns. (16)

Finally, Hans-Jürgen Ehmer, Head of Production at Volkswagen de Mexico explained in 1984 why rationalization was necessary for Volkswagen,

> We are forced to constantly modernize and rationalize if we want to keep the Federal Republic of Germany a production site for the automobile industry in the long-term. There is no 'Worldwide-Stop-Rationalization-Agreement,' as the competition also tries to keep or reduce their manufacturing costs through constant rationalization. (Ehmer 1984: 5; translation mine)[3]

Wir müssen uns unbedingt auf amerikanische Fabrikation einstellen, immer natürlich unter Berücksichtigung deutscher Qualität" (Stahlmann 1992: 159).

2 Original German text: "demgegenüber muß ein Konzept, für das die weitere Entfaltung der Produktivitäts- und Innovationsressourcen und der Kampf um Technologieführerschaft im Zentrum steht, auf die Pflege und den Ausbau der Produktionsintelligenz und des kreativen Humanvermögens setzen" (Kern and Schumann 1998: 13).

3 Original German text: "Wir sind zur ständigen Modernisierung und Rationalisierung gezwungen, wenn wir den Produktionsstandort Bundesrepublik Deutschland für die Automobilindustrie auf Dauer erhalten wollen. Es gibt keine 'Weltrationalisierungs-Stop-Abkommen',

With no global constraints, all firms must rationalize to survive.

All these quotes share the same preoccupation with productivity, reflecting aspects of how the social domination of maintaining the socially necessary standard of productivity is a constant concern for management and labor alike. They demonstrate how both value-regimes were caught up in this capitalist historical dynamic. They must run production at the socially necessary pace or risk negative economic and social outcomes. This historical dynamic forms the core of the critical theory of automation and technological displacement.

2 Productivity Pressure as Social Domination

Modern capitalist societies exhibit a historical dynamic characterized by continuous pursuit of productivity that continuously redefine productivity norms and value. The highest level of productivity sustained in any production process changes what is considered "normative production" within a given time frame, for example, the benchmark of how many hours it takes to manufacture a vehicle. Since value is rooted in *socially necessary* labor time, redefining what is *socially necessary* redefines the standard of value. Valorization processes that fail to meet the socially necessary standard are 'pulled' by a kind of 'gravity' to meet or exceed the productive standard because failing to meet the socially necessary productive norm is disadvantageous. Strictly within the valorization process, failing to meet the socially necessary norm means the value of commodities from the slow production process is higher than that of value-systems that meet the productive norms, which usually results in higher production costs and higher prices, which is especially unfavorable when price competition is salient.

What characterizes modern capitalism from other forms of human organization is how, by universalizing valorization and capital accumulation as foundational social imperatives, *productivity increases become integral to the system* which makes production transformations routine and ongoing. No production processes are ever set in stone, nor can they afford to be, as the never-ending pursuit for higher efficiency 'devalues' processes slower than the socially necessary standard. To paraphrase Marx (1963 [1852]: 15), capital and labor make commodities, but they do not make them just as they please; they do not make them in production processes chosen by themselves, but under circumstances directly encountered, given, and transmitted from the past. This

auch die Konkurrenz versucht, ihre Herstellkosten durch ständige Rationalisierung niedrig zu halten bzw. zu senken" (Ehmer 1984: 5).

"given and transmitted past" encompasses all past productivity developments that have become socially necessary productive standards. The gravitational pull of value and socially necessary labor time *delimits feasible combinations of capital and labor.*

Businesses and workers alike are subject to "impersonal, increasingly rationalized, structural imperatives and constraints that cannot fully be grasped in terms of class domination, or, more generally, in terms of the concrete domination of social groupings or of institutional agencies of the state and/or the economy" (Postone 2017: 47). This is the *first sense* in which social domination is *social*, i.e., that these dynamics, imperatives, and constraints originate from *capitalism as a social form based on value in motion*, rather than the concrete operations of any single or collective labor organization, business, or government. These temporal dynamics also *lie outside direct control by any of these systems*, as even though temporal processes within individual systems can be controlled, the socially compelling temporal norms for systems of that type (e.g., auto companies) are set beyond the control of any individual system.[4] Thus, as Rosa (2015: 309) argues, temporal acceleration of technical, organizational, and social change is "almost entirely impervious to social or political interventions." Because there is no determinate locus of social domination, these dynamics do not appear to be 'social' at all, just as fish do not notice the water they swim in (Postone 2017: 47).

The *second sense* in which social domination is social is how systems support productivity pressure through communication. Among the relevant social

4 This analysis moves beyond approaches that center class struggle as *the* way to understand capitalist modernity. E.g., in 'traditional Marxism,' capitalism is analyzed as class relations grounded in private property and mediated by the market (Postone 2015: 7). 'Social domination,' in this view, is framed as class domination and exploitation with contradiction arising from the capitalist relations of production coming into conflict with the forces of production, understood as the working class (Marx 1978 [1859]: 4; Postone 2015: 7). Domination of the capitalist class over the working class was certainly present in the historical narrative, especially in the US. However, the social domination elaborated here goes beyond management versus labor or company versus company dynamics to identify social domination as the compulsion of temporal productive norms rooted in the fundamental structure of capital as value in motion. Once the foundational categories and processes of capitalist modernity—e.g., commodity, value, capital—are solidified, universalized, and put into motion, the dynamics they generate take on a 'life of their own,' a reality *sui generis*, that place imperatives and constraints on social action. Thus, the 'traditional' framework that argues the workers are unfree, but the capitalists are free is incomplete. Both are free in certain ways and unfree in others. Social domination signifies the domination of the social whole by capitalism, including capitalists and workers. In fact, the unfreedom experienced by capitalists mediates the unfreedom of the working class as their actions that appear as domination by management often are pressured by capital's domination of society.

systems, high productivity is nearly universally framed as positive, which obscures how maintaining productivity at the socially necessary level entails social domination. Because conforming to productivity norms is 'desirable' and systems actively participate in maintaining them, the *compulsion* to conform to them appears unremarkable—unless *failing to conform* to them produces disturbance or crisis. Even workers, who are generally against high labor intensity for themselves, are usually in favor of increasing productivity within firms or society generally, especially if the responsibility for productivity increase falls to machines instead of workers and doing so increases wages and benefits. As Greenhouse (2019) recounts from the president of the clothing workers' union, "I even believe in helping an employer function more productively … For then, we will have a claim to higher wages, shorter hours, and greater participation in the benefits of running a smooth industrial machine" (337). Pure Luddism did not appear in any statements from labor or management of either country because they both benefited from keeping value in motion and implicitly understood that doing so required maintaining certain productive norms. The US and Germany developed different value-regimes in path dependent directions that at times helped or hurt their auto industries in adapting to these everchanging productive norms, but nevertheless all parties accepted that, no matter how their production processes and industrial relations are arranged, they must always somehow address the 'productivity problem.'

2.1 *Competition and 'Competitiveness'*

In Marxian theory, competition is the primary means by which productive norms generalize. As Marx (1976 [1867]) explains,

> The law of the determination of value by labor-time makes itself felt to the individual capitalist who applies the new method of production by compelling him to sell his goods under their social value; this same law, acting as a coercive law of competition, forces his competitors to adopt the new method. (436)

Pressure to adopt new productive norms does not always require direct economic competition, as observed in how communications from social systems, e.g., the Harbour Report, supplement economic pressure with socio-communicative influence. The forced rationalization of Germany under the Nazis also demonstrated how direct competition is not necessary to compel change if there is a more productive model to emulate and the will and resources necessary to emulate it. Thus, pressure to conform to socially necessary productive norms has a *social aspect beyond economic market outcomes.*

In addition, other forms of competition beyond direct market competition have increased as Brown (2015: 36) argues that under neoliberalism more domains of life have become modeled on the competitive market, where individuals and firms are expected to accrue capital, maximize ratings, and enhance competitive positioning. Competing for the best hours per vehicle, quality awards, or other competitive rankings reflects the proliferation of different forms of competition that encourage convergence toward the socially necessary productive norm.

Though competitive dynamics are consequential, rhetoric surrounding 'competitiveness' is a fetishistic term that obscures the underlying capitalist dynamic. At their core, competitive struggles are about *controlling time*. Competition around HPV benchmarks is obviously about time, but even quality competitions reflect how defects emerge as a 'cheating' of time in production passed on as externalities to consumers. Development and design processes are placed under productivity pressure too as shortening the time it takes to design and release products has declined since the 1990s under pressure from lean competitors who developed faster and cheaper product development and design processes and new computer design technologies (Womack et al. 2007 [1990]: 105–140; Krzywdzinski 2020a: 22–29). The quasi-autonomous moments of value in motion each have their own evolutionary histories that intersect with the valorization processes discussed here, e.g., in realization/circulation with the acceleration of turnover times or advances in transportation, distribution with the changing geographies of production and struggles over wages, and in investment such as the invention of financial instruments and technologies (Marx 1978 [1885], 1981 [1894]; Sturgeon et al. 2009; Covarrubias and Ramírez Perez 2020b, 2020c). Equally detailed histories could be written about productivity development, competition, and social domination in these other arenas.

2.2 *Mastering Time*

The key to pioneering socially necessary productivity norms is to *master time* comprehensively throughout production, including product development, preventing defects, maintaining peaceful labor relations to prevent disruption, and deploying technology and labor at the level of skill, sophistication, and speed deemed socially necessary. There is not one single productive arrangement that accomplishes this, but nevertheless each process has a socially necessary labor time norm that needs to be reached to achieve the expected valorization. Time is not a given unmoving frame but is actively made by processes. These processes do not just occur *in time* but *create temporal worlds* which are reformulated with each productivity increase (Harvey 2017).

To effectively master time, social domination must become *self-domination*. Self-discipline or self-subjectivation to internalize this processual and temporal domination aids in fitting the socially necessary temporal pattern (see Foucault 1995 [1975]; Brown 2015; Postone 2017: 47–48). The idea that hard work is necessary and beneficial for every person has been ingrained into the core of modern identity since the Protestant Reformation (Weber 2002 [1905]). Through education, religious teaching, parenting, and work, people are inculcated with messages that encourage this self-discipline, and they become accomplices to social domination as workers perform according to productivity norms and productivity improvements are pursued. This socialization aligns private interests with the socially determined interests set by social conditions independent of the private individual, e.g., self-valorization requires work performance according to socially necessary labor time standards (Nicolaus 1968: 48). This is not totalizing, however, as workers also seek to shape productivity norms to be more ergonomic or humanized. This is why industrial relations can be a source of divergence, as mastery over time requires industrial relations to mediate the labor-management struggle resulting from an imperfect internalization of the productivity imperative among workers, especially when productivity norms approach or exceed sustainable physical and mental limits.

Cooperative industrial relations may foster time-mastery on the shopfloor within the value-regime and yet still experience social domination from productive norms outside the value-regime. Global productivity standards became increasingly important over the course of the 20th century as automakers transnationalized sales and production, so that even if workers and management mutually consented to a certain level of productivity within a value-regime, the global determination of socially necessary labor time may still apply productivity pressure on a macro level. Systems can choose to lag in productivity, but this comes with tradeoffs, e.g., less use values, the tradeoffs that come with trade restrictions, or results in lower profits or financial losses. Productivity leadership confers advantages in capital accumulation, e.g., by underselling the competition to gain market share, but maintaining this position requires vigilance, a constant search for innovation, and ensuring labor peace to maintain time mastery. *There are consequences to avoiding social domination just as there are to conforming to the socially necessary norms*. The viable socio-historic combinations of labor and capital are delimited by these norms and all systems must respond to the challenge these norms represent. This constitutes *an immanent necessity and a form of unfreedom* (Postone 2017: 43).

If modernity under the *dialectic of enlightenment* entails a constant struggle for survival, then the temporal processes of social domination reflect *how the parameters of that struggle are continuously redefined* (Postone 1993; Horkheimer and Adorno 2001 [1947]). In the beginnings of the American industry, mastering time entailed utilizing skilled workers on multipurpose machines, but a decade later firms that adopted the assembly line, flow orientation, and single purpose machines thrived. The Fordist challenge necessitated rationalization for survival, which made some skills more valuable while others, e.g., the skills of fitters, disappeared. The terms of what it took to master time and survive changed for both workers and firms in tandem with the transformations of socially necessary temporal-productive norms.

We have observed that consequential productive developments occurred in decades-long waves of creative destruction. The rise of Fordism in the US, the development of automation in the 1950s, and the rise of lean production can be categorized as major trends that impacted the long-term productive trajectory of automakers. Each development had its own characteristics and effects on companies and workers but nevertheless were patterned in similar ways. Each movement constituted a major leap in productivity that established new productivity leaders and laggards with different positive or negative consequences depending on how the new productivity problem was tackled within different value-regimes. Each development saw the rise and fall of automakers depending on their capacity to adapt to new socially necessary norms and/or evade the productivity pressure via alternative strategies. Change was not always linear, as the productivity gap between the standard-bearer and the competition varied, sometimes narrowing, sometimes widening, but nearly always pushing productivity forward over time. Narrowing the productivity gap sometimes took decades, as observed in the German industry up until the 1950s or the US industry between the 1980s and the 2000s. The usefulness of this theoretical approach is how the dynamics of each era can be explained through the theory, not because the dynamics are identical, but because the capitalist historical dynamic remains valid as long as modern societies are based on capital as value in motion.

2.3 *Automation and/or Productivity*

From the industry's beginnings until the 1970s, it was axiomatic that new technology and automation were nearly synonymous with productivity improvements. This assumption was challenged since the 1970s as lean methods did not center on automating production to increase productivity, and lean producers were hesitant to adopt automation that interfered with the flexibility of production processes (Ohno 1988; Liker 2021). Automation efforts in the 1980s in both value-regimes were disappointing and failed to sufficiently narrow the productivity gap with lean competitors (Finkelstein 2003; Jürgens et al.

1993; Jürgens 2023). A technological determinist would find this baffling, but this critical theory posits that *fixed capital also faces productivity pressure* just like workers. The advanced technologies deployed at Halle 54 or Hamtramck were not immune from productivity pressure because they are machines. The lean assembly lines with less automation set the standards of socially necessary labor time, thus applying productivity pressure on the lagging processes, both machines and workers alike. It is not enough for new *theoretically* more productive technologies to exist, but they only become socially necessary if they are concretely applied to valorization processes and genuinely trivialize time and space more than the alternatives. In this sense, neither technology nor management dominate workers on their own, but *social domination* appears as the consequence of capital accumulation and the continuous pursuit of productivity. Technology *can* be used to strategically empower or disempower workers, and management exploits workers to extract surplus labor (see Marx 1967 [1867]; Reynolds 1989; Kern and Schumann 1987; Meyer 2004). However, *social domination* should be distinguished analytically from technological or class domination even as they are also intertwined.

Both fixed capital and labor are subsumed within value in motion and are both pressured to continuously pursue higher productivity. In the contemporary auto industry, the flexibility of humans makes them essential to areas like assembly, while others are dominated by machines because their speed and precision far outstrip human capability, with convergence of automation levels in nearly all major auto companies (see Jürgens and Meißner 2005: 42; Jürgens and Krzywdzinski 2020a; Jürgens 2021; Jürgens 2023). The increasing complexity of vehicles and adjusting to the changing product requirements meant a linear process from less to more automation did not always occur, but nevertheless production processes were under productivity pressures to maintain efficiency regardless of these challenges. If technologies cope with speed, accuracy, and flexibility challenges better than human workers, then they can become socially necessary. There is a struggle between the mental and physical capabilities of the human body, which possess great adaptability and flexibility but limited stamina, speed, and precision, versus the limited adaptability and flexibility of machines that usually have greater stamina, speed, and precision. Capital as value in motion determines which combinations of capital and labor become socially necessary in which production processes based on what sustainably sets the norms of socially necessary labor time.

There can be no adequate autonomous theory of automation and technological displacement without understanding social domination. Technological displacement only becomes a social problem in capitalist society and is generated through its historical dynamics. Automation only becomes an imperative when it coincides with the broader social imperative to increase productivity and fulfills the requirements to become socially necessary. Recognizing this explains why automation succeeds and why it sometimes fails. There is no linear climb from less to more automation in all production processes, but a dynamic struggle between multiple—sometimes contradictory—demands for speed, ergonomics, precision, flexibility, efficiency, low-costs, innovation, and productivity. Concrete production processes with varied emphases differed between value-regimes but nevertheless were evaluated against the socially general productive norms that exerted a kind of gravity to pull production toward those norms. Tendencies toward convergence and divergence appeared, with differences both in how automation was implemented and how the consequences of technological displacement were mitigated. Nevertheless, major trends were detectible, e.g., the adoption of Fordism, the rise of transfer machines and later robots, and the hybridization of lean principles. This demonstrated how concerns with increasing productivity played a major role in these movements, illuminating the underlying historical dynamic operating in the *Longue Durée* development of industrial history.

2.4 *Micro, Mezzo, and Macro Level Productivity Pressure*

It is useful to distinguish how these dynamics played out on different scales. Theorizing on a micro, mezzo, and macro level reveals different expressions of productivity pressure and social domination on each level.

First is the *micro level* productivity pressure to manage the daily control of production on the shopfloor with given combinations of machines, workers, and materials. At this level are struggles to operate the machines without breakdowns and for workers to utilize their brains and bodies in the expected movements. It involves both concrete labor processes, e.g., the physical labor of machines and muscles, and the abstract valorization of workers and objects according to socially necessary labor time standards. Questions of mastering time involve whether production is on schedule to meet quotas or how to solve production problems. Workers and foremen often struggle over productivity by implicitly or explicitly negotiating effort-wage bargains. Workers also negotiate with other workers in relation to abstract time expectations, making statements to each other such as "Slow down … if you work too quickly, they're going to raise your rate," or "if you [work quickly], then I'm expected to do it, too" (Stockman 2021: 100–101). Grievances are dealt with first on this level, and shopfloor actions from absenteeism to strikes can disrupt or stop the flow of value in motion (Norsworthy and Zabala 1985).

The second *mezzo level* constitutes productivity pressure within the value-system and/or the value-regime. The structural arrangements on the micro and mezzo level are shaped by the legal and contractual framework of the value-regime, e.g., the New Deal/Treaty of Detroit framework in the United States versus the codetermination system with works councils, unions, and representation on company boards in Germany. The legal framework provides the 'rules of the game' of industrial relations which shape productivity development. Culture and history are important as different cultural affinities and educational systems produced different skill resources between the value-regimes. Productivity pressure applies here in terms of managing labor and capital conflict on a larger scale through collective bargaining and/or codetermination to develop medium to long-term investments in productivity development, e.g., worker training or fixed capital investment. Productivity pressure through competition may apply between firms operating within the same value-regime and/or between plants within the same value-system or value-regime.

The third *macro level* productivity pressure comprises the pressure to conform to the *global standard* of socially necessary labor time for production processes. Here, the productive capacity and the advantages and disadvantages of value-regime arrangements come to the fore to shape productivity differences between value-systems. Productivity gaps matter most at this level as penetration of foreign competition into value-regimes through transplants or imports has consequences for the employment and financial health of the domestic firms. Globalization makes international competition and benchmarking more important, thus increasing this macro level productivity pressure for all participants in the global industry. Management-labor coordination is imperative as productivity pressures come from *outside the direct control* of either party, and firm survival is often on the line when macro level pressures are intense. The question is whether a value-regime *enables or hinders* value-systems to become the productivity leader or to narrow productivity gaps should they emerge.

The 'productivity problem' always needs to be addressed in some form on all three levels. There is pressure to maintain productivity from the expectations of individual worker productivity to plant or collective bargaining to the competition between foreign and domestic automakers. There is both *generic time pressure* to be productive according to the capacities of the built system and an *ever-changing specific productivity pressure* to valorize at the speed of socially necessary labor time. Both the productivity leaders and non-leaders are dominated by time and the need for productivity in different ways. The productivity leader must further improve productivity to remain productivity leader, while the others are pressured to raise productivity even faster than the leader to catch up, or they will continue to face disadvantages if the productivity gap is not addressed. How to meet these expectations is variable by value-regime, but that productivity pressure *must be addressed* is invariable.

There are circumstances where a certain level may be more important to manage than the others. For example, in the US during the 1970s–1980s, macro level productivity pressure from Japan was the most urgent problem, but closing the productivity gap took major reforms from the shopfloor to the bargaining table. Productive weaknesses and difficulty adapting to change stemming from combative industrial relations from the micro level to the mezzo level hurt the ability of the domestic firms to effectively respond to macro level productivity pressures. For Germany during this period, the relative lack of competition made mezzo concerns more pressing, i.e., how to codetermine the execution of the diversified quality production strategy through new production concepts and humanization for long-term productivity development. Imbalances at this level generated a crisis that prompted reforms that were partially inspired by the macro level standard of lean production (Krzywdzinski 2020b). In the first half of the 20th century, micro and mezzo developments were more important in the US as clear productivity leadership made the macro level irrelevant, and struggles were primarily over how to distribute the gains resulting from high productivity. Meanwhile, the 'American Challenge' made macro level pressures a major concern in Germany as the growth model focused on exports, making automation imperative to achieve the mass production standard (Hilger 2003; Baccaro and Pontusson 2016). Identifying productivity pressure at all three levels and the different concerns within each is useful for expanding the concept of social domination.

3 Communication and the Social Logic of Capital

Multiple social systems regularly communicate about productivity including corporations, labor unions, governments, scientists, news media, consultant firms, and technology developers. A range of communicative mediums facilitate this including press releases, advertisements, technology conferences, social research, benchmarking studies, and news reports. Each plays a role in how social systems observe and communicate about productivity developments and what constitutes modern 'progress.' In their communications, participants, analysts, and observers make distinctions between productive/unproductive, profitable/unprofitable, innovative/noninnovative, viable/nonviable business decisions and so on. Such distinctions enforce social domination as value-systems seek to be categorized on one side of the distinction and not the other.

Statistics such as HPV, production quotas, sales figures, and market share also communicate as systems decide whether the numbers signify positive or negative developments for a value-system. From a Luhmannian systems theory perspective, communications between systems describe how social domination takes on a specifically *social* character.

These communications are so ubiquitous that the term *domination* may appear strange. This ubiquity, however, is precisely how domination is exercised *because* it is normalized, not despite it. The more convergence of communicative patterns appears around certain distinctions in multiple social systems (e.g., high productivity is positive, and low productivity is negative) the easier it becomes to negatively label systems falling short of expectations and compel them to change. Even though Luhmannian theory rejects the concept of 'common sense' or a 'collective consciousness,' close agreement among relevant social systems may still appear, e.g., in how unions, governments, and companies all agreed that high productivity is desirable in the abstract—even if unions may resist when certain forms of productivity pressure are applied to workers. To the extent that high productivity is understood as both desirable and necessary, the less pursuing productivity increases 'feels' like domination. Perfect agreement among systems is impossible, and workers are typically ambivalent about 'doing what it takes' to increase productivity because of possible negative effects, but nevertheless, if any concept could be considered nearly universally valued in modern societies productivity is a good candidate.

This reflects how labor and management simultaneously have opposing *and* shared interests. There are opposing class interests over exploitation, pay, benefits, and working conditions but also mutual structural interests in the overall health of the value-system, the operations of which valorize both factions, that gives labor and management reason to be concerned with the flow of value in motion. This explains why, at different points in both value-regimes, workers were willing to support automation or work reforms viewed as 'necessary' for the preservation of jobs—since jobs are a precious commodity guarded by workers as jealously as capitalists guard money and property (see Knowles 2017: 245–246; Stockman 2021). Thus, social domination entails not just a convergence tendency toward socially necessary production methods, but also a convergence of communications about increasing productivity to both maintain jobs and accumulate capital. Class antagonism and worker interest in a humanized workplace with more autonomy is not eliminated, but under certain circumstances improving productivity to maintain jobs was salient over these other interests. There was also recognition that 'modernization' can raise living standards, create jobs, and generate economic growth, and autoworkers bargained for their contracts to benefit from this. To the extent these goals were shared by labor and management, both classes made the implicit agreement to adhere to the prevailing productive norms, because adhering to these norms enabled the increased flow of value that benefited both labor and management while eschewing these norms could cause decline or crisis. Therefore, both at least implicitly agreed to follow the norms of socially necessary labor time and the logic of capital, even if doing so was motivated foremost by their class interests (Nicolaus 1968: 48).

Communication mediates social domination without identifying or rigorously understanding it. Some communications are straightforward, e.g., "[Toyota plant] Takaoka was almost twice as productive and three times as accurate as [GM plant] Framingham in performing the same set of standard activities on our standard car" (Womack et al. 2007 [1990]: 81). This statement relies on data comparison to state facts that become imbued with meaning in a modern capitalist social context that values higher productivity. In that context, the meaning behind the statement is not merely the bare fact that one factory is more productive than the other, but that the lagging factory ought to become more productive and close the productivity gap. Other statements are mediated and coded, e.g., "A plant that doesn't have a competitive product, a competitive workforce, and a competitive level of quality isn't going to survive" (Vasilash 1997). The precise meaning of 'competitive' is rarely clarified but can be described as mediating the fundamental message that the *temporality of certain processes is out of step with the socially necessary time determined for those processes*. Other codewords such as 'world-class,' 'benchmark,' 'optimization,' 'efficiency' etc. can all be linked back to a fundamental admonishment that temporal processes either do or do not match the socially necessary standard. Concepts such as 'market forces,' 'competitive pressures,' and 'market dictates' point toward social domination without spelling it out, pointing toward quasi-metaphysical powers or 'economic laws' that implicitly coerce observed outcomes. This critical theory seeks to identify and explain precisely what is elided in most communications surrounding these issues. Luhmannian systems theory elucidates how systems participate in obscuring and mediating social domination, while also pushing productivity pressure onto value-systems through communication.

The book *The Machine that Changed the World* (Womack et al. 2007 [1990]) published by MIT researchers is a prime example of how social domination is mediated through communication. Through its study of the relative 'competitiveness' of each system compared to the lean production benchmark, self-conscious descriptions of benchmark productivity, quality, design, logistics, and other factors were described in detail, both communicating what the benchmarks were and what practices allowed a system to reach the benchmarks. It made its case that future market success depended on adopting lean production to stay competitive. While some predictions did not come to pass and some practices, particularly the ones most based in Japanese culture, claimed to be 'lean' did not generalize, there is no doubt that the book influenced governments, businesses, and unions in their decision-making, with most value-systems hybridizing lean production principles (Adler et al. 1997; Pries 2003; Helper and Henderson 2014; Wittrock 2015; Krzywdzinski 2020b; Jürgens 2023). Multiple publications cite the book as prompting a 'Japanese shock' that reverberated around the world and initiated or spurred on the hybridization processes (e.g., Jürgens 1993, 1995; Boyer and Freyssenet 1995, 2002; Parker and Slaughter 1995; Babson 1995b, 1995c; Krzywdzinski 2020b). Thus, the IMVP project generated communications that sparked further communications that eventually reshaped production processes. Publications from consultancy and research firms such as the Harbour Report pushed this further, multiplying the communications about comparative productivity and benchmarking within the global auto industry. Explanations that rely on economic competition or 'market pressures' alone cannot fully grasp these dynamics.

Communicative patterns change in tandem with the socially necessary temporal norms. When Toyota reaches a new HPV benchmark, communications describing the more productive/less productive distinction change to reflect the new benchmark. Even improving systems end up on the less productive side of the distinction if they fall behind the benchmark. The systems are not 'objectively' productive or unproductive but are assigned so based on comparison to the socially necessary temporal norm. At different times, both US and German systems were described on the negative side of various distinctions because their productivity failed to meet the benchmark. The same dynamics applied when discussing high and low costs, which always stand in relation to the socially general magnitude of value expected for any given commodity. For example, the German model was often considered a high-cost system in part because their temporal production processes were slower than the socially necessary temporal norm. This was not the case 'objectively' but grounded in comparison to other systems. Thus, socially necessary temporal norms and the comparison between different systems influence how individuals and systems understand and communicate about the world. They provide the language, categories, and distinctions by which these communications are understood. These facts and their social meaning are recontextualized based on the socially necessary norms. In this way, all individuals and systems participate in reinforcing social domination and understand it intuitively, even if 'unconsciously.' Simply put, Social domination, productivity pressure, and temporal productive norms shape the sociology of knowledge in modern societies (see Horkheimer 1975 [1937]; Postone 1993; Mannheim 2015 [1936]).

Observations and communications occur within social systems. For example, the archives of various UAW and AFL-CIO officials held numerous writings from journalistic, academic, company, and labor sources discussing automation, technological displacement, and productivity developments. Such materials synthesized the system's self-description of the issues and communicated them through disseminating media, e.g., policy papers, press releases, speeches and so on. For example, both the UAW and IG Metall held conferences where global labor leaders discussed their views on these issues (e.g., CIO Automation Conference 1955; IG Metall 1960: 54; 1968: 79; Weinberg 1965). Communication begat communication as systems evolved based upon their observations and communications with other systems. The reactions are fundamentally contingent but nevertheless fall into perceivable patterns. Throughout the analysis, communications about productivity, automation, and technological displacement exhibited patterns that reinforced the capitalist historical dynamic to increase productivity for the sake of valorization for workers, capital accumulation for management, and national prosperity for value-regimes.

Workers in both value-regimes argued that automation and increasing productivity was desirable if measures were enacted to guard against the negative consequences of automation and technological displacement (e.g., Reuther 1962; Brumlop and Jürgens 1983; Autogramm 1984; Steigerwald 2010). Increased productivity was not truly 'progress' unless it improved working conditions and/or worker self-valorization. In principle, however, workers favored productivity increases since it promised increased economic abundance, growth, and job security. Corporations used automation to extract surplus value and to advertise their self-descriptions as representing industrial 'modernity' or 'progress.' They aimed to promote superiority in manufacturing to aid in realization and accumulate capital (e.g., Nordhoff 1958a; Ford Motor Company Archives 1952c). This discourse is also tied to other industries such as the machine tool or robotics industry which design and manufacture new means of production. Such companies approach the auto industry to sell their machines and robots promising that efficiency and productivity will increase and costs will decrease (e.g., Hounshell 2000; Association for Advancing Automation 2023). These systems wanted to stay on the positive side of these distinctions and worked to align the facts of their operations with these norms—both the temporal norms of socially necessary labor time and the socially valued normative distinctions. They likewise sought to avoid being described on the other side of these distinctions e.g., backward, inefficient, low quality, uncompetitive etc.[5]

5 For workers, this involves using worker collective power to bargain for working conditions that are both productive but socially humane so that even if the maximum productivity potential is restricted, the socially necessary productivity norm constitutes the work structure

To do so required not just assertions, but the actions of management and the workforce that aligned facts and norms, i.e., making work processes match or exceed the norms of what makes a *productive* workforce and *productive* industrial enterprise in that historical context.

The relationship of socio-communicative discourse and temporal productive norms resembles Marx's (1978 [1859]) dialectical concepts of base and superstructure. As Marx (1978 [1859]) describes,

> In the social production of their life, men enter into definite relations that are indispensable and independent of their will, relations of production which correspond to a definite stage of development of their material productive forces. The sum total of these relations of production constitutes the economic structure of society, the real foundation, on which rises a legal and political superstructure and to which correspond definite forms of social consciousness. The mode of production of material life conditions the social, political and intellectual life process in general. It is not the consciousness of men that determines their being, but, on the contrary, their social being that determines their consciousness. (4)

Similarly, patterns of communication in business, labor, and government constitute a superstructural discourse that supports the development of the productive forces. Thus, base and superstructure dialectically shape and maintain each other. The Luhmannian analysis reveals a superstructure that delimits legitimate and viable communications that tend to agree that increasing productivity is important, desirable, and necessary—even as concrete rationalization processes are variable and contested. This is not a deterministic analysis where base determines superstructure, but superstructural claims to 'progress' or 'efficiency' need to be backed by the demonstrated efficacy of concrete technical-temporal production processes to be legitimated and not fall into the negative side of these distinctions.

Both the base and superstructure transform simultaneously with increases in productivity. For example, just as the productive base of auto production was based on transfer machine automation during the 1950s and 1960s, the

---

and pace workers' desire. This plan is foiled if/when not all value-regimes/value-systems are equally restrained by labor so that productivity pressure to conform to the unconstrained productivity leader appears. Thus, though workers may endeavor to sometimes restrain productivity, this is only insofar as productivity increases negatively effects working conditions, and their goal is to readjust the socially general productivity norm, rather than to restrain productivity for its own sake.

superstructural discourse surrounding it coalesced around transfer machines as the necessary tool to increase productivity, improve quality, and remain competitive (see Hounshell 2000; Steigerwald 2010; Jürgens 2023). Thus, the superstructure reinforces the capitalist historical dynamic which transforms the material productive forces and the economic structure of society. Luhmannian analysis goes beyond Marx in theorizing how communications emerge contingently from social systems, forming a dynamic discourse that may nevertheless exhibit certain patterns that rhetorically support this historical dynamic.

Reflecting on past productive developments and modern 'progress,' there is an implicit agreement that certain transformations of labor and technologies were socially necessary. For example, phone operators lost their jobs from the 1920s to the 1940s in the US (see Feigenbaum and Gross 2020), but who today argues that operator automation or cellphone technology should be dismantled so every call would be handled by a human operator for the sake of more jobs? As Henry Ford (1922: 46) hypothesized and evidenced by the "inefficient low-quality craft production" of China until around 2000 (Womack et al. 2007 [1990]: 275; Wenten 2020), tens of millions of jobs *could* be created if all automakers tried to meet existing demand while dismantling their technologies, automation, and lean work structure to return to the 1900s craft system based on skilled fitters. Yet, no one seriously advocates for this, and the possibility is rarely imagined. This 'blank space' of what is *not communicated* also reveals how social domination shapes social discourse. When the German auto industry journal *Automobil Produktion* stopped publicizing body shop automation levels because they were nearly universally close to full automation, it signaled that high body shop automation became so socially necessary that it does not warrant comment (Krzywdzinski 2020a: 18–19). Perhaps productivity norms are at their strongest when they are so obvious that they are not communicated about, with no controversy or issues, but are nevertheless implemented anyway. This dynamic that limits what is thought and communicated demonstrates how social domination is a form of *power* in Lukes' (2005 [1974]) sense of the third dimension of power.

Technological displacement may be controversial as it occurs, but the more time passes the more productivity increases and their subsequent disruptions are retrospectively justified and appear 'inevitable' or as 'progress.' This can be described as another manifestation of *commodity fetishism*. Just as a commodity does not betray the labor power or working conditions used to produce it, so too does it obscure the history of productive development, automation, and job displacement that occurred to produce the contemporary commodity. Thereby, *what is communicated and what is not communicated* both support social domination. Beyond economic competition, productivity pressure is exerted through socio-communicative processes, demonstrating how the *social logic of capital* shapes social discourse and productive development down to our epistemologies, categories, and imaginations.

4 Convergence and Divergence of Productive Systems

This comparative historical analysis is useful for explicating what is contingent and what is heteronomous in the productive development of both value-regimes. Both the US and Germany faced similar productive problems which placed heteronomous pressures on their choices, but they nevertheless approached these problems differently based on their divergent socio-historic circumstances, thereby generating different outcomes. Neither an analysis that unduly emphasizes contingency nor heteronomy is adequate. Only a nuanced explanation can provide an analytically powerful critical theory.

Throughout the narrative, each value-regime addressed productivity problems driven by the pursuit of capital accumulation, was inspired by (or felt threatened from) internal and external comparisons (internal versus external benchmarking), and through a desire to communicate productive strengths to project 'modernity' and 'progress.' Different combinations of human and machine labor were deployed, shopfloor cultures developed, and business-labor-government relations emerged in each regime to tackle these problems at the micro, mezzo, and macro level. There were value-regime characteristics that both enabled and facilitated as well as hindered and inhibited efforts to approach or exceed the productivity frontier. Some of these characteristics were transformed to aid in the implementation of automation or more productive work arrangements, while others remained nearly constant as productive development ran along value-regime specific path dependencies. Even as benchmark standards outside the value-regime generated productivity pressures, e.g., lean production since the 1970s, the conditions for matching the standards were often value-regime specific and therefore were difficult or impossible to replicate due to the differences between value-regimes. In such cases, the productivity problem had to be addressed via a combination of hybridized adaptation and alternative methods, or the costs of not conforming to socially necessary labor time were borne out, e.g., higher costs, lower profits, job losses, or industrial decline. For these reasons, among others, adaptation to the productivity challenge took many paths that were characterized by struggle and not all efforts were successful. Based on the business-labor-government combinations analyzed, three major productive trajectories emerged. Three factors are highlighted here: industrial relations as either combative or cooperative, the prevalence of skilled labor in the workforce, and whether the system is more oriented toward accumulating capital or achieving other, usually humanistic, objectives.

4.1 *The United States: Combative Relations, Low Skill, Capital Orientation*

In the United States, management exerted authoritarian Taylorist control over work processes at the expense of worker autonomy that resulted in *combative industrial relations*. It was mediated by a grievance system constructed by New Deal legislation and collective pattern bargaining. This system enabled rapid technological and productivity development during the first two thirds of the 20th century which generated unrivaled capital accumulation. Macro level concerns were nonexistent because the Big Three were unopposed productivity leaders, with productive power and capacity so far beyond other value-regimes that there was essentially no serious global competition, especially in the US which remained the largest market throughout the 20th century. However, combative industrial relations became a weakness when lean producers outperformed the Big Three in productivity and quality (Lam et al. 1991; Womack et al. 2007 [1990]; Helper and Henderson 2014). Until that point, tense industrial relations at the micro and mezzo level proliferated for decades *but were acceptable if conflict was managed* and higher profits for management and higher wages and benefits for labor continued uninterrupted. Since the shift in productivity leadership, there was a slow decline in the Big Three's prominence both domestically and internationally, which was difficult to ameliorate due to the long legacy of distrust and contentiousness at the micro and mezzo levels. Only by slowly overcoming these problems at the lower levels, i.e., by labor-management cooperation—even if motivated by fear of job loss—was it possible to catch up to the socially necessary labor time standards set by lean producers. The efforts were not enough to save GM and Chrysler from bankruptcy, however, and the arrival of transplants and market share loss meant hundreds of thousands of UAW jobs were lost, jobs that remained had lower wages and benefits, and the value-regime became split between union and nonunion plants.

The historical analysis reveals how structural weaknesses in the US value-regime, especially its *combative nature* and *generally lower level of worker training*, at first enabled but later inhibited productivity development. Management prerogative to hire and fire, shape production processes, and *orientation toward expanding mass markets for maximum capital accumulation* facilitated technological and organizational developments that expanded volume enormously, and the dearth of worker power precluded effective resistance against deskilling, technological displacement, and the alienation of the assembly line (Meyer 1981, 2004; Braverman 1998 [1974]; Crumm 2010). Thus, Fordism made the US the cradle of mass production and the mass consumption society, even as it entailed high human costs. The New Deal and the rise of the UAW provided a counterbalance to management excess, and contracts after the Treaty of Detroit helped establish the American middle class who continued the Fordist-Keynesian cycle of growth that benefited both management and labor. Productivity development, primarily based on automating workers of all skill levels to discipline them and reduce their bargaining leverage (Reynolds 1989; Meyer 1981, 2004), was driven and directed by management through Taylorist scientific management—though work standards conflicts were a legitimate reason to strike. The technological orientation of productivity development reflected the combative nature of industrial relations, as management did not want to broadly train workers in ways that increased the firm's reliance on skilled work and improved the UAW's bargaining leverage. This too was not a major obstacle before the loss of productivity leadership because technological solutions appeared to be the key to high productivity until lean producers demonstrated how systematically eliminating waste and reorganizing both human workers and machines could push the productivity frontier further. The shift to lean was especially difficult for the US precisely because successful implementation required worker motivation, cooperation, multiskilled training, and could not be implemented via obedient machines—nearly the opposite approach of how US firms preferred to increase productivity (Finkelstein 2003; Crumm 2010, Helper and Henderson 2014). The automation 'leapfrog' in the 1980s partially failed because of the lack of worker training, demonstrating how lack of skill investment hurt productivity gains (Jürgens et al. 1993; Crumm 2010; Jürgens 2023). The history of distrust and disempowering labor at every opportunity hurt the Big Three as the norms of social necessity adjusted so that cooperative relations, worker participation, and reliance on a multiskilled workforce became vital to securing higher productivity.

In sum, the *combative industrial relations, generally lower skill level, and orientation toward capital accumulation* characterized the US value-regime. These attributes facilitated—or at least did not seriously hinder—the creation of the Fordist-Taylorist mass production system, but the first two characteristics became obstacles to moving beyond aspects of that system that held back productivity development. Though these three factors do not explain the entire history, they are major factors in explicating how value-regime characteristics shaped the Big Three response to the productivity problem. The system generated a mass production society that made the US a major world power but also contained weaknesses that led to the domestic industry's slow decline and the value-regime's increasing heterogeneity since the 1970s.

4.2 *Germany: Cooperative Relations, High Skill, Humanist Orientation*

German capital-labor relations were *exceptionally cooperative,* and the *high skill German workforce* supplied the resources necessary to achieve high productivity, perhaps with the latent potential to exceed the productivity frontier. However, the *systemic arrangement, power structure, and orientation* of the cooperative relations in Germany meant that the system balanced a capitalist and humanist orientation that frequently undermined attempts to improve productivity. This was most apparent until the rise of fascism as worker power to resist restrictions of their autonomy, ambivalence toward mass production, and economic troubles made early German automakers like Daimler and Benz stick to a craft production system (Bellon 1990; Stahlmann 1992; Hachtmann and Von Saldern 2009). Though this system was by no means static and there were efforts to rationalize, the productivity gap between American and German producers remained so large that German automakers were of no serious threat to worldwide American dominance. The Nazi modernization programs resolved the contradictions by enforcing modernization at the expense of workers, but also provided the capital equipment necessary to engage in mass production after WWII.

The quick reestablishment and subsequent strengthening of the legal and contractual apparatus that enabled cooperative relations after the war meant that the productivity problem was largely solved peacefully at the micro and mezzo level in the German auto industry. This enabled a rapid response to the 'American Challenge' during the *Wirtschaftswunder* decades as the productivity gap narrowed and Volkswagen became a serious rival to the Big Three on the world stage (Tolliday 1995a; Hilger 2003). This required implementing extensive automation and the assembly line, which German workers previously resisted, but in the context of high growth and a foreign/domestic division of labor, this was accepted so long as technological displacement was managed through codetermination (Rationalization Agreement 1968; Brumlop and Jürgens 1983). Here, the German value-regime demonstrated its ability to effectively respond to macro level pressures to automate, rapidly improve productivity, *and* maintain cooperative relations at the mezzo and micro level. It demonstrated how cooperative relations and reliance on highly skilled workers were *not incompatible* with high growth and high productivity.

When the era of high growth ended in the 1970s and more intense competition appeared in export markets, the cooperative relations and high skilled workforce enabled the alternative strategies of diversified quality production, new production concepts, and the humanization of work. With growth slowdown, strategies that maximally increased productivity would not be tolerated by German workers and were generally prevented by codetermination rights. Instead, the orientation of productivity development shifted to balancing the desires of increasing productivity and lowering costs for management with worker desires for humanization of work, job security, enriched interesting jobs, and German quality work (Kern and Schumann 1984, 1987; Lüdtke 2009). This entailed implementing further automation in all production areas, including assembly, that were controlled by the highly skilled workers, which, in theory, would greatly improve productivity in the long-run (Kern and Schumann 1987; 1998). The diversity and quality strategy attempted to shield the value-regime from productivity pressure by establishing quality-based market niches and achieving realization via alternative competitive criteria (Streeck 1991; Sorge and Streeck 2016). Thus, a contingent shift occurred where the response to the low growth environment was to focus on alternative development and business strategies rather than aggressively improve productivity as the Japanese did (see Ohno 1988). The cooperative relations and highly skilled workforce signified that an aggressive push to improve productivity was likely possible, if consented to by management and labor, but the humanist orientation mediated this. This makes sense given the German orientation toward *humanist codetermination* rather than codetermination oriented toward maximum capital accumulation.

Issues appeared when mezzo level cost imbalances and macro level competition placed productivity pressure on German workers. Since the 1990s crisis, the need to balance interests was renewed as lean reforms improved efficiency, but German workers restrained this somewhat to prevent 'management by stress' (Krzywdzinski 2020b). Reforms were implemented through codetermination and compromise, while the remaining productivity gap and high wages were subsidized by production and sales abroad, especially in China, and by low-wage Eastern European suppliers (Jürgens 2008; Jürgens and Krzywdzinski 2009; Jürgens 2021). The balance appeared to be maintained up until the 2020s as Chinese automakers ramp up exports and global EV adoption accelerates, which threatens the contemporary German model. New compromises are needed in the transition to EVs and the reshaping of the global competitive landscape (Bormann et al. 2018; Automotive News Europe 2024).

In sum, the *cooperative industrial relations, generally higher skill level, and orientation toward humanist productive development* characterized the German value-regime. Though cooperation was not as strong in the early 20th century, the strength of German labor systems and the broad ambivalence toward Fordism made it so Germany did not catch up to the American productive standard. Thus, German society motorized much slower and German auto firms accumulated comparatively little capital (Bellon 1990; Hachtmann and von Saldern 2009). During the mid-century period of high growth, these characteristics appeared to work in harmony—although the humanist drive was not as prominent, especially for foreign workers (Tolliday 1995a; Brumlop and Jürgens 1983). The humanist orientation both enabled and restricted productivity growth along a distinctly German path in the 1970s and 1980s, but overall productivity was behind American and Japanese competitors. Since the 1990s crisis, lean productivity reforms were again balanced with humanist interests. Thus, the humanist orientation of German systems and the 'constructive' constraints they apply on productive development constitutes the throughline in explaining the evolution of the German 'model' (Kern and Schumann 1984; 1987; Sorge and Streeck 2016).

The German system struggled to maintain this codetermined orientation despite stark productivity pressures. Maintaining this outlook is a struggle because it *works against* rather than *coincide with the logic of capital.* The capitalist historical dynamic as a form of *unfreedom* means that cooperation at the micro and mezzo level *is not enough* to ensure successful autonomous productive development. Macro level social domination means that German development must not fall too far behind the globally determined socially necessary norms or face negative consequences. The early 90s crisis was one manifestation of such negative consequences, while forming a *de facto* two-tier divide through aggressive globalization manages the 'costs of noncompliance' today. Thus, while German codetermination may be preferred over US industrial relations, especially in managing productivity problems at the micro and mezzo level, German codetermination by no means overcomes the imperatives and constraints of social domination at the macro level. For this reason, a class analysis that diagnoses the German system as having successfully muted class antagonism through codetermination and thus achieved a quasi-socialist 'utopia' of industrial relations and working conditions misses how *German automakers are influenced by the capitalist historical dynamic to improve productivity and maintain high production standards*. The despotism of time in the factory is still in effect even as labor-management relations appear harmonious. This is because the 'despot' is neither labor nor management, who cooperatively consented to this humanist orientation, but the social domination that constantly pushes the German model to align more with the social logic of capital and follow the *global* norms of socially necessary labor time.

4.3 *Japan: Cooperative Relations, High Skill, Capital Orientation*

The emergence of the Japanese value-regime as productivity leader since the 1970s made the lean production system an important foil to the US and German systems. Generally, the Japanese value-regime is characterized by *cooperative relations with high worker motivation and participation, multiskilled workforces, and an orientation toward continuous improvement and eliminating waste*—a capital orientation *par excellence* (Ohno 1988; Womack et al. 2007 [1990]; Liker 2021). Japanese firms did not have the same problems of worker distrust and discontent that the US dealt with at the micro and mezzo levels (Lam et al. 1991) and fostered motivation and commitment through lifetime employment, intense socialization, performance pay, and 'enterprise' unions (Babson 1995c: 238–242). Though skill formation and cooperation differed between Germany and Japan, both nevertheless had the advantages that emerge from cooperative relations and a high skilled workforce (see Jürgens 1995: 298). The major difference between the two was that Japanese automakers had a strong orientation toward *maximizing capital accumulation* by structuring and stressing the production process so that waste is revealed and eliminated (Ohno 1988; Liker 2021). Thus, the Japanese system possessed the 'best' combination of factors from the *standpoint of capital accumulation.* Japanese workers may have suffered from 'management by stress,' but if this was tolerated so production was not disrupted, then lean producers could create production processes that continually redefine the productivity frontier through kaizen and enjoy competitive advantages as productivity leader.

Marx in *Capital* (1976 [1867]: 545) predicted that labor would become increasingly deskilled and subordinated to the machine (see Braverman 1998 [1974]), but there is evidence that if skilled labor aligns their interests with management for the sake of capital accumulation then a far higher level of productivity can develop. Inherently contradictory class interests make this difficult, but regardless of *how* the *de facto* alignment of class interests in concrete production processes came to be—e.g., continuous growth, corporate socialization, Japanese culture, job guarantees etc. (see Babson 1995c; Wittrock 2015), the fact that it was possible for lean producers was all that was necessary for the achieved level of productivity to become socially necessary and exert productivity pressure on the rest of the global industry. Even if the conditions that facilitated lean production in Japan could not be replicated in the US or Germany, the pressure to approximate the lean productivity standard persisted.

The Japanese and German comparison also demonstrates how cooperative relations and highly skilled workforce do not guarantee high productivity and efficiency. Indeed, Germany has generally been the least productive of the three value-regimes since the 1970s despite its cooperative relations. Though cooperative relations may be a *necessary precondition* to reaching higher levels of productivity, they are not the *only precondition*, as German humanist codetermination made production processes less productive than the Japanese capital-oriented codetermination of kaizen. Because the Japanese value-regime was structured to improve the flow of value rigorously and continuously, Japanese lean producers were rewarded with high productivity, lower costs, high quality, and more accumulated capital. The success of this system on the market and socially through communication shaped the global auto industry as all value-systems were compelled to align their flow of value in motion with the lean producers, thus pressuring toward convergence of lean production principles and a similar orientation toward capital accumulation to survive.

4.4 *Dynamics of Convergence and Divergence*

Productive development is always shaped by the value-regime in which it occurs. Divergences appear based on these socio-historical characteristics and path dependencies. Yet, pressures toward convergence also appear as socially necessary productive norms change over time. The question is whether these value-regimes can adapt when necessary to match the productive norms, or if the disadvantages from lagging can be compensated in some way. What is not possible, however, is to remain static or fall too far outside the productive norms if a system is to survive. Regardless of the desirability of the German or American system in the abstract, each system must be evaluated on its ability to adapt to the changing requirements of capitalist survival based on continually transforming norms of socially necessity. Contingency is always present, but social domination represents a restriction of viable choices and a compulsion to make certain choices that help a value-system survive in the capitalist market.

Systems (e.g., unions and companies) can make choices that result in lower profits, lower market share or even crisis, as occurred in both value-regimes at different times, but neither management nor labor wants to face the outcomes from these choices for the sake of maintaining capital accumulation and worker valorization. Thus, the heteronomy of capitalism restricts certain choices and forces others—including the compulsion to automate certain processes or maintain certain levels of productivity. Experiments are run, trial and error occur, and the efficacy of any given measure may be uncertain, but nevertheless the value-systems converged in certain ways even as the value-regimes diverged in others.

Is it a coincidence that the producers with the highest level of productivity typically accumulated the highest capital, e.g., the Big Three until the 1970s and the lean producers thereafter? Is it a coincidence that those who were behind the productive benchmarks for long periods of time often faced decline or crisis? This is not to argue that those with the most efficient productive systems always dominates the competition, there are other dynamics in realization (e.g., competition in product design), distribution (e.g., levels of economic inequality), and investment (e.g., VW's serendipitous early investments in China) that can shape outcomes. Likewise, the argument is not that relative inefficiency cannot exist for long or that there is a totalizing tendency toward convergence in all aspects of the industry. Rather, the issue is identifying how productivity leadership confers advantages that spur on dynamics toward convergence and how these pressures interact with tendencies of value-regime divergence to produce different outcomes.

Tendencies to overemphasize divergence or convergence are not uncommon. *The Machine That Changed the World* (Womack et al. 2007 [1990]) explicitly claims that the entirety of their depiction of lean production ought to be adopted by firms around the world, as the authors argue, "Institute lean production as quickly as possible … Otherwise lean competitors will overwhelm you …" (91). Yet, the wholistic lean package was never fully adopted by any firm, just as Fordism required adjustment to fit into the German value-regime. The adaptation to lean principles appears to be nearly universal (Pries 2003; Weyer 2011), but this was also variable and hybridized. Predictions of lean dominance were too specific without understanding the tension and contradiction between *contingent and divergent* national trajectories and *convergent* productivity pressures. They correctly identified that lean production represented a challenge to the global industry but did not articulate theoretically how or why its adoption is necessarily hybridized and shaped by different value-regimes. Thus, for Womack et al. (2007 [1990]) the *challenge of macro level social domination is identified*, but the possibility of micro and mezzo level hybridization and diversity is underappreciated.

There are also approaches that place undue emphasis on contingency and divergence. For example, Boyer and Freyssenet (1995) claim that,

> The long run history of manufacturing industries and productive system has recurrently shown that over a century long period and whatever the country, there is not at all any convergence towards the productivity levels and organizations which are supposed to be at the technological frontier. Quite on the contrary, the *long run persistence of productive diversity is a well-established* Tact. (8; emphasis in original)

Evidence throughout this analysis demonstrated that labor and management in both countries have at times consciously aimed to increase productivity, including specifically to approach the productivity leader. There is productive diversity, but this diversity also leads to a diversity of market outcomes with less productive firms tending to fare less well in the long-run than more productive ones. Productivity has *not been the first or only priority of all automakers at all times* but is nevertheless an important concern that becomes salient under certain conditions, e.g., intense competition or large productivity gaps. Even Boyer and Freyssenet (1995: 3, 2002) admit that there is not an infinite number of productive models, identifying only five viable models throughout the industry's history. Furthermore, as the early history of Daimler-Benz illustrated, even the most 'backward' and 'inefficient' craft systems implemented rationalization programs and experienced pressure to conform to American standards, indicating that no 'productive model' is perpetually sustainable or immune from productivity pressure (Bellon 1990; Stahlmann 1992; Jürgens 2023). Boyer and Freyssenet (1995, 2002) correctly highlight the possible diversity and divergence at the micro and mezzo levels but undervalues social domination at the macro level. The approach developed here ameliorates these deficits through a nuanced analysis that balances the tendencies of divergence and convergence at all three levels. Neither technological determinism nor denial of convergence pressures in favor of contingency is helpful for confronting industrial history. A sophisticated and nuanced theory is needed to address the balance between the two approaches.

5 Mediations and Limitations

No theory can explain all phenomena, and there are always contingencies that it may not explain. The elaboration thus far expands the critical theory of automation and technological displacement theory by examining concrete history and navigating the divide between convergence and divergence within value-regimes. For the sake of nuance, the following examines strategies the auto firms apply to modify or ameliorate productivity pressure and discusses the limitations of the theory.

While possessing the highest productivity undoubtedly confers advantages, market success is not guaranteed by productivity alone. Issues may emerge at the level of realization, distribution, or investment that negate productivity advantages. The Model T crisis in the mid-1920s and the Beetle crisis in the early 1970s demonstrated how high productivity means nothing if the value of the product is not realized due to changing wants, needs and desires (Hounshell 1985; Tolliday 1995b; Jürgens 1998). Starting in the 1990s, SUVs and pickup trucks became increasingly popular, especially in the United States, which brought high profits to the Big Three who specialized in these vehicles while the Japanese did not. Here, product specialty and realization were *more decisive* than productivity as US firms still lagged in productivity yet supplied the products American consumers demanded (Ingrassia 2011; Albert 2019: 256–257). The discussion covered major turning points in product development and realization trends, but did not comprehensively outline how product development, design, and realization trends contribute to business success. Thus, the full causality of what leads to market success or failure cannot be explained by the social domination thesis alone. Nevertheless, automation and the pursuit of productivity did play an important role in competition and industrial development and was a major concern for the companies and unions in different ways in each period.

As a study limited in scale, scope, and industry, the dynamics discussed here do not perfectly align with dynamics observed in other industries within either country. Automobiles are expensive durable consumer commodities composed of thousands of parts, many of which are similar but not identical between different companies (Jürgens and Meißner 2005; Sturgeon et al. 2009). This prevents establishing maximum economies of scale in production and economies of scope in design (Chandler 1990; Sturgeon et al. 2009: 9). Other manufacturing industries have established "industry-level technical and business process standards" which may make socially necessary standards clearer and more universally followed, but this may also make it difficult to establish new standards to gain a competitive advantage because operational improvements can be easily imitated (Lieberman and Dhawan 2005: 1073; Sturgeon et al. 2009: 9). Though market position, design, marketing etc. play a role in automaker success, Lieberman and Dhawan (2005: 1074) argues that because the auto industry has many producers that are similarly positioned and there is "common agreement regarding the best practice," that gaps in "operational effectiveness" are *more consequential* in auto manufacture than other factors. If the structure of the auto industry makes it more sensitive to productivity gaps, then the productivity pressures described here might not be as prominent in other industries. For example, it may be difficult to gain substantial productivity advantages in other industries or competition in other arenas is more prominent. Many of the developments discussed here emerged from waves of creative destruction, which may not appear in other industries. Non-manufacturing industries likely have very different dynamics and time pressures. There are theoretical reasons to assume that the basic theory, i.e., that capital as value in motion entails imperatives and constraints that result in a historical dynamic that pushes productivity forward, may be observable in all capitalist industries, but the specific dynamics in these industries and how they play out in different value-regimes cannot be answered here. This analysis only indirectly suggests that similar dynamics may be observable in the history of other industries.

5.1 *Productivity, Wages, and Class Struggle*

This analysis focused on how firms increased productivity to reduce costs, but decreasing worker valorization was also frequently used to cut costs. Struggles over wages are important as the value of labor can be manipulated more easily than material or fixed capital costs, are faster to implement than productive reforms that require training and capital investment, and are a simple means to increase profit. Decreasing management salaries and bonuses or accepting lower profits are also valid options, though the power imbalance between labor and management usually meant that the preservation of management valorization and profits was prioritized over worker valorization, especially in the US (see Russo 1984; Lukes 2005 [1974]). Both value-regimes experienced crises since the 1970s that aided management in procuring concessions from workers to improve profitability and lower the breakeven point. However, cutting wages and benefits without improving productivity would not have been a viable long-term solution because of the cost disadvantages that accrue from large productivity gaps. As an extreme example, it would be nearly impossible to pay low enough wages paired with pre-1914 production processes and technologies to make high volumes of vehicles that could sell profitably in contemporary markets. Therefore, when under productivity pressure or sales decline, the pressures to cut wages (including management salaries and bonuses), save on non-labor costs, outsource to low-wage locations, and increase productivity are all present, and combinations of approaches were taken to tackle these dilemmas, with German compromises typically considered more 'humane' than American solutions.

High wages were easier to secure when growth, productivity, and labor solidarity was high. Wage and benefit improvements were made through difficult collective bargaining and/or codetermination but were nevertheless easier to attain due to the success of the companies. When value-systems are healthy, and especially when they are growing, the capital and labor struggle over distributing the rewards of success can result in higher wages and lower profits or vice versa depending on the contingent struggle of unions and/or works councils and management. This critical theory complements these analyses with a wider view of how productive developments and dynamics at the micro, mezzo, and macro level influenced the class struggle. For example, one precondition for the high wages and benefits UAW members won from the 1950s to the 1980s was due in part to the global dominance of the Big Three stemming from massive productive advantages. Once productivity leadership was lost and sales declined, concessions were justified by management as necessary. No concession or contract was 'inevitable,' but each gain or loss for labor was shaped by the circumstances of the value-system that were subsequently influenced by productivity pressures and global competitive conditions.[6]

Backgrounding struggles for work and wages are the dynamics of the continuously changing norms of production that redefine what it takes to survive in modern capitalism. The question of a just distribution of income cannot be settled once and for all but can be reexamined with each change in production. The saliency of the productivity question or the distribution question varies based on the socio-historic circumstances, e.g., whether sales are growing or declining or whether a firm is productivity leader or there is a substantial productivity gap. Workers are always motivated to self-valorize just as capitalists are motivated by profit. Workers in both value-regimes sought self-valorization as bourgeois sellers of labor power, thereby accepting these fundamental 'rules of the game.' Yet, in this endeavor, automation and technological displacement can decrease valorization opportunities but may be understood as socially necessary by both factions if a productivity gap threatens the health of the value-system.[7] Yet workers are not hapless victims but resist technological displacement, concessions, or increased exploitation. Labor organizations in both value-regimes fought against management prerogative and struggled to affirmatively valorize themselves. What the social domination thesis adds is illuminating how the imperatives and restraints of capital as value in motion shaped efforts to self-valorize and how value-regimes facilitated this differently.

In this framework, both workers and management are dominated by time and placed under systemic imperatives and constraints. Approaches that focus *solely* on class struggles miss how the dynamics of capital, as a system both parties participate in but are beyond their control, influence class struggles and their outcomes. Social justice oriented scholars and writers frequently analyze

6 Management and top executives also seek self-valorization, and the rapid rise in income inequality and executive pay in the last several decades makes distribution struggles increasingly contentious. This is especially prominent in the US due to how the vastly unequal capital accumulation of management generates power imbalances in union-management struggles and how American workers do not have codetermination rights (see Russo 1984; Ingrassia 2011; Milanović 2016; Piketty 2014, 2020).

7 Lower wages may make automation less attractive in instrumental cost/benefit analysis. However, this is less pressing in the auto industry because of the proven efficiency of automation and the historically high wages for autoworkers that, despite waves of concessions in recent decades, remains relatively high compared to all jobs (Jürgens et al. 1993: 98–108; Cutcher-Gershenfeld 2015; Jürgens 2023).

labor and implicitly or explicitly advocate for labor resistance and increasing workers power in these struggles (e.g., Parker and Slaughter 1988; Babson 1995b; Cutler 1998; Kern and Schumann 1998; Holmes 2004; Meyer 1981; 2004), while business-oriented scholars and writers advocate for management prerogative over labor (e.g., Womack et al. 2007 [1990]; Ingrassia 2011; Harbour 2017; Whyte 2020). Typically missing from both sides is an analysis of the historical dynamics of capitalism and its structural heteronomy. The intention here is to reframe the history of the auto industry in both value-regimes with a focus on these dynamics and how they operate within and beyond class struggles.

5.2 *Government and Trade*

Governments play a vital role in constructing value-regime specific systems and attributes through laws and regulatory agencies. They served as rule makers and conflict mediators which framed how labor and management coped with the challenges of automation, technological displacement, and increasing productivity. The US federal government established the NLRB which enabled unionization in the 1930s. However, rules for unionization and state right-to-work laws also helped transplants remain nonunion, which facilitated the increasing heterogeneity of the value-regime. This system and the contractual grievance system were designed to mediate labor-management conflict that *was assumed to be inevitable* rather than legally mandate representation and cooperation as with German codetermination. The grievance system outlined what would be handled by the multi-step grievance process and what were legitimate grievances to authorize strikes. Thus, the American government and company-union contracts outlined labor relations in the US, which became characterized by their combativeness. Aside from the fascist era, the German government shaped labor relations through the codetermination and works council laws. They formed the foundation for the additional labor systems and codetermination rights that were absent in the US. These laws provided 'constructive' restraints that influenced the development of the German system. Efficacious worker power enabled workers wide-ranging influence over production, including how to fairly handle technological displacement and ergonomically improve working conditions.

In both value-regimes, government investments, especially before and during WWII, set up the industry for the explosive postwar growth (Flink 1988; Tolliday 1995a). Government commitment to the domestic firms extended to when they encountered crisis, e.g., when US government intervened to save Chrysler in 1980 and bailout GM and Chrysler after the 2009 bankruptcy (Flink 1988; Ingrassia 2011). Thus, value-systems relied on governments not only as rule makers but as investors and sources of extra-market support. This supports the analytical importance of value-regimes, i.e., how national configurations give special treatment to domestic industries to protect jobs and support the flow of value within the regime.

Governments, to varying degrees at different times, also sought to shield domestic industries from social domination through tariffs, voluntary import restraints, or other regulations that make it more difficult for foreign companies to export to domestic markets (Noyes 1938; Flink 1988: 252–254; Berry, Levinsohn, and Pakes 1999; Benjamin 1999; Wenten 2020). These measures *partially nullified social domination* because they decreased the cost advantages derived from higher productivity so that lagging domestic firms faced less productivity pressure to reform their production processes and impetus to close the productivity gap. This can allow domestic industries and jobs to be maintained despite more productive foreign competition but may retard product and productivity development compared to other value-regimes.

Relative openness to 'free trade' or trade restrictions is another important characteristic of value-regimes. The government's ability to control market openness and exposure to competition and globalization can influence the strength of pressures to globalize, outsource, automate, and increase productivity. The more open a value-regime is, the more the domestic industries are pressured to conform to the *global* macro level standards of socially necessary labor time to survive. A regime can choose to erect tariffs or import constraints, but this has its own opportunity costs.

For example, the Iron Curtain made communist Eastern and capitalist Western Europe evolve along two divergent paths of auto industry development, both in terms of production processes and products, with much less capacity, volume, and technology in the East than in the West (see Ciesla 2009; Grieger 2009; Fava 2009). This resulted in far less motorization in Eastern Europe and production processes were unfavorably compared to the highly productive American factories (Hounshell 2000: 101). When the Soviet Union fell and Eastern Europe became exposed to Western European capitalism, firms like Škoda, which stood little chance of competing on their own, were bought by conglomerates like Volkswagen, and other transnational corporations used Eastern European countries to establish low-wage, low-cost parts suppliers (Jürgens and Krzywdzinski 2009; Guzik, et al. 2020). In the auto industry, the divergent development between East and West made it so today there is a large gulf between the value generated and the quality of jobs between the value-regimes of Eastern and Western Europe (Jürgens and Krzywdzinski 2009; Guzik, et al. 2020). National governments can manipulate and somewhat control socially necessary productive norms at the mezzo level by closing off domestic industries from competition, but they cannot control the globally determined socially necessary productive norms at the macro level. Therefore, governments have tools that can mediate productivity pressure but ultimately cannot control it, demonstrating how social domination also imposes heteronomy on governments.

5.3 *Business Strategies to Avoid Productivity Pressure*

Certain business strategies, including diversified quality production or a productive model based on 'innovative' niche products, help automakers avoid social domination (Streeck 1991; Boyer and Freyssenet 2002; Sorge and Streeck 2016). The aim is to enact strategies that, while production processes might be behind the socially general standard, can achieve profitability by distinguishing the product from standard mass volume vehicles. For example, offering wide-ranging variants or customizability options, selling a brand based on high quality or luxury, unique or 'innovative' designs, and offering fundamental product changes with environmental benefits like EVs, constitute business strategies that may allow firms to sell commodities not based on price but on other characteristics (Boyer and Freyssenet 2002; Holweg 2008; Sorge and Streeck 2016). If successful, sales become dependent on the desirability of these characteristics, and productivity may be less than the socially general norm because of how the unique characteristics affect production, and/or, in the case of Germany, because of the unique work model of the value-regime. Discerning customers who seek out these special characteristics may be willing to pay high prices to fulfill their desires, which can cover the costs of productive inefficiency and still result in profit. Smaller companies like Chrysler needed innovative designs to retain market share against Ford and GM, Tesla offered luxury EVs, and German companies, especially luxury brands like Daimler-Benz and BMW, pioneered this approach with the DQP strategy in the 1980s forward (Flink 1988; Boyer and Freyssenet 2002; Sorge and Streeck 2016).

However, these strategies did not preclude either German or American firms, both volume and luxury producers, from adapting major productivity developments such as assembly line Fordism, transfer lines, or lean production to their production processes (Moll 1961; Hounshell 1985; Flink 1988; Jürgens et al. 1993; Krzywdzinski 2020b; Jürgens 2023). Why did this occur? First, although these strategies attempt to avoid competition and productivity pressure, they do not negate the generic desire to improve productivity within production processes at the micro and mezzo level, whatever they may be. In Germany in the 1990s, the diversity strategy was successful for almost two decades but ran into problems when the companies' cost structure—including their comparatively inefficient production processes—became unbalanced and required productivity-based reforms to bring down the breakeven point and regain profitability (Jürgens 2004). Adopting hybrid lean practices and the platform strategy lowered HPV and costs across the European auto industry while retaining many aspects of the diversity and quality strategy (Holweg 2008; Jürgens 2008; Grieger and Lupa 2015; Sorge and Streeck 2016).

Thus, even when focusing on diversity, quality, or product innovation at the expense of maximum productivity, there is still productivity pressure to maintain high productivity so that cost disadvantages do not hurt realization or the firm's financial health. Even though a Mercedes-Benz is more complex than a Chevrolet, Volkswagen, or Toyota, and therefore cannot achieve comparable HPV, the lean principles, high automation, and the platform strategy can still save costs. Enhancing productivity can still derive advantages against the limited competition and communications about benchmarking and comparisons still push the *social* productivity imperative (Womack et al. 2007 [1990]: 88–91; Weyer 2011; Harbour 2017). Even though there are business strategies that deflect the productivity pressure of mainstream auto production, there are other forms of productivity pressure that are applicable. The industry's history demonstrated that no major company, whether volume, luxury, or niche, perfectly avoided social domination to develop autonomously without regard to technological change or productivity standards.

5.4 *The Growth Imperative*

High economic growth is frequently a solution to the issues of automation and the threat of technological unemployment because technological displacement is offset by growth in overall production that requires more jobs. Higher productivity can assist as cost and other competitive advantages generates growth opportunities even in low-growth mature markets, e.g., the gradual gain in market share for Japanese firms in the US. This was beneficial for Japanese and American transplant workers but disastrous for the Big Three, reflecting how growth in such conditions can be a zero-sum game. Thus, there were few viable growth opportunities to offset the displacement and downsizing that occurred in the Big Three during these decades. Only in the late 1990s forward did new markets like China and India became major sources of profit for the Big Three (Wenten 2020). The same applied to German automakers as Chinese growth greatly supported the overall sales growth of German firms (Bormann 2018). Thus, while growth always remains a hypothetical answer to the problems of technological displacement and unemployment, compensating growth is not always possible for socio-historic reasons outside the control of value-systems.

Nevertheless, the growth imperative is omnipresent, same as the productivity imperative. The imperatives are interrelated as growth ameliorates displacement problems and increasing productivity is usually a precondition for growth. There may be contingent growth opportunities for less productive firms, e.g., serving niche demands, but large productivity advantages make price competition viable so that more productive firms can take the market share of less productive firms. A running current throughout the historical narrative is the push and pull between automation and growth. Just as Marx (1976 [1867]) described, workers are pushed out of production via automation and then pulled back in by industrial growth—displaced and reabsorbed in quick succession. The theory developed here adds additional dynamics by discussing how different productive trajectories and productivity gaps influence the possibilities for growth—providing growth opportunities for productivity leaders and restricting opportunities for laggards.

5.5 *Globalization and Outsourcing*

There are tensions between explanations that center job displacement and automation and those that center globalization and outsourcing. Automation constitutes a 'push factor' of displacing jobs with technology, while globalization is a 'pull factor,' with jobs being drawn elsewhere in pursuit of low wages. This approach theorizes globalization and automation as 'two sides of the same coin' in the sense that both are exercised for the sake of capital accumulation. These processes are analytically distinct yet should not be viewed as antithetical to one another or as mutually exclusive alternatives but as interconnected and with the same underlying motivation. Certain conditions and technologies must be in place for outsourcing and globalizing to be both possible and desirable, just as certain technologies are needed to automate (Klein and Pettis 2020). It is useful to view both as two options among many to deal with capital accumulation or cost problems based on the socio-historic circumstances.

In recent decades, economic growth has been driven by globalization and framed as a 'cure-all' for financial woes including high costs and stagnating domestic sales. Globalization opens markets to global competition and thus the pressure of social domination to reach the global benchmark standards often becomes more intense (Pries 2003; Weyer 2011; Krzywdzinski and Jürgens 2015; Wenten 2020). It also encourages outsourcing to low-wage locations and more sales markets that may lessen the urgency of productivity reforms because export or transplant sales are growing rapidly in unsaturated markets. Setting up production and sales in Eastern Europe, Mexico, China and others may be the lifeblood of the auto industry right now, but what will happen if/when these markets mature and/or wages increase (see Wallerstein 2004; Wallerstein 2013)? The extent of globalization may be limited in its breadth and depth, as Earth is not a totally open system that can expand infinitely (see Dahms 2023). Neither are the 'good' job opportunities, e.g., high pay and benefits, infinitely expandable in the auto industry, especially given the high automation, the continual transformations of labor, and the productivity pressures to eliminate waste (see Knowles 2023a). Globalization is also not a net gain for all, e.g., outsourcing in communities like Detroit, where decades of automation and outsourcing have degraded much of the industrial heart of the city (Martelle 2014). Struggles over value distribution occur between firms, plants within firms, labor and management, nation-state value-regimes, and local communities through globalization and productivity pressures.

The typical imagining of 'our manufacturing jobs' is still oriented around the nation-state, demonstrating the ideological power of the imagined community (Anderson 1983). American and German domestic firms were largely centered on production within their own value-regimes, but globalization entails an increasing transnationalization of corporations in terms of their operations and sales, complicating the ties of the companies to value-regimes (see Robinson 2004, 2014). Yet, transnationalization of government authority remains territorial, and union and labor systems are difficult to upscale and coordinate (Holmes 2004; Robinson 2004; Hertwig, Pries, and Rampeltshammer 2011). It appears management has an advantage in successfully evading their supposed responsibility to the value-regime and setting up production in low-cost locations, though worker power in Germany has made this pursuit more favorable for domestic German workers than for the UAW dealing with the Big Three (Holmes 2004; Jürgens 2008; Jürgens and Krzywdzinski 2009; Covarrubias 2020).

Globalization modifies and amplifies the temporal processes discussed here and provides new ways to handle and disperse their effects. Though globalization is transforming the global economy, this analysis centers the "abstract constraints and imperatives that drive capital's dynamic" through temporal and processual terms rather than spatial terms like globalization (Postone 2017: 53). In this framework, globalization constitutes a spatial 'fix' to the pressure of these temporal processes and is fundamentally intertwined with these dynamics, simultaneously generating pressures to outsource, automate, lower costs, and transform labor.

5.6 *Possibilities of an Automation Crisis*

Technological automation differs from the original conception of Taylorism (increasing efficiency within given methods), or increasing productivity via increased labor intensity (e.g., line speed-up and many lean methods) in that automation directly changes what Marx (1976 [1867]: 577–578) calls the "organic composition of capital" where production processes develop a higher ratio of "constant capital," e.g., machines and materials, to "variable capital," i.e., workers (Postone 1993: 132). Absolute numbers of workers may rise in high growth conditions, but the ratio of machines to workers still increases when processes are automated. This has occurred in most auto production processes, except assembly, while other production reforms, e.g., lean production, typically improve efficiency without changing the organic composition of capital. However, they all share the similarity that each practice can push productivity norms forward and become socially necessary. Nevertheless, automation is of special importance because of technological displacement and the possibility of technological unemployment or a general anachronism of human labor (Postone 1993, 2015, 2017).

The organic composition of capital has radically changed in many auto production processes as they became increasingly automated until many processes today are near full automation. However, humans have never been fully excised from the system as indirect repair, maintenance, and monitoring workers are still needed. Technological displacement in these areas was mostly handled via internal transfers, though both countries coped with this via different programs, e.g., rationalization agreements to regulate transfers or a Jobs Bank (Rationalization Agreement 1968, 1987; Brumlop and Jürgens 1983; Schoenberger 2009; Ingrassia 2011). Meanwhile, hundreds of thousands of workers in both countries were employed in assembly due to their higher flexibility and the limitations of assembly automation. Overall, the auto industry automated most areas of production over the decades, leaving a small contingent of workers to tend the machines, while assembly was left as the last bastion of labor-intensive work (Meyer 2004; Krzywdzinski 2020a; Jürgens 2021; Jürgens 2023). New technological developments, including Industry 4.0, new advances in robotics, and the EV transition, may change this situation in the future, but this has not been the trend since the 1990s, and what new automation would entail remains to be seen.

As the discussion has been limited to one industry in two countries, while the organic composition of capital greatly changed in many production areas and technological displacement occurred, it is difficult to generalize the results to society at large. Since the industry retained a large assembly workforce, it is difficult to conclude that all production areas *inevitably* increase their organic composition of capital, even if all remain under productivity pressures. Postone (2015) argues that the historical dynamics of capitalism point toward the historical possibility of a new social form not centered on human labor,

> [Our productive capacities] open up the historical possibility of a future form of social production that no longer is based on the expenditure of

> direct human labor in production ... On the other hand, the necessity of the present is constantly reconstituted. Yet that necessity becomes increasingly anachronistic ... The emergence of the possibility of a future, in which surplus production no longer must be based on the labor of an oppressed class, is, at the same time, the emergence of the possibility of a disastrous development in which the growing superfluity of labor is expressed as the growing superfluity of people. (20–21)

Present limitations mean that a definitive statement on this possibility cannot be made. Even as human workers became superfluous in many auto production areas, it cannot be said with certainty this happened similarly in other industries. Thus, questions of whether developments in the auto industry signify a general trend where human labor becomes increasingly anachronistic cannot be fully answered here.

However, this critical theory is useful in explaining why automation and technological displacement occurs and how this is driven by the continuous pursuit of productivity. In this way, dealing with the 'productivity problem' can be described as responding to a constant 'crisis.' A critical theory of productivity is not narrowly concerned with 'obvious' periodic crises counterposed to the assumption of 'normalcy.' Rather, it takes this underlying 'crisis' as the 'normal' state of affairs and examines the different ways this 'crisis' is coped with and productivity pushed forward. This endeavor is not just descriptive but embeds historical analysis in the dynamics of capitalism. Future research may illuminate more historical-empirical evidence to further refine the theory.

6 Political Implications

The findings here have numerous political implications open to interpretation. A conservative may argue that this study provides evidence that maintaining a strict orientation around maximum capital accumulation through efficiency optimization and increasing productivity is always preferred. Workers, a conservative might argue, ought to temper their demands for limiting productivity through humanization to work cooperatively with management to maximally accumulate capital and maintain jobs. If technological displacement is inevitable, then the best way to handle it is to maximize productivity to ensure maximum capital accumulation so transfer procedures can be erected and firm growth prevents layoffs. This interpretation is perhaps best summed up in the admonition from Henry Ford II (1955) that,

> Part of the price of progress may be the willingness to accept change in the time, place, and type of employment that is available. In order to reap the full advantage of the new technologies, we must avoid the fatal freezing of men, machines and methods into rigid patterns. (16)

Such an interpretation holds that if pressures to increase productivity and automate cannot be stopped, that one should accept where 'market forces' lead even if that means a race to the bottom for labor. I would argue, however, that drawing this conclusion is a misinterpretation that limits the imagination. Identifying and analyzing forces of convergence is not an endorsement of such forces and misses how divergence and resistance can nevertheless persist. It implicitly accepts capitalist realism, i.e., that it is impossible to imagine a coherent alternative to capitalism (Fisher 2009).

One alternative is to ask: *what would it take to consciously control social domination rather than be controlled by capital's imperatives and constraints*? One potential answer is global regulation of production and control of technological development and implementation, because regulation at the mezzo level of the value-regime has been shown to not be enough to stem productivity pressures at the macro level (see Rosa 2015). A global regulatory system could set international policies regarding automation, technological displacement, and productivity development, e.g., not letting productivity gaps go too far ahead of regulatory limits or mandating transfers or job training for technologically displaced workers.

Perhaps a "Worldwide-Stop-Rationalization-Agreement" (*Weltrationalisierungs-Stop-Abkommen*) as described by Ehmer (1984: 5) would be necessary to control the constant pressures to rationalize and automate. Such measures would entail opportunity costs, i.e., the costs of limiting production and economic growth, but this may be desirable in the context of limited resources, climate change, and environmental degradation (Dahms 2023). Such efforts may be necessary if the goal is to 'live within our means' or de-grow the economy (see Frase 2016: 91–119).

However, what if instead of regulation limiting productive development, global governance systems *consciously and intentionally* pushed productivity forward to reduce both socially necessary labor time and *socially necessary labor* to a minimum. This recalls Marx's (1978 [1894]: 439–441) contention that communism necessarily entails the reduction of the "realm of necessity" and an opening up of the "realm of freedom" (see Knowles 2017: 168–169). With global coordination, openness to experimentation, and agreements to support participating workers and businesses, it may be possible to develop effective assembly line automation to finally free the alienated assembly line worker (Meyer 2004). The millions of global assembly line workers would presumably need new jobs, but global coordination could also facilitate job retraining and reassignment. The global governance systems could also work toward fixing this problem by orienting toward a 'post-work' future (see Srnicek and Williams 2015; Knowles 2017). For example, these aggressive automation experiments could be paired with a universal basic income to facilitate smooth job transfers and support technologically displaced workers in all industries as the world works toward a post-work, post-scarcity, and post-capitalist global social order (see Srnicek and Williams 2015; Bregman 2017; Knowles 2023b). Aggressive automation could be paired with globally enforced lower working hours so that, even in areas of high labor intensity, the amount of working time respects human limitations (Srnicek and Williams 2015; Bregman 2017). Such measures are aimed at protecting human interests in the process of intentionally and radically accelerating productivity.

Any political intervention to control social domination requires a global scale because, as was demonstrated again and again throughout the narrative, neither government intervention nor codetermination at firms could control productivity pressures at the macro level. Governments may manipulate productivity pressure via trade restrictions or regulations, and firms can create collectively bargained or codetermined productive norms within a firm, but neither can control the setting of socially necessary labor time determined at the global level. This is why codetermination or more democratic firm governance structures like Workers Self-Directed Enterprises (WSDE) are not sufficient to nullify productivity pressure or social domination. According to Wolff (2012: 13–14) all workers in a WSDE are also the firm's directors, so workers collectively have the full power to decide what to produce, where to produce, *how to produce*, and what to do with the surplus. Wolff (2012) claims that the fundamentally different structure of WSDEs enables them to make qualitatively different decisions in handling technical displacement, automation, investment, and responding to crisis than traditional capitalist firms (123–137). This may be true but having the directors and workers of a firm become one and the same does not negate the pressures all firms experience to conform to socially necessary labor time. Individual WSDEs in the context of capital as value in motion are still subject to capital. They may have exceptional control over the micro and mezzo levels to self-determine their own processes but still lack control over macro level pressures. There are good theoretical reasons why WSDEs would not be immune to productivity pressure, just as similar German automakers were at times compelled to adapt and improve productivity. Perhaps a critical mass of coordinated WSDEs could sufficiently control capital, but this too entails working toward control at a global scale. The identification of capital's global imperatives and constraints was why Marx (1976 [1867]) insisted on a *global* socialist revolution leading to a dictatorship of the proletariat in recognition that nothing less could enact the kind of coordination and control necessary to solve not just the problem of capitalist class domination but of the *social domination of capital.* The choice is not between a dictatorship of the proletariat or the freedom of capitalism, but between continuing to live under the *dictatorship of capital* and a genuine alternative that somehow escapes or rationally controls the imperatives and constraints capital places on social action.

Any establishment of a global governance system to consciously control capital and its social domination would undoubtedly be difficult and involve tradeoffs. If capital constitutes the social core of modern society (Postone 1993), then controlling capital means nothing less than controlling society down to its core processes and categories. Directing them also necessarily transforms them into new dynamics and structures. Unprecedented effort and costs would be necessary, but there are also costs to letting the status quo continue. The motivation is to ask, as Skidelsky (2020) put it, "how can humans be enabled to 'feel at home' in world governed by an inhuman and, if not intentionally, inhumane logic" (21). We conclude by drawing attention to these historical processes to prompt thinking about potential alternatives.

7 Conclusion

To conclude, the discussion invites a deconstruction of 'progress' in modern society. Conventionally understood, much progress has taken place in the auto industry as it has put millions of people to work and provided means of personal transportation to millions more. Thanks to advances in productivity and automation, the time it takes to make an automobile has gone from hundreds or even thousands of hours at the turn of the 20th century to less than 20 hours total for some vehicles today. But is it also 'progress' when someone loses their job to a machine? Is it progress when workers are deskilled or transferred to less well-paid work due to automation (Knowles 2023a)? This begs the question, who are the 'winners' and 'losers' from modern progress and how many lives must be disrupted for industrial development to *not* be labeled as progress? Yet, it is undeniable that the benefits of productivity and wealth produced from the global economy are enormous, just as are the human costs in terms of alienation, exploitation, and the negative effects of technological displacement. Progress is double-sided, producing results that, from a human point of view, appear as both 'progressive' and 'regressive' simultaneously (Horkheimer and Adorno 2001 [1947]; Allen 2016; Knowles 2017: 252). There is both 'progress' in freedom as well as 'progress' in domination under capitalism. Here, social domination is identified as the *price paid for progress*, it is a 'deal with the devil' that society makes to gain the advantages of higher productivity and more material wealth. In short, it is an often unrecognized hidden cost of modernity. But just as with any commodity, paying the price does still mean we get something in exchange. The political question is whether the exchange is worth it after all. Progress is thus loaded with contradictions and ideology, and a recognition of the contradictory nature of modern progress is necessary now more than ever (Horkheimer and Adorno 2001 [1947]; Allen 2016; Knowles 2017: 253).

Critical Theory does not superficially accept the concept of progress in modern societies. As Horkheimer (1975 [1937]: 207) explains, "[Critical Theory] is suspicious of the very categories of better, useful, appropriate, productive, and valuable, as these are understood in the present order, and refuses to take them as nonscientific presuppositions about which one can do nothing." This suspicion is warranted because progress is not a neutral term but reflective of capitalist society and its priorities, including the drive to increase productivity and accumulate capital. Many human costs are wrapped up in modern progress, betraying how the modern concept of progress is oriented toward capital, not humanity. Horkheimer (1975 [1937]) also explains how social scientists often forget how they are embedded in society, failing to critically examine how their work reflects the notions of 'progress' shaped by modern capitalism. He emphasizes the need to recognize the "two-sided character of the social totality," i.e., that it is both a totality created by human beings and thus always contingent and open to change, and yet human beings also "experience the fact that society is comparable to nonhuman natural processes" and that the world is "not their own but the world of capital" (207–208). In other words, there is a struggle between the individual and collective ability to realize *autonomy and agency* in society because the social world, especially the dynamics of capitalism, appears like a *heteronomous* force of nature that no individual could hope to control (see Horkheimer and Adorno 2001 [1947]; Postone 1993). Capital operates like a 'subject' whose existence is its own purpose that self-valorizes eternally in the spiral of value in motion (Postone 1993; Harvey 2017). Both workers and management participate in and have an interest in perpetuating this 'subject' by pushing forward progress *simultaneously with* the forces of heteronomy that compel and constrain them.

Any attempt to overcome the contradictions of modern progress must intimately understand their dynamics. This should be the task of a critical social science, including efforts to understand the dynamics of automation, technological displacement, and productivity development (Knowles 2017: 254). Doing so requires examining how *the gravity of concrete socio-historical conditions exert pressures on the process of illuminating those conditions* (Dahms 2015: 12). Identifying and analyzing these *social forces of gravity*, including social domination, is ultimately the purpose of critical theory. The critical theory developed here should be considered successful to the extent it demonstrates the importance of understanding these processes through rigorous examination of concrete historical processes—illuminating what lies behind phenomena like automation, technological displacement, and the social imperative of productivity.

Archival Bibliography

Congressional Quarterly

Congressional Quarterly. 1927. "The Status of the Automobile Trade." *CQ Researcher*. Retrieved August 30, 2021. (http://library.cqpress.com/cqresearcher/cqresrre1927121000).

Lee, Kendrick. 1943. "Labor in Government." *CQ Researcher*. Retrieved August 30, 2021. (http://library.cqpress.com/cqresearcher/cqresrre1943042900).

Masci, David. 2000. "Auto Industry's Future." *CQ Researcher*. Retrieved October 28, 2021. (https://library.cqpress.com/cqresearcher/document.php?id=cqresrre2000012100).

Noyes, Charles E. 1938. "The Market for Automobiles." *CQ Researcher*. Retrieved August 30, 2021. (https://library.cqpress.com/cqresearcher/document.php?id=cqresrre1938090200).

Patch, Buel W. 1932. "Outlook for the Automobile Industry" *QR Researcher*. Retrieved August 30, 2021. (http://library.cqpress.com/cqresearcher/cqresrre1932102600).

Riefler, D. B. 1929. "Condition of the Automobile Industry." *CQ Researcher*. Retrieved August 30, 2021. (https://library.cqpress.com/cqresearcher/document.php?id=cqresrre1929121000).

Ford Motor Company Archives

Barnes, J. E. 1982. "Meeting the Japanese Auto Challenge: an American Progress Report." 1982 Meeting the Japanese Auto Challenge AR-74-18056_016_135. Ford Motor Company Archives.

Ford, Henry II. 1955. "Horsepower and Horse Sense." Ford Motor Company Archives.

Ford, Henry II. 1959. "Wanted: An Economic Breakthrough." Ford Motor Company Archives.

Ford, Henry II. 1961. "Suggested Comments, Report on Automation, President's Advisory Committee on Labor-Management Policy." Ford Motor Company Archives.

Ford, Henry II. 1964. "Imperatives for Progress." Ford Motor Company Archives.

Ford, Henry II. 1982. "The Challenge of the 1980s." Ford Motor Company Archives.

Ford Motor Company Archives. 1952a. "1952 Serpentine Dragon Cleveland Engine AR-74-18056_SAFE1-347."

Ford Motor Company Archives. 1952b. "1952 Cleveland Engine Plant Electronic Brains AR-74-18056_SAFE1-295."

Ford Motor Company Archives. 1952c. "1952 Cleveland Engine Plant General Story AR-74-18056_SAFE2-005."

Ford Motor Company Archives. 1953a. "1953 DS Harder Bio AR-74-18056_SAFE2-307."

Ford Motor Company Archives. 1953b. "1953 Expansion Since WWII AR-74-18056_SAFE2-256."

Ford Motor Company Archives. 1954. "1954 Automation Speech Press Release."

Ford Motor Company Archives. 1981. "1981 Manufacturing Technology AR-74-18056_015_234."

Ford Motor Company Archives. 2015a. "Ford Trains Thousands of Kansas City Assembly Plant Workers to Support Upcoming F-150 Production."

Ford Motor Company Archives. 2015b. "Kansas City Assembly Plant Comes on Line as Second U.S. Factory Building All-New Ford F-150."

Poling, H. A. 1982. "1982 Poling Speech Strategic Planning AR-74-18056_016_155." Ford Motor Company Archives.

Sullivan, Ray H. 1953. "1953 Industrial Relations Conference Speech AR-74-18056_SAFE2-255." Ford Motor Company Archives.

General Motors Heritage Center

General Motors Heritage Center. 1954. "heritage-collection-GM_NR_03041954_4."

General Motors Heritage Center. 1959. "heritage-collection-GM_NR_11121959."

General Motors Heritage Center. 1984. "heritage-collection-AP_NR_08131984002."

General Motors Heritage Center. 1982. "For Release Thursday, March 25, 1982."

General Motors Heritage Center. 1985. "General Motors Annual Report 1985."

General Motors Heritage Center. 1987. "heritage-collection-GM_NR_08051987001."

General Motors Heritage Center. 1992. "For Release Friday, May 22, 1992."

General Motors Heritage Center. 1991. "Fore Release Wednesday, August 7, 1991."

General Motors Heritage Center. 1994. "General Motors Public Interest Report Nineteen Ninety-Four."

General Motors Heritage Center. 1994. "General Motors Annual Report 1994."

General Motors Heritage Center. 2019. "GM 101: An Overview of Our Legacy and Business Employee Manual."

IG Metall Vorstand

IG Metall. 1953. "IG Metall Geschäftsbericht 1950–1952." Frankfurt, Germany: IG Metall.

IG Metall. 1954. "IG Metall Geschäftsbericht 1952–1953." Frankfurt, Germany: IG Metall.

IG Metall. 1956. "IG Metall Geschäftsbericht 1954–1955." Frankfurt, Germany: IG Metall.

IG Metall. 1958. "IG Metall Geschäftsbericht 1956–1957." Frankfurt, Germany: IG Metall.

IG Metall. 1960. "IG Metall Geschäftsbericht 1958–1959." Frankfurt, Germany: IG Metall.

IG Metall. 1962. "IG Metall Geschäftsbericht 1960–1961." Frankfurt, Germany: IG Metall.

IG Metall. 1968. "IG Metall Geschäftsbericht 1965–1967." Frankfurt, Germany: IG Metall.
IG Metall. 1974. "IG Metall Geschäftsbericht 1971–1973." Frankfurt, Germany: IG Metall.
IG Metall. 1983. "IG Metall Geschäftsbericht 1980–1982." Frankfurt, Germany: IG Metall.
IG Metall. 2007. "IG Metall Geschäftsbericht 2003–2006." Frankfurt, Germany: IG Metall.

M@RS—The Digital Archives of Mercedes-Benz Classic

Könecke, Fritz. 1956a. "Production without Workers?" M@RS—The Digital Archives of Mercedes-Benz Classic. Pp. 21–23 in Press Information 1956, PRINT1300. Retrieved March 11, 2022. https://bit.ly/40nD81I.
Könecke, Fritz. 1956b. "To all Daimler-Benz Employees." M@RS—The Digital Archives of Mercedes-Benz Classic. Pp. 84–85 in Press Information 1956, PRINT1300. Retrieved March 11, 2022. https://bit.ly/40nD81I.
The Digital Archives of Mercedes-Benz Classic. 1969. "Worth/Rhine The new Daimler-Benz truck assembly plant." M@RS—The Digital Archives of Mercedes-Benz Classic. Press Information 1969, PRINT2094. Retrieved April 8, 2022. https://bit.ly/4h0Jb3r.
The Digital Archives of Mercedes-Benz Classic. 1978. "Kennziffern und Schaubilder." M@RS—The Digital Archives of Mercedes-Benz Classic. Pp. 17–30 in Press Information June 16, 1978, PRMIT7401. Retrieved March 11, 2022. https://bit.ly/3WrCnDo.
Woltereck, Hans. 1956a. "Auf dem Wege zur 'Automation:' Höhere geistige, aber geringere körperliche Anforderungen." M@RS—The Digital Archives of Mercedes-Benz Classic. Press Information March 17, 1956, PRMIT16340. Retrieved March 25, 2022. http://bit.ly/3PKDMS6.
Woltereck, Hans. 1956b. "On the way to Automation: Higher intellectual, but lower physical demands." M@RS—The Digital Archives of Mercedes-Benz Classic. Pp. 24–27 in Press Information 1956, PRINT1300. Retrieved March 11, 2022. https://bit.ly/3Ws9BCZ.
Zahn, Joachim. 1978 "Ausführungen von Prof. Dr. Joachim Zahn Vorsitzender des Vorstandes der Daimler-Benz AG bei der Bilanz-Pressekonferenz am 9. Mai 1978." M@RS—The Digital Archives of Mercedes-Benz Classic. Pp. 1–11 in Press Information June 16, 1978, PRMIT7401. Retrieved March 11, 2022. https://bit.ly/3WprVwc.

Volkswagen Aktiengesellschaft Corporate Archives

Autogramm. 1984. "Wir wollen den Fortschritt sozial beherrschbar machen." *Autogramm*, Februar. Wolfsburg, Germany: Volkswagen Aktiengesellschaft Corporate Archives.
Die Presse. 1965. "Nordhoff vor Industriellen VW-Chef uber technische, menschliche und soziale Aspekte der Automatisierung." *Die Presse*, October 15. Wolfsburg, Germany: Volkswagen Aktiengesellschaft Corporate Archives.

Ehmer, Hans-Jürgen. 1984. "Rationalisierung trotz Arbeitslosigkeit?" Wolfsburg, Germany: Volkswagen Aktiengesellschaft Corporate Archives.

Enz und Metter Bote. 1958. "Nordhoff. Automatisierung bedeutet nicht Arbeiter-Entlassung, 07.11.1958." *Enz und Metter Bote*, November 7. (62/20/1). Wolfsburg, Germany: Volkswagen Aktiengesellschaft Corporate Archives.

Nordhoff, Friedrich. 1958a. "Speech Delivered by Friedrich Nordhoff June 3, 1958." Wolfsburg, Germany: Volkswagen Aktiengesellschaft Corporate Archives.

Nordhoff, Friedrich. 1958b. "Nordhoff Bemerkungen zum Thema Rationalisierung: Vortrag vor der Industrie- und Handelskammer Braunschweig Dezember 5, 1958." (373/84/1). Wolfsburg, Germany: Volkswagen Aktiengesellschaft Corporate Archives.

Rationalization Agreement. 1968. "Abkommen zum Schutze der Arbeitnehmer (Lohnempfänger und Angestellte) vor Folgen der Rationalisierung." 1968. Wolfsburg, Germany: Volkswagen Aktiengesellschaft Corporate Archives.

Rationalization Agreement. 1987. "Tarifvertrag zur sozialen Sicherung der Arbeitnehmer bei technischen und arbeitsorganisatorischen Änderungen. 11. February 1987." (1119/106/1). Wolfsburg, Germany: Volkswagen Aktiengesellschaft Corporate Archives.

Volkswagen. 1954. "vw-Konzernarchiv 373 Nr. 796/1." Wolfsburg, Germany: Volkswagen Aktiengesellschaft Corporate Archives.

Volkswagen. 1965. "vw-Konzernarchiv Z 174 Nr. 1562/17." Wolfsburg, Germany: Volkswagen Aktiengesellschaft Corporate Archives.

Wolfsburger Allgemeine. 1966. "Bizeps allein genügt nicht, Nordhoff: Automation stellt höhere Anspruche an Wissen und Bildung." *Wolfsburger Allgemeine*, Oktober 19. (62/147/2). Wolfsburg, Germany: Volkswagen Aktiengesellschaft Corporate Archives.

Wolfsburger Nachrichten. 1965b. "Automatisierung hilft dem Menschen: Vortrag Professor Nordhoffs im Braunschweigischen Hochschulbund." *Wolfsburger Nachrichten*, May 24. Wolfsburg, Germany: Volkswagen Aktiengesellschaft Corporate Archives.

Walter P. Reuther Library

Auto Plant Closures and Employment, 1992–1994, Box: 6, Folder: 15. Walter P. Reuther Library. (Yettaw 1994).

Automation by Jack Conway, Admin. Assist. To W. P. Reuther, 1955–56, Box: 42, Folder: 18. Walter P. Reuther Library. (Conway 1955).

Automation Committee, 1954–64, Box: 45, Folder: 10. Walter P. Reuther Library. (Automation Committee 1954).

Automation Committee, 1954–64, Box: 45, Folder: 16. Walter P. Reuther Library. (Murrow 1957).

Automation; G. G. Murie, 1955, Box: 26, Folder: 61. Walter P. Reuther Library. (Murie 1955).

Abner, 19Automation: Speech by W. Abner, 5/1963, Box: 7, Folder: 8. Walter P. Reuther Library. (Abner 1963).

CIO Automation Conference, 1955, Box: 4, Folder: 17. Walter P. Reuther Library. (CIO Automation Conference 1955).

CIO pamphlet; Guaranteed Annual Wages, 1953, Box: 1, Folder: 46. Walter P. Reuther Library. (CIO 1953).

Germany, IGM Conference, Nat Weinberg; speech, 1965 Mar, Box: 100, Folder: 31. Walter P. Reuther Library. (Weinberg 1965).

GM "Meeting the Competitive Challenge" Speeches, 1988, Box: 12, Folder: 4. Walter P. Reuther Library. (Selvala 1988).

"Job Enrichment," N. Weinberg, 1974, Box: 9, Folder: 41. Walter P. Reuther Library. (Weinberg 1974).

Letters and speeches, 1981, 1986, Box: 1, Folder: 5. Walter P. Reuther Library. (Westfall 1981).

"Towards a Union Perspective on QWL," D. MacLeod, Box: 9, Folder: 20. Walter P. Reuther Library. (MacLeod n.d.).

Bibliography

Abelhauser, Werner. 1975. *Wirtschaft in Westdeutschland 1945–1948*. Stuttgart, Germany: Deutsche Verlags-Anstalt.

Abernathy, W. J. 1978. *The Productivity Dilemma. Roadblock to innovation in the automobile industry*. Baltimore, MD: John Hopkins University Press.

Abernathy, W. J., Clark, K. B., and Kantrow, A. M. 1983. "The New Industrial Competition." Pp. 72–131 in *Survival Strategies for American Industry*, edited by A. M. Kantrow. New York, NY: Harvard Business Review Executive Book Series.

Abolhassani, Amir, Harner, James E., and Jaridi Majid. 2018. "Empirical analysis of productivity enhancement strategies in the North American automotive industry." *International Journal of Production Economics*. 208(2019): 140–159.

Acemoglu, Daron and Robinson, James. 2012. *Why Nations Fail: The Origins of Power, Prosperity, and Poverty*. New York, NY: Crown Business.

Adler, Paul. 1993a. "Time-and-Motion Regained." *Harvard Business Review*. Retrieved August 25, 2022 (https://hbr.org/1993/01/time-and-motion-regained).

Adler, Paul. 1993b. "The 'Learning Bureaucracy': New United Motor Manufacturing, Inc." *Research in Organizational Behavior*. 15: 111–194.

Adler, Paul, Kochan, Thomas A., MacDuffie, John Paul, Pil, Frits K., and Rubinstein, Saul. 1997. "United States: Variations on a Theme." Pp. 61–83 in *After Lean Production: Evolving Employment Practices in the World Auto Industry*, edited by T. A. Kochan, R. D. Lansbury, and J. P. MacDuffie. Ithaca, NY: Cornell University Press.

Africa Wire. 2008. "US automakers narrow productivity gap with Asian rivals." Gale OneFile: Business. Retrieved August 2, 2022 (link.gale.com/apps/doc/A179774476/ITBC?u=tel_a_utl&sid=bookmark-ITBC&xid=1cdb1e5d).

Albers, Detlev, Goldschmidt, Werner, and Oehlke, Paul. 1971. *Arbeitskämpfe in Westeuropa. England, Frank-reich, Italien*. Reinbek bei Hamburg: Rowohlt Taschenbuch Verlag.

Albert, Dan. 2019. *Are We There Yet?: The American Automobile Past, Present, and Driverless*. New York, NY: W. W. Norton & Company.

Albert, Michel. 1993. *Capitalism Against Capitalism*. London: Whurr Publishers.

Allen, Amy. 2016. *The End of Progress: Decolonizing the Normative Foundations of Critical Theory*. New York, NY: Columbia University Press.

Alternative Fuels Data Center. 2024. "Electric Vehicle Registrations by State." *U.S. Department of Energy*. Retrieved October 14, 2024 (https://afdc.energy.gov/data/10962).

Anderson, Benedict. 1983. *Imagined Communities: Reflections on the Origin and Spread of Nationalism*. London, UK: Verso.

Anderson, Brad. 2025. "Germany's EV Sales Crash 28% In First Full Year Without Subsidies." *Carscoops*. Retrieved January 15, 2025 (https://www.carscoops.com/2025/01/ev-sales-in-germany-plunge-over-27-in-2024-after-subsidies-were-scrapped/).

Arnold, Horace Lucien, and Faurote, Fay Leone. 1915. *Ford methods and the Ford shops*. New York, NY: The Engineering Magazine Company.

Arrighi, Giovanni. 2010. *The Long Twentieth Century: Money, Power, and the Origins of Our Times*. Updated Edition. New York: Verso.

Asher, Robert and Edsforth, Ronald. 1995. "A Half Century of Struggle: Auto Workers Fighting for Justice." Pp. 1–37 in *Autowork*, edited by R. Asher and R. Edsforth. New York, NY: SUNY Press.

Asher, Robert. 1995. "The 1949 Speed Up Strike and the Post War Social Compact, 1946–1961." Pp. 127–154 in *Autowork*, edited by R. Asher and R. Edsforth. New York, NY: SUNY Press.

Association for Advancing Automation. 2023. "Unimate: the First Industrial Robot." *Association for Advancing Automation*. Retrieved December 12, 2022 (https://www.automate.org/a3-content/joseph-engelberger-unimate).

Automotive News. 2009. "Detroit must pay (cash) for past manufacturing sins." Gale General One File. Retrieved August 2, 2022 (link.gale.com/apps/doc/A195030297/ITOF?u=tel_a_utl&sid=bookmark-ITOF&xid=7e248d27).

Automotive News Europe. 2024. "VW could cut up to 30,000 jobs in Germany, report says." *Automotive News Europe*. Retrieved October 15, 2024 (https://europe.autonews.com/automakers/vw-said-plan-30000-job-losses-germany).

Autor, David, Levy, Frank, and Murnane, Richard. 2003. "The Skill Content of Recent Technological Change: An Empirical Exploration." *The Quarterly Journal of Economics*. 118(4): 1279–1333.

Babson, Steve. 1993. "Lean or mean: the MIT model and lean production at Mazda." *Labor Studies Journal*. 18(2): 3–12.

Babson, Steve. 1995a. "Whose Team? Lean Production at Mazda U.S.A." Pp. 235–246 in *Lean Work: Empowerment and Exploitation in the Global Auto Industry*, edited by S. Babson. Detroit, MI: Wayne State University Press.

Babson, Steve. 1995b. "Lean Production and Labor: Empowerment and Exploitation." Pp. 1–40 in *Lean Work: Empowerment and Exploitation in the Global Auto Industry*, edited by S. Babson. Detroit, MI: Wayne State University Press.

Babson, Steve. 1995c. "Restructuring the Workplace: Post-Fordism or Return of the Foreman?" Pp. 227–256 in *Autowork*, edited by R. Asher and R. Edsforth. New York, NY: SUNY Press.

Baccaro, Lucio and Pontusson, Jonas. 2016. "Rethinking Comparative Political Economy: The Growth Model Perspective." *Politics & Society*. 44(2): 175–207.

Bainbridge, L. 1983. "'Ironies of automation.' Analysis, Design and Evaluation of Man-Machine Systems." *Automatica*. 19(6): 775–779.

Barclay, H. W. 1936. *Ford Production Methods*. New York, NY: Harper & Brothers.

Behr, Peter. 1986. "Some Advice on Saving GM From Itself." *Washington Post*. Retrieved on December 24, 2022. (https://www.washingtonpost.com/archive/business/1986

/12/11/some-advice-on-saving-gm-from-itself/5bbc748e-ada0-4cee-9600-f87264598058/).

Bellon, Bernard. 1990. *Mercedes in Peace and War: German Automobile Workers, 1903–1945*. New York, NY: Columbia University Press.

Beniger, J. R. 1986. *The Control Revolution: Technological and Economic Origins of the Information Society*. Cambridge, Mass: Harvard University Press.

Benjamin, Daniel. 1999. "Voluntary Export Restraints on Automobiles." *PERC Reports* 17(3).

Berggren, Christian. 1994. "NUMMI vs. Uddevalla." *Sloan Management Review*. 35(2).

Berggren, Christian. 1995. "Are Assembly Lines Just More Efficient? Reflections on Volvo's 'Humanistic' Manufacturing." Pp. 277–291 in *Lean Work: Empowerment and Exploitation in the Global Auto Industry*, edited by S. Babson. Detroit, MI: Wayne State University Press.

Berry, Steven, James Levinsohn, and Ariel Pakes. 1999. "Voluntary Export Restraints on Automobiles: Evaluating a Trade Policy." *American Economic Review*. 89(3): 400–30.

Biggs, Lindy. 1995. "Building for Mass Production: Factory Design and Work Process at the Ford Motor Company." Pp. 39–63 in *Autowork*, edited by R. Asher and R. Edsforth. New York, NY: SUNY Press.

Book, Simon, Demling, Alexander, Fahrion, Georg, Giesen, Christoph, Hage, Simon, and Hesse, Martin. 2024. "An Existential Crisis in the German Auto Industry." *Der Spiegel*. Retrieved January 13, 2025 (https://www.spiegel.de/international/business/electric-shock-an-existential-crisis-in-the-german-auto-industry-a-266bd037-b63a-4c9b-97b5-423866d7080f).

Bormann, René, Fink, Philipp, Holzapfel, Helmut, Rammler, Stephen, Sauter-Servaes, Thomas, Tiemann, Heinrich, Waschke, Thomas, and Weirauch, Boris. 2018. "The Future of the German Automotive Industry: Transformation by disaster or by design?" *Division for Economic and Social Policy Friedrich-Ebert-Stiftung*. Retrieved September 9, 2022 (https://library.fes.de/pdf-files/wiso/14450.pdf).

Boudette, Neal E. 2018. "Inside Tesla's Audacious Push to Reinvent the Way Cars Are Made." *New York Times* Retrieved November 18, 2021 (https://www.nytimes.com/2018/06/30/business/tesla-factory-musk.html).

Boutdette, Neal E. 2024. "A Loss at Mercedes-Benz Slows U.A.W.'s Southern Campaign." *New York Times*. Retrieved January 9, 2025 (https://www.nytimes.com/2024/05/18/business/uaw-mercedes-benz-alabama-election.html).

Boyer, Robert and Freyssenet, Michel. 2002. *The Productive Models: The Conditions of Profitability*. London and New York: Palgrave.

Boyer, Robert and Freyssenet, Michel. 1995. "Productive models, between business history and social sciences. The world that changed the machine." Fifth International Steering Committee of "Emergence of Industrial Models" Program. Gif-sur-Yvette, France: GERPISA.

Boyle, Kevin. 1995. "Auto Workers at War: Patriotism and Protest in the American Automobile Industry, 1939–1945." Pp. 99–126 in *Autowork*, edited by R. Asher and R. Edsforth. New York, NY: SUNY Press.

Braverman, Harry. 1998 [1974]. *Labor and Monopoly Capital*. New York, NY: Monthly Review Press.

Braudel, Fernand. 2009 [1960]. "History and the Social Sciences: The Longue Duree." *Review*. 32(2): 171–203.

Bregman, Rutger. 2017. *Utopia for Realists*. New York, NY: Back Bay Books.

Bright, James R. 1958. *Automation and Management*. Norwood, Mass.: Plimpton Press.

Brooks, Chris. 2019. "Why the UAW Lost Again in Chattanooga." *Labor Notes*. Retrieved January 9, 2025 (https://labornotes.org/2019/06/why-uaw-lost-again-chattanooga).

Brown, Wendy. 2015. *Undoing the Demos: Neoliberalism's Stealth Revolution*. New York, NY: Zone Books.

Brumlop, Eva and Jürgens, Ulrich. 1983. "Rationalization and Industrial Relations: A Case Study of Volkswagen" *International Institute for Comparative Social Research/Labor Policy*. 83(216): 1–59.

Brynjolfsson, Erik and McAfee, Andrew. 2011. *Race Against the Machine*. Lexington, Mass: Digital Frontier Press.

Brynjolfsson, Erik and McAfee, Andrew. 2014. *The Second Machine Age*. New York: W. W. Norton & Company.

Business Wire. 1995. "Nissan is again North America's most productive plant." *Business Wire*. Gale General One file.

Butollo, Florian, Jürgens, Ulrich, and Krzywdzinski, Martin. 2018. "From Lean Production to Industrie 4.0. More Autonomy for Employees?" *WZB—Discussion Paper*, SP III 2018(303): 1–24.

Calabrese, Giuseppe Giulio. 2020. "The Italian Automotive Industry: Between Old and New Development Factors." Pp. 163–202 in *New Frontiers of the Automobile Industry*, edited by A. V. Covarrubias and S. M. Ramírez Perez. Cham, Switzerland: Palgrave Macmillan.

Caplan, Lincoln. 1983. "Back to Industrial Basics" *New York Times*. Retrieved March 12, 2023 (https://www.nytimes.com/1983/10/16/books/back-to-industrial-basics.html).

Chandler, Alfred D. 1964. *Giant enterprise: Ford, General Motors, and the automobile industry. Sources and Readings*. New York, Burlingame: Harcourt, Brace & World.

Chandler, Alfred D. 1990. *Scale and Scope: The Dynamics of Industrial Capitalism*. Cambridge, Mass: Belknap Press.

Chandler, Alfred D. 1977. *The Visible Hand: The Managerial Revolution in American Business*. Cambridge, Mass: Belknap Press.

Chilton, Chris. 2024. "Chinese Buyers Are Ditching German Cars For Local Brands, And That's Bad News." *Carscoops*. Retrieved January 13, 2025 (https://www.carscoops.com/2024/10/german-automakers-are-scrambling-to-stay-afloat-in-china/).

Ciesla, Burghard. 2009. "Difficult Relations: German Automobile Construction and Economic Alliance in Eastern Europe, 1945–1990." Pp. 87–100 in *Towards Mobility. Varieties of Automobilism in East and West*, edited by M. Grieger, U. Gutzmann, and D. Schlinkert. Wolfsburg, Germany: Volkswagen AG.

Clark, R. 1979. *The Japanese Company*. New Haven, CT: Yale University Press.

Clelland, Donald A. 2014. "The Core of the Apple: Dark Value and Degrees of Monopoly in Global Commodity Chains." *Journal of World-Systems Research*. 20(1): 82–111.

Clibborn, Stephen, Lansbury, Russell D., and Wright, Chris F. 2020. "Who Killed the Australian Automotive Industry: The Employers, Government or Trade Unions?" Pp. 255–276 in *New Frontiers of the Automobile Industry*, edited by A. V. Covarrubias and S. M. Ramírez Perez. Cham, Switzerland: Palgrave Macmillan.

Clinton, Bentley C. and Steinberg, Daniel C. 2019. "Providing the Spark: Impact of financial incentives on battery electric vehicle adoption." *Journal of Environmental Economics and Management*. 98: 102255.

Collis, Danielle. 2024. "Luxury German automaker must urgently win back market share." *News.com.au*. Retrieved January 13, 2025 (https://www.news.com.au/technology/motoring/luxury-german-automaker-must-urgently-win-back-market-share/news-story/6638f980fb81e1933fc7ef78e7823ce6).

Cook, Lorne. 2024. "The EU is imposing duties on electric vehicles from China after trade talks fail." *The Associated Press*. Retrieved January 14, 2025 (https://apnews.com/article/eu-china-trade-electric-vehicles-duties-ev-9c720558b83316fdb6e1a0f9c2b55a15).

Covarrubias, Alex V. 2020. "The Boom of the Mexican Automotive Industry: From NAFTA to USMCA." Pp. 323–348 in *New Frontiers of the Automobile Industry*, edited by A. V. Covarrubias and S. M. Ramírez Perez. Cham, Switzerland: Palgrave Macmillan.

Covarrubias, Alex V. and Ramírez Perez, Sigfrido, M. 2020a. *New Frontiers of the Automobile Industry*. Cham, Switzerland: Palgrave Macmillan.

Covarrubias, Alex V. and Ramírez Perez, Sigfrido, M. 2020b. "Introduction: Changing Geographies and Frontiers of the Automotive Industry." Pp. 1–38 in *New Frontiers of the Automobile Industry*, edited by A. V. Covarrubias and S. M. Ramírez Perez. Cham, Switzerland: Palgrave Macmillan.

Covarrubias, Alex V. and Ramírez Perez, Sigfrido, M. 2020c. "Wrapping Up: The New Geographies and Frontiers of the AI have Arrived. Who is Taking the Lead?" Pp. 455–494 in *New Frontiers of the Automobile Industry*, edited by A. V. Covarrubias and S. M. Ramírez Perez. Cham, Switzerland: Palgrave Macmillan.

Crumm, Thomas A. 2010. *What is Good For General Motors: Solving America's Industrial Conundrum*. New York, NY: Algora Publishing.

Cutcher-Gerschenfeld, Joel, Brooks, Dan, and Mulloy, Martin. 2015. "The Decline and Resurgence of the U.S. Auto Industry." *Economic Policy Institute*. Retrieved April 17, 2023 (https://www.epi.org/publication/the-decline-and-resurgence-of-the-u-s-auto-industry/).

Cutler, Jonathan. 1998. *A Slacker's Paradise: The Fight For 30 Hours Work at 40 Hours' Pay in the United Automobile Workers, 1941–1966*. PhD. Dissertation, Sociology, City University of New York.

Cutler, Jonathan. 2004. *Shorter Hours, the UAW, and the Struggle for American Unionism*. Philadelphia, Pennsylvania: Temple University Press.

Dahms, Harry F. 2002. "Sociology in the Age of Globalization: Toward a Dynamic Sociological Theory." *Current Perspectives in Social Theory*. 21: 287–320.

Dahms, Harry F. 2008 "How Social Science is Impossible without Critical Theory: The Immersion of Mainstream Approaches in Time and Space." Pp. 3–61 in *No Social Science without Critical Theory*, edited by H. F. Dahms. Bingley, UK: Emerald Publishing Limited.

Dahms, Harry F. 2015. "Which Capital, Which Marx? Basic Income between Mainstream Economics, Critical Theory, and the Logic of Capital." *Basic Income Studies*. 10(1): 115–140.

Dahms, Harry F. 2023. *Planetary Sociology: Beyond the Entanglement of Identity and Social Structure*. Bingley, UK: Emerald Publishing Limited.

Dassbach, Carl. 1994. "Where is North American Automobile Production Headed?: Low-Wage Lean Production" *Electronic Journal of Sociology*. 1(1).

Degan, Ronald Jean. 2011. "Fordism and Taylorism are responsible for the early success and recent decline of the U.S. motor vehicle industry." *Center of Research in International Business & Strategy*. 81: 1–29.

DeMarines, Ron. 2000. "GM Parts/Vehicles Productivity Soar Says Harbour Report." *Autoparts Report* 13(24). Gale One File Business. Retrieved August 2, 2022 (link.gale.com/apps/doc/A63676236/ITBC?u=tel_a_utl&sid=bookmark-ITBC&xid=5825c7b0).

Der Spiegel. 2024. "Erstmals fahren die meisten Neuwagen in China elektrisch." *Der Spiegel*. Retrieved January 13, 2025 (https://www.spiegel.de/auto/china-elektroautos-im-juli-2024-erstmals-mehrheit-der-neuwagen-a-82301ec8-7162-4522-84aa-aee9f4afd368).

Deutsche Welle. 2024. "Ford looking to cut thousands of jobs in Europe." *Deutsche Welle*. Retrieved January 13, 2025 (https://www.dw.com/en/ford-looking-to-cut-thousands-of-jobs-in-europe/a-70832943).

Dias, Jaclyn. 2022. "Elon Musk dares United Autoworkers to try to unionize Tesla." *National Public Radio*. Retrieved March 30, 2023 (https://www.npr.org/2022/03/03/1084366833/elon-musk-dares-united-autoworkers-to-try-to-unionize-tesla).

Donnelly, Tom, Mellahi, Kemal, and Morris, David. 2002. "The European automobile industry: escape from parochialism." *European Business Review*. 14(1): 30–39.

Doran, James. 2005. "GM angers union with plan to cut 30,000 jobs." *Times*. Gale Academic One File. Retrieved August 2, 2022 (link.gale.com/apps/doc/A139011765/AONE?u=tel_a_utl&sid=bookmark-AONE&xid=f879c4b7).

Drucker, Peter F. 1946. *Concept of the Corporation*. New York, NY: John Day.

Durkheim, Emile. 1984 [1893]. *The Division of Labor in Society*. Translated by W. D. Halls. New York, NY: The Free Press.

Eaton, Adrienne. 1995. "The Role of the Union and Employee Involvement in Lean Production." Pp. 70–78 in *Lean Work: Empowerment and Exploitation in the Global Auto Industry*, edited by S. Babson. Detroit, MI: Wayne State University Press.

Eddy, Melissa. 2021. "He's Steering Volkswagen, With His Eyes on Beating Tesla." *New York Times*. Retrieved January 14, 2025 (https://www.nytimes.com/2021/11/24/business/volkswagen-ceo-herbert-diess.html#:~:text=Diess%20repeatedly%20stresses%20the%20gap,3%20or%20ID.).

Edsforth, Ronald and Asher, Robert. 1995. "The Speedup: The Focal Point of Workers' Grievances, 1919–1941." Pp. 65–98 in *Autowork*, edited by R. Asher and R. Edsforth. New York, NY: SUNY Press.

Edsforth, Ronald. 1995. "Why Automation Didn't Shorten the Work Week: The Politics of Work Time In the Automobile Industry." Pp. 155–179 in *Autowork*, edited by R. Asher and R. Edsforth. New York, NY: SUNY Press.

Elbaum, Bernard. 1989. "Why apprenticeship persisted in Britain but not in the United States." *The Journal of Economic History*. 49(2): 337–349.

Ewing, Jack. 2017. *Faster, Higher, Farther: The Volkswagen Scandal*. New York, NY: W. W. Norton & Company.

Fava, Valentina. 2009. "Skill Formation in Škoda's Path to Mass Production: Reworking Imported Technological and Organizational Knowledge." Pp. 111–120 in *Towards Mobility. Varieties of Automobilism in East and West*, edited by M. Grieger, U. Gutzmann, and D. Schlinkert. Wolfsburg, Germany: Volkswagen AG.

Feigenbaum, James and Gross, Daniel P. 2020. "Automation and the Fate of Young Workers: Evidence from Telephone Operation in the Early 20th Century." *NBER Working Paper* no. 28061: 1–42.

Ferguson, E. S. 1968. *Bibliography of the History of Technology*. Boston, Mass: MIT Press.

Fine, Sidney. 1969. *Sit-Down: The General Motors Strike of 1936–1937*. Ann Arbor, MI: University of Michigan Press.

Finkelstein, Sydney. 2003. "GM and the great automation solution." *Business Strategy Review*. 14(3): 18–24.

Fisher, Mark. 2009. *Capitalist Realism: Is There No Alternative?* Winchester, UK: Zero Books.

Fisher, Paul. 1951. "Labor Codetermination in Germany." *Social Research*. 18(4): 449–485.

Flink, James J. 1988. *The Automobile Age*. Cambridge, Mass: The MIT Press.

Ford, Henry. 1922. *My Life and Work*. Public Domain.

Ford, Martin. 2014. *The Rise of the Robots*. New York, NY: Basic Books.

Ford Motor Company. 2021. "2021 Annual Report." Ford Motor Company. Retrieved July 26, 2022 (https://s205.q4cdn.com/882619693/files/doc_financials/2021/ar/Ford-2021-Annual-Report.pdf).

Foucault, Michel. 1995 [1975]. *Discipline & Punish: The Birth of the Prison*. New York, NY: Vintage Books.

Frase, Peter. 2016. *Four Futures: Life After Capitalism*. London, UK: Verso.

Frey, Carl and Osborne, Michael. 2013. "The Future of Employment: How Susceptible are Jobs to Computerization?" Oxford, UK: Oxford Martin Programme on Technology and Employment.

Frey, Carl. 2019. *The Technology Trap: Capital, Labor, and Power in the Age of Automation*. Princeton, NJ: Princeton University Press.

Friedman, Milton. 2002 [1962]. *Capitalism and Freedom*. Chicago: University of Chicago Press.

Fridenson, Patrick. 2009. "Corporate Culture in the French Automobile Industry: the Changes from 1944 to 2004." Pp. 165–174 in *Towards Mobility. Varieties of Automobilism in East and West*, edited by M. Grieger, U. Gutzmann, and D. Schlinkert. Wolfsburg, Germany: Volkswagen AG.

Galbraith, John Kenneth. 1993 [1952]. *American Capitalism: The Concept of Countervailing Power*. New York, New York: Routledge.

General Motors. 2020. "2019 Annual Report." General Motors. Retrieved July 19, 2022 (https://www.sec.gov/Archives/edgar/data/1467858/000146785820000028/gm2019 10k.htm).

Granel, M. 1985. "Auswirkungen des Robotereinsatzes auf die Arbeitsorganisation" *REFA-Nachrichten*. 38(4): 15–21.

Greenhouse, Steven. 2019. *Beaten Down, Worked Up: The Past, Present, and Future of American Labor*. New York, NY: Alfred A. Knopf.

Grieger, Manfred. 2009. "Business with the Socialist Automotive Industry. Volkswagen's Economic Relations with the Soviet Union and the German Democratic Republic." Pp. 101–110 in *Towards Mobility. Varieties of Automobilism in East and West*, edited by M. Grieger, U. Gutzmann, and D. Schlinkert. Wolfsburg, Germany: Volkswagen AG.

Grieger, Manfred and Lupa, Markus. 2015. *From the Beetle to a Global Player. Volkswagen Chronicle*. Wolfsburg, Germany: Volkswagen Aktiengesellschaft.

Guzik, Robert Bolesław, Domański, and Krzysztof Gwosdz. 2020. "Automotive Industry Dynamics in Central Europe." Pp. 377–397 in *New Frontiers of the Automobile Industry*, edited by A. V. Covarrubias and S. M. Ramírez Perez. Cham, Switzerland: Palgrave Macmillan.

Hachtmann, Rüdiger and von Saldern, Adelheid. 2009. "'Gesellschaft am Fließband' Fordistische Produktion und Herrschaftspraxis in Deutschland." *Zeithistorische Forschungen*. 6: 186–208.

Hachtmann, Rüdiger. 2008. "Fordismus und Sklavenarbeit. Thesen zur betrieblichen Rationalisierungsbewegung 1941 bis 1944." Potsdamer Bulletin für Zeithistorische Studien. 43–44: 21–34.

Haipeter, Thomas. 2006. "Recent Developments in Co-determination at Volkswagen: Challenges and Changes." *Journal of Industrial Relations*. 48(4): 541–547.

Haipeter, Thomas, Inger Korflür and Gabi Schilling. 2018. "Neue Koordinaten für eine proaktive Betriebsratspolitik. Erfahrungen aus dem Gewerkschaftsprojekt 'Arbeit 2020 in NRW'." *WSI-Mitteilungen*. 70(3): 219–226.

Hall, Peter A. and Soskice, David. 2003 [2001]. "An Introduction to Varieties of Capitalism." Pp. 1–68 In *Varieties of Capitalism: The Institutional Foundations of Comparative Advantage*, edited by Peter A. Hall and David Soskice. Oxford, UK: Oxford University Press.

Harbour, Ron. 2017. "Are Robots 'Stealing' Productivity from Humans?" *BRINK News*. Retrieved April 12, 2022 (https://www.brinknews.com/are-robots-stealing-productivity-from-humans/).

Harvey, David. 1990. "Between Space and Time: Reflections on the Geographical Imagination." *Annals of the Association of American Geographers*. 80(3): 418–434.

Harvey, David. 2017. *Marx, Capital and the Madness of Economic Reason*. New York, NY: Oxford University Press.

Hayek, Friedrich. 1944. *The Road to Serfdom*. Chicago: University of Chicago Press.

Heim, Stéphane. 2020. "The Japanese Automotive Industry Since 2000: Causes and Impacts of Growth Disparities." Pp. 203–226 in *New Frontiers of the Automobile Industry*, edited by A. V. Covarrubias and S. M. Ramírez Perez. Cham, Switzerland: Palgrave Macmillan.

Helper, Susan and Henderson, Rebecca. 2014. "Management Practices, Relational Contracts, and the Decline of General Motors." *Journal of Economic Perspectives*. 28(1): 49–72.

Herrigel, Gary. 1996. "Crisis in German Decentralized Production: Unexpected Rigidity and the Challenge of an Alternative Form of Flexible Organization in Baden Württemberg." *European Urban and Regional Studies*. 3(1): 33–52.

Herrigel, Gary. 2000. "Social Theory and the Transformation of Capitalism in the Twentieth Century." *International Journal of Politics, Culture and Society*. 13(3): 405–426.

Herrigel, Gary and Sabel, Charles F. 1999. "Craft Production in Crisis: Industrial Restructuring in Germany During the 1990s." Retrieved November 25, 2021 (https://bpb-us-w2.wpmucdn.com/voices.uchicago.edu/dist/f/1260/files/2018/07/33-craft_production_in_crisis-1d43myg.pdf).

Hertwig, Markus, Pries, Ludger, and Rampeltshammer, Luitpold. 2011. "Stabilizing effects of European Works Councils: Examples from the automotive industry." *European Journal of Industrial Relations*. 17(3): 209–226.

Hicks, Michael and Devaraj, Srikant. 2015. "The Myth and Reality of Manufacturing in America." *Ball State University Center for Business and Economic Research*.

Hilger, Susanne. 2003. "Pacemakers of Globalization in German Industry: Corporate Strategies at Siemens, Daimler-Benz, and Henkel, 1945–1975." *Business and Economic History On-Line* (1): 1–15.

Hiott, Andrea. 2012. *Thinking Small: The Long, Strange Trip of the Volkswagen Beetle.* New York, NY: Ballantine Books.

Hirsch, Barry T., Macpherson, David A., and Even, William E. 2024. "Union Membership, Coverage, and Earnings from the CPS." Retrieved January 9, 2025 (https://www.unionstats.com/).

Hobsbawm, Eric. 1996 [1962]. *The Age of Revolution.* New York, NY: Vintage Books.

Holmes, John. 2004. "Re-scaling collective bargaining: union responses to restructuring in the North American auto industry." *Geoforum.* 35(2004): 9–21.

Holweg, Matthias. 2008. "Beyond Mass and Lean Production: On the Dynamics of Competition in the Automotive Industry." Pp. 13–34 in *Build to Order: The Road to the 5-Day Car,* edited by G. Parry and A. Graves. London, UK: Springer.

Hoppenstedt, Max. 2024. "USA planen Verbot für moderne Autos aus China." *Der Spiegel.* Retrieved October 15, 2024 (https://www.spiegel.de/netzwelt/netzpolitik/usa-planen-verbot-fuer-autos-aus-china-wegen-ernsthafter-gefahr-fuer-die-nationale-sicherheit-a-e7336ebe-108d-4cdc-a1a5-de0deabeb506).

Horkheimer, Max. 1975 [1937]. "Traditional and Critical Theory." Pp. 188–243 in *Critical Theory: Selected Essays.* New York, NY: Continuum International Publishing Group.

Horkheimer, Max and Adorno, Theodor W. 2001 [1947]. *Dialectic of Enlightenment: Philosophical Fragments.* Stanford, CA: Stanford University Press.

Horst, Kern and Sabel, Charles F. 1991. "Trade Unions and Decentralized Production: A Sketch of Strategic Problems in the West German Labor Movement" *Politics and Society.* 19(4): 373–402.

Hounshell, David. 1985. *From the American System to Mass Production, 1800–1932: The Development of Manufacturing Technology in the United States.* Baltimore, MD: Johns Hopkins University Press.

Hounshell, David. 2000. "Automation, Transfer Machinery, and Mass Production in the US Automobile Industry in the Post-World War II Era." *Enterprise & Society.* 1(1): 100–138.

Howell, Larry J. and Hsu, Jamie C. 2002. "Globalization within the Auto Industry" *Research Technology Management.* 45(4): 43–49.

Howes, Candace. 1995. "Are Japanese Transplants Restoring U.S. Competitiveness or Dumping Their Social Problems in the U.S. Market?" Pp. 156–180 in *Lean Work: Empowerment and Exploitation in the Global Auto Industry,* edited by S. Babson. Detroit, MI: Wayne State University Press.

Hyde, Charles K. 2013. *Arsenal of Democracy: The American Automobile Industry in World War II.* Detroit, Michigan: Wayne State University Press.

Ingrassia, Paul. 2011. *Crash Course: The American Automobile Industry's Road to Bankruptcy and Bailout—and Beyond.* New York, NY: Random House.

Ingrassia, Paul and White, J. B. 1994. *Comeback: The Fall and Rise of the American Automobile Industry.* New York, NY: Simon and Schuster.

International Energy Agency. 2024a. "EV Life Cycle Assessment Calculator." *International Energy Agency.* Retrieved October 14, 2024 (https://www.iea.org/data-and-statistics/data-tools/ev-life-cycle-assessment-calculator).

International Energy Agency. 2024b. "Electric car sales, 2012–2024." *International Energy Agency.* Retrieved October 14, 2024 (https://www.iea.org/data-and-statistics/charts/electric-car-sales-2012-2024).

International Energy Agency. 2024c. "Global EV Data Explorer." *International Energy Agency.* Retrieved October 14, 2024 (https://www.iea.org/data-and-statistics/data-tools/global-ev-data-explorer).

Isidore, Chris. 2024. "Shawn Fain was Kamala Harris' most forceful union backer. It could cost him his job." *CNN.* Retrieved January 9, 2025 (https://www.cnn.com/2024/12/27/business/shawn-fain-risk-taker/index.html).

Jolly, Jasper. 2024. "Volkswagen hit by 60% fall in profits as sales in China slump." *The Guardian.* Retrieved January 14, 2025 (https://www.theguardian.com/business/2024/oct/30/volkswagen-hit-by-fall-in-profits-sales-in-china-slump).

Jouet, Mugambi. 2017. *Exceptional America: What Divides Americans from the World and from Each Other.* Berkeley, CA: University of California Press.

Jürgens, Ulrich. 1994. "VW at the turning point: success and crisis of a German production concept." Pp. 91–108 in Université d'Evry-Val d'Essonne, Groupe d'Etudes et de Recherches Permanent sur l'Industrie et les Salariés de l'Automobile (Evry) (Ed.): Des trajectoires des firmes aux modèles industriel, Université d'Evry-Val d'Essonne, Groupe d'Etudes et de Recherches Permanent sur l'Industrie et les Salariés de l'Automobile.

Jürgens, Ulrich. 1995. "Lean Production and Co-Determination: The German Experience." Pp. 292–310 in *Lean Work: Empowerment and Exploitation in the Global Auto Industry*, edited by S. Babson. Detroit, MI: Wayne State University Press.

Jürgens, Ulrich. 1997a. "Germany: Implementing Lean Production." Pp. 109–116 in *After Lean Production: Evolving Employment Practices in the World Auto Industry*, edited by T. A. Kochan, R. D. Lansbury, and J. P. MacDuffie. Ithaca, NY: Cornell University Press.

Jürgens, Ulrich. 1997b. "Rolling Back Cycle Times: The Renaissance of the Classic Assembly Line in Final Assembly." Pp. 255–273 in *Transforming Automobile Assembly: Experience in Automation and Work Organization*, edited by K. Shimokawa, U. Jürgens, and T. Fujimoto. Berlin, Germany: Springer.

Jürgens, Ulrich. 1998. "The Development of Volkswagen's Industrial Model, 1967–1995." Pp. 273–310 in *One best Way? Trajectories and Industrial Models of the World's*

Automobile Producers, edited by M. Freyssenet, A. Mair, K. Shimizu, and G. Volpato. New York, NY: Oxford University Press.

Jürgens, Ulrich. 2004. "An Elusive Model—Diversified Quality Production and the Transformation of the German Automobile Industry." *Competition and Change*. 8(4): 411–423.

Jürgens, Ulrich. 2008. "Globalization and Employment Relations in the German Auto Industry." Pp. 49–72 in *Globalization and Employment Relations in the Auto Assembly Industry*, edited by R. Blanpain and R. D. Lansbury. The Netherlands: Kluwer Law International BV.

Jürgens, Ulrich. 2009. "The Final Chapter of the 'VW Model'? The VW Trajectory, 1995–2005." Pp. 225–243 in *The Second Automobile Revolution*, edited by M. Freyssenet. New York, NY: Palgrave Macmillan.

Jürgens, Ulrich. 2021. "Automation, Lean Production, Industrie 4.0: The Trajectory of the German Model." *Keizaigaku-ronsan/The Journal of Economics*. 61(3–4): 1–20.

Jürgens, Ulrich. 2023. *Automatisierung und Arbeit in der Automobilindustrie: Von Henry Ford zu Industrie 4.0*. Baden-Baden, Baden-Württemberg: Nomos.

Jürgens, Ulrich and Krzywdzinski, Martin. 2006. "Standort- und Beschäftigungssicherungsvereinbarungen in der deutschen Automobilindustrie zwischen 1993 und 2006" *WZB Discussion Article* SP II 2006–303.

Jürgens, Ulrich and Krzywdzinski, Martin. 2009. "Changing East-West Division of Labour in the European Automotive Industry." *European Urban and Regional Studies*. 16(1): 27–42.

Jürgens, Ulrich and Krzywdzinski, Martin. 2015. "Competence development on the shop floor and industrial upgrading: case studies of auto makers in China." *The International Journal of Human Resource Management*. 26(9): 1204–1225.

Jürgens, Ulrich, Malsch, Thomas, and Dohse, Knuth. 1993. *Breaking from Taylorism: Changing Forms of Work in the Automobile Industry*. New York, NY: Cambridge University Press.

Jürgens, Ulrich and Meißner, Heinz-Rudolf. 2005. *Arbeiten am Auto der Zukunft: Produktinnovationen und Perspektiven der Beschäftigten*. Edition Sigma.

Just-auto.com. 2007. "US: Domestics close productivity gap." Gale One File: Business. Retrieved August 2, 2022 (link.gale.com/apps/doc/A164275040/ITBC?u=tel_a_utl&sid=bookmark-ITBC&xid=fb835e9d).

Just-auto.com. 2018. "VW Wolfsburg wins lean production award." Gale Academic One File. Retrieved August 2, 2022 (link.gale.com/apps/doc/A547314703/AONE?u=tel_a_utl&sid=bookmark-AONE&xid=2701055f).

Kaplan, Jerry. 2015. *Humans Need Not Apply*. New Haven, CT: Yale University Press.

Keller, Maryann. 1993. *Collision GM, Toyota, Volkswagen and the Race to Own the 21st Century*. New York, NY: Currency/Doubleday.

Kennedy, Scott. 2024. "The Chinese EV Dilemma: Subsidized Yet Striking." *Center for Strategic & International Studies*. Retrieved January 13, 2025 (https://www.csis.org/blogs/trustee-china-hand/chinese-ev-dilemma-subsidized-yet-striking).

Kemezis, Paul. 1975. "Volkswagen. Puts '74 Loss at $336-Million." *New York Times*. Retrieved February 23, 2022 (https://www.nytimes.com/1975/05/13/archives/volkswagen-puts-74-loss-at-336million-336million-loss-in-74-is.html).

Kern, Horst and Schumann, Michael. 1984. *Das Ende der Arbeitsteilung?: Rationalisierung in der industriellen Produktion*. Munich: C. H. Beck Verlag.

Kern, Horst and Schumann, Michael. 1987. "Limits of the Division of Labor. New Production and Employment Concepts in West German." *Economic and Industrial Democracy*. 8: 151–170.

Kern, Horst and Schumann, Michael. 1998. "Kontinuität oder Pfadwechsel? Das deutsche Produktionsmodell am Scheideweg." *SOFI-Mitteilungen*. 26(1998): 7–15.

Keynes, John Maynard. 1964 [1936]. *The General Theory of Employment, Interest and Money*. New York, NY: Harbinger.

Keynes, John Maynard. 1963 [1930]. "Economic Possibilities for our Grandchildren." Pp. 358–373 in *Essays in Persuasion*. New York: W. W. Norton & Co.

Klein, Matthew C. and Pettis, Michael. 2020. *Trade Wars Are Class Wars: How Rising Inequality Distorts the Global Economy and Threatens International Peace*. New Haven, Connecticut: Yale University Press.

Klier, Thomas and Rubenstein, James. 2020. "Overview of the U.S. Automobile Industry." Pp. 41–66 in *New Frontiers of the Automobile Industry*, edited by A. V. Covarrubias and S. M. Ramírez Perez. Cham, Switzerland: Palgrave Macmillan.

Knowles, Anthony J. 2017. "Automation, Work, and Ideology: The Next Industrial Revolution and the Transformation of 'Labor.'" Master's Thesis, Sociology, University of Tennessee TRACE.

Knowles, Anthony J. 2021. "Sociology as Social System: Luhmann, Enlightenment, and the Gap Between 'Facts' and 'Norms.'" *Current Perspectives in Social Theory*. 37: 159–192.

Knowles, Anthony J. 2023a. "The Futility of Human Capital? Contradictions of 'Neoliberal Ethics,' Heteronomy, and Automation." *Current Perspectives in Social Theory*. 40: 91–115.

Knowles, Anthony J. 2023b. "Universal Basic Income, Social Justice, and Marginality: A Critical Evaluation." *Social Justice*. 48(4): 1–31.

Kochan, Thomas A., Lansbury, Russell D., and MacDuffie, John Paul. 1997. "Conclusion: After Lean Production?" Pp. 303–324 in *After Lean Production: Evolving Employment Practices in the World Auto Industry*, edited by T. A. Kochan, R. D. Lansbury, and J. P. MacDuffie. Ithaca, NY: Cornell University Press.

Krafcik, John F. 1988. "Triumph Of The Lean Production System." *Sloan Management Review*. 30(1): 41–52.

Krisher, Tom, and Hall, Kristin M. 2024. "Tennessee Volkswagen employees overwhelmingly vote to join United Auto Workers union." *Associated Press*. Retrieved January 9, 2025 (https://apnews.com/article/volkswagen-union-vote-united-auto-workers-chattanooga-5154459od8ao6efddfa2f6ac7dboofbe).

Krzywdzinski, Martin. 2020a. "Automation, Digitalization, and Changes in Occupational Structures in the Automobile Industry in Germany, the United States, and Japan: A Brief History from the Early 1990s Until 2018." *Weizenbaum* Series 10: 1–68.

Krzywdzinski, Martin. 2020b. "Lean Production in Germany: A Contested Model." Pp. 507–528 in *The Cambridge International Handbook of Lean Production*, edited by T. Janoski and D. Lepadatu. Cambridge, UK: Cambridge University Press.

Krzywdzinski, Martin and Jürgens, Ulrich. 2015. "Variations in Convergence China's Automotive Industry Is Characterized by Global Standards—and National Traditions." *WZB Report*. Retrieved August 7, 2022 (https://www.academia.edu/14876816/Variations_in_Convergence_China_s_Automotive_Industry_Is_Characterized_by_Global_Standards_and_National_Traditions).

Kuhlmann, Martin, Barbara Splett and Sascha Wiegrefe. 2018. "Montagearbeit 4.0? Eine Fallstudie zu Arbeitswirkungen und Gestaltungsperspektiven digitaler Werkerführung." *WSI-Mitteilungen*. 70(3): 182–188.

Kuhlmann, Martin, Sperling, Hans Joachim, and Balzert, Sonja. 2004. *Konzepte innovativer Arbeitspolitik. Good-Practice-Beispiele aus dem Machinenbau, der Automobil-, Elektro- und Chemischen Industrie*. Berlin, Germany: Sigma.

Kumar, Rajeev Ranjan, and Alok, Kumar. 2020. "Adoption of electric vehicle: A literature review and prospects for sustainability." *Journal of Cleaner Production*. 253: 119911.

Kurz, Robert. 2014 [1986]. "The Crisis of Exchange Value: Science as a Productive Force, Productive Labor, and Capitalist Reproduction." Pp. 17–75 in *Marxism and the Critique of Value*, edited by Neil Larson, Mathias Nilges, Josh Robinson, and Nicholas Brown. Chicago: MCM Publishing.

Kurz, Robert. 1999. "Marx 2000." *Exit!* Retrieved August 14, 2017 (www.exit-online.org/druck.php?tabelle=transnationales&posnr=67).

Lam, Alice C., Norsworthy, J. R., and Zabala Craig, A. 1991. "Labor Disputes and Productivity in Japan and the United States" Pp. 411–435 in *Productivity Growth in Japan and the United States*, edited by C. R. Hulten. Chicago, Il: University of Chicago Press.

Lawder, David. 2024. "U.S. locks in steep tariff hikes on Chinese EVs, other raw minerals." *Automotive News*. Retrieved October 15, 2024 (https://www.autonews.com/china/us-locks-steep-china-ev-tariff-hikes-some-industries-warn-disruptions).

Lee, Daniel. 2000. "The Society of Society: The Grand Finale of Niklas Luhmann." *Sociological Theory*. 18(2): 320–330.

Leland, Henry M. 1966. *Master of Precision*. Detroit, MI: Wayne State University Press.

Lichtenstein, Nelson. 1986. "Life at the Rouge: A Cycle of Worker's Control." Pp. 237–259 in *Life and Labor: Dimensions of American Working-Class History*, edited by C. Stephenson and R. Asher. New York, NY: New York State University.

Lichtenstein, Nelson. 2024. "The 'Stand-Up' Strike of 2023 Takes Its Place in UAW History." *New Labor Forum*. 33(2): 48–55.

Lieberman, Marvin B. and Dhawan, Rajeev. 2005. "Assessing the Resource Base of Japanese and U.S. Auto Producers: A Stochastic Frontier Production Function Approach." *Management Science*. 51(7): 1060–1075.

Liker, Jeffery K. 2021. *The Toyota Way: 14 Management Principles from the World's Greatest Manufacturer, 2nd Edition*. New York, NY: McGraw Hill.

Lipset, Martin Seymour. 1996. *American Exceptionalism: A Double-Edged Sword*. New York: W. W. Norton & Co.

Lipset, Martin Seymour and Marks, Gary. 2000. *It Didn't Happen Here: Why Socialism Failed in the United States*. New York: W. W. Norton & Co.

Lüdtke, Alf. 2009. "'German Quality Work'—Did it Shape the Production of Automobiles in (West-) Germany after 1945?" Pp. 175–190 in *Towards Mobility. Varieties of Automobilism in East and West*, edited by M. Grieger, U. Gutzmann, and D. Schlinkert. Wolfsburg, Germany: Volkswagen AG.

Luhmann, Niklas. 1994. "What is the Case? And 'What Lies behind it?' The two Sociologies and the Theory of Society." *Sociological Theory*. 12(2): 126–139.

Luhmann, Niklas. 2012 [1997]. *The Theory of Society Volume 1*. Stanford, CA: Stanford University Press.

Luhmann, Niklas. 2013 [1997]. *The Theory of Society Volume 2*. Stanford, CA: Stanford University Press.

Lukes, Steven. 2005 [1974]. *Power: A Radical View 2nd edition*. New York, NY: Palgrave Macmillan.

Lüthje, Boy, Luo, Siqi and Zhang, Hao. 2013. *Beyond the Iron Rice Bowl: Regimes of Production and Industrial Relations in China*. Frankfurt, Germany: Campus.

Lutz, Hannah and Walsh, Dustin. 2014. "Harbour gave it to automakers straight; Efficiency analyst shook up industry." *Automotive News*. 89(6638). Gale One File: Business. Retrieved August 2, 2022 (link.gale.com/apps/doc/A382797276/ITBC?u=tel_a_utl&sid=bookmark-ITBC&xid=79bbf828).

MacDougall, William. 2020. "The Automotive Industry in Germany." *Germany Trade & Invest*. Retrieved November 25, 2021 (https://www.gtai.de/resource/blob/64100/817a53ea3398a88b83173d5b800123f9/industry-overview-automotive-industry-en-data.pdf).

MacDuffie, John Paul and Fujimoto, Takahiro. 2010. "Why Dinosaurs Will Keep Ruling the Auto Industry." *Harvard Business Review*. Retrieved November 28, 2022 (https://hbr.org/2010/06/why-dinosaurs-will-keep-ruling-the-auto-industry).

MacDuffie, John Paul and Pil, Fritz K. 1995. "The International Assembly Plant Study: Philosophical and Methodological Issues." Pp. 181–196 in *Lean Work: Empowerment and Exploitation in the Global Auto Industry*, edited by S. Babson. Detroit, MI: Wayne State University Press.

Mannheim, Karl. 1936. *Ideology and Utopia*. New York, NY: Martino Publishing.

Mantoux, Paul. 2006 [1928]. *The industrial revolution in the eighteenth century: An outline of the beginnings of the modern factory system in England*. London, UK: Routledge.

Martelle, Scott. 2014. *Detroit A Biography*. Chicago, IL: Chicago Review Press.

Martineau, Jonathan. 2015. *Time, Capitalism and Alienation: A Socio-Historical Inquiry into the Making of Modern Time*. Chicago: Haymarket Books.

Marx, Karl. 1932 [1844]. "Economic and Philosophic Manuscripts of 1844." Retrieved August 10, 2020 (https://www.marxists.org/archive/marx/works/download/pdf/Economic-Philosophic-Manuscripts-1844.pdf).

Marx, Karl. 1963 [1852]. *The Eighteenth Brumaire of Louis Bonaparte*. New York, NY: International Publishers.

Marx, Karl. 1973 [1858]. *The Grundrisse: Foundations of the Critique of Political Economy*. London, UK: Penguin Classics.

Marx, Karl. 1976 [1867]. *Capital: Volume 1: A Critique of Political Economy*. London, UK: Penguin Classics.

Marx, Karl. 1978 [1859]. "Marx on the History of His Opinions." Pp. 3–6 in *The Marx-Engels Reader*, edited by R. Tucker. New York, NY: W. W. Norton and Company.

Marx, Karl. 1978 [1894]. "Capital, Volume 3." Pp. 439–442 in *The Marx-Engels Reader*, edited by R. Tucker. New York, NY: W. W. Norton and Company.

Marx, Karl. 1978 [1885]. *Capital: Volume 2: A Critique of Political Economy*. London, UK: Penguin Classics.

Marx, Karl. 1981 [1894]. *Capital: Volume 3: A Critique of Political Economy*. London, UK: Penguin Classics.

Marx, Roberto, Marotti de Mello, Adrianna, and Ferreira de Lara, Felipe. 2020. "The New Geography of the Automobile Industry: Trends and Challenges in Brazil." Pp. 349–376 in *New Frontiers of the Automobile Industry*, edited by A. V. Covarrubias and S. M. Ramírez Perez. Cham, Switzerland: Palgrave Macmillan.

Maynard, Micheline. 2007. "G.M. talks with union said to be breaking down." *New York Times*. Retrieved August 2, 2022 (https://www.nytimes.com/2007/09/17/business/17gm.html).

McClean, Aidan. 2022. *Electric Revolution: Myths & Truths about Electric Vehicles and Climate Disaster*. Self published.

McCracken, Jeffery. 2003. "U.S. automakers improve productivity according to report, sources say." *Knight Ridder/Tribune News Service*. Gale General One File. Retrieved August 2, 2022 (link.gale.com/apps/doc/A103551796/ITOF?u=tel_a_utl&sid=bookmark-ITOF&xid=3ddbbad9).

McKenney, Zachary J. 2018. "The State of the Union? Transnational Manufacturing and the US Labor Movement." PhD Dissertation, Sociology, University of Tennessee TRACE.

McKerracher, Colin. 2024. "China's Batteries Are Now Cheap Enough to Power Huge Shifts." *Bloomberg*. Retrieved January 13, 2025 (https://www.bloomberg.com/news/newsletters/2024-07-09/china-s-batteries-are-now-cheap-enough-to-power-huge-shifts).

McNeill, J. R. and Engelke, Peter. 2014. *The Great Acceleration: An Environmental History of the Anthropocene since 1945*. Cambridge Mass.: The Belknap Press of Harvard University Press.

Mercedes-Benz. 2023. "Reconstruction 1945–1949." *Mercedes-Benz Group AG*. Retrieved February 8, 2023 (https://group.mercedes-benz.com/company/tradition/company-history/1945-1949.html).

Meyer, Stephen. 1981. *The Five Dollar Day: Labor Management and Social Control in the Ford Motor Company 1908–1921*. Albany, NY: SUNY Press.

Meyer, Stephen. 2002. "'An Economic "Frankenstein"': UAW Workers' Responses to Automation at the Ford Brook Park Plant in the 1950s." *Michigan Historical Review*. 28(1): 63–89.

Meyer, Stephen. 2004. "The Degradation of Work Revisited: Workers and Technology in the American Auto Industry, 1900–2000." *Automobile in American Life and Society*. Retrieved December 3, 2022 (http://www.autolife.umd.umich.edu/Labor/L_Overview/L_Overview1.htm#meyer).

Meyer, Steve. 2009. "The End of the Line: American Corporate Cultures and the Growth and Decline of the Automobile Industry, 1945–1990." Pp. 151 in *Towards Mobility. Varieties of Automobilism in East and West*, edited by M. Grieger, U. Gutzmann, and D. Schlinkert. Wolfsburg, Germany: Volkswagen AG.

Milanović, Branko. 2016. *Global Inequality: A New Approach for the Age of Globalization*. Cambridge, MA: Harvard University Press.

Misa, T. J. 1995. *A Nation of Steel. The Making of Modern America 1865–1925*. Baltimore, MD: The John Hopkins University Press.

Moll, H. H. 1961. „Die Entwicklungstendenzen der Automatisierung und Schlußfolgerungen für die Ausbildung in der Automobilindustrie." Pp. 51–68 in *Zentralstelle zur Erforschung und Förderung der Berufserziehung: Automatisierung und Berufsausbildung*. Bielefeld, Germany: Bertelsmann Verlag.

Monden, Y. 1983. *Toyota Production System. Practical Approach to Production Management.* Atlanta, GA: Institute of Industrial Engineers.

Mortier, W. L-F. 1924. "Workers, Machinery, and Production in the Automobile Industry." *Monthly Labor Review.* 19(4): 735–760.

Mossalgue, Jennifer. 2024. "Volkswagen to cut 35,000 jobs but keep factories open." *Electrek.* Retrieved January 13, 2025 (https://electrek.co/2024/12/26/volkswagen-to-cut-35000-jobs-but-keep-factories-open/).

Muller, Helen J., Rehder, Robert R., and Bannister, Geoffrey J. 1998. "The Mexican-Japanese-US Model for Auto Assembly in Northern Mexico." *Latin American Business Review.* 1(2): 47–67.

Nevins, A. and Hill, F. E. 1957. *Ford: Expansion and Challenge: 1915–1933.* New York, NY: Charles Scribner's Sons.

Nevins, A. and Hill, F. E. 1963. *Ford: Decline and Rebirth: 1933–1962.* New York, NY: Charles Scribner's Sons.

Nicholson, Philip Yale. 2004. *Labor's Story in the United States.* Philadelphia, PA: Temple University Press.

Nicolaus, Martin. 1968. "The Unknown Marx." *New Left Review.* 1(48): 41–61.

Norsworthy, J. R. and Zabala, Craig A. 1985. "Worker Attitudes, Worker Behavior, and Productivity in the U.S. Automobile Industry, 1959–1976." *Industrial and Labor Relations Review.* 38(4): 544–557.

Ohno, Taiichi. 1988. *Toyota Production System: Beyond Large-Scale Production.* Portland, Oregon: Productivity Press.

OICA. 2023. "2019 Production Statistics." *International Organization of Motor Vehicle Manufacturers.* Retrieved March 29, 2023 (https://www.oica.net/category/production-statistics/2019-statistics/).

Oré, Diego. 2024. "Exclusive: Mexico, facing US pressure, will halt incentives to Chinese EV makers." Reuters. Retrieved January 14, 2025 (https://www.reuters.com/business/autos-transportation/mexico-facing-us-pressure-will-halt-incentives-chinese-ev-makers-2024-04-18/).

Ou, Shiqi, Lin, Zhenhong, He, Xin, Przesmitzki, Steven, Wu, Zhixin, Zheng, Jihu, Lv, Renzhi, and Qi, Liang. 2020. "China's Booming Plug-in Electric Vehicle Market—How Will It Continue?" Pp. 215–256 in *Who's Driving Electric Cars: Understanding Consumer Adoption and Use of Plug-in Electric Cars,* edited by M. Contestabile, G. Tal, and T. Turrentine. Cham, Switzerland: Springer Nature.

Pardi, Tommaso. 2020. "Searching for Industrial Policy: The Long Decline of the French Automotive Industry." Pp. 113–136 in *New Frontiers of the Automobile Industry,* edited by A. V. Covarrubias and S. M. Ramírez Perez. Cham, Switzerland: Palgrave Macmillan.

Perl, Peter. 1984. "Fear, Frustration Underlie GM-United Auto Workers Negotiations." *Washington Post*. September 9, p. A3.

Perkins, Greg and Murmann, Johann Peter. 2018. "What Does the Success of Tesla Mean for the Future Dynamics in the Global Automobile Sector?" *Management and Organization Review*. 14(10): 1–10.

Peterson, Joyce. 1987. *American Automobile Workers 1900–1933*. New York, NY: SUNY Press.

Piketty, Thomas. 2014. *Capital in the Twenty-First Century*. Cambridge, MA: Harvard University Press.

Piketty, Thomas. 2020. *Capital and Ideology*. Cambridge, MA: Belknap Press of Harvard University Press.

Piore, Michael J. and Sabel, Charles F. 1984. *The Second Industrial Divide: Possibilities for Prosperity*. New York, NY: Basic Books.

Postone, Moishe. 1993. *Time, Labor, and Social Domination*. New York, NY: Cambridge University Press.

Postone, Moishe. 2015. "The Task of Critical Theory Today: Rethinking the Critique of Capitalism and its Futures." *Current Perspectives in Social Theory*. 33: 3–28.

Postone, Moishe. 2017. "The Current Crisis and the Anachronism of Value: A Marxian Reading." *Continental Thought & Theory: A Journal of Intellectual Freedom*. 1(4): 38–54.

Pries, Ludger. 1999. "Emerging New Production Systems in the Transnationalization of German Carmakers: The Case of BMW/Spartanburg and DaimlerChrysler/Tuscaloosa." *Actes du GERPISA*. 30: 1–24.

Pries, Ludger. 2003. "Emerging production systems in the transnationalization of German car manufacturers: adaption, application or innovation?" *New Technology, Work and Employment*. 18(2): 82–100.

Pries, Ludger and Wäcken, Nils. 2020. "The 2015 Volkswagen 'Diesel-Gate' and Its Impact on German Carmakers." Pp. 89–111 in *New Frontiers of the Automobile Industry*, edited by A. V. Covarrubias and S. M. Ramírez Perez. Cham, Switzerland: Palgrave Macmillan.

PR Newswire. 2006. "Productivity Gap Among North American Automakers Narrows in Harbour Report 2006." Gale One File Business. Retrieved August 2, 2022 (link.gale.com/apps/doc/A146481451/ITBC?u=tel_a_utl&sid=bookmark-ITBC&xid=18f36b7e).

Pulignano, Valeria. 2020. "The Automaker that Changed the World. High Automation, Total Quality Management and Digitalization at FIAT Chrysler Automobiles (FCA). A Comment on 'Working conditions within Italian FCA Group plants' by Matteo Gaddi." *Sociologica*. 14(2): 303–307.

Quinn, Dennis Patrick. 1988. *Restructuring the Automobile Industry: A Study of Firms and States in Modern Capitalism*. New York, NY: Columbia University Press.

Rabson, Mia. 2024. "Canada to hit China with tariffs on electric vehicles, aluminum, steel." *Winnipeg Free Press*. Retrieved October 15, 2024 (https://www.winnipegfreepress.com/canada/2024/08/26/cp-newsalert-canada-to-hit-china-with-tariffs-on-electric-vehicles-aluminum-steel).

Rehder, Robert R., and Thompson, Judith Kenner. 1994. "Nissan U.K.: the Japanese transplant beachhead in Europe." *Columbia Journal of World Business*. 29(3): 92–102.

Reuters. 2025. "Chinese EV makers extend buying incentives as price war enters third year." *Reuters*. Retrieved January 13, 2025 (https://www.reuters.com/business/autos-transportation/chinese-ev-makers-extend-buying-incentives-price-war-enters-third-year-2025-01-02/).

Reuther, Walter P. 1962. "Policies for Automation: A Labor Viewpoint." *The Annals of the American Academy of Political and Social Science*. 340: 100–109.

Reynolds, Douglas. 1989. "Engines of Struggle: Technology, Skill, and Unionization at General Motors, 1930–1940." *Michigan Historical Review*. 15(1): 69–92.

Rifkin, Jeremy. 2014. *The Zero Marginal Cost Society: The Internet of Things, the Collaborative Commons, and the Eclipse of Capitalism*. New York: St. Martin's Press.

Rinehart, James. 1999. "The International Motor Vehicle Program's Lean Production Benchmark: A Critique." *Monthly Review*. 50(8): 19–27.

Ritter, G. A. and Tenfelde, K. 1992. *Arbeiter im Deutschen Kaiserreich 1871 bis 1914*. Berlin, Germany: Verlag J. H. W. Dietz.

Robinson, William I. 2004. *A Theory of Global Capitalism: Production, Class, and State in a Transnational World*. Baltimore: John Hopkins University Press.

Robinson, William I. 2014. *Global Capitalism and the Crisis of Humanity*. New York, NY: Cambridge University Press.

Rooke, Rob. 2008. "A brief socialist history of the automobile." *Links International Journal of Socialist Renewal*. Retrieved November 22, 2021. (https://links.org.au/brief-socialist-history-automobile).

Rosa, Harmut. 2015. *Social Acceleration: A New Theory of Modernity*. New York: Columbia University Press.

Rostow, W. W. 1990 [1960]. *The Stages of Economic Growth: A Non-Communist Manifesto*. 3rd ed. Cambridge, UK: Cambridge University Press.

Rothstein, Jeffery S. 2006. "The Uncertain Future of the American Auto Industry." *New Labor Forum*. 15(2): 65–73.

Rothstein, Jeffery S. 2008. "Lean Times: The UAW Contract and the Crisis of Industrial Unionism in the Auto Industry." *New Labor Forum*. 17(2): 60–69.

RP News Wires. 2007. "Harbour Report: Detroit Three close productivity gap." Retrieved August 2, 2022 (https://www.reliableplant.com/Articles/Print/12134).

Ruben, George. 1985. "GM-Toyota settle with UAW." *Monthly Labor Review*. 108(9): 51.

Rubinstein, Saul A., and Kochan, Thomas A. 2001. *Learning from Saturn: Possibilities for Corporate Governance and Employee Relations*. Ithaca, NY: Cornell University Press.

Russo, John. 1984. "Killing Jobs with 'Cooperation': the GM Memo." *Labor Research Review*. 1(5): 61–68.

Rüttimann, B. and Stöckli, M. 2016. "Lean and Industry 4.0—Twins, Partners, or Contenders? A Due Clarification Regarding the Supposed Clash of Two Production Systems." *Journal of Service Science and Management*. 9: 485–500.

Salter, Chuck. 2004. "The Truth Shall Set You Free." *Fast Company*. 78–83.

Scheiber, Noam. 2021. "What Will It Take for Electric Vehicles to Create Jobs, Not Cut Them?" *New York Times*. Retrieved March 30, 2023 (https://www.nytimes.com/2021/09/22/business/economy/electric-vehicles-jobs.html).

Schmidt, Gert. 2007 [2005]. "The Vision of a Reasonable Automobile and the Fiction of a Reasonable Automobilism." Pp. 231–252 in *Und es fährt und fährt*, edited by G. Schmidt, H. Bungsche, T. Heyder, and M. Klemm. Berlin, Germany: Sigma Verlag.

Schoenberger, Robert. 2009. "GM and UAW will drop jobs bank program that paid employees when there was no work." *Cleveland.com*. Retrieved December 10, 2022 (https://www.cleveland.com/business/2009/01/gm_and_uaw_agree_to_drop_jobs.html).

Schor, Juliet B. 1992. *The Overworked American: The Unexpected Decline of Leisure*. New York, NY: Basic Books.

Schumann, Michael, Kuhlmann, Martin, Sanders, Frauke, and Sperling, Hans Joachim. 2006. *VW Auto5000: ein neues Produktionskonzept. Die deutsche Antwort auf den Toyota-Weg?* Hamburg, Germany: VSA.

Schumpeter, Joseph. 2003 [1942]. *Capitalism, Socialism, and Democracy*. New York, NY: Routledge.

Schumpeter, Joseph. 2017 [1939]. *Business Cycles: A Theoretical, Historical, and Statistical Analysis of the Capitalist Process*. Eastford, CT: Martino Fine Books.

Schwab, Klaus. 2016. *The Fourth Industrial Revolution*. Geneva, Switzerland: Portfolio Penguin.

Shepardson, David. 2024. "UAW membership fell 3.3% in 2023 to 370,000 workers." *Reuters*. Retrieved January 9, 2025 (https://www.reuters.com/business/autos-transportation/uaw-membership-fell-33-2023-370000-workers-2024-03-29/).

Skidelsky, Robert. 2020. "The Future of Work." Pp. 9–22 in *Work in the Future*, edited by R. Skidelsky and N. Craig. Cham, Switzerland: Palgrave Macmillan.

Thompson, Heather Ann. 1995. "Auto Workers, Dissent, and the UAW: Detroit and Lordstown." Pp. 181–208 in *Autowork*, edited by R. Asher and R. Edsforth. New York, NY: SUNY Press.

Srnicek, Nick and Williams, Alex. 2015. *Inventing the Future: Postcapitalism and a World Without Work*. London, UK: Verso.

Serrin, William. 1985. “Saturn Labor Pact Assailed by UAW Founder” New York Times, October 28, p. A13.

Servan-Schreiber, Jean Jacques. 1968. *The American Challenge*. New York, NY: Atheneum.

Sewell, Jr., William H. 2008. “The temporalities of capitalism.” *Socio-Economic Review* (6): 517–537.

Shenhav, Y. 1999. *Manufacturing Rationality. The Engineering Foundations of the Managerial Revolution*. New York, NY: Oxford University Press.

Sierzchula, William, Bakker, Sjoerd, Maat, Kees, and van Wee, Bert. 2014. “The influence of financial incentives and other socio-economic factors on electric vehicle adoption.” *Energy Policy*. 68: 183–194.

Sloan, Alfred. 1963. *My Years with General Motors*. New York, NY: Doubleday.

Smith, Adam. 2014 [1776]. *The Wealth of Nations*. Lexington, KY: Shine Classics.

Smith, Chris and Meiksins, Peter. 1995. “System, Society and Dominance Effects in Cross-National Organizational Analysis.” *Work, Employment & Society*. 9(2): 241–267.

Sorge, Arndt and Streeck, Wolfgang. 2016. “Diversified Quality Production Revisited: The Transformation of Production Systems and Regulator Regimes in Germany.” *MPIfG Discussion Papers*. 16(13): 1–19.

Special to People's World. 2024 [1991]. “General Motors' 1991 Christmas Massacre: 21 plants, 74,000 jobs gone.” *People's World*. Retrieved January 2, 2025 (https://peoplesworld.org/article/general-motors-1991-christmas-massacre-21-plants-74000-jobs-gone/).

Springer, Roland. 1999. “The End of New Production Concepts? Rationalization and Labour Policy in the German Auto Industry.” *Economic and Industrial Democracy*. 20: 117–145.

Stahlmann, Michael. 1992. “Management, Modernisierungs- und Arbeitspolitik bei der Daimler-Benz AG und ihren Vorläuferunternehmen von der Jahrhundertwende bis zum Zweiten Weltkrieg.” *Zeitschrift für Unternehmensgeschichte*. 37(3): 147–180.

Statista. 2021a. “Automotive industry worldwide.” *Statista*. Retrieved December 7, 2021 (https://www.statista.com/study/9644/automotive-industry-statista-dossier/).

Statista. 2021b. “Volkswagen” *Statista*. Retrieved December 7, 2021 (https://www.statista.com/study/15785/volkswagen-statista-dossier/).

Statista. 2021c. “General Motors” *Statista*. Retrieved December 7, 2021 (https://www.statista.com/study/22199/general-motors-statista-dossier/).

Statista. 2021d. “Ford” *Statista*. Retrieved December 7, 2021 (https://www.statista.com/study/21309/ford-statista-dossier/).

Statista. 2022. “Motor vehicle production of the United States and worldwide from 1999 to 2021.” *Statista*. Retrieved April 10, 2023 (https://www.statista.com/statistics/198488/us-and-global-motor-vehicle-production-since-1999/).

Stockman, Farah. 2021. *American Made: What Happens to People When Work Disappears*. New York, NY: Random House.

Steigerwald, David. 2010. "Walter Reuther, the UAW, and the dilemmas of automation." *Labor History*. 51(3): 429–453.

Streeck, Wolfgang. 1991. "On the Institutional Conditions of Diversified Quality Production." Pp. 21–61 in *Beyond Keynesianism: The Socio-Economics of Production and Full Employment*, edited by E. Matzner and W. Streeck. Aldershot, UK: Edward Elgar Publishing.

Sturgeon, Timothy J., Memedovic, Olga, Biesebroeck, Johannes Van, and Gereffi, Gary. 2009. "Globalisation of the automotive industry: main features and trends." *International Journal of Technological Learning, Innovation, and Development*. 2(1/2): 7–24.

Susskind, Daniel. 2020. *A World Without Work: Technology, Automation, and How We Should Respond*. New York, NY: Metropolitan Books.

Sweezy, Paul M. 2009. "Cars and cities—'automobilisation' and the 'automobile-industrial complex'." *Links International Journal of Socialist Renewal*. Retrieved February 14, 2023 (https://links.org.au/paul-m-sweezy-cars-and-cities-automobilisation-and-automobile-industrial-complex).

Terrell, Ellen. 2016. "When a quote is not (exactly) a quote: General Motors." *Library of Congress Blogs*. Retrieved January 14, 2025 (https://blogs.loc.gov/inside_adams/2016/04/when-a-quote-is-not-exactly-a-quote-general-motors/).

Tesla. 2023. "Manufacturing: Build a Sustainable Future." Retrieved March 30, 2023 (https://www.tesla.com/en_eu/manufacturing).

The Economist. 2017. "General Motors is getting smaller but more profitable." *The Economist*. Retrieved August 16, 2022 (https://www.economist.com/business/2017/06/24/general-motors-is-getting-smaller-but-more-profitable).

Thomas, W. I. and Thomas, D. S. 1928. *The child in America: Behavior problems and programs*. New York, NY: Knopf.

Thompson, E. P. 1967. "Time, Work-Discipline, and Industrial Capitalism." *Past and Present*. 38: 56–97.

Thompson, Heather Ann. 1995. "Auto Workers, Dissent, And The UAW: Detroit And Lordstown." Pp. 181–208 in *Autowork*, edited by R. Asher and R. Edsforth. New York, NY: SUNY Press.

Tolliday, Steven. 1995a. Enterprise and State in the West German Wirtschaftswunder: Volkswagen and the Automobile Industry, 1939–1962. *The Business History Review*. 69(3): 273–350.

Tolliday, Steven. 1995b. "From 'Beetle Monoculture' to the 'German Model': the Transformation of Volkswagen, 1967–1991." *Business and Economic History*. 24(2): 111–132.

Tribune Business News. 2003. "Report Finds U.S. Automakers Boosting Productivity, but Japanese Still Lead." Gale One File Business. Retrieved August 2, 2022 (https://go-gale-com.utk.idm.oclc.org/ps/retrieve.do?tabID=T004&resultListType=RESULT_LIST&searchResultsType=SingleTab&retrievalId=7964b57b-cfb5-487f-abce

-7ba37736c6b3&hitCount=1&searchType=AdvancedSearchForm&currentPosition=1&docId=GALE%7CA103653388&docType=Article&sort=RELEVANCE&contentSegment=ZBCI&prodId=ITBC&pageNum=1&contentSet=GALE%7CA103653388&searchId=R3&userGroupName=tel_a_utl&inPS=true).

Turner, Lowell. 2009. "Institutions and Activism: Crisis and Opportunities for a German Labor Movement in Decline." *Industrial and Labor Relations Review*. 62(3): 294–312.

Vasilash, Gary S. 1997. "Assembly plants: how they compare." *Automotive Manufacturing & Production* 109(8). Gale General One File. Retrieved August 2, 2022 (link.gale.com/apps/doc/A20855370/ITOF?u=tel_a_utl&sid=bookmark-ITOF&xid=1f132311).

UAWD. 2023. "REJECT ELECTRIC VEHICLE TIERS." *Unite All Workers For Democracy*. Retrieved March 31, 2023 (https://uawd.org/noevtiers/).

U.S. Department of Energy. 2024. "Federal Tax Credits for Plug-in Electric and Fuel Cell Electric Vehicles Purchased in 2023 or After." www.fueleconomy.gov. Retrieved October 15, 2024 (https://fueleconomy.gov/feg/tax2023.shtml#requirements).

Wald, Ellen. 2024. "The US wants to end its reliance on Chinese lithium. Its policies are doing the opposite." *New Atlanticist*. Retrieved January 13, 2025 (https://www.atlanticcouncil.org/blogs/new-atlanticist/the-us-wants-to-end-its-reliance-on-chinese-lithium-its-policies-are-doing-the-opposite/).

Wallerstein, Immanuel. 2004. *World-Systems Analysis*. Durham, NC: Duke University Press.

Wallerstein, Immanuel. 2013. "Structural Crisis, or Why Capitalists May No Longer Find Capitalism Rewarding." Pp. 9–36 in *Does Capitalism Have a Future*, edited by I. Wallerstein, R. Collins, M. Mann, G. Derluguian, and C. Calhoun. New York, NY: Oxford University Press.

Wall Street Journal. 2008. "America's Other Auto Industry." *Wall Street Journal*. Editorial, December 1. Retrieved May 23, 2023 (https://www.wsj.com/articles/SB122809320261867867).

Ward's Auto World. 2001. "Efficiency by the Numbers; Japanese still lead in Harbour productivity rankings." Gale One File: Business. Retrieved August 2, 2022 (link.gale.com/apps/doc/A76320582/ITBC?u=tel_a_utl&sid=bookmark-ITBC&xid=65ef50ce).

Ward's Auto World. 2006. "Critical Differences." Gale General One File. Retrieved August 2, 2022 (link.gale.com/apps/doc/A146392108/ITOF?u=tel_a_utl&sid=bookmark-ITOF&xid=aeab9a06).

Wayland, Michael. 2022. "Toyota dethrones GM to become America's top-selling automaker in 2021." *CNBC*. Retrieved May 24, 2023 (https://www.cnbc.com/2022/01/04/toyota-dethrones-gm-to-become-americas-top-selling-automaker-in-2021.html).

Weber, Max. 2002 [1905]. *The Protestant Ethic and the "Spirit" of Capitalism and Other Writings*. New York, NY: Penguin Classics.

Weber, Max. 2012. *Max Weber: Collected methodological writings*. Edited by H. H. Bruun and S. Whimster. New York, NY: Routledge.

Weber, Max. 2013 [1922]. *Economy and Society.* Edited by Guenther Roth and Claus Wittich. Berkeley: University of California Press.

Webster, Joseph. 2024. "China has become an electric vehicle export behemoth. How should the US and EU respond?" *Atlantic Council.* Retrieved October 15, 2024 (https://www.atlanticcouncil.org/blogs/new-atlanticist/china-has-become-an-electric-vehicle-export-behemoth-how-should-the-us-and-eu-respond/).

Weinthal, Ben. 2003. "German Union Suffers First Defeat in 50 years." *Labor Notes.* Retrieved June 13, 2022 (https://labornotes.org/2003/07/german-union-suffers-first-defeat-50-years).

Wenten, Frido. 2020. "The Automotive Industry in China: Past and Present." Pp. 279–300 in *New Frontiers of the Automobile Industry,* edited by A. V. Covarrubias and S. M. Ramírez Perez. Cham, Switzerland: Palgrave Macmillan.

Weyer, Johannes. 1997. "Die Risiken der Automationsarbeit" *Zeitschrift für Soziologie.* 26(4): 239–257.

Weyer, Matthias. 2011. "Hours-per-vehicle controlling—the renaissance of staff productivity." *International Journal of Production Research.* 49(11): 3271–3284.

Winter, Drew. 1992. "Harbour study is not the last word on efficiency." *Ward's Auto World* 28(11). Gale General One File. Retrieved August 2, 2022 (link.gale.com/apps/doc/A12942855/ITOF?u=tel_a_utl&sid=bookmark-ITOF&xid=98d2efb3).

Winter, Drew. 2003. "Productivity Gains." *Ward's Auto World* 39(7). Gale General One File. Retrieved August 2, 2022 (link.gale.com/apps/doc/A105897602/ITOF?u=tel_a_utl&sid=bookmark-ITOF&xid=d452ec3e).

White House. 2022. "FACT SHEET: President Biden's Economic Plan Drives America's Electric Vehicle Manufacturing Boom." Retrieved March 30, 2023 (https://www.whitehouse.gov/briefing-room/statements-releases/2022/09/14/fact-sheet-president-bidens-economic-plan-drives-americas-electric-vehicle-manufacturing-boom/).

Williams, Karel, Haslam, Colin, Williams, John and Cutler, Tony with Adcroft, Andy and Johal, Sukhdev. 1992. "Against lean production." *Economy and Society.* 21(3): 321–354.

Wittrock, Christian. 2015. "Re-embedding lean: The Japanese Cultural and Religious Context of a World Changing Management Concept." *International Journal of Sociology.* 45(2): 95–111.

Woirol, Gregory. 1996. *The Technological Unemployment and Structural Unemployment Debates.* Westport, CT: Greenwood Press.

Wolff, Richard. 2012. *Democracy at Work: A Cure for Capitalism.* Chicago, IL: Haymarket Books.

Womack, James P., Jones, Daniel T., and Roos, Daniel. 2007 [1990]. *The Machine That Changed the World: The Story of Lean Production—Toyota's Secret Weapon in the Global Car Wars That Is Now Revolutionizing World Industry.* New York, NY: Free Press.

Whyte, Ken. 2020. *The Sack of Detroit: General Motors and the End of American Enterprise*. New York, NY: Knopf.

Yates, Charlotte. 1992. "North American Autoworkers' Response to Restructuring." Pp. 111–145 in *Bargaining for change: union politics in North America and Europe*, edited by M. Golden and J. Pontusson. Ithaca, NY: Cornell University Press.

Zabala, Craig A. 1995. "Sabotage In An Automobile Assembly Plant: Worker Voice On The Shopfloor." Pp. 208–225 in *Autowork*, edited by R. Asher and R. Edsforth. New York, NY: SUNY Press.

Index

Printed in the United States
by Baker & Taylor Publisher Services